China's Engine of Environmental Collapse

China's Engine of Environmental Collapse

Richard Smith

PLUTO  PRESS

First published 2020 by Pluto Press
345 Archway Road, London N6 5AA

www.plutobooks.com

British Library Cataloguing in Publication Data
A catalogue record for this book is available from the British Library

ISBN   978 0 7453 4155 2   Hardback
ISBN   978 0 7453 4157 6   Paperback
ISBN   978 1 7868 0662 8   PDF eBook
ISBN   978 1 7868 0664 2   Kindle eBook
ISBN   978 1 7868 0663 5   EPUB eBook

Typeset by Stanford DTP Services, Northampton, England

Contents

Preface

As I write the last pages of this book in late December, the Australian continent is ringed with wildfires and temperatures are soaring to 45°C (113°F) in Sydney, breaking all historical records. The incineration of tens of thousands of square miles of forests, pine and eucalyptus plantations, farms, exurban houses, cows, kangaroos, and koala bears in terrible "fire tornadoes" has thrown into sharp relief, as no other environmental catastrophe has yet done, the insoluble contradiction between the capitalist drive for infinite growth and finite planet we live on, and the ringing truth of Greta Thunberg's cry: "The house is on fire. We need to act like it."

Nowhere are out-of-control economic growth and blind denialism greater than in China today. For decades, Western economists, academics, and media have celebrated China's economic "miracle," for many good reasons: In 1979, at the outset of Deng Xiaoping's Reform and Opening, China was a very poor, stagnant, and isolated Stalinist "socialism-in-poverty." From then until 2018, China's real annual GDP growth averaged 9.5 percent, a pace described by the World Bank as "the fastest sustained expansion by a major economy in history." Such growth has enabled China to raise hundreds of millions of people out of poverty and create an urban middle class roughly equal in size to the entire population of the United States. In 1979, China's economy accounted for just 1.8 percent of global GDP, as against 26 percent for the US. Today, China accounts for 15.5 percent of global GDP while the US share has dropped to 23.6 percent. China has become the world's second-largest economy, largest manufacturer, largest merchandise trader, and largest holder of foreign exchange reserves.

Australia's own economic boom over the past three decades has been powered by China's rise, as Australia ramped up exports of coal, iron ore, and liquified natural gas, in large part to fuel China's engines. China, Australia's largest trading partner, takes 40 percent of those exports (and 31 percent of all Australian exports). Australia's GDP grew more than ten-fold from 1979 to 2018, largely on the strength of its coal exports to China (and Japan, South Korea, and Taiwan). Mining-related equipment, technology, and services currently account for 15 percent of Australia's GDP, and one in ten Australian jobs.

The other side of the coin is that China's Stalinist-capitalist economic "miracle" is not just unsustainable, it's suicidal. China's reckless cheap-and-dirty mode of development has savaged its environment and ecology. Uncontrolled dumping has defiled rivers, lakes, and aquifers. Long stretches of China's rivers are officially classed as "too toxic to touch." In 2016 the government reported that 80 percent of tested water wells across the North China Plain (home to 400 million people) were "so badly contaminated with industrial and other pollutants as to be unsafe for drinking or home use," but urban residents and farmers have little choice but to drink those waters and irrigate crops with them. In 2013 the Ministry of Land and Resources conceded that three million hectares (11,580 square miles) of farmland, an area the size of Belgium, was "too toxic to farm" because of the overapplication of fertilizers and pesticides, irrigation with toxic industrial wastewater, and the dumping of toxic waste on fields. China's leaders trumpet the country as a "new model" society destined to supersede the "declining West," but their police state can't even guarantee safe water, food, or medicines in any city or rural village in China. Builders and manufacturers have built shiny new cities and infrastructure at "China speed" as *People's Daily* likes to brag. But in their haste to build and overbuild, they've wasted staggering quantities of natural resources and racked up the worst industrial health and safety record of any nation on earth, with more than 100,000 workplace deaths per year in recent decades. Even discounting for China's larger workforce this is many times the rates found in the US, Europe, or Japan. The government spends billions of dollars on high-tech life-science parks and biotech, medical, and pharmaceutical research institutes in the quest for scientific glory and industrial prowess, but it can't provide decent basic health care or even general practitioners for its citizens. The privatizing of health care in the 1990s resulted in what is probably the most corrupt medical system in the world, while leaving the uninsured and underinsured (which is almost everyone) unable to cover the costs of serious illnesses. Desperate parents or spouses have even been forced to sell organs to pay for cancer treatment for a loved one.

But of all the disasters resulting from China's economic "miracle," the most urgent threat is this: In its race to "catch up and overtake the US," soaring CO_2 emissions have made China by far the leading driver of global climate collapse. In 2018 China's CO_2 emissions were nearly as much as those of the five next-largest emitters (the US, India, Russia, Japan, and Germany) combined.[1] Yet China's population was only 68 percent as large as the total population of those five countries, and its GDP was just 32 percent as large as their combined GDPs.

What explains these incredible and shocking anomalies and contradictions? This book asks questions like these—and it proposes to answer them with a Marxist "mode of production" theorization of China's political economy that explains why these contradictions are built into the nature of its hybrid bureaucratic-collectivist capitalism and the framework of Communist Party rule. This book contends that both capitalism and China's hybrid economic system are completely unsustainable, and that the drive to planetary climate collapse cannot be reversed with carbon taxes, tech fixes, and marginal environmental cleanups. I contend, with Greta, that the time for half measures has passed.

Since the first international climate negotiations at Kyoto in 1992, all efforts to suppress CO_2 emissions (voluntary reductions, cap-and-trade schemes, and carbon taxes) have been subordinated to maintaining economic growth, because all parties understand that there's no magic trick to "dematerialize" production, no way to suppress emissions without suppressing growth, and therefore without closing or downsizing many of the world's leading companies. Of the ten largest companies on the Fortune Global 500 list, six are oil companies and two are auto manufacturers. How can we suppress emissions without shutting down or, at very minimum, drastically downsizing those companies? Given capitalism, profit maximization must be prioritized over all other considerations, including emissions reductions, or companies will fail, the economy will collapse, and mass unemployment and starvation will result. Climate change will kill us in the long run but suppressing economic growth will kill us in the short run—and so we keep kicking the can down the road until we now find ourselves at the precipice. Australia shows us that the long run is not far off.

I contend that sooner or later Australia is going to have to shut down its coal production, most of its iron mines, and more. That will hurt. But watching Sydney, Canberra, and Melbourne go up in flames will hurt more. China is going to have to shut down, phase out, or downsize thousands of fossil fuel-based, unsustainable industries across the economy (see Chapter 7). The same goes for the US, the European Union countries, Japan, India, and the other nations that presently account for the bulk of CO_2 emissions. And when we shut down, phase out, or retrench those industries, we're going to have to create new low- or no-carbon jobs for the hundreds of millions of workers who will be unavoidably displaced. That's going to be a huge problem, no doubt. But what's the alternative? Either we organize a rationally planned, democratically managed industrial drawdown of fossil fuel producers and downstream fossil fuel-dependent industries—including transportation, energy generation, petrochemicals, mining and manufacturing, plastics, synthetics, disposables, industrial farming, cement and construction, and tourism—or Mother Nature is going to shut them down for us in a much less pleasant manner. There will be no jobs and no profits on a dead planet. The Chinese and the world as a whole need to face this fact and deal with it.

A NOTE ON THE AUTHOR AND THE ORIGINS OF THIS BOOK

I wrote my doctoral thesis (UCLA Department of History, 1989) on the contradictions of market reform under Deng Xiaoping during the first decade of Reform and Opening (1978–89), and I learned enough Chinese to read government documents and research in China. I held postdoctoral appointments at the East–West Center in Honolulu, Hawaii and Rutgers University. But I didn't pursue a career in China studies. I was trained as a comparative economic historian not a China specialist and I had other interests and options. The specialization required of historians, the limited job opportunities, and the immobility of academic life didn't appeal to me, so I opted to work in industry and pursued my intellectual interests on the side. Working as a part-time independent scholar has obvious disadvantages. But I can write without academic jargon, on the topics of my choice across a range of fields from the Chinese revolution to ecological economics, with no concern for tenure and promotion. And I've not had to censor myself as I would have had to do in academia (and not only in China studies).

Taking my cue from Marx's dictum that "philosophers have only interpreted the world in various ways; the point, however, is to change it," my research and writing has centered on the analysis, and comparative analysis, of the two social systems or modes of production that dominate our world today: Capitalism and bureaucratic-collectivism (by which I mean Stalinism, Maoism, and China's current brand of hybrid bureaucratic-collectivist capitalism). My objectives have been, first, understanding the potentials and limits of reform within those systems, and second, figuring out how to change them. Since the 1990s, my work has mainly focused on environmental issues.

My interest in China's environmental problems grew out of my dissertation research, which revealed that while market reforms certainly spurred growth they also exacerbated many of the economic irrationalities of the old Stalinist-Maoist system, while adding new capitalist irrationalities on top of those. Nowhere was this more apparent than with respect to the environment. I published several articles on China's developing environmental problems in the late 1990s and began researching this book in 2000. But I set it aside in 2005 to engage the growing debate around capitalism and the environment in the West. I wrote a series of essays criticizing the two leading mainstream schools of ecological economics—the steady-state/degrowth school led by Herman Daly, Serge Latouche and others, and the "green capitalism" school of Paul Hawken and Lester Brown. A collection of those were published as *Green Capitalism: The God That Failed* in 2016.

By the 2010s, China's "airpocalypses," "cancer villages" and other environmental disasters were making headlines around the world. Yet there is still nothing in the literature to explain the drivers of China's extraordinary pollution and resource consumption, and how they differ from "normal" capitalism, why officials find it rational to produce mountains of unsaleable steel and aluminum, "ghost cities," and so on, and why, paradoxically, the Communist Party's iron-fisted dictatorship can't seem to suppress pollution from its own industries. Thus, the time seemed right to resume the China environment project. Hence this book.

Acknowledgements

I first want to thank Professor Robert Brenner who taught me Marxist mode of production theory, the theoretical framework of this book, and supervised my doctoral thesis. I want to thank my friend Jin Xiaochang who has shared with me his experience and deep knowledge of Chinese politics and economics over the decades, and who read and criticized this manuscript in drafts. Thanks also to Xiaochang and his wife Liu Hui for helping me with translations. Thanks to Evan Grupsmith for research assistance. Thanks to energy engineer Simon Göß of the German consultancy firm Energy Brainpool GmbH & Co. who generously read Chapter 4, updated some statistics, and let me reproduce his tables on energy generation. Thanks to my friend and comrade, Professor Jenny Chan of Hong Kong Polytechnic University, who read and criticized the first chapter of this book and kept me abreast of workers' and students' struggles in Shenzhen. Jenny also kindly provided the photos of the Jasic supporters which can be found in Chapter 8. A big thank you to the environmental researchers and writers at Chinadialogue, Greenpeace Beijing, and *Caixin* whose critically important work has informed this book. Thanks to Sébastien Budgen and Andrew Hsiao who supported this project from its inception. Thanks to Mark Selden, Gregor Benton, Charlie Hore, and Simon Pirani who read an earlier version of this book and offered sage advice, which I accepted. I especially want to thank Edward Fullbrook, founder and editor of the *Real-World Economics Review*, who has enthusiastically supported my work from the first essay that I sent him in 2010. I also want to thank David Castle at Pluto Press, who warmly embraced this project from the beginning. And finally, my deepest appreciation goes to my muse, spouse, and best friend, Professor Nancy Holmstrom whose wisdom, unfailing support, and editing skills have made this a better book. I remain solely responsible for any remaining errors of fact or interpretation.

Richard Smith
New York, December 30, 2019

A Note on the Names of Rivers in this Volume

The Yangtze River is referred to in modern Chinese as the Chang Jiang, meaning "long river," while the name Yangtze is reserved for a small section of the river near its mouth. The Lancang Jiang, meaning "turbulent river," is the modern Chinese name for the Mekong River as it passes through China; the Mekong is the common Western name for the river's entirety, although it has many names as it runs through Thailand, Cambodia, Myanmar, Laos, and Vietnam. The Yarlung Tsangpo is the Tibetan name for the upper reaches of what is known as the Brahmaputra River after it enters the Indian subcontinent.

Introduction
China as an Environmental Rogue State

THE PARADOX OF AUTHORITARIAN CONTROL
AND OUT-OF-CONTROL POLLUTION

Government, the military, society and schools, north, south, east and west—the Party leads them all.

– Xi Jinping, October 2017

The Party must control all tasks.

– Xi Jinping, December 2018[1]

This book began life in 2015 as an article that asked a simple question: "Why is pollution so horrific in China, so much worse than in 'normal' capitalism most everywhere else?"[2] What's more, why can't China's ferociously authoritarian government suppress pollution from its own industries? Take CO_2 emissions: In 1990 China's CO_2 emissions were half those of the United States (Table 1.1). Fifteen years later those emissions had more than doubled, overtaking the US. Then in just twelve years, from 2005 to 2017, China's CO_2 emissions nearly doubled again to more than twice those of the US. Yet China's GDP was only 63 percent as large as the US GDP in 2017.

Table 1.1   US vs. China CO_2 emissions, 1990–2017 [in million metric tons of CO_2 equivalent]

Year	US	China
1990	6,371	3,265
2005	7,339	7,908
2017	6,457	13,110

Source: Climate Action Tracker global emissions time series[3]

Given that China has 1.4 billion people, four times as many as the US, and given that it became the world's second-largest economy in 2006, it's no surprise that its emissions have grown. What is surprising however is that in comparison with the US and the five next-largest emitters, China's emissions are so out of proportion to the size of its economy and so far beyond the limits to which China's leaders know that they must hold if we are to prevent runaway global warming.

For more than a century the US was the world's largest CO_2 emitter by far. But its emissions declined from their peak of 7,370 million MtCO2e (metric tons of CO_2 equivalent) in 2007 to 6,457 million MtCO2e in 2017, reflecting the ongoing replacement of coal-fired power plants with solar, wind, and lower-emissions natural gas energy sources.[4] The emissions of the European Union countries have also trended downward over the past three decades, from 5,654 million MtCO2e in 1990 to 4,206 million MtCO2 in 2017.[5] To be sure, those declines are far from sufficient to reverse global warming—they aren't even enough to meet their commitments to the 2015 Paris Agreement on Climate Change—but at least they were declines. By contrast, China's carbon emissions have relentlessly grown, quadrupling from 3,265 million MtCO2e in 1990 to 13,442 million MtCO2 in 2018.[6]

Flouting the Intent of the Paris Agreement

China presents a climate crisis paradox. It is the largest producer of photovoltaic panels and wind turbines; it leads the world in installed capacity of both, accounting for about 30 percent of global total in 2018, with the US at a distant 10 percent. It has invested more money in renewable energy and electric vehicles than the rest of the world combined.

Furthermore, President Xi Jinping has stated his aspiration to lead the fight against global warming. In June 2017, when President Trump announced that the US would withdraw from the Paris Agreement, Xi termed it a "hard-won achievement" that "all signatories must stick to." Walking away from the pact would endanger future generations, he said. Xi pledged that China would fulfill its obligations under the Paris Agreement, and said that China would be in the "driver's seat" when it came to "international cooperation" on climate change. He received near universal praise for those statements.[7] In October 2018, the United Nations Intergovernmental Panel on Climate Change (UN IPCC) issued a major report which said that primary energy from coal would need to be virtually phased out by mid-century to have a reasonable chance of holding global warming to 1.5°C. Meeting this target would require that global CO_2 emissions be reduced by 55 percent by 2030, and to virtually zero by 2050.[8]

There is no chance that Xi is unaware of that report. Yet his government has prioritized maintaining economic growth at state-set targets of 6–8 percent per year. China has also prioritized energy self-sufficiency, even at the cost of driving up fossil fuel consumption and emissions, flouting the intent of its Paris Agreement pledge, defying climate science, and scotching Xi's "climate savior" aspirations.

The Paris Agreement—the result of the 2015 United Nations Climate Change Conference in Paris—set a goal of limiting global warming to less than 2°C above pre-industrial levels. In response to criticism that this target was too low, the final version further committed parties to "pursue efforts to limit the temperature increase to 1.5°C above pre-industrial levels."[9] Under the terms of the agreement, each country put forward a proposal to curtail its greenhouse gas emissions between 2015 and 2030 (their "nationally determined contribution," or NDC). More than four years later, no major industrial country is on track to fulfill its pledge.[10] Worse, after slowing in 2015–16, the growth in global carbon emissions spiked in 2017–18, breaking new records in 2018, led again by China.[11]

China stands apart both for the easy targets that it set for itself and for its record of soaring emissions and relentlessly growing investment in coal-fired power production, regardless of its pledges. The US set its NDC target as reducing net greenhouse gas emissions by 26–28 percent below 2005 levels by 2025. Current US policies are projected to reduce emissions by only 11–13 percent below 2005 levels; insufficient to limit warming to 2°C, let alone the tougher 1.5°C target. But China did not actually pledge to cut its emissions at all by 2030. In ratifying the Paris Agreement in September 2016 it set itself the lowest possible bar, virtually no bar at all. China's NDC pledged that it would "peak" its CO_2 emissions "around 2030," and at an unspecified level; reduce carbon emissions per unit of GDP ("carbon intensity") by 60–65 percent below 2005 levels by 2030; increase the share of non-fossil fuel energy generation from 15 percent in 2015 to "around 20 percent" by "around 2030"; and increase its forest stock volume by 4.5 billion cubic meters compared with 2005 levels.[12] In other words, China reserved the unrestricted right to continue growing its CO_2 emissions between 2015 and 2030. And that's just what it has done.

Xi's government has repeatedly promised to reduce coal-fired power production, only to renege on those commitments. In 2016, speaking to the National Energy Commission (NEC) which he chairs, Premier Li Keqiang called on producers to "increase the proportion of renewables in the energy mix," and to "accelerate" such a transition. The next year, China's National Energy Administration canceled more than 100 coal-fired power plants as Li pledged to cut 150 million tons of coal capacity. Yet this did not happen. Instead, China added 194 million tons of new capacity by 2018. Satellite photos show that the government never actually shut down most of those coal plants. Instead, a "massive cohort of hundreds of new coal-fired power plants" is on course to be added to the "already overbuilt Chinese coal plant fleet" by provincial and local officials, while in Beijing, the power industry lobbies for hundreds more.[13] In October 2019, speaking again to the NEC, Li signaled a major policy reversal—coal power would be a top priority in the government's next Five-Year Plan (2021–25). He stressed China's need for energy security and downplayed the importance of a rapid transition away from fossil fuels. He called for speeding up the construction of large-scale coal transportation infrastructure, talked up "safe and green coal mining" and the "clean and efficient development of coal-fired power," and called for "developing and utilizing coalbed methane."[14] In short, coal is still king in China.

China isn't replacing fossil fuels with renewables so much as building more capacity of *both*.[15] It's building new wind and solar infrastructure at a rapid pace, but it's also building new coal- and natural gas-fired power plants as fast if not faster than renewables. And not only in China. Chinese state-owned enterprises (SOEs) are building hundreds of coal-fired power plants across Asia, Europe, Africa, and South America.[16] What's more, as we'll see in Chapter 4, for all the solar and wind power capacity that China has built, it's not building this fast enough, and they still contribute a trivial share of its electricity generation.[17] As a result, CO_2 emissions are surging despite clean energy gains.[18] Powered by sharply rising demand for electricity, steel, and cement, China's emissions grew by 4.7 percent in 2018, nearly double the growth of US emissions, and this increase was on top of a total emissions base that was by then twice that of the US.[19] In the first six months of 2019, China's emissions grew by another 4 percent, according to Greenpeace.[20] Although China claims to have cut carbon intensity by 45 percent from 2005 levels (a considerable step towards its target of a 65 percent reduction by 2030), with overall GDP up 390 percent since 2005, the emissions saved by intensity reduction have been offset many times over by its relentless growth.[21]

It's often said in China's defense that while its emissions may lead the world, its per capita emissions are a fraction of those of the US, and that America's historical emissions dwarf those of China. Yet after three decades of breakneck growth, China is catching up fast. Per capita CO_2 emissions surged past those of the EU six years ago and are now half those of the US (7.45 MtCO2e vs. 15.56 MtCO2e in 2018). Yet China's per capita GDP was just 15 percent that of the US in 2018 ($9,627 vs. $62,904).[22] Similarly, China's cumulative emissions between 1965 and 2018 are now more than two-thirds those of the US, and according to one assessment, based on present trends "China will be responsible for the most atmospheric carbon dioxide in less than 20 years."[23] The atmosphere doesn't care about per capita emissions, only total atmospheric CO_2 concentrations.[24] As the world's largest emitter by far—accounting for 30 percent of total global emissions, against 15 percent for the US, 10 percent for the EU and 7 percent for India—"socialist" China is by far the leading driver of planetary climate collapse.

Flouting the Montreal Accord

The disregard shown by the Chinese government and its industrial producers goes further. In May 2018 researchers for the Environmental Investigation Agency (EIA) discovered that China was violating the 1987 Montreal Protocol, which banned production of the ozone-depleting industrial gas chlorofluorocarbon-11 (CFC-11). CFC-11 is used in refrigerants, aerosol propellants, foam insulation, and in other sectors, but it also depletes the atmosphere's protective ozone layer and is a "super global warmer," 20 to 50 times more powerful than CO_2. The ban on the production of ozone-depleting substances under the terms of the Montreal Protocol, which China signed, was regarded at the time as the single most successful environmental agreement ever enacted, resulting in Western companies developing safer alternatives. Yet even though chlorofluorocarbon (CFC) production was also banned in China in 1991, Chinese producers of air-conditioners and foam insulation for refrigerators and buildings, keen to cheapen production and heedless of mere legalities, avoid purchasing CFC replacements because they're licensed by foreign companies. Instead, they've been illegally producing and using the cheaper CFC-11. China's producers know perfectly well this is both extremely dangerous and illegal. In 2007 the government ordered that "relevant companies must demolish equipment involved in the production of CFC substances," adding that offenders "would be punished according to the law." But the producers don't care, and apparently neither do the government regulators and local officials who are complicit in permitting this illegal-but-profitable production to continue. When the EIA report appeared, Beijing blamed "a few companies," but investigators "found that these are not isolated incidents but common practice throughout the industry."[25]

Given the planetary climate emergency that we face, these are just shocking, criminally irresponsible, and ultimately suicidal policies and trends. It's difficult to comprehend the Chinese Communist Party's insouciant disregard for the specter of planetary collapse. Of course, the same could be also said about America's own rogue president. Yet while Trump is doing plenty of damage, he doesn't own the economy. He can tweet all he likes about saving the coal industry but American utility operators have already decided in favor of wind and solar renewables, the cheap prices of which are driving fossil fuels out of the market for new power plants.[26] The entire auto industry initially defied Trump's plan to scrap Obama's tightened fuel economy standards, though some eventually caved fearing retribution. But California is defying Trump's plan to loosen pollution restrictions, suing the administration, with the potential to tie up Trump's jihad against regulation until he's out of office.[27] In contrast, China's government owns most of the economy and controls the rest, so it can do pretty much what it wants. Right now, what it wants is to maximize growth and electricity generation, even if burning all this fossil fuel sets China, and the world, on fire.

Driving the Sixth Extinction

What's more, the pattern we see with supersized carbon emissions extends across the whole economy. China's voracious consumption of natural resources is out of all proportion to any rational economic need, and flagrantly disregards local and international environmental regulations and laws.[28] Conservationists liken China to "a giant vacuum cleaner of the natural world."[29]

China is the leading driver of global deforestation, consuming more lumber than the rest of the world put together.[30] It is also the largest importer of illegally logged lumber. While protecting its own forests, China is leveling forests from Siberia to South America to satisfy the voracious appetite of its construction companies, papermakers, and flooring and furniture manufacturers. A recent headline in the *South China Morning Post* read: "Chinese consumers' crazy rich demand for rosewood propels drive toward its extinction."[31]

Chinese loggers are also destroying the habitats of Siberian tigers, Amur leopards, Indonesian orangutans, and dozens of rare birds, driving an untold number of species to the edge of extinction.[32] Just as there's no market in China for ecologically certified lumber, neither is there a market for ecologically certified palm oil, beef, seafood, or agricultural products.[33] Xi's self-styled "ecological" government doesn't care about such things. Just the opposite. China is the largest consumer by far of illegally poached wildlife— elephants, lions, tigers, rhinos, sharks, pangolins, and dozens of exotic bird species—for its booming trade in traditional medicine.[34] With state media fully occupied trumpeting patriotic propaganda about "Amazing China,"[35] its citizens have no idea that their country leads the world in CO_2 emissions, nor that their country is almost single-handedly responsible for the industrial-scale slaughter of exotic fauna and flora at the center of the "sixth extinction." Surrounded by Xi's totalitarian "Great Firewall" which effectively blocks out all such unpleasant news from the West, how would they learn these elementary facts?

Many assumed that China's obsession with traditional medicine would wane as the country modernized. There is no scientific proof of any medicinal use for rhino horn, tiger bone, or so many other feudal-era nostrums. To placate the growing fury of international conservation groups the government has occasionally banned the trade in rhinos, tigers, and other endangered species, though enforcement has been spotty. But since Xi took over in 2012 and began extolling this superstitious quackery as "a gem of ancient Chinese science," ordered schools to teach this nonsense, and instructed China's general hospitals to give "equal emphasis" to traditional medicine and so-called "Western medicine," the State Council has rescinded said bans and legalized the use of rhino horns and tiger bones for "medical research or in healing."[36] That may spell doom for more rare species. But if China doesn't suppress its CO_2 emissions many if not most of the world's species will face extinction, including humans.

In the last century, the US was the leading resource consumer and American industries and consumers were the main drivers of global warming and environmental destruction. But as mathematical ecologist Robert Wilson writes: "China has now passed America and is now the most physically important country on the planet. No other country has a more important influence on the biosphere, whether in terms of what we take from it or what we dump into it."[37]

The Authoritarian "Advantage"?

The foregoing examples of out-of-control CO_2 emissions and out-of-control local officials might seem surprising given that China's totalitarian Party-state is laser-focused on, as Xi says, total control of "all tasks." Indeed, it's often argued in the West that China's dictatorship should be an *advantage*, in that it should be able to compel polluters to stop polluting. Likewise, an authoritarian government should be able to ram through the transition to renewables. So why don't they?

In fact, China has comprehensive environmental protection laws on the books. It has its own equivalents of the EPA (Environmental Protection

Agency) and FDA (Food and Drug Administration) in the US. Yet those agencies can't guarantee safe food, medicines, or drinking water, even in major cities. The government can move industries away from Beijing to clear the capital's air a bit but that just redistributes the smog elsewhere, and for decades they've been largely powerless to prevent the dumping of toxic pollutants into the country's rivers, lakes, and aquifers. As a result, cancers and other intestinal and organ diseases are rife (see Chapter 3). Well, why is the government incapable of suppressing pollution from its own industries? After all, Xi's fearsome police state jails, tortures, and even occasionally executes officials (such as the head of the State Food and Drug Administration, who was executed in 2007 after widely publicized scandals involving toxic drugs, food, pet food, toothpaste, and toys),[38] and has no difficulty policing the internet, suppressing dissidents, labor activists, democracy campaigners, feminists, and Marxist students. So why can't China's leaders enforce their own environmental laws and regulations? Why can't they force through the transition to renewable energy? And why are China's leaders determined to maintain a 6.5 percent annual economic growth rate even as they know very well that this can only end in collective ecological suicide?

This prompts related questions: Why is there so much overproduction in China? Why do state-owned steel and aluminum mills produce metals that only pile up in stockyards or get dumped on the world market at below the cost of production? And not only metals. State-owned companies massively overproduce cement, plate glass, chemicals, dams, highways, cars, electric cars, appliances, and even solar and wind power plants. Production for the sake of production. Local officials strive to build their own relatively self-contained industrial structures, with their own steel mills, machinery manufacturers, auto plants, and power plants. Some provinces and even municipalities have their own airlines, resulting in needless duplication, lost economies of scale, and massive resource waste.

Why is there so much overconstruction? Why do China's builders put up miles and miles of apartment blocks with no prospective buyers, huge office towers with no prospective tenants, even entire "ghost cities" that sit nearly empty for years, some for more than a decade now, while builders are putting up still more? Right now, local governments and builders are said to be planning and building some 3.4 billion residences, this for a country with 1.4 billion people, most of whom have already been rehoused since the 1990s.[39] In Wuhan and other cities local governments dynamite blocks and blocks of brand new but unsold apartment towers to start construction all over again. Construction for the sake of construction. Why can't China's authoritarian government suppress what it calls "blind growth," "blind construction," and "blind demolition" by its own companies and stop all this needless waste and pollution?

Why is corruption so out of control? As we'll see, corruption is a major driver of resource overconsumption, pollution, and environmental destruction in China. The government arrests crooked officials every day, exhibits them in retro-Maoist confessions on primetime television. According to Amnesty International, China has the highest rate of executions in the world, more than the rest of the world put together (upwards of 15,000 per year in the 1990s). Yet official corruption only grows worse year by year, while the amounts of money involved reach ever more astounding sums. Party officials were found to be the most numerous account holders revealed by the Panama Papers leak in 2016. Well, why can't Xi's fearsome police state discipline its own officials?

Finally, given the foregoing, one can't help but ask the most basic question, at least for those on the left: What went wrong with the Chinese revolution? We're hardly surprised when capitalist corporations and governments plunder and pollute the world. But the Communist Party claims that China is a socialist country with a leadership dedicated to "serving the people." And Xi has repeatedly declared his intention to turn China into an "ecological civilization."[40] So why would its leaders pursue policies that doom its own people and the planet too?

A MODE OF PRODUCTION THEORY OF CHINA'S POLITICAL ECONOMY, ITS DYNAMICS, AND THE DRIVERS OF ENVIRONMENTAL DESTRUCTION

The answers to these questions begin with a wholesale reinterpretation of the nature and dynamics of China's political economy, one that is consistent with the evidence and patterns summarized above and presented in detail in subsequent chapters. This book presents a Marxist "mode of production" theorization of China's bureaucratic-collectivist political economy, its class structure, surplus extraction relations, its drivers, contradictions, and tendencies in which the foregoing policies and practices can be understood as built into, rational, and even necessary for ruling-class reproduction in this system. I argue that the Stalinist bureaucratic-collectivist system established by Mao Zedong, and then modified 30 years later with Deng Xiaoping's marriage of capitalism and bureaucratic-collectivism, is driven in the main by statist-nationalist extra-economic drivers that are at least as powerful, if not more powerful than the market drivers of capitalism. We'll see how the merger of capitalism and bureaucratic collectivism has resulted in the worst of both worlds for the environment, exacerbating many of the irrationalities of the old system, while compounding them with new irrationalities of capitalism that didn't exist in Mao's day. We'll see how China's "communist capitalism" has created enormous wealth and raised living standards for millions while destroying the environment and the ecological basis on which life depends in the process.

After Chapter 1, which deals with the foreign-invested Special Economic Zones (SEZs), the book turns its focus to the state-owned, state-controlled economy, because this is the main engine of the economy, because it overdetermines the rest, and because this sector is the largest driver of environmental destruction in China, responsible for the bulk of CO_2 emissions. This state-owned hybrid bureaucratic-collectivist capitalist sector is what's distinctive about China's pattern and trajectory of development as compared with "normal" capitalism elsewhere.

In conclusion this book argues that even though China's bureaucratic-collectivist capitalism is the leading driver of climate collapse, "normal" capitalism, even "green" capitalism, is no solution for China (or the rest of the world either), because both systems are unsustainable and suicidal. I contend that given the state of the planet today, the only way to prevent runaway global warming is to slam the brakes on economic growth in both China and the US, shut down entire swathes of useless, superfluous, harmful, and destructive industries, and replace these political-economic systems with an ecosocialist world economy based on public ownership of most means of production, democratically planned production for need, and democratic management of the economy and society.[41]

ORGANIZATION OF THE BOOK

Chapter 1 begins with an examination of the export engine that turned China into the "workshop of the world." Whereas previous studies have largely focused on labor exploitation, I'm equally concerned with what the export zones actually produce, and the consequences for people and planet. Chapters 2–4 survey the current state of China's environment—its polluted air, water, and farmland—and the proximate causes like overproduction, overconstruction, overdevelopment, profligate resource consumption, and the wanton dumping and venting of pollutants. Chapters 5 and 6 present a theorization of the political-economic drivers of this destruction—the dynamics, contradictions, and tendencies of China's hybrid Stalinist-capitalist economy—showing how market reforms compounded the irrationalities of the old bureaucratic-collectivist system with the irrationalities of capitalism, resulting in an environmentally ruinous "miracle" economy, and explaining why Beijing's fearsome police state can't discipline its own subordinates. In Chapter 7, I discuss what the Chinese (and the rest of the world) will need to do to brake the drive to planetary collapse. Finally, in Chapter 8 I discuss the political crisis currently facing the Party regime, survey resistance and speculate about the nature and potential of the next (third) Chinese revolution—improbable as that may seem at present.

1

The "China Price": Police-State Capitalism and the Great Acceleration of Global Consumption

CHINA AND THE SECOND INDUSTRIAL REVOLUTION

In her gripping exposé of human misery and environmental ruin, *The China Price*, Alexandra Harney writes that "American companies have been moving manufacturing offshore for decades . . . But never has one country yielded such visible price declines on such a wide range of goods in such a short period of time [as China]. It is as though the world has been watching a second industrial revolution unfold."[1] China's rise was

Figure 1.1

Credit: Dan Wasserman, Tribune Content Agency

made possible by revolutionary changes in technology and manufacturing processes—computerization, the internet, and the modularization of production that permitted sourcing components from several nations. Taken together, these opened the way for Western companies to relocate entire industries to distant shores and source inputs and products "just in time" from multiple (and often competing) factories around the world.

What gave China the advantage as an export platform over, say, India—which had at least as many millions of hungry jobless workers—was that China had a highly organized and effective developmental party-state that could not only furnish labor and control labor costs, but could also clear land and concentrate resources to plan and build the industrial parks, and the infrastructure to facilitate the development of the SEZs (power plants, ports, roads, railways, telecommunications, and so on), and could also build and staff industry-focused technical schools, universities, and research centers. Milton Friedman liked to ridicule Stalinism by insisting that central planning was "impossible," and could "never work." That was before China. By comparison, India's dysfunctional ruling class can't even provide toilets for its citizens, or pick up the trash, let alone provide electricity, modern container ports, high-speed trains, or a skilled industrial work force. In the twenty-first century, hundreds of millions of Indians remain unconnected to an electrical grid.[2] Unmanaged refuse accumulates into "mountains" that collapse killing people and cause tuberculosis, dengue fever, and poisoned ground water.[3] India's air pollution is now as bad as if not worse than China's despite having far less industry.[4] And Prime Minister Narendra Modi wants to compete with China?

The "Miracle" of China's Police-State Capitalism

Over the past four decades China's comparative advantage in the world economy has lain in three crucial factors:

- Dramatic cost reductions made possible by the provision of vast numbers of semi-coerced ultra-cheap workers to power light manufacturing for export—kept cheap, at least up to the mid-2000s, by the police state-led militarization of employment in the export zones, including the suppression of worker resistance and unionization efforts.[5] Even with wage increases since the mid-2000s, no other developing country, such as Vietnam, can match China's provision of such huge numbers of skilled, experienced workers, or match its infrastructure. And nowhere else would workers work around the clock.

As Susan Helper, the former chief economist at the US Department of Commerce puts it: "China is not just cheap. It's a place where, because it's an authoritarian government, you can marshal 100,000 people to work all night for you."[6]

- Further dramatic cost reductions have been made possible by contempt for, and lack of spending on, environmental protection. The "China price" is due to investors' freedom to pollute as much as to their freedom to exploit ultra-cheap labor.[7] Lots of industries— chemicals, plastics, tanneries, metal plating, painting, textile dyeing, electronics, and others—moved to China mainly to escape "oppressive" environmental and health and safety regulations in the US, Japan, and Europe.

- The capacity of China's developmental state to work closely with foreign and domestic investors to build the physical infrastructure, the schools and universities, and teach English to millions of young people.[8]

By comparison, India suffers from numerous disadvantages in its bid to become an export powerhouse. High on this list is its political system— democracy. Modi complains that democracy is a barrier to development because he can't get his parliament to overhaul labor laws that favor workers. Nor can he get rid of land laws that prevent the converting of farmland to factory sites. India's workers strike when they feel aggrieved, as they did when Modi attempted to make it easier to fire them.[9] By contrast, independent trade unions are illegal in China, the right to strike was deleted from the national constitution in 1982, and labor organizers are routinely locked up, or worse. Chinese workers have nevertheless fought back, in waves of illegal strikes and protests in the early 1990s and the early 2000s; and from 2010 they succeeded in winning wage increases, improvements in working conditions, reductions in employer abuse, legal limits on overtime, and other gains.[10] But Xi's government has taken an increasingly hard line against labor unrest in recent years, closing down labor-focused NGOs and arresting strikers en masse.[11]

Furthermore, China's land developers don't have to bother with public hearings, environmental impact statements, or recalcitrant legislatures. Since the government owns all the land in China, local officials have had the law on their side when they've evicted hundreds of millions of farmers from their land—with or without compensation—to build new dams, ports, industrial parks, and railways, or to expand existing conurbations and build entirely new cities. By contrast, the Indian government, founded in 1947, still doesn't even fully control its own territory. Since the 1960s, New Delhi has waged an on-and-off war with armed Maoist rebels who control sizeable rural strongholds across the center of the country and often side with peasants against industrial expropriators.

It's difficult to overstate the importance of this advantage for speeding industrialization and modernization. China has built entire subway systems in 22 cities since 2008. This was only possible because the central government could mobilize and concentrate funds and resources on massive infrastructure projects like this and because local officials could, by fiat, dig up entire neighborhoods to install tunnels and stations.

China has other important social and cultural advantages over India. Notably, the absence of feudal-era caste barriers, and the presence of an organized, modernizing ruling class not unlike Japan's Meiji rulers. China has also benefited from the close proximity to wealthy ethnically Chinese industrialists and investors in Hong Kong, Taiwan, and Singapore, many with family connections in the coastal provinces and all of them keen to get into China on the ground floor. Those investors and industrialists provided the bulk of foreign direct investment (FDI) capital in the early years of Reform and Opening (*gaige kaifang*) in the 1980s. These advantages played important roles, but China's most crucial systemic comparative advantage was and is its highly organized, police state-backed model of capitalism.

The "China Price"

China's masses of cheap migrant workers were a magnet for the world's most labor-intensive manufacturing and assembly industries. The unbeatable combination of seemingly limitless supplies of ultra-cheap industrial workers; state-guaranteed labor peace and political stability; and good roads, railways, ports, and telecommunications attracted vast inflows of Western capital and modern means of production into China's export zones from the 1980s, turning China into an export manufacturing powerhouse. By the 1990s China had more than 104 million manufacturing workers, about twice as many as the US, Canada, Japan, Germany, France, Italy, and the UK combined. They worked shifts of between 8 and 16 hours, often 7 days a week, for an average of $0.57 per hour in 2002—less than British handloom operators earned in the early Industrial Revolution by one estimate. This "China price" set the global floor for high-volume light-industrial manufacturing from the 1980s and enabled companies to produce consumer goods at between half and a tenth (or less) of the cost of manufacturing them in the US, Europe, or Japan.[12]

Those export earnings in turn underwrote the fastest national industrialization and modernization in history. In 1990, China's share of the world's manufacturing output by value was just 2.4 percent. By 2006 this had risen to more than 12 percent, and to nearly 25 percent by 2015. By 2015 China produced 80 percent of the world's air-conditioners, 70 percent of its smartphones, and 60 percent of its shoes, while accounting for 43 percent of global clothing exports.[13] China became the world's largest exporter in 2009, overtaking Germany, and world's largest manufacturer in 2015, ending America's 110-year run at the top. Its export industries now produce everything from basic consumer goods to computers, cars, and components for Boeing aircraft. In 1980 China's per capita GDP was just $250, less than that of Pakistan. By 2014, total GDP had surpassed Japan to rank second behind the US. China's economy grew by more than 10 percent per year between 1992 and 2011. "Looking back," Vaclav Smil writes, "it is now clear that China's three post-1980s decades added up not only just to the fastest, but also to the largest, economic advance in history."[14]

Figure 1.2 Newly installed nets to prevent workers from jumping to their deaths at one of Foxconn's factory buildings in the township of Longhua in Guangdong province on June 2, 2010. Ten workers died at the company's base in southern China in 2010, all apparently suicides. The deaths triggered investigations by Apple and other big clients, including Dell Inc.

Credit: Bobby Yip/Reuters/Newscom

Figure 1.3 Foxconn workers' dormitory in Shenzhen, with windows clad in bars to prevent suicides.

Credit: Courtesy of Jenny Chan, 2018

Unfree Labor in China's Militarized Special Economic Zones

Even the machine is nodding off
Sealed workshops store diseased iron
Wages concealed behind curtains
Like the love that young workers bury at the bottom of their hearts
With no time for expression, emotion crumbles into dust
They have stomachs forged of iron
Full of thick acid, sulfuric and nitric
Industry captures their tears before they have the chance to fall

Time flows by, their heads lost in fog
Output weighs down their age, pain works overtime day and night
In their lives, dizziness before their time is latent
The jig forces the skin to peel
And while it's at it, plates on a layer of aluminum alloy
Some still endure, while others are taken by illness
I am dozing between them, guarding
The last graveyard of our youth.
             – "The Last Graveyard" by Xu Lizhi[15]

China's rise has however come at horrific social and environmental costs. Numerous reports and studies have documented the pitiless exploitation that hundreds of millions of migrant industrial workers have endured for decades in the militarized export factories of the SEZs. Working conditions are shockingly dangerous, safety is callously disregarded, management is paramilitary, and competition is Darwinian.[16]

**WORK HARD ON THE JOB TODAY
OR WORK HARD TO FIND A JOB TOMORROW**
             – Wording of a banner at the Foxconn Chengdu plant[17]

With 1.3 million employees in 2012,[18] Apple's Taiwanese subcontractor Hon Hai Precision Industry Co. Ltd., better known as Foxconn, is emblematic of this industrial regime.[19] Foxconn is China's largest employer. Its factories assemble iPhones, iPads, and devices for other vendors, and are notorious for excruciating exploitation. Slavery was certainly more brutal; wages were always cheaper in Bangladesh; but no other large-scale factory system anywhere has squeezed more labor out of workers for lower wages than Foxconn. The founder, chairman, and general manager of Foxconn Terry Gou has perfected Taylorism in his electronics assembly sweatshops, driving desperate young migrants to work twelve-to-sixteen-hour days with barely a day or two off per month. Foxconn workers spend months and even years working at a single task consisting of high-speed repetitive motions, are exposed to dangerous chemicals and dust, and suffer humiliating and physically brutal punishments—until they simply wear out, their health or eyesight fails, and they quit, or even commit suicide.[20]

"Suicide Express"

China's migrant workers live in conditions of unfreedom unmatched anywhere outside of North Korea. Despite some limited reforms over the years their "socialist" government has treated them as second-class citizens and denied them full citizenship rights; the *hukou* (household registration) necessary to live permanently in the cities where they work; the right to urban social services; and the right to bring their families and send their children to public schools. Their "workers' state" has routinely backed employers in disputes, denying workers the right to form trades unions or strike, and has arrested, imprisoned, tortured, and sometimes killed labor activists.[21] Given all this it's perhaps not surprising that by the 2000s, workers in the SEZs had begun turning to suicide in final desperate acts of protest.[22]

Jenny Chan writes movingly of one such young woman, seventeen-year-old Tian Yu, who in despair tried to end it all by jumping from the fourth floor of her Foxconn dormitory building, only to survive, paralyzed for life:

[Tian Yu endured] the accumulated effects of endless assembly line toil, punishing work schedules, harsh factory discipline, a friendless dormitory, rejection from managers and administrators, compounded by the company's failure to [pay] her, and then her inability to make contact with friends and family . . . "I was so desperate my mind went blank," [she said].[23]

Since 2010 dozens of migrant workers at factories operated by Foxconn and other companies have committed or attempted suicide; including mass suicides—jumping from buildings in groups, or collectively swallowing pesticides in public. Foxconn responded to the wave of suicides by wrapping factories and dorms with "suicide prevention nets" and forcing workers to sign this pledge in order to be hired:

Should any injury or death arise for which Foxconn cannot be held accountable (including suicides and self-mutilation), I hereby agree to hand over the case to the company's legal and regulatory procedures. I myself and my family member will not seek extra compensation above that required by the law so that the company's reputation would not be ruined and its operation remains stable.[24]

We haven't seen this since the Middle Passage, when slave ship captains hung up "anti-jumping nets" to prevent slaves from ending it all before they reached their fate on American plantations. In his brilliant comparative historical study of modern neo-slavery and resistance in Shenzhen,

Goodbye iSlave: A Manifesto for Digital Abolition, Jack Qiu writes that "suicides—more than four centuries ago on the slave ships, or in Foxconn neighborhoods in 2010—result from existential despair," and are "at the same time, an ultimate act of defiance to free oneself from that despair while denying [others] the right of ownership."[25]

How Long Can the "Miracle" Built on iSlave Labor Last?

Chan, Qiu and others show that what's really "special" about the SEZs is that workers can be subjected to extreme exploitation only because the CCP has created such an all-embracing police state that migrant workers have become virtually slaves, coerced by their employers, sometimes even unable to quit their jobs.[26] China's celebrated "miracle economy" and its "comparative advantage" in world trade are built above all on semi-slave labor.

That's why, when Gou tried to replicate his profit "miracle" in Brazil and elsewhere—including building a new factory in Wisconsin in 2018—the economics didn't work. He couldn't pull it off because he found that in capitalist states, unlike in "socialist" China, workers are free to organize and strike and they don't have to submit to sixteen-hour days and Industrial Revolution-era wages; so Foxconn beat a retreat back to China.[27]

That's also why, when workers began fighting back and striking from the 1990s, and as their strikes and protests forced the government to raise minimum wages at the turn of the century, Foxconn and other employers turned to exploiting tens of millions of teenage "student interns" from trade schools and colleges.[28] The government coerces schools which in turn coerce teachers who then coerce students by preventing them from graduating if they don't submit to spending a summer or even a whole year working twelve-hour shifts and six-day weeks in Foxconn's "iSlave" factories, under conditions and pay that violate the government's own labor laws. As one "student-iSlave" assembler of Hewlett-Packard computers told the *Wall Street Journal*: "I was suddenly told I had to spend the summer making computers or I couldn't graduate. I feel like I was tricked." Such interns comprised 15 percent of the million-strong labor force in Foxconn's factories during the summer of 2010, and the use or abuse of teenage student interns has continued.[29] But with these student iSlaves resisting and organizing too, it's not clear how long China's comparative advantage in semi-slave labor can last.

DISPOSABLE WORKERS PRODUCING DISPOSABLE PRODUCTS
FOR A DISPOSABLE WORLD

That's the labor side of the story. But I also want to draw attention to another side of this exploitation—the environmental costs of what those workers make. As Harney notes, the advent of the "China price" enabled export industries backed by Western investment to effect the deepest cuts in the production costs of light industrial goods since the Industrial Revolution. This price revolution in turn demolished industry after industry around the world, especially in the US. First, plummeting costs enabled foreign-owned China-based exporters to wipe out the last categories of what had been consumer durables—shoes, garments, furniture, appliances, and home and office electronics—and replace them with cheap and/or rapidly obsolescing disposables. Secondly, technological innovations, especially in electronics, created continuous waves of entirely new products and categories, new "needs" that included laptops, smartphones, tablets, games consoles, drones, and so on, mostly produced in China. Thirdly, the transition to capitalism in China itself, and capitalist expansion in other developing nations since the 1980s, has dramatically increased the number of global "mass consumers" which, together with the changes just noted above, has powered what social scientists have termed the "great acceleration" of global consumption since the mid-twentieth century.[30]

When China launched Reform and Opening in the early 1980s and invited foreign investors to set up joint ventures, and later wholly owned foreign-invested enterprises in its coastal SEZs, the combination of ultra-cheap labor and minimal environmental restrictions attracted many of the world's dirtiest and least sustainable industries. Steel, coke, aluminum, cement, chemicals and petrochemicals, metal plating, leather tanning, plastics, paints and finishes, synthetic fibers and textile production, fabric dyeing, paper production—facing increasingly tough environmental restrictions at home in the US and Europe—relocated to China after 1980.[31] Furthermore, China became the world's biggest car battery and electronics recycling center. Seventy percent of the world's e-waste has been dumped in China since the 1980s (that is until the government finally banned those imports in January 2018).[32]

Cheap Chinese labor spurred the biggest boom in global consumption in history. From the 1980s, as prices fell year after year, Western consumers bought more and more of almost everything that China exported. The West lost millions of industrial jobs to China but Western consumers benefited from the free fall of prices for most light-industrial goods. While the cost of housing, cars and fuel, air travel, medical care, higher education, and other needs has steadily risen in the US, the price of clothes, shoes, toys, most tools and appliances, furniture, and consumer electronics has plummeted. The sudden availability of such a huge pool of ultra-cheap workers also spurred a minor industrial revolution, enabling producers to annihilate most of the remaining categories of durable goods and replace them with cheaper, disposable alternatives. With the disposables revolution, local tailors and alteration shops, shoe repair shops, appliance repair shops, television repairmen, furniture restorers, re-upholsterers, and the like all but vanished in the West as it became cheaper to toss and replace than repair. This in turn spurred an unprecedented acceleration of global natural resource plunder.

"Trashion Fashion": The Environmental Costs of the Disposable Garments Revolution

If H&M really want to move towards a sustainable future, they kind of have to not exist.

– Jemima Kelly, the *Financial Times*[33]

Take clothing. In 1960 the average American household spent over 10 percent of its income on clothing and shoes—the equivalent of roughly $4,000 today—but the average person purchased fewer than 25 garments per year. Today the average American household spends less than 3.5 percent of its budget on clothing and shoes—under $1,800—yet it buys nearly three times as many garments, an average of 70 per person per year, more than one per week.[34] Shoe consumption has increased even more rapidly as prices have plummeted with the advent of disposable shoes and sneakers that can't be re-soled.

"Fast fashion"—or "trashion fashion"—from H&M, Target, Zara, and others, now rules the apparel market, with clothes so cheap it's often not worth the cost of dry cleaning them. As Elizabeth Cline relates in *Overdressed: The Shockingly High Cost of Cheap Fashion*: "Seasonal shopping patterns have given way to continuous consumption." Zara delivers new lines twice a week, while H&M and Forever 21 stock new styles *every day*. The number of fashion seasons has increased from two a year in the 1960s—spring/summer and autumn/winter—to as many as 100 "micro-seasons" today. The average American is now purchasing 60 percent more items of clothing compared with the year 2000, but each garment is kept for half as long.[35] In Cline's words, "buying so much clothing and treating it as if it is disposable, is putting a huge added weight on the environment and is simply unsustainable." Between the pesticides, chemical dyes, synthetic fibers, and water consumption, garments consume enormous quantities of natural and industrial resources. Apparel is one of the world's most polluting industries.[36] The $2.5-trillion global clothing and footwear industry is also said to be responsible for 8 percent of global greenhouse gas emissions, nearly as much as the EU.[37]

Cotton, which accounts for one third of all fibers found in textiles, is a thirsty crop. The cotton needed to produce one shirt requires 2,700 liters of water—what one person drinks in two and a half years. Growing so much cotton severely stresses water reserves. In Central Asia the Aral Sea has nearly disappeared because cotton farmers have diverted the rivers that used to fill it. In other places, aquifers are being drawn down unsustainably to grow cotton. Cotton farming consumes 24 percent of insecticides and 11 percent of pesticides, despite using about 3 percent of the world's arable land.[38] The US cotton crop requires the application of 22 billion pounds of toxic pesticides every year. Synthetic fibers like polyester have less impact on water and land than natural fibers like cotton, but they have other deleterious environmental consequences. A polyester shirt is responsible for more than twice the carbon emissions of a cotton shirt. Polyester production for textiles released about 1.5 trillion pounds of greenhouse gases in 2015, the equivalent of about 185 coal-fired power plants.

Most fibers are dyed or bleached, treated in toxic chemical baths to make them brighter, softer, more fade resistant, waterproof, or less prone to wrinkles. Upholstery fabrics and children's pajamas are treated with ghastly chemicals to make them fireproof or stain resistant. These toxic baths consume immense quantities of chemicals and water, and in China the chemicals have been routinely dumped in rivers and lakes, untreated, for decades (see Chapter 3). Then, after all these chemical treatments, the fabrics are dried under heat lamps. These processes consume enormous quantities of energy. The textile industry is one of the largest sources of greenhouse gas emissions in the world, and it's growing exponentially.

In 1950, when there were about 2.5 billion people on earth, they consumed around 10 million tons of fabric for all uses. Today the world population has exceeded 7 billion, but we consume more than 70 million tons of fabric annually, nearly 3 times as much per capita. Producing 70 million tons of fabric consumes astounding quantities of resources, including more than 145 million tons of coal and between 1.5 and 2 trillion gallons of fresh water, every year. Synthetic fibers like polyester are the worst, consuming between 10 and 25 times as much energy to produce as natural fibers. What's more, synthetic fibers are "poisoning our waterways and food chain on a massive scale," and plasticizing the oceans.[39] In short, fast fashion is accelerating the disposal of Planet Earth.[40] At the end of the day, the only solution to fast fashion-led planetary destruction is to stop making the stuff, shut down the production lines and retail operations, and produce durable clothing instead.

"iPhones Hardly Have a Shelf Life Greater Than a Loaf of Bread"

And what's true for China's garment industry has been true for most of the rest of China's export industries. From cheap disposable shoes and clothes, toys, tools, housewares, Christmas junk, and flimsy plastic appliances to meticulously made and expensive (but nevertheless designed-to-be-obsolesced) iPhones and 60-inch flat-screen televisions, most of the world's light-industrial goods are made in China and they are, for the most part, deliberately designed to be technically or fashionably obsolesced—unrepairable and mostly unrecyclable. Responding to Apple's attempt to greenwash its energy-hogging, resource-wasting, suicide-riddled Chinese iFactories by issuing so-called "green bonds," one critic complained that

> Maybe Apple could actually put environmental credentials into their products by making them have repairable, replaceable and non-proprietary parts, not issuing a new model every few months with ever so minor "upgrades." iPhones hardly have a shelf life greater than a loaf of bread . . . 100% renewable energy? What a joke. What they mean by that is the use of energy at their offices, not at the companies they outsource their manufacturing to, and not to the companies that provide the materials, which are both far more energy intensive.[41]

What's more, with its exciting new leasing plan, "eager gadget fans" can now get "A new iPhone every year," as one headline in the *Daily Mirror* read in 2015. That's obviously a good thing from the standpoint of Apple and the advert-hustling *Mirror* but they don't pause to consider the environmental cost of our disposable world. At a product event in March 2016, Apple's vice president for worldwide marketing remarked that it was "really sad" that more that 600 million computers in use today are more than five years old. Sad not for the users, because the technology is such that it's not really necessary to frequently upgrade your computers, but sad for Apple's balance sheet if they can't sell you trivially upgraded versions every year.[42]

Globally, we toss 300 million computers and a billion smartphones a year. Americans alone toss 100 million smartphones. The environmental cost of all this e-waste is staggering. The environmental cost of production begins with the degradation wrought by lithium, cobalt, and nickel mining for all those batteries.[43] Then there's the environmental cost of the energy consumed to power the mines and factories that are producing and reproducing these billions of gadgets. And then there are the costs of disposal—e-waste, including smartphones, contains all manner of toxic metals and chemicals, including mercury, lead, arsenic, cadmium, selenium, chromium, and flame retardants. Notoriously, for decades 70 percent of the world's e-waste was "recycled" in impoverished coastal Chinese villages where children cooked motherboards over open fires to melt out the tiny bits of gold and silver while their parents burned piles of electrical cables to salvage the copper, or smashed lead-acid car batteries to get the lead out. The health of children and parents alike was destroyed in the process while the rural farm soils and water courses were devastated. And after the metals were salvaged, the bulk of the e-waste—mainly plastics of one sort or another, with all their toxic and carcinogenic dioxins—was incinerated because it couldn't really be recycled, and crowded China has little room for landfills, sending more toxics into the world's atmosphere. Alternatively, e-waste was simply dumped into the world's oceans, adding to the giant plastic gyres covering vast stretches of the oceans. The government concedes that China is the world's leading dumper of plastics into the oceans.[44]

Appliances used to last decades, even generations. Now you're lucky if they last a few years. In the case of furniture, IKEA and others brought us "fast furniture"—flat-packed, flimsy, pressed-particle chipboard or MDF furniture, kitchen cabinets, and so on—essentially sawdust bound together with chemicals and resin, and heat-pressed into panels. Chipboard furniture, as you've probably experienced, sags and swells, corners break, and edge-taping breaks off. As a result, after a short lifespan most items get thrown out, often to be replaced with another just like it. Over the years people spend more on this junk than if they had bought a well-made, even second-hand piece of furniture in the first place. This is no small contributor to resource exhaustion—IKEA is the third-largest consumer of wood on the planet and sources at least a quarter of its wood from illegal loggers in Russia—which is often then milled in China.[45] Particle board also consumes significant energy to produce—wood scraps must be shredded, dried, and mixed with chemicals and adhesives, all before the heating and panel pressing process begins. Chipboard furniture also releases formaldehyde and other toxics in our homes, offices, schools and commercial spaces, and here too, it can't really be recycled because it's full of chemicals, so most is left to leach in landfills or burned in incinerators. Fast furniture, like fast fashion, is speeding planetary collapse.

Products We Don't Need and Planet Earth Can't Afford

Needless to say, we have benefited immensely from the availability of afford-able computers and smartphones. But there is no technical reason why these devices could not be produced as durable products—upgradeable, repair-able, rebuildable, fully recyclable—so that they could last decades, instead of being designed to be tossed and replaced every two years.[46] The same goes for flimsy plastic appliances, chipboard IKEA furniture, shoes that can't be re-soled, H&M clothes so cheap they're not worth the cost of dry cleaning, and so on. The ruinous economic logic of disposable products would not have mattered so much in Adam Smith's day, when factories were small, products few, and there were only a billion of us on Planet Earth. But today, when huge Chinese factories employ millions of workers manufacturing endless waste streams of disposable products and ever more pointless new "needs"—products designed not for the needs of people but for the needs of companies *to sell to* people—this kind of economic logic matters. It's not just irrational and wasteful. It's suicidal.

The production of disposable goods like these can't really be "greened" in any meaningful sense. Like mining, metallurgy, smelting, and oil and gas drilling, much manufacturing can't really be cleaned up beyond narrow limits, or within reasonable costs. That's why they moved to China in the first place. Unfortunately, China's "rise" since the 1980s has been largely based on just these sorts of industries. That's a huge problem for the Chinese and for the world, but it's a problem that has to be faced squarely if we hope to preserve a planet habitable for human beings. As the great American ecologist Barry Commoner used to say about toxics, "there is no 'away.'" After all is said and done, the only real solution is to stop making unneces-sary toxics and rigorously control the toxics we can't yet do without.[47]

2

"Blind Growth": Scenes of Planetary Destruction from the Twelfth Five-Year Plan

The first time that Li Gengxuan saw the dump trucks from the nearby factory pull into his village, he could not believe his eyes. Stopping between the corn-fields and the primary school playground, the workers dumped buckets of bubbling white liquid onto the ground. They then turned around and drove right back through the gates of their factory compound without a word. In March 2008 Li and other farmers in Gaolong, a village in the central plains of Henan province near the Yellow River, told a *Washington Post* reporter that workers from nearby Luoyang Zhonggui High-Technology Co. had been dumping this industrial waste in fields around their village every day for nine months. The liquid was silicon tetrachloride, the byproduct of poly-silicon production and a highly toxic substance. When exposed to humid air, silicone tetrachloride turns into acids and poisonous hydrogen chloride gas, which can cause dizziness and breathing difficulties. Ren Bingyan, a pro-fessor at Hebei Industrial University, told the *Post* that "the land where you dump or bury it will be infertile. No grass or trees will grow in its place . . . It is . . . poisonous, it is polluting. Human beings can never touch it." When the dumping began crops wilted from the white dust, which sometimes rose in clouds several feet off the ground and spread over the fields as the liquid dried. Village farmers began to faint and became ill. At night, villagers said, "the factory's chimneys released a loud whoosh of acrid air that stung their eyes and made it hard to breath." "It's poison air. Sometimes it gets so bad you can't sit outside. You have to close all the doors and windows," said Qiao Shipeng, a truck driver worried about the health of his one-year-old child. Reckless dumping of industrial waste is everywhere in China today. But what caught the attention of the *Post* was that Luoyang Zhonggui High-Technology Co. was a "green energy" company producing polysilicon destined for solar panels sold around the world. Indeed, it was a major supplier to Suntech Power Holdings, then the world's leading producer of solar panels, whose founder Shi Zhengrong topped the 2008 Hurun China Rich List.[1]

Silicon tetrachloride is an unavoidable byproduct of polysilicon production. But reckless pollution of farm villages is not unavoidable, and today China is the only country in the world where such criminal behavior and cynical disregard for the health and lives of farmers and workers has become standard practice on a national scale, countenanced by officials at every level, even as the government's own environmental agencies decry such behavior and struggle, mostly in vain, to stop it.[2] One Chinese researcher told the *Post* that "if this happened in the United States, you'd be arrested." But in China environmental regulations are regularly flouted by state-owned and private industries alike, while protesting peasants, workers, and environmental activists (and their lawyers) are arrested, jailed, and beaten. Polysilicon production produces about four tons of liquid silicon tetrachloride waste for every ton of polysilicon produced. In Germany, where Siemens produces solar panels, pollution recovery technology is installed to process the silicon tetrachloride waste and render it harmless. But such environmental protection technology is expensive. In 2008 the cost to produce polysilicon safely was about $84,500 per ton. Chinese companies were producing it for $21,000–$56,000 per ton, saving millions of dollars a month, by just dumping the toxic waste on helpless rural communities. Gaolong village is a mirror to China. It illustrates how the marriage of capitalism and Stalinist-Maoist bureaucratic-collectivism has created a diabolically ruinous hybrid economic system that is ravaging China's environment, destroying the health of its people, driving the country to ecological collapse, and threatening the whole planet.

CHINA SELF-DESTRUCTS

For more than three decades, China's economy has been the envy of the world. Since 1979, China's GDP has grown by an average of just under 10 percent per year. Never, the World Bank tells us, has a nation industrialized and modernized so quickly, or lifted so many millions out of poverty in such a short time. From a backward, largely agrarian "socialism-in-poverty," Deng Xiaoping brought in foreign investors, introduced market incentives, set up export bases and turned China into the light-industrial workshop of the world. In turn, growing trade surpluses funded the renovation and expansion of China's huge state-owned industries. Four decades of surging economic growth lifted China from the world's tenth-largest economy in 1979 to the second-largest by 2010, and by some measures the largest as of 2018.[3] What's more, after decades of export-based growth generated by the exploitation of desperately poor migrant laborers, China's twelfth Five-Year

Plan (2011–2015) refocused the economy toward internal market demand, with the intention of turning China into a mass consumer society modeled on the US. As China sailed through the global near-collapse of 2008–2009, hardly missing a beat while Western capitalist economies struggled to climb out of recession, even a market-fundamentalist, Thatcherite publication like *The Economist* had to concede that China's state capitalism was perhaps the wave of the future.[4]

But the cheap and dirty production that built that "miracle" has come at horrific social and environmental cost. It's difficult to grasp the demonic violence and wanton recklessness of China's state-driven and profit-driven assault on nature and its own people. In a March 2005 interview with *Der Spiegel*, Pan Yue, the eloquent young vice minister of China's State Environmental Protection Agency (SEPA) said that

> The Chinese miracle will end soon because the environment can no longer keep pace . . . We are using too many raw materials to sustain [our] growth . . . Our raw materials are scarce, we don't have enough land, and our population is constantly growing. Currently there 1.3 billion people living in China, that's twice as many as 50 years ago. In 2020 there will be 1.5 billion . . . but desert areas are expanding at the same time; habitable and usable land has been halved over the past 50 years . . . Acid rain is falling on one third of Chinese territory, half of the water in our seven largest rivers is completely useless, while one fourth of our citizens do not have access to clean drinking water. One third of the urban population is breathing polluted air, and less than 20 percent of the trash in cities is treated and processed in an environmentally sustainable manner . . . Because air and water are polluted, we are losing between 8 and 15 percent of our gross domestic product. And that doesn't include the costs for health . . . In Beijing alone, 70 to 80 percent of all deadly cancer cases are related to the environment.

Criticizing Western economists who reassure us that more growth is the key to repairing the environmental damage caused by growth, Pan added that

> There is yet another mistake . . . It's the assumption that economic growth will give us the financial resources to cope with the crises surrounding the environment, raw materials, and population growth. [But] there won't be enough money, and we are simply running out of time. Developed countries with a per capita gross national product of $8,000 to $10,000 can

afford that, but we cannot. Before we reach $4,000 per person, different crises in all shapes and forms will hit us. Economically we won't be strong enough to overcome them.[5]

Pan's searing honesty got him demoted and sidelined, but if anything he understated the speed, scale, and ferocity of a regime of environmental destruction that extends far beyond China itself.

Consuming the Planet to Support Unsustainable Growth

As China's growth took off in the 1980s and 1990s, the industrial boom rapidly depleted the country's resources—especially lumber, oil, and minerals—forcing Beijing to turn outward to feed its voracious engines of growth. The manic and thirsty industrialization boom in northern industrial cities drained freshwater aquifers, leaving some 600 cities, including Beijing, facing dire water shortages, and severely polluting most remaining reserves. Profit-hungry loggers cut down most of what was left of forests, recklessly denuding mountains and precipitating such extensive flooding and loss of life in 2009 that the government banned domestic logging. Chinese loggers then turned to plundering Siberia, Malaysia, and Indonesia—even New Guinea and parts of Africa. China has limited crude oil reserves, so industrialization and automobilization quickly turned it from a modest oil exporter into a net importer by 1993, and the world's largest oil importer by 2013. Iron ore, copper, and other critical industrial mineral reserves have also been rapidly drawn down, forcing the country to import growing quantities of minerals.[6] Today, with 18.5 percent of the world population, China is by far the largest consumer of primary industrial raw materials (cement, metal ores, industrial minerals, fossil fuels, and biomass). As of 2008 China was consuming 32 percent of global output of these resources, nearly four times as much as the US, the second-largest consumer. China consumes just over half of global coal output and one-third of oil output each year. As the leading producer and consumer of steel (45.7 percent of global output), China now depends on imports for 77 percent of its iron ore.[7] The one natural resource that China has plenty of, unfortunately, is coal.

As we noted in the Introduction, China has become the world's largest consumer of lumber and forest products, leveling forests from Siberia to Southeast Asia, New Guinea, Congo, and Madagascar.[8] By 2006 it was importing half of all tropical trees globally; many, if not most, of which are felled illegally.[9] Ninety percent of Mozambique's lumber exports go to China, and 70 percent of Gabon's and Cameroon's. Indonesian teak, Cambodian rosewood, Cameroonian bouma, Malaysian pacific maples, Gabonese kevazingo, Indonesian merbau, New Guinean white tulip pine, Siberian birch and pine, and more—most of the world's tropical and boreal forests are going to China.[10] According to the UN, most of Indonesia's forests will be gone by 2022, along with its charming orangutans.[11] The same goes for Cambodia and Myanmar. Whereas much of this wood used to be processed and re-exported to the US and Europe as flooring, furniture, and the like, by 2005 more than 92 percent of wood products made in China were consumed in China, most in its non-stop building boom.[12] Greenpeace has concluded that if China and other developed countries don't curb their demand for wood "future generations will be living on a planet without ancient forests."[13]

China does not import water in the same way, but it controls the headwaters of at least ten of Asia's transboundary rivers, including the Brahmaputra, which flows into India and Bangladesh; the Mekong, which flows down through Cambodia, Burma, Vietnam, Laos, and Thailand; and two rivers that flow into Kazakhstan and Russia. China's furious dam building and water diversion projects are reducing supplies and disrupting seasonal flow patterns for billions of people whose livelihood depends on those rivers.[14]

Of course, China has the world's largest population and is industrializing from a comparatively low level just four decades ago, so it's hardly surprising that it consumes lots of resources to build infrastructure and modernize. But the fact is that most of these resources have been squandered on a stupendous scale, and for all the waste and pollution, most Chinese have gotten surprisingly little out of it all.[15]

Chinese demand is driving poaching of everything from elephants and rhinos to seahorses and mushrooms. Edward O. Wilson calls the global extinction crisis "an Armageddon." As the nouveau riche indulge their millennia-old beliefs in traditional medicinal cures—supposedly enhancing their virility by eating pangolins, tiger bones, and bear paws—China has become the largest and fastest-growing market for illegally traded wildlife, funding the industrialized extinction of exotic species around the globe. Tanzania has lost two-thirds of its elephants since 2006 and Chinese officials are accused of being "huge buyers" of illegal ivory. While urging East Africans to "protect their wild animals" on a state visit to Tanzania in 2013, Xi Jinping's own entourage "smuggled out thousands of kilos of ivory" which was "sent to China in diplomatic bags on the presidential plane," according to the EIA.[16]

Irrational Exuberance with Chinese Characteristics

In Chapter 1 we considered resource waste in the Chinese export economy, especially in the production of disposable goods. When we turn to the domestic economy the overconsumption and waste is breathtaking but the modalities of overproduction and waste in the state-owned economy are very different in many respects from those of capitalist export bases like Shenzhen. A 2013 UN report warned that China's resource consumption was "unprecedented in human history."[17] As its economy opened to the West and exports began returning billions of dollars in trade surplus foreign exchange, Beijing's central planners launched wave after wave of gargantuan development projects, beginning in the 1990s. These included the world's largest and second-largest dams (the Three Gorges Dam, begun in 1992 and completed in 2012; and the Baihetan Dam, begun in 2017); vast urban renewal projects and new cities, along with subways, sewerage systems, ports, airports, hospitals, schools and universities, and museums; a national high-speed railway system and express highway system; and telecoms and internet services infrastructure. This stunning modernization blitz accomplished most of what the US built over a century in not much more than 30 years.

To be sure, the Chinese have benefited enormously from all this new infrastructure and housing, which, together with the parallel explosion in consumer goods, restaurants, modern conveniences, and high-tech gadgets, has met pent-up demand suppressed under decades of Maoist austerity. But China's state-owned producers don't stop when they've produced and built enough. Beijing regularly complains that local officials squander resources in building superfluous housing, redundant infrastructure, and useless vanity projects that the country simply does not need. From the start this investment boom has been characterized by overproduction, profligate waste of resources and energy, and needless pollution. In the early 2010s China's economy was consuming 7.9 times more energy per dollar of GDP than Japan, and 3.9 times more than the US.[18] It was also consuming 5.6 times more water per dollar of GDP as Japan's economy, and 2.9 times more than the US economy.[19]

"Making Too Much"

In the early years of market reform in the 1980s and 1990s, Chinese and Western boosters argued that marketization would rationalize China's state-owned producers, disciplining them, and compelling them to suppress overproduction, waste, and redundancy.[20] Instead, for the most part it resulted in massive overproduction of basics like steel, aluminum, plate glass, cement, coal, and electricity, as well as colossal overconstruction of apartment blocks, shopping malls, expressways, ports, industrial parks, railways, subways, airports, skyscrapers, and even entire "ghost cities."[21]

As Vaclav Smil writes: "The pace of China's concretization and its overall scale has been stunning. In 1980 the country produced just short of 80 Mt [megatons] of cement . . . by 2010 that total had tripled and reached 1.88 Gt [gigatons] (nearly 24 times the 1980 total and 57 percent of the global production for less than 20 percent of the world's population), and it rose further to 2 Gt in 2011." Perhaps no other comparison illustrates the scale of this concretization better than this: "China poured more cement (5.5 Gt) in just the three years between 2009 and 2011 than builders in the United States poured during the entire twentieth century (about 4.56 Gt)."[22]

Cement production accounted for about 5 percent of global CO_2 emissions in 2010, up from 2 percent in 1975, largely due to China's binge pouring in the 1990s and 2000s. According to Smil, in 2011 China's CO_2 emissions from cement production alone were only about 12 percent less than Japan's total CO_2 emissions from all sources.[23] Chart 2.1 below, by Robert Wilson at Plymouth Marine Laboratory, comparing China's current annual emissions from cement production with those of the nineteen

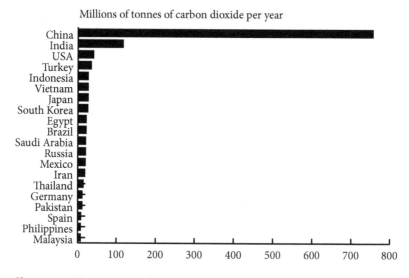

Chart 2.1 CO_2 emissions from cement production by country, 2018

Chart by Robert Wilson @countcarbon with data from Robbie M. Andrew, Global CO_2 emissions from cement production, 1928–2018, *Earth System Science Data* no. 10 (2019): 1675–1710, www.earth-syst-sci-data.net/11/1675/2019/essd-11-1675-2019.pdf.

next-largest producers, shows how China's emissions are many times larger than every other producer.

Lauri Myllyvirta of Greenpeace Beijing notes that "China and Indonesia have very similar GDP per capita and urbanization rates and trajectories," but while China has five times the population, its cement production "generates 28 times more CO_2 emissions per capita per year than Indonesia's."[24] That would appear to be due both to the inefficiency of China's antiquated small-scale cement producers (discussed in Chapter 5) and to the over-construction of infrastructure: The (little-used) national express highway system, (underutilized) national high-speed railway system, the thousands of superfluous dams, (discredited) south–north water transfer project (the biggest cement pour in history), and all the new cities.

Yet even as the country became glutted with zombie factories, redundant highways, little-used airports, and ghost cities, government organs at all levels relentlessly push for more expansion.[25] Where, in any normal capitalist economy, would one read headlines like these?

"Booming municipalities defy China's effort to cool economy"
– *Wall Street Journal*, September 15, 2006

"New capital projects unchecked: Beijing inspectors learned"
– *Xinhua*, October 28, 2006

"China urges auto makers to limit their expansion"
– *Wall Street Journal*, December 27, 2006

"China can't curb steel mills"
– *Wall Street Journal*, March 13, 2013

"China bans capacity expansion in cement, glass sectors"
– *Xinhua*, August 14, 2018

"Making too much"
– *Beijing Review*, October 31, 2013

"Beijing warns local officials against allowing expansion in industries with overcapacity"
– *South China Morning Post*, November 5, 2013

"In China, Beijing fights losing battle to rein in factory production"
– *Wall Street Journal*, July 16, 2014

Perpetually growing supply with no demand. You don't see this kind of waste in Shenzhen; waste there is different. That's one reason why China's hybrid economy cannot be understood as simply capitalist, or even state capitalist.

SCENES OF PLANETARY DESTRUCTION
FROM THE TWELFTH FIVE-YEAR PLAN

Since Deng Xiaoping initiated Reform and Opening, consecutive Five-Year Plans have set annual industrial growth rate targets of around 8 percent and promoted successive sets of "pillar" and strategic industries. The eleventh Five-Year Plan (2006–2010) prioritized armaments, power generation, oil and petrochemicals, telecoms, civil aviation, shipping, autos, metals, construction, and machinery. The twelfth Five-Year Plan (2010–2015) called for the development of "seven strategic emerging industries" to be the backbone of the next phase of industrial modernization and technological development: 1) Energy efficient and environmental technologies (like "clean coal"); 2) next-generation IT, cloud computing, and the "Internet of Things"; 3) biotechnology; 4) high-tech vehicles and aircraft; 5) new-generation nuclear power and more solar and wind energy systems; 6) new materials, including the development of rare-earth elements, special glass and ceramics, high-performance fibers, and composite materials; 7) new-energy vehicles, motor batteries, drive motors, electronic controls, plug-in hybrid and electric vehicles, and low-emissions vehicles.[26]

Scene 1: The "Car Craze" that China and Planet Earth Didn't Need

The twelfth Five-Year Plan called for "enhancing China's independent capacity to manufacture automobiles," including "domesticating production of all key parts," along with the "large-scale commercialization" of energy-efficient and hybrid vehicles, and the building of "world-famous brands and core competencies."[27] Up to 1979, China produced around 160,000 motor vehicles per year, with trucks and buses accounting for 90 percent of the output. People largely got around on bicycles, buses, and trains. In 1990 China had just 5.5 million cars, trucks, and buses on the road. By 2013 it had become the world's largest auto assembler and the largest auto market, producing 18.7 million cars and light vehicles, more than twice the output of the US in that year. By 2017 China was producing 25 million cars per year, and another 4 million commercial vehicles. What's more, it had 300 million registered vehicles on its roads, surpassing (of course) the

269 million registered vehicles in the US. Analysts predict that it could have between 390 million and 532 million cars on the road by 2050.[28]

Why does China need such a huge auto industry, particularly given the climate crisis that we face? In the US, transportation became the leading source (28.5 percent) of greenhouse gas emissions in 2016, surpassing electricity generation (28.4 percent).[29] Vehicle emissions are surging around the world just when we need to be drastically suppressing emissions.[30] As far back as 1990, studies showed that the combination of trains, buses, and bicycles was the most energy-efficient, least polluting, and healthiest way of facilitating urban transit.[31] China could have just modernized the system that they already had, instead of banning bicycles on major streets and building ring road after ring road around Beijing, which is what they did instead.

The automobilization of China has brought three profound changes. First, it has dramatically lengthened the time it takes to get anywhere within gridlocked cities (the average speed on Beijing's ring roads is nine miles per hour) and created epic, world-historic traffic jams on highways feeding into these cities. One such traffic jam near Beijing in 2010 stretched over 100 kilometers and lasted for nearly *two weeks*.[32] Secondly, it has added a dense new layer of smog on top of the already thick layers of smog that are smothering the country's cities. In 2015 the government reported that 31 percent of Beijing's smog came from motor vehicles, 22 percent from burning coal, 18 percent from industrial production, and 14 percent from construction dust.[33] Thirdly, it has paved over much-needed farmland and wetlands, and wasted enormous resources that China does not have to waste. This did not have to happen. All these results were predicted back in the 1990s and were entirely avoidable.[34] China did not have to repeat the same mistakes that were made in Los Angeles all over again.

The Communist Party promoted joint venture-based auto production as a "pillar" industry in the 1990s for three reasons. First, once the government embarked on its market reform strategy, abandoning lifetime employment, it needed to push growth to generate private- and state-sector jobs, like capitalist governments everywhere. The auto industry has generated lots of jobs in China. By 2000 automobile manufacturing and related industries accounted for about 27 million jobs, one out of every eight urban jobs in China (and this excludes road building, another big employer).[35] Secondly, the Party promoted the car craze to bolster status-seeking, middle-class political support. In the 1980s, the Party supported modest consumerism. But after the Tiananmen Square protests in 1989, it opted for expansive

Figure 2.1 Beijing at rush hour on January 1, 1985, before the car craze.
Credit: Alamy

Figure 2.2 Smoggy Beijing in the midst of the car craze, on February 23, 2011.
According to the Beijing Municipal Transportation Commission, 44 percent of
the capital's motor vehicles travel less than five kilometers per trip—a distance that
one used to be able to cover in 15–20 minutes by bicycle but which today can take
hours when the roads are congested.
Credit: AP Images

consumerism to win back the support of the working and middle classes.[36] Hence the car craze, the condominium craze, the shopping mall craze, the high-speed train craze, the tourism craze, and so on.[37] Thirdly, the cadres wanted fancy imported cars for themselves, their wives, and their children, and they got them. China is the world's largest market for Ferrari, Lamborghini, Bentley, Mercedes-Benz, and BMW.

It is no small irony that just as the CCP was ramping up auto production and banning bicycles from public roads in the 1990s, European countries were moving in the opposite direction—barring cars from many central city streets, promoting bicycles and car sharing, and expanding public transit. China didn't begin expanding its urban subways in earnest until the late 2000s, after two decades of automobilization had gridlocked its cities and dramatically increased air pollution.

Figure 2.3   Copenhagen missed the car craze. Pictured is the late morning rush hour at the heavily bicycle-trafficked crossroads at Frederiksborggade, Søtorvet, heading towards central Copenhagen on August 16, 2016. Fifty percent of Copenhagen's residents commute by bicycle. In the 1960s, Copenhagen, unlike Stockholm and many European and American cites, rejected the modernist "utopia" that called for leveling old city centers and replacing them with freeways, high-rise office buildings and apartment blocks. Today it's one of the most vibrant, livable, healthy, and walkable cities in the world. It retains its historic housing stock, strong bicycle culture, and has added extensive pedestrianized zones—an urban model that many "modernized," auto-centered cities around the world are now desperately trying to revive.

Credit: Alamy

Scene 2: The Roads Not Taken

As China was racing to surpass the US as the world's largest car market, the CCP decided that China should also "catch up and overtake" the US Interstate Highway System as well. Thus by 2010 China had built 53,000 miles of intercity expressways, surpassing the US Interstate Highway System's 47,000 miles. This program, built at huge cost and by tearing through cities and paving over thousands of square miles of valuable farms, wetlands, and so on, is mostly yet another ill-conceived prestige project. Except for a few highways near major cities like Beijing or Shenzhen, China's expressways are often little used. In some places, farmers dry their crops on empty superhighways. Commenting on an image of an empty eight-lane highway running through a small city, journalist Tom Lasseter writes:

> One often hears about the traffic jams in the big cities of China. But here's the flip side of the coin: In rural towns and cities in China, local officials like to build big showcase projects, displaying grandiosity but little utility. I was in the city of Fengzhen in Inner Mongolia yesterday. By Chinese standards, it is a small place, maybe 200,000 people. So imagine my surprise as we leave the downtown to come across [an] eight-lane highway going past a mammoth new City Hall. Nary a car on it. A passerby could keel over with a stroke on that highway and not risk getting run over for many hours. The city is already in hot water for building a power plant that Beijing says is unneeded. Across China, there are plenty of largely empty hotels, brand new empty highways, modern airports that lose money for lack of traffic, etc. What happens is that unelected local officials, not particularly responsive to local needs, find that pharaonic projects give their municipalities a luster that can attract investment, which is their path to promotion within the one-party system. So for every eight-lane road you see like this, there is a happy bureaucrat pondering a bright career ahead.[38]

How much cement has been poured, how much iron rebar has been forged, and how much coal has been burned to produce the energy to pave over so much of China—for no useful purpose?

In January 2017, *People's Daily* reported that China was in the process of building the world's highest-altitude ring road in Lhasa, Tibet:

> The road, with a total length of nearly 100 kilometers, will feature seven tunnels and 27 bridges. Lhasa has an average elevation of more than 3,600

meters; thus, the ring road is designed with a speed limit of 60 km/h. It will take less than two hours to circle the city. The road is expected to be completed and open to traffic by June 2017.

Impressive. But Lhasa has an urban population of just 257,000 ex-yak herders and monks, fewer people than, say, Jersey City (263,000) across the Hudson River from where I'm sitting right now in Manhattan. The urban area of Lhasa occupies just 23 square miles (Jersey City takes up 21 square miles). Try as I might, I can't envision a 100-kilometer (62.5-mile) ring road with 7 tunnels and 27 bridges surrounding *Jersey City*. What on earth does Lhasa need with such a ridiculous construction? How much cement, steel, and other resources have been wasted, and how much coal has been burned to make the cement and produce the electric power to build this two and a half-mile high white elephant? Useless vanity projects like this are everywhere in China.[39]

To make matters worse, the pollution generated by all China's needless overproduction and overconstruction is melting Tibet's glaciers. Scientists

Figure 2.4 The construction site of the world's highest ring road, around Lhasa, Tibet on January 5, 2017. Never one to shy away from a world record, no matter how meaningless, China is already bragging about constructing the world's highest ring road around the Tibetan capital. China's urban planners love ring roads. Shanghai has four, and Beijing six. Beijing's Sixth Ring Road is approximately 220 kilometers long. The government says Lhasa's new ring road will "contribute to Tibet's glorious 'golden age.'"

Credit: AP Images/Imagine China

tell us that the collapse of Tibet's glaciers will be catastrophic for the more than two billion Chinese, Indian, and Southeast Asian people who depend on rivers fed from Tibet, the "roof of the world."[40]

Scene 3: Too Many Trains, Too Many Stations, Too Many Subways

How much steel, aluminum, copper, cement, and electricity has been consumed to build China's huge national high-speed rail network? By 2013, China had already built more high-speed railways than the rest of the world combined. But the twelfth Five-Year Plan budgeted hundreds of billions of dollars to expand the system's total track length to 45,000 kilometers by 2020. No doubt many of these lines fulfill a useful function. But the scale of this project shows that it's more about prestige and "make-work" jobs than modernizing necessity. Most high-speed lines make no economic sense and run at reduced capacity. Grandiose but empty stations have been built in rural towns where only a couple of trains pass by per day, accommodating fewer than a dozen passengers.[41] China's *Caixin* spoke to Professor Zhao Jian of Beijing Jiaotong University, who said that

> It is unwise to continue building high-speed rail lines while the current high-speed network has a hard time getting enough passengers and is operating at a loss . . . The country has built more than 10,000 kilometers of high-speed rail lines and most lines are losing money because of inadequate demand.

Some lines run at only 30 percent of capacity, Zhao said, and even the busiest, such as the train from Beijing to Shanghai, "will run a loss for a long time . . . The rush to build high-speed rail networks indicates that the old investment-driven growth model has hardly changed."[42] Zhao reckons that only 5,000 of the planned 45,000 kilometers will be in areas where there are enough people to justify the cost.[43] Chinese rail companies have also tried to sell their high-speed trains overseas. But there too, few proposed lines justify the huge cost so they're not selling.

China's subway construction boom faces the same problems. Twenty-two cities already have subway systems, and money was budgeted in 2012 to build subways in another sixteen cities by the end of 2018. But Wang Mengshu, a subway engineer who helped design China's first subway in Beijing in 1965, says that most of these are unnecessary, excessively expensive prestige projects more than they are public services. "Second-, third-, fourth-tier cities . . . those cities don't need to build subways. Even if they can afford to build them, they can't afford to run them. But a lot of places think that if they have a subway, then they are a big city," he said.[44] As economist Nouriel Roubini told *Reuters* in 2011:

> I was recently in Shanghai and I took their high-speed train to Hangzhou . . . The brand-new high-speed train is half-empty and the brand-new station is three-quarters empty. Parallel to that train line, there is also a new highway that looked three-quarters empty. Next to the train station is also the new local airport of Shanghai and you can fly to Hangzhou. . . There is no rationale for a country at that level of economic development to have not just duplication but triplication of those infrastructure projects.[45]

Duplication, triplication, and waste is everywhere in China. Yet even as its rail system is already overbuilt and losing money, it's full speed ahead for new capital investment in rails.[46]

Scene 4: China as a "Major Aerospace and Air-Travel Power"

The twelfth Five-Year Plan also called for a push to make China a "major aerospace and air-travel power." Plans were laid out for spending nearly $200 billion on nearly 100 new airports and thousands of new airliners, helicopters, business jets, and small aircraft of all varieties. In 2017 Boeing forecast that Chinese carriers would need to purchase more than 7,000 new airliners alone over the subsequent twenty years, worth $1.1 trillion, to meet robust demand for domestic and international travel.[47] Great for Boeing and Airbus, but China does not "need" an aviation industry on a scale anything like this—and neither does the rest of the world. It's just suicidal for developing countries like China to repeat the environmental blunders of the West. The UN IPCC calculates that aviation is currently responsible for about 3.5 percent of anthropogenic climate change, a tiny share. But with air travel growing by 5 percent per year, by 2050 aviation could account for a quarter of all emissions.[48] Aviation is already the fastest-growing source of global CO_2 emissions, and if it continues to grow at its current rate it will overwhelm all the cuts engineers have managed to make elsewhere.[49] There are no practical alternatives to kerosene-based fuels for commercial jet aircraft; and biofuels, the much-hyped "renewable" alternative, are destroying rainforests from Indonesia to the Congo. This is why, after surveying the literature on the potential for mitigating greenhouse gas emissions with alternative forms of transportation, George

Monbiot concludes that while some forms of transport can be rendered a bit greener, there's virtually nothing we can do with aviation based on present or foreseeable technologies:

> There is, in other words, no technofix. The growth in aviation and the need to address climate change cannot be reconciled. Given that [efficiency gains tend to be canceled out by growth] a 90 percent cut in emissions requires not only that growth stops, but that most of the planes which are flying today are grounded. I recognize that this will not be a popular message. But it is hard to see how a different conclusion could be extracted from the available evidence.[50]

In a world where climate scientists tell us that we need to cut global CO2 emissions by 90 percent by 2050, global aviation emissions are on course to double by 2030. Absent some technological miracle, the only way to suppress aviation emissions is to ground planes, ration air travel, abandon air shipping,[51] and not add hundreds of millions more people to the global overtourism problem.[52] That's what Xi and the rest of the world will have to do if we really want an "ecological civilization." Even the aviation industry is beginning to see the problem.[53] Coming to grips with this reality may not be popular in China or the US, but the alternative is not going to be popular either.

Scene 5: Construction Frenzies and Ghost Cities

Wasteful as the foregoing examples are, nothing compares with the resources squandered on China's frenzied home- and city-building juggernaut. Since the 1990s, five-year plans have set quotas for increased urbanization. The 12th Five-Year plan called for 52 percent of Chinese to be urban residents by 2015. In response, mayors have been on a non-stop building boom like no other in history. Millions of residents of Beijing and Shanghai have been summarily evicted to make way for skyscrapers, new SOE headquarters, apartment blocks, shopping malls, theme parks, expressways, and ring roads.[54] Across the country, hundreds of millions have been evicted from farms and villages to make way for new highways, ports, airports, and dams, or their land has been sold off to developers for urban expansion. Operating on the principle of "build it and they will come," cities and provinces compete to build cloud-piercing skyscrapers even if they have no prospective tenants for them. By 2020, twelve of the planet's twenty tallest towers are expected to be in provincial Chinese cities like Shenyang, Wuhan, and Suzhou. By 2015 the office vacancy rate in Shenyang was nearly

Figure 2.5   A man plays basketball alone in front of the empty Ordos Kangbashi Public Library on a cold morning in October 2015.

Credit: Raphael Oliver

Figure 2.6   An empty street in a newly developed residential area on the southwestern outskirts of Ordos Kangbashi, October 2015.

Credit: Raphael Oliver

30 percent, yet three more towers—all taller than the Chrysler Building—were under construction, and another twelve were on the drawing board.[55] Beijing's premier architectural atrocity, the Rem Koolhaas-designed China Central Television Headquarters building—dubbed the "Big Underpants" by locals (and which prompted Xi's call for an end to "weird architecture" in Beijing)—was completed in 2008, but still sat mostly empty in 2014.[56] Cities compete to build ersatz "Wall Street-style" financial centers, as in Beijing (abandoned) and Tianjin (abandoned and unfinished); and oft-abandoned knockoff Disneylands.[57] Stunningly lavish Party offices are built everywhere (see Figures 2.8–2.9 below). China's coast has multiple redundant ports, some nearly empty, but more are planned.[58] Planning officials complain that cities are "blindly spreading out like big pancakes."[59] A national land survey found that 130,000 square kilometers of farmland, equal to half the area of Germany, was paved over in the urbanization frenzy between 1996 and 2009, and it hasn't slowed since. When cities can't find room to build so-called "new districts" or "new areas" because they're hemmed in by mountains, some have just leveled mountains to create land to sell off to developers. In Lanzhou "more than a thousand excavators at a time were unleashed on 700 mountains . . . so that a massive new district could be built."[60]

Words can't do justice to China's ghost cities (but have a look at the videos and satellite photos).[61] The largest ghost city, Ordos Kangbashi in Inner Mongolia, about 500 kilometers west of Beijing—a "marvel of urban planning, 137 square miles of shining towers, futuristic architecture and pristine parks carved out of the grassland"— is surreal.[62] It's got everything—office towers, administrative centers, hospitals, schools, a futuristic airport, museums, a beautiful public library, theaters, sports fields, a shopping mall, miles of apartment blocks, subdivisions of middle-class duplexes—a thoroughly modern city lacking just one thing, people.[63] Almost no one lives there. Something else is missing too, jobs. Ordos Kangbashi sits atop one of China's largest coal deposits and was built in expectation of booming coal production. But coal prices have fallen, and the government is closing many coal mines, so it is deeply in debt. Fourteen years after construction began, by dint of pressure and subsidies, the government has coaxed a few thousand bureaucrats and migrant workers to live there, paying almost no rent. With no industrial, commercial, or government jobs out in the middle of the grasslands, no one wants to move there. Yet even with no prospect of recovering the colossal waste of money already sunk into this white elephant, construction continues apace. Since 2010 the government has built more skyscrapers, added three sports stadiums (with neither teams nor spectators), and even a Formula 1 racing circuit (lacking race cars, drivers, and spectators).[64]

Figure 2.7   A few of the many unfinished and eerily empty office and residential tower blocks of the New Yujiapu Financial District, part of the Binhai New Development Area in Tianjin. May 5, 2014.
Credit: Alamy

Or consider Yujiapu in Tianjin, east of Beijing. In another burst of irrational exuberance local officials spent tens of billions of dollars to build the Yujiapu Financial District, a knockoff Manhattan complete with "Rockefeller Center," "Lincoln Center," and "Twin Towers." Yujiapu Financial District was intended to be "the biggest financial center in the world" (of course). That was in 2008. Today, mile after mile of office buildings sit mostly unoccupied, many unfinished and abandoned, despite massive government spending to attract residents and businesses.[65] Meanwhile, here and there new buildings are still going up amid the mostly empty complexes. Rob Schmitz of *Marketplace* recounts the following comments from a local property industry insider:

"It was a failure before it even started," says Gao Fei inside the Tianjin office of Centaline Property, where he works as director of investment consulting. "The most important thing for Tianjin's government has always been a high GDP rate. That means the government has to spend a lot of money on huge projects like this one. In China, these kinds of wasteful projects are everywhere."

For years, high GDP growth has ensured local officials promotions within the Chinese Communist Party. In the case of the faltering Manhattan replica of Yujiapu, it helped boost Tianjin's GDP growth rate to around 16 percent for three years, the fastest in China at the time. And *that* helped former Tianjin mayor Zhang Gaoli get promoted—to Vice Premier of China. In Zhang's rearview mirror on his way to Beijing: a failed project and mountains of debt.[66]

Ordos Kangbashi, Yujiapu, Binhai New Area, Caofeidian, Lanzhou New Area—China is littered with hundreds of ghost cities and new areas, mostly sitting empty and massively indebted. Optimists retort that these empty cities will eventually fill up because the government wants to move another 250 million farmers off their land and into cities. Indeed, some new areas are filling up. But Tom Miller, author of *China's Urban Billion: The Story Behind the Biggest Migration in Human History*, cautions that those with the best prospects are on the fringes of richer, first-tier cities—like Shanghai's Pudong district, the original Chinese ghost city that stood empty for years but eventually filled up, contradicting skeptics.[67] Most ghost cities and new areas have been built near poorer provincial cities, or far from commercial or industrial centers where the land was cheap, but without regard for jobs (or water, or infrastructure). They're not filling up. There's just no accounting for irrational planning by self-serving bureaucrats. Instead of letting cities grow organically, their preference, like Soviet planners before them, for self-glorifying showcase projects often predisposes them to build in wildly inappropriate locations.[68] Yujiapu, just an hour from Beijing and next door to Tianjin, is superfluous, useless. Beijing ordered it to be shelved. There was no need to build it in the first place. Caofeidian, built near Tangshan on the Bohai Sea, cost $100 billion. In 2006, local officials promised it would be "the world's first fully-realized eco-city," and would house one million people. Today it's mostly abandoned and only a few thousand people live there.[69]

And those 250 million farmers? Well, the housing built in China's ghost cities isn't affordable for ex-farmers.[70] It's mostly luxury condos and villas built for speculation, and many of them have already been sold to speculators who have no intention of ever living there. They're looking to preserve the value of their investments, not fill them with jobless ex-farmers who can't afford the purchase price or pay an economic rent. Since 2016, the government has also ordered a raft of affordable housing to be built. But with capped prices, builders skimp and put them up in even less desirable locations. Consequently, "the[se] cramped, poor-quality units that are far from anywhere lie mostly empty."[71] Meanwhile, builders are still building future ghost cities even as the population is projected to begin contracting by 2027, and drop to 90 percent of its current level by 2065.[72] As Miller writes: "Time for a reality check on China's ghost cities."

That reality check is coming right now. Today, more than one in five urban apartments in China sit unoccupied, roughly 65 million, enough to house half the population of the US. The bulk of these were built for speculation. Twenty-one percent of China's urban residents own two urban apartments, and many own three or four—all bought for speculation. The Chinese call them "gold bricks." Middle-class savers have few options to invest their savings. Bank interest is close to zero. They can't invest abroad. The stock market is a rollercoaster. So most have put their savings in housing speculation. For three decades the government has promoted real estate speculation as a safe investment and propped it up with loans to builders and easy mortgages for buyers.[73] Since the 1990s, property speculation in China has been a one-way bet. Yet economists have long warned that what China is really building is the biggest real estate bubble in history. Decade after decade state-owned and private builders have confidently assumed that local governments would pay the bills because the government fears collapse more than it fears local debt. So far this has been a good bet. But China's dramatic economic slowdown since 2015 has precipitated a sharp drop in housing prices. Developers have cut prices by up to 30 percent as demand for new housing plummets. Protests by homeowners who "overpaid" have become so common that a new term has appeared on social media—*fangnao*, or "property troublemaking."[74]

Scene 6: Versailles in Harbin

Besides the waste of useless empty cities, in a country where two-thirds of the population lives on less than $10 a day, China's citizens endure further insult as Party cadres squander social wealth on stunningly extravagant vanity projects. These include at least two full-scale replicas of the White House, complete with Oval Offices (in Fuyang and Wuxi),[75] copycat Eiffel Towers and French chateaux, and Disneyesque replicas of entire English and Continental European towns.

In Yangzhong, Jiangsu province one local official built a 2,100-ton, 15-story brass-clad "puffer fish tower" complete with "night-time light show to lure visitors" at a cost of more than $11 million.[76] At least it's original, and there are plenty more.[77]

Figure 2.8   Isn't this what you'd expect the headquarters of a provincial state-owned pharmaceutical company to look like? The Harbin Pharmaceutical Group Sixth Factory in Harbin, Heilongjiang province caused a public uproar for squandering tax revenue on this mini-Versailles, complete with gold-tinted walls and chandeliers. See Joanna Corrigan, "Oh la la! Chinese state factory decked out to look like the Palace of Versailles (much to the disgust of neighbors)," *Daily Mail*, September 8, 2011, www.dailymail.co.uk/news/article-2034679/Chinese-state-factory-decked-look-like-Palace-Versailles.html.

Credit: Str/AFP/Getty Images

Figure 2.9   Versailles in Harbin.

Credit: Str/AFP/Getty Images

Figure 2.10 The $11 million, 2,300-ton, 295-foot-long puffer fish tower.
Credit: AP Images/Imagine China

Scene 7: China's Big Invention—Disposable Housing

"China speed" amazes world.
– *People's Daily*, November 30, 2015

Construction is breathtakingly fast in China.[78] But it can also be breathtakingly shabby and dangerous. The problems begin with the most common of all building materials, concrete. As Vaclav Smil writes:

> Inevitably, such a pace of construction guarantees that a substantial share of newly poured concrete will be of substandard quality, a conclusion confirmed by the obvious dilapidation of China's concrete structures built during the late 1980s and early 1990s, the first period of China's construction boom. The quality of concrete used to construct many of China's new dams . . . is of particular concern, even more as thousands of them are located in areas of repeated, vigorous seismic activity. Even if the initial quality of the concrete posed no problems, the US experience of extensive concrete-based infrastructure offers a sobering view of what lies ahead for China.[79]

China's local building regulators, like its food safety and environmental regulators, are subordinate to local officials, who partner with, and profit from, the very construction companies that they are nominally supposed to regulate. As a result, safety is often subordinated to time and cost savings, with predictable results. The Chinese call it "tofu construction." Beijing concentrates its best builders on showcase infrastructure and prestige projects in the big, first-tier cities. But out in the suburbs and provinces quality falls off. Between July 2011 and August 2012, eight major bridges collapsed in China. One Australian reporter counted four collapsed bridges in just *nine days* in July 2012.[80] Buildings too collapse, and sometimes even simply topple over.

Figure 2.11   A 60-meter section of Jintang Bridge fell onto a cargo ship near the eastern port city of Ningbo on March 27, 2008. Four crew members were missing and presumed dead. For more photos see Mamta Badkar, "Look at all the major Chinese bridges that have collapsed in recent years," *Business Insider*, August 28, 2012, www.businessinsider.com/china-bridge-collapses-2012-8.

Credit: AP Images/Xinhua/Huang Shengang

Tens of millions of citizens have been displaced by urban renewal projects or cleared off their land and dumped in satellite new towns where shoddy new housing is already crumbling as they move in. In 2010, China's Ministry of Housing and Urban-Rural Development conceded the low quality of construction and warned that "China's newly-built houses can only last for 20 or 30 years."[81] After the collapse of an apartment in Fenghua, Zhejiang province in April 2014, officials warned of a "coming wave of such accidents as the 'fast food' buildings built in the 1980s and 1990s enter their 20s and

30s." Building safety experts warned people not to purchase apartments in certain localities known to be particularly risky. Most "won't last 50 years, or in some cases about 25 years," and they present constant safety hazards.[82]

Figure 2.12 On a Sunday morning in June 2009 this nearly finished thirteen-story apartment building in Shanghai just toppled over, killing a construction worker.

Credit: Newscom

Officials call for tougher regulation but most Chinese blame corruption. Bid-rigging is the norm and there are no checks or balances on the procurement process. "We do have relevant laws regarding the bidding process, but there is a lack of enforcement. The bidding process is only a show," says Zhu Lijia, a professor at the Chinese Academy of Governance in Beijing. One college student, Zeo Niu, interviewed by NPR after a major bridge collapse in 2012, knew the system well. Her uncle ran a construction company in central China. She called the use of substandard material while charging for high-quality goods "very, very common" and said that it was "not news." What really upset her was that because so many projects collapse, people had become overwhelmed: "I will never remember those victims' names in this accident, and people won't remember it. It will be buried by the next accident," she said.[83]

In the early afternoon of May 12, 2008, a magnitude-7.9 earthquake struck Sichuan province, with the epicenter near the town of Wenchuan some 80 kilometers north of Chengdu. Dozens of towns and villages were

Figure 2.13 This building in Fenghua city in eastern China's Zhejiang province collapsed on April 4, 2014. It buried seven people, killing one. Inspectors warned that the rest could also collapse.

Credit: Newscom

leveled, 1.5 million mostly mud-brick houses collapsed. Reinforced concrete office buildings, factories, schools, and hospitals were heavily damaged, and many collapsed. More than 87,000 people were killed and 4.8 million left homeless. Most horrifying was the collapse of school buildings, which caused the death of so many children. Some 7,000 classrooms collapsed and upwards of 9,000 students were crushed in the rubble. This stood in glaring contrast to Communist Party office buildings, some of which stood virtually next door. They emerged largely unscathed. It was plain for all to see that the Party had taken care that in this earthquake-prone region their own buildings were built to proper standards. Not so the shabbily built schools. It took all the Party's efforts, years of lies and cover-ups, "unifying" the press to celebrate heroic rescue efforts, brutal imprisonment of protesters, payoffs of parents, and rebuilding to quell the anger of parents whose bitterness remains to this day.[84] No one was held accountable. The artist Ai Weiwei made a film right after the earthquake in which he walks through collapsed school buildings with a construction expert who points out how the builders had skimped on iron rebar reinforcement of concrete columns, leaving them too weak to withstand the earthquake. Apparently, no building inspectors reported these shortcomings or shut down those sites, whereas they were evidently diligent at Party buildings. Ai salvaged tons of that rebar, straightened it all out, and turned it into an extraordinarily moving piece of political art, entitled "Straight," which was installed in a huge space in the Brooklyn Museum as his film of the wreckage played on screens around the room.[85] In a subsequent installation in 2009, entitled "Remembering," he hung 9,000 children's backpacks on an armature across the entire 348-foot length of Munich's Haus der Kunst museum, representing the 9,000 children who perished on that day.[86]

Figure 2.14 Against a background of blue backpacks, huge characters in five colors spell out "For seven years she lived happily on this earth," a sentence with which the mother of one of the earthquake victims commemorated her daughter.

Credit: Joerg Koch/DDP/AFP/Getty Images

THE WORST INDUSTRIAL SAFETY RECORD IN THE WORLD

We are treated like ants . . . not humans . . . I sold my life to Shenzhen. If I had known the danger of pneumatic drilling, I would never have done the work, no matter how poor I am.
    – Wang Zhaogang, silicosis-stricken construction worker[87]

China's shoddy construction practices are mirrored by its abysmal industrial safety record. The devastating chemical dump explosion that incinerated

43

more than 100 people in Tianjin on the night of August 11, 2015 was the twelfth reported chemical accident that year and was soon followed by two more fatal explosions in other cities in early September. Like building safety, industrial health and safety has never been a priority in China, but since the turn to the market in the 1980s, explosions at factories, chemical dumps, and gas pipelines, along with factory fires, construction mishaps, collapsing coal mines, and similar industrial "accidents" have soared along with the national GDP. Hundreds of thousands of such events occur every year. Coal mining accidents alone have killed more than 6,000 miners per year for decades.[88] In 2011 two factories exploded when clouds of aluminum dust from milling iPad cases ignited, killing 4 and injuring 77. In 2013 a blaze at a poultry slaughterhouse in northeastern China killed 120 workers. A pipeline blast in Qingdao in November 2013 killed 55 and left 11 missing, not far from where huge oil tanks exploded in 1989, killing 19. In January 2014, 16 people died when a fire tore through a shoe factory in Zhejiang province. In August 2014 a factory in eastern Jiangsu province that polished wheel rims for General Motors exploded, killing 68 workers and injuring 187. In August 2018 a power plant exploded in Hubei killing at least 21

Figure 2.15 Tianjin, August 13, 2015. A man walks past the charred remains of new cars in a parking lot near the site of the world's largest-ever industrial explosion, on August 12, which killed 173 people and underscored concerns about corruption, incompetence, and the inability to police pollution and industrial safety.

Credit: AP Images/Ng Han Guan

people. In March 2019, a chemical factory not far from Shanghai that had been fined and warned multiple times over unsafe conditions exploded, killing 78 and injuring more than 600.[89] And on it goes. As Gerry Shih of the *Washington Post* writes:

> A deadly factory explosion in 2007 didn't kill Ren Guanying. Nor did the chlorine gas leak that sparked mass panic in 2010. When countless smaller industrial accidents struck this smog-choked belt of Jiangsu province over the years, they spared her too. The 58-year-old factory worker's luck ran out on March 21st . . . "We used to always worry whenever we heard a blast, until we got numb to it" [said her daughter, Ma Li] in her shattered home about half a mile from the chemical plants. "This place was like a time bomb. It finally got my mom."[90]

The next nearby blast came a week later, taking seven more lives.[91] As Geoffrey Crothhall of China Labour Bulletin says: "Every time this happens, the government goes through the same routine. They carry out an investigation, they say lessons will be learned, the guilty will be punished, measures will be taken. But nothing changes."[92]

More Than One Million Workplace Deaths per Decade

Terrible industrial accidents occur in normal capitalist countries too. Mercury poisoning killed and severely injured thousands of residents of Minimata, Japan in the 1960s. The Bhopal toxic gas release in 1984 killed more than 4,000 people. The Rana Plaza garment factory collapse in Bangladesh in 2013 killed 1,129 garment workers. But these are trivial numbers compared with China, where official reports indicate that more than one million workers have died in industrial accidents per decade since the 1980s. During the boom years of the 2000s the government reported that workplace accidents regularly claimed more than 10,000 lives a month, and more than 115,000 lives a year—more than *twenty times* the average number of workplace fatalities in the US in the same period. In 2005 more than 127,000 workers were reportedly killed on the job in China vs. 5,734 in the US.[93]

Even allowing for the fact that China's labor force is five times larger than the US labor force, its workplace death rate is still shocking. What's more, the government concedes that official counts of workplace deaths substantially understate the actual totals because local officials routinely cover up deaths to protect themselves. A *China Daily* editorial in 2010 asked: "Why do industrial enterprises such as coal mines and steel plants always cover up workplace accidents? Why do they always try to dilute the seriousness of an accident by reporting fewer number of deaths than a disaster has actually claimed?" The editorial cited a case in which the actual number of accidental deaths was found to be three times higher than the officially reported total. The real totals are thus certainly higher, perhaps as much as two or three times higher than the official figures.[94]

Even more workers are injured, or suffer from silicosis, chemical poisoning, cancers, and other industrially induced diseases.[95] These injuries are even less likely to be reported and typically receive inadequate compensation, if any is offered at all.[96] Chinese health authorities and researchers say that around 23 million are suffering and dying from silicosis, many of them the construction workers who drilled the tunnels and built the foundations of China's cities and infrastructure with little or no safety equipment, sacrificing their lives to build and overbuild the country at "China speed." This compares with 11.5 million silicosis-impaired workers in India, 2 million in the US and 1.7 million in Europe.[97] What's worse is that the bulk of those millions of migrant workers, the main workforce on construction sites, are left to fend for themselves. Many repeatedly appeal to the government for help, usually to no avail. Desperate workers who've protested against the government have been met with batons and tear gas. Unsurprisingly, some prefer the quick death of suicide to the extended horror of a slow but inevitable death by suffocation as their lungs give out.[98]

Yes, China has comprehensive industrial health and safety regulations. The government has its own equivalent of the Occupational Safety and Health Administration (OSHA) in the US, the State Administration of Workplace Safety. It promulgated the Occupational Disease Control Act in 2001 and the Work Safety Act in 2002, ratified the International Labor Organization's "Occupational Safety and Health Convention, 1981" in 2007 and the "Chemical Convention, 1990" in 1995. The problem is that these are all routinely ignored, little-enforced, and inspectors are regularly bribed. Top to bottom, the government has been unable or unwilling to enforce its own health and safety codes. One executive from a toy industry multinational with extensive operations in Guangdong told the *Far Eastern Economic Review* in 1993 that "industrial safety is the last thing that anybody worries about in Shenzhen, or anywhere else in the province."[99] Or anywhere else in China.

TWENTY MORE YEARS OF THIS?

In 2014 Justin Yifu Lin, the former chief economist and senior vice president of the World Bank, and a close advisor to senior leaders in Beijing, said that he was confident China could sustain its 8 percent annual average growth rate for the foreseeable future. He predicted "20 more years of roaring growth" for China."[100] Indeed? This is how capitalist—especially Chicago School—economists think. They are obsessed with numbers, oblivious to the real world of human suffering and environmental devastation that results from that growth. On paper, the mathematical projections work. But where does Lin imagine the resources are going to come from for this scale of consumption? And what will be the human costs and environmental consequences or "externalities" (in economist-speak) of extracting them?

As it happens, in 2011 the Earth Policy Institute at Columbia University calculated that if the Chinese economy were to keep growing by around 8 percent per year, average per capita consumption would reach current US levels by around 2035. But to provide the natural resources for China's 1.4 billion people to consume on a per capita basis like 330 million Americans consume today, the Chinese—currently 18.5 percent of the world's population—would consume as much oil as the entire world consumes today. It would also consume more than 60 percent of other critical resources.

Table 2.1   Annual consumption of key resources in China and US, latest year, with projections for China to 2035 compared to current world production

Commodity	Unit	Consumption, latest year		Projected consumption, 2035	
		US	China	China	World
Grain	Million tons	338	424	1,505	2,919
Meat	Million tons	37	73	166	270
Oil	Million barrels per day	19	9	85	86
Coal	Million tons oil equiv.	5	1,714	2,335	3,731
Steel	Million tons	102	453	456	1,329
Fertilizer	Million tons	20	49	91	214
Paper	Million tons	74	97	331	394

(Projected Chinese consumption in 2035 is calculated assuming per capita consumption will be equal to current US consumption, based on projected GDP growth of 8 percent annually. Latest-year figures for grain, oil, coal, fertilizer, and paper are from 2008; latest-year figures for meat and steel are from 2010.)

Source: Earth Policy Institute, 2011

If China were to consume like that, what would the rest of the world live on? As Michael T. Klare describes in *The Race for What's Left: The Global Scramble for the World's Last Resources*, existing reserves of oil, minerals, and other resources are already "being depleted at a terrifying pace and will be largely exhausted in the not-too-distant future." A 2013 United Nations Environment Program (UNEP) report warned that China was "consuming natural resources at a speed and scale the world has never seen":

China's dramatic economic growth over the past few decades has increased demands for natural resources within and beyond the country itself in ways that are unprecedented in human history ... In the last three decades, China has grown from a modest user of minerals, fossil fuels and other primary materials to become the world's largest consumer.

The country consumed 22.6 billion tonnes of such materials in 2008 – nearly a third of the world's total – up from 1.7 billion tonnes in 1970. It consumes four times as much as the United States, the second-biggest user. . . .

The country's population grew to 1.3 billion from 816 million over the 38-year period. But the amount of resources used by every citizen has also soared as their living standards improved. Per capita resource consumption rose from 31 per cent of the world average in 1970 to 1.62 times the world average in 2008, with the sharpest rise coming after 2000.[101]

Despite continuous improvement in resource efficiency—growing at a rate of 3.91 percent annually (still) in 2009, China used 2.5 times more energy than the global average to produce each unit of economic growth.[102] In short, with an economy just two-thirds the size of the US, China not only consumes four times more natural resources but even consumes nearly twice as much per capita as the rest of the world. Imagine the world, Mr. Lin, after twenty more years of this kind of plunder.

3

The Damage Done: The Poisoning of China's Water, Soil, and Foods

CHINA AS TOXIC WASTE DUMP

If China's smog is appalling, the contamination of its rivers, lakes, reservoirs, underground aquifers, and farm soils can only be described as apocalyptic. In less than four decades of reckless growth China has managed to severely pollute most of its freshwater resources while rendering extensive areas of farmland too polluted to grow food crops. No other nation has wrecked its environment so quickly and on such a scale.[1] The industries that are most responsible for this disaster are mining and chemicals. Of all the dirty industries that the West shipped to China in the 1990s, chemicals were the worst, and by the 2000s China had become the largest manufacturer of industrial chemicals. "Chemical plants were popping up by the hundreds of thousands—alongside train tracks, public housing complexes, rivers and farms," as Javier C. Hernandez puts it.[2] Soon thereafter China also had the world's largest number of lead- and chemical-poisoned children. Chemical pollution was not merely contained to urban industrial zones, as around Lake Tai to the west of Suzhou (see below). In the remote tropical villages of Yunnan province, mining for cadmium, zinc, chromium, copper, and other minerals leached heavy metals into water courses, wells, and farm soils. Poisoned rice and corn soon engendered widespread stomach, colon, kidney, liver, breast, and blood cancers, nearly wiping out whole towns, "as if a super-virus romped through them." "Forced to choose between starvation and poison, villagers ate the toxic rice or sold it to others and still do so today," writes environmental investigative journalist He Guangwei.[3] By the 2000s, China was also importing 70 percent of the world's e-waste, to be "recycled" in ramshackle coastal villages where villagers and their children now suffer from lead poisoning and other ailments. As fast as China became the workshop of the world, it also became the toxic waste dump of the world.[4]

The threat that chemical poisoning poses to public health in China can't be overstated. Basic food production is at risk for most of the country. Large areas have become virtually unlivable, with hundreds of millions of people trapped in cancer-ridden and smog-smothered communities, forced to consume toxic water and food, and breathe arsenic- and mercury-laden air.[5] Worse, unlike with smog, rivers, lakes, wells, reservoirs, and polluted farmlands cannot be cleaned up by just turning off the coal-fired power plants. With soil and water contamination, the damage is done, and it's not clear if it can ever be undone.[6] In a nation in which 18.5 percent of the world's population is trying to feed themselves on just 7 percent of its farmland, the enormity of this public health catastrophe is staggering. And yet even as it becomes increasingly urgent to find solutions, the government finds itself divided and powerless to reverse these trends.[7]

China's Rivers Run Black or Red or White or . . .

China's freshwater sources are contaminated by all manner of industrial chemicals, dyes, heavy metals, pesticides, fertilizers, and other toxics.[8] Gushing pollutants turn long stretches of rivers bright red, purple, milky white, or inky black. Its largest rivers resemble vast open cesspools and for much of their length the banks are strewn with refuse, dead fish, and dead farm animals, even dead people. Sewage is routinely dumped, mostly untreated, in the same rivers from which many cities take their drinking water, imperiling the health of hundreds of millions. Rivers are also assaulted by huge accidental spills of toxic chemicals—benzene, xanthogenate, analine, cadmium, and so many others—that happen every year, and in some places seemingly every day.[9] In September 2004, Jim Yardley reported on the situation in the Huai River basin, upstream from Shanghai, after a huge chemical spill created an 82-mile-long band of water that killed nearly every living thing and was too polluted even to safely touch (the Huai, Yardley pointed out, was supposed to have been a government "success story").[10] In April 2014, it was a major leak of benzene that poisoned the drinking water for millions in Gansu province.

Rivers Polluted Beyond any Human Use

In 2012 the government reported that 40 percent of China's rivers were "seriously polluted" (Grade 4) and 20 percent were so polluted their water was "too toxic even to touch" (Grade 5).[11] In northern China, the fabled and once-mighty Yellow River is so depleted from overuse that it now sometimes runs completely dry before reaching the sea. The 300 rivers that drain the North China Plain are "open sewers if they are not completely dry," in

Figure 3.1   Boats collect garbage floating on the Yangtze River next to the Three Gorges Dam in Yichang city, Hubei province on July 17, 2013. Layers of rubbish floating in the Yangtze regularly threaten to jam the massive dam. The garbage is so thick in parts of the river that people can walk on the surface. More than 150 million people live upstream from the dam. In several nearby cities, household garbage is dumped directly into the river, China's longest, because municipalities are ill-equipped for trash disposal. The China Three Gorges Corporation reportedly spends about 10 million yuan ($1.6 million) every year to clear floating waste.

Credit: AP Images/Imagine China

the words of Ma Jun, China's leading authority on the country's water crisis. More than a third of China's fish species had gone extinct by 2007.[12] Ma observed that "even when the river is flowing, its water has become virtually useless in many places along the lower reaches." One study indicated potable water was only available in 31 percent of the entire drainage area of the Yellow River, and most of that was in its undeveloped western regions. For more than two-thirds of its length, the river has toxicity levels of Grade 4 or 5 (unfit for any human use, not even for industry or agriculture).[13]

The Yangtze River is, if anything, worse. Pollution, damming, and increased shipping has caused a sharp decline in aquatic life, with victims including the legendary Yangtze Baiji dolphin, the first large aquatic mammal to have been declared extinct in more than 50 years. Even common species like carp "are gasping for survival," one government report said.[14] And as

if the Three Gorges Dam project on the Yangtze didn't have enough problems, once the 400-mile-long reservoir filled up, largely untreated sewage,
industrial effluent, and refuse from huge upstream cities like Chongqing
turned it into the world's largest cesspool.[15] Instead of properly collecting,
processing, and recycling refuse in upriver cities like Chongqing, staggering quantities are just tossed into the river for overwhelmed refuse scows to
fish out before it clogs the dam's turbines (see Figure 3.1).[16] As *China Daily*
recently reported, citing officials: "More than 150 million people live near
the dam and its upper stream. But a number of cities remain unequipped
with garbage disposal equipment. Residents dump their household garbage directly into the river and the practice affects dam safety in the rainy
season."[17] The same goes for sewage, which, in most places, is pumped directly into the river without treatment. Then there are the industrial waste
discharges from the thousands of factories that line the Yangtze. Thus, it
was no surprise that in May 2006 *Shanghai Daily* reported the following:

> Experts warned yesterday that the Yangtze River has become so "cancer-
> ous" with pollution that it is threatening the safety of drinking water in
> Shanghai and other cities along its banks. The effluents in some sections
> of China's longest river are getting worse, and the Yangtze will become as
> filthy as the Yellow and Haihe rivers in five to [ten] years if action isn't
> taken soon.[18]

The dumping hasn't stopped.[19] A 2012 investigation by Greenpeace found
a wide range of hazardous substances in the effluent of communal wastewater treatment plants from industrial zones in Zhejiang province south
of Shanghai, where a high proportion of China's textile manufacturing and
dyeing is concentrated (producing fabrics for H&M, Nike, Esprit, Calvin
Klein, Levi's, and Liz Claiborne, among others).[20] Effluent from the Binhai
and Linjiang industrial zones was being discharged into the Qiantang River
to the south of Shanghai. Samples found toxic and hazardous chemicals
including carcinogenic chlorinated anilines (used in dyes), highly persistent
and bioaccumulative perfluorooctanoic acid (PFOA)[21] and PFCs (used in
textiles), carcinogenic nitrobenzene and chlorinated benzenes (CNBs), carcinogenic ethylene dichloride (EDC), and dibutylphthalate (DPB) which is
toxic to reproduction. The most shocking aspect of the Greenpeace study
was that their samples were taken from water that had *already been processed* by a water treatment plant specifically set up for these factories. Yet
it completely failed to remove toxic chemical compounds. Greenpeace con-

cluded that this demonstrates the inherent problems with "end-of-pipe" wastewater treatment:

There are intrinsic problems associated with the pollution control approach and its emphasis on wastewater treatment plants. While these are effective at cleaning up certain types of pollution—such as sewage or other biological wastes—they cannot cope with many hazardous chemicals. Some will pass through the treatment process unchanged and be discharged into the surface waters where they can enter the food chain and build up in the downstream sediments. Others can be converted into other more hazardous substances that are also discharged and/or can accumulate in other wastes generated during the treatment process. Hazardous wastes in the form of treatment plant sludge are therefore created, which in turn are disposed of, into landfills or through incineration, releasing the hazardous substances or their by-products into the environment.[22]

In the final analysis, Greenpeace concluded that "the dispersal of hazardous chemicals into water systems can only be addressed by the rapid and transparent *elimination of their use at source.*"[23]

As if this daily inundation of toxic chemicals, garbage and sewage weren't enough, in March 2013 residents of Shanghai suffered further insult as some 16,000 rotting pig carcasses floated down the Huangpu River into the Yangtze (a source of city's drinking water). Later that year, the government reported that the upper Yangtze ecology had "collapsed," with mass die-offs and extinctions from the relentless assaults of pollution, dams, and other ills.[24] At the other end, where the Yangtze empties into the East China Sea at Shanghai, the effluent of urban and industrial pollutants from China's rivers is said to be "wiping out" life up and down the coast.[25]

Eighty Percent of Groundwater is Undrinkable

If the water from China's rivers is unsafe to drink or irrigate crops, the groundwater from China's wells is no better. Sixty percent of China's population gets its drinking water from groundwater wells, which in rural areas is normally drunk untreated. Well water is also used extensively for agriculture in the north of the country. In February 2013, a survey of eleven cities undertaken by the China Geological Survey indicated that 64 percent of water sources were severely polluted, and 33 percent were moderately polluted. Only 3 percent of sources were graded as clean.[26] This is why the number of birth defects "is constantly increasing in both urban and rural areas," soaring by 40 percent in just six years from 2001 to 2007, while cancer too is at elevated levels.[27]

In 2016 the Ministry of Water Resources reported that 80 percent of the 2,103 water wells tested across the heavily populated plains of northern China were "so badly contaminated by industrial and agricultural runoff that their water was unfit for drinking and home use"; this was a marked increase on 2014 levels. In the 2016 study 33 percent of wells tested had Grade 4-quality water, which meant that it was "fit only for industrial uses," while an additional 47 percent of wells were even worse, Grade 5, extremely polluted and "unfit for any use." No wells tested had Grade 1 water ("clean"), and barely 19.9 percent of wells tested were rated Grade 2 ("usable if filtered"). Contaminants included manganese, fluoride, and triazoles, a set of compounds used in fungicides. In some areas, there was pollution by heavy metals.[28] In other words, hundreds of millions of Chinese living in rural areas have little choice but to drink toxic, even mutagenic and cancerous, groundwater.

The survey studied wells relatively close to the surface, the sort used by farmers, villages, and towns. Large cities get much of their water from reservoirs that are hundreds or even thousands of feet deep. Yet other studies indicate that reservoirs and deep wells are seriously polluted as well.[29] "From my point of view, this shows how water is the biggest environmental issue in China. People in the cities, they see the smog every day, so it creates huge pressure from the public. But in the cities, people don't see how bad the water pollution is. They don't have the same sense," said Dabo Guan, a Tsinghua University professor. The government's plans to improve water quality and safety are failing. The twelfth Five-Year Plan goal of "completely solving rural drinking water issues" by the end of 2015 will not be met, and "some villages are going backward because of scarcity and pollution."[30] Urban water safety has not improved.[31]

Urban Chinese who can afford it drink bottled water. But a 2014 survey showed that more than half, 59 percent, drink the water that comes out of their taps. Yet bottled water is no solution to China's drinking water crisis. First, bottled water itself is often contaminated (and frequently counterfeit) because regulation of bottled water is no more stringent than regulation of public water provision, and there have been numerous scandals regarding unsafe bottled water.[32] Secondly, bottling water needlessly consumes oil and energy, wastes water, and generates unnecessary pollution: One study showed that producing one bottle of water requires three bottles of freshwater and a quarter of a bottle of oil. Then there are all the environmental costs of producing and disposing of the billions of plastic bottles. Bottled water in China, like everywhere else, is a huge problem, not a solution.[33] On top of all this, plastic waste in China is mostly incinerated, releasing dioxins and other pollutants.

In 2017, Greenpeace published a comprehensive study of changes in surface water quality over the period of the twelfth Five-Year Plan (2011–2015). It found that 14 (if not 16) out of 31 provinces and province-sized municipalities failed to meet their water quality improvement targets (insufficient long-term data ruled out conclusions about Chongqing and Tianjin), even though these were not high bars. The study found that "while water quality improved on a national scale during the first two years of the . . . period, improvements flattened off beginning in 2013." In eight provinces "more than half of the water in major rivers was deemed unsuitable for human contact [Grade 4 or worse]." Water pollution in key urban areas was "particularly severe." By 2015, "85.3% of water in Shanghai's major rivers was categorized as [Grade 4] or worse." In Beijing the figure was 40 percent, and in Tianjin 95 percent of surface water was "unsuitable for human contact." Only Grades 1 and 2 are safe for drinking from the tap without filtration or purification. No city in China today consistently delivers Grade 1 or 2 "potable" (clean, safe, unpolluted) tap water.[34] Most are lucky to reach Grade 3.[35]

WASTE MANAGEMENT WITH CHINESE CHARACTERISTICS

It is an astonishing fact that China, the second-largest industrial power in the world, has no comprehensive management and disposal system for industrial toxic waste. For all the billions of dollars that the government has squandered building useless industries, ghost cities, expressways to nowhere, and brand new antique aircraft carriers, the country still lacks the most basic infrastructure. This includes systematic household and commercial refuse collection and recycling, modern sewerage systems, and safe procedures for handling toxic waste. Those have just not been priorities for planners in Beijing, who are more concerned with fatuous prestige projects. As a result, waste management is chaotic, underfunded, understaffed, and often effectively unregulated.

Cities Surrounded by Trash Mountains

Beijing has more than 1,000 unregulated landfills scattered in and around the city, some right next to waterways.[36] Environmental experts "blame these sites for severe pollution of the soil, air and ground water because garbage is dumped without any treatment [or lining underneath]."[37] The city does have a few properly lined landfills but not enough to keep up with its surging population and the explosion of consumer refuse. As a result, "more and more garbage is being dumped randomly by residents in unregulated landfills," as well as along roadways, in vacant lots, and so on.[38] The same is true all over the country. In December 2015, 77 people were buried alive when a mountain of construction waste gave way and flooded into Shenzhen, flattening factories and toppling apartment blocks. In July 2016, Hong Kong beaches were hit with a record "tsunami" of plastic waste washed out from illegal mainland dumps. The same month, 20,000 tons of waste was illegally dumped on a lakeshore in the famously beautiful city of Suzhou, west of Shanghai.[39] In Xi'an, the country's largest official landfill—700,000 square meters of unsorted refuse in piles reaching 50 stories high—is closing 20 years ahead of schedule because of a deluge of refuse that has grown tenfold over the past 25 years. Instead, since Xi'an is too far west to be able to dump its refuse in the ocean like coastal cities do, the city will burn the waste—plastic, toxics, and all.[40] Brilliant.

China's Pacific Ocean Waste Dump

In 2017, China banned imports of electronic and plastic waste. Although this was a positive step (albeit with many Chinese electronics recyclers just relocating to Thailand instead),[41] it was taken mainly because the country now has its own consumerism-led waste problems to deal with. Since it has no comprehensive waste management system, the plastic refuse that's not buried in legal-but-unregulated peri-urban landfills is either incinerated or dumped in rivers and sent out to sea. Scientists estimate that in 2015 the Yangtze River deposited 367,000 tons of plastic debris into the ocean, more than any other river in the world, twice as much as the amount carried by the Ganges. The world's third- and fourth-most polluted rivers are also in China.[42] China is now the world's leading dumper of plastic waste into the oceans—of the eight million tons of plastic that pollute the world's oceans every year, 3.5 million tons come from China's rivers. And this is growing sharply, with 2018 levels 27 percent higher than those of 2017. Environmental groups complain that, desperate to clean up its rivers, China "is dumping increasing amounts of trash in its seas instead."[43]

In July 2018, Shanghai introduced a pilot program of household waste sorting. Four color-coded bins were introduced for dry, wet, recyclable, and hazardous waste. Better than nothing. But increasingly the bulk of household refuse in China—as in the US—is unrecyclable plastic wrappings, bags, Styrofoam, composite plastic-paper-foil packaging and containers, and so on. All this has been greatly magnified in recent years with the incessant promotion of online shopping frenzies and the food delivery craze.[44] A friend in Shanghai told me that "in China, ordering a cup of coffee delivered to your twentieth-floor office or apartment is actually considered a sane thing to do." There's no doubt, however, that burning all this plastic waste is truly insane. It releases hundreds of toxics, including dioxin, which is why Chinese communities have been battling municipal governments over polluting refuse incinerators for decades.[45] Refuse incineration is the police state's way to make a problem go away. But it's a growing public health menace, the opposite of what one would expect from a government that says it wants to clean up its environment and build an "ecological civilization" (see Chapter 5).[46] Dumping it out at sea is hardly an ecological solution either. At the end of the day, the only rational and environmentally responsible solution for disposing of plastic waste is to stop making it. We got along without "plastic everything" in the 1950s, we weren't living in caves, and whales weren't dying because their guts were filled with plastic trash.[47]

Great Walls of Sludge

Then there's the sewerage problem. China has built more than 700 wastewater treatment facilities in cities across the country since the 1990s, but wastewater quality standards are routinely flouted because the government implements no compulsory monitoring of water quality and no independent testing. Water monitoring and treatment is mostly left up to the officials who run the local treatment facilities, and who naturally are inclined to send up good reports on their work. As the British NGO Chinadialogue reported:

> Self-testing is widespread. In China, there are only a couple of water-quality monitoring bureaus that are independent of water-treatment plants. The bulk of the monitoring work—whether you're talking about the unit at the housing ministry, national or local monitoring stations—is done by the internal laboratory at the water-treatment plant in question. You get two names on paper, but it's the same group of people behind the results.[48]

What's more, wastewater treatment plants often sit idle because facilities have nowhere to put the resulting sludge.[49] China's sewage treatment facilities generate more than 34 billion cubic meters, 22 million tons, of sludge each year—more than all the water held in the Three Gorges Dam reservoir. But even when cities utilize treatment plants, the Ministry of Agriculture and Rural Affairs won't permit the resulting sludge to be spread on farmland as fertilizer because household sewage is mixed with toxic industrial waste containing pathogens, heavy metals, dioxins, and hundreds of toxic industrial chemicals. Peking University researchers say these toxics are not "countryside manure," but "a concentration of the dirtiest things in wastewater." As such, they "pose a long-term threat to the environment and the food chain."[50] Toxic industrial waste can't really be removed from sludge, at least with any practicable technology. It should never have been mixed with household sewage in the first place. But since it is, and since it's illegal to spread sludge on farms, China's millions of tons of toxic sludge just end up being illegally dumped into the rivers, illegally poured out on melon fields, or heaped on malodorous "sludge piles" around the cities. In 2016 suburban Beijingers protested the growing piles of toxic sludge encircling the city: "It's hard to know which is more outrageous: staring at stinking Great Walls of sludge or eating melons and corn and peanuts grown in fields around Beijing where more thousands of tons of the stuff is trucked out and dumped on farm fields every day as 'fertilizer,'" one said.[51]

The Toxic Waste Nightmare

China has had laws on the books banning the dumping of toxic chemicals and industrial waste on land, in rivers, and in underground aquifers since 1990.[52] But the Ministry of Ecology and Environment (MEE, formerly the Ministry of Environmental Protection) and subordinate agencies have no systematic means of enforcement. Local officials easily resist providing essential data on toxic effluents from factories under their supervision (the better to keep such sources of jobs and tax revenue going). Regulating agencies have too few inspectors: Often a single inspector is expected to supervise hazardous waste disposals at hundreds of factories. And though the MEE theoretically has the power to levy fines and even send egregious offenders to prison for up to seven years, "experts say courts handling such cases have generally leaned toward light sentences—or none at all."[53] Little wonder then that local officials routinely ignore environmental laws and regulations. As William Kelly and Chip Jacobs write:

For some local bosses, regulations were advisory, not mandatory. "We don't think these decisions apply to us," one Guangdong official said of pollution controls.[54]

There are obvious economic incentives to just dump the toxic waste into the nearest river, lake, or field. As one environmental NGO officer explained:

Illegal disposal is definitely a money-saving way to get rid of nasty chemicals and other waste. Properly disposing of a ton of hazardous waste can cost up to 6,000 yuan . . . but a firm that hires a midnight dumper can cut that cost to just 1,200 yuan per ton.[55]

Yet even when industrial bosses want to be law-abiding, that can be hard to do in China. One official explained that "because China doesn't have enough licensed waste disposal facilities to meet the demand . . . it is not uncommon for a company with hazardous waste to wait six months to use a licensed disposal facility. And even after a long wait, the request may be rejected for a lack of space."[56]

The basic problem is that safely processing toxic waste requires cutting-edge technology and very expensive facilities, as we noted in Chapter 2. If Western and domestic Chinese companies actually had to pay the costs of properly processing their toxic waste, this would only further diminish China's slipping competitive advantages in the world market.

Just "Pump it into the Ground"

If all this weren't awful enough, China's groundwater is also being *deliberately poisoned* as textiles and pharmaceuticals factories, printing and dyeing mills, and chemical plants, looking to avoid fines for dumping their effluents into rivers, have instead turned—in a kind of demonic take on carbon capture and storage—to drilling and pumping their industrial waste directly into the earth, which is to say, directly into both shallow and deep aquifers. Companies increasingly use "high-pressure pumps to discharge huge volumes of their wastewater directly underground." Such waste disposal drilling operations have become big business. One scientist said that this "deliberate, malicious waste discharge by factories has already become endemic."[57] Here again, at the end of the day, the solution to toxics is to stop making the ones we don't absolutely need, and rigorously control those we do need to protect people and planet, which would require at the minimum, a society based on rule of law.

THE BAD EARTH: TOXIC FOOD AND "CANCER VILLAGES"

Made in China makes us terrified.
    – A Chinese parent reacting to the latest fake vaccine scandal

Farmers won't eat what they produce.
    – Hu Kanping, Chinese Ecological Civilization Research
    and Promotion Association

Decades of senseless pollution of rivers, lakes, reservoirs, and aquifers from overapplication of chemical fertilizers and pesticides, industrial dumping, and dumping of untreated sewage has ruined much of China's farmland and contaminated food supplies.[58] The government carried out its first comprehensive survey of farmland pollution between 2006 and 2010 but then spent years suppressing the report as a "state secret," out of concern for public panic. In May 2013, the Food and Drug Administration of Guangzhou, the capital of Guangdong province, shocked the country by revealing that eight out of eighteen samples of rice tested from local canteens and restaurants had cadmium levels far surpassing national limits. Officials said the rice came from adjacent Hunan province, where expanding factories, smelters, and mines had been built alongside rice paddies. Cadmium is used in coatings and in batteries for cellphones, cameras, and computers. It can cause liver, kidney, and respiratory tract damage, weaken bones, and has been linked to several cancers.[59] Hunan province is China's rice granary. As He Guangwei wrote in 2014:

> Hunan is also known for the non-ferrous metals mines that produce almost 50 million tons of waste a year. Wastewater from mining is frequently used to irrigate farmland, and mine tailings, which contain cadmium amongst other pollutants, tend to be poorly managed. It was cadmium from Hunan's mine waste that had leaked into the soil and contaminated the rice . . . The government has set a "red line" of 297 million acres of arable land to be protected in order to ensure China's food security, but the situation continues to deteriorate. Lack of regulation or lack of enforcement in many areas allows untreated wastewater to be used to irrigate farmland and the dumping of slag and sludge by industrial enterprises continues . . . heavy metal pollution in the province is still getting worse, with once-isolated patches of contamination spreading to affect larger areas.[60]

It is incredible and outrageous that industrial effluent containing all manner of toxic chemicals, heavy metals, and pathogens is routinely and apparently legally used to irrigate crops in China because of freshwater shortages. Across China, huge harvests are irrigated with toxic industrial effluent and agricultural runoff.[61]

Government surveys show that nearly 28,000 square kilometers (11,000 square miles), fully 13 percent of the total area of Hunan province, is contaminated with mining waste and heavy metals including cadmium, mercury, chromium, lead, and arsenic. Samples of river bottoms have found cadmium at 1,800 times the official safe limit, lead at 52 times the official limit, and so on.[62] Shocking as this is, environmentalists suspect that published figures vastly understate the true extent of soil contamination.[63] Fish (and fishermen) have also been found to be contaminated with high levels of cadmium, mercury, and lead.[64]

It was only in response to widespread protests after the cadmium-tainted rice panic and the 2013 "airpocalypse" over northern China that the government finally released some limited information. In December 2013, the Ministry of Land and Resources reported that three million hectares of China's farmland have become "too polluted to grow crops on." Researchers also said that "as much as 70 percent" of China's farmland was likely contaminated to some degree.[65] In April 2014, the Ministry of Environmental Protection (MEP) conceded that almost 20 percent of China's arable land, 10 percent of its woodlands, and 10 percent of its grassland soils were seriously polluted by heavy metals including cadmium, mercury, arsenic, lead, chromium, zinc, and nickel, and inorganic compounds including DDT. The report summed up the nation's farmland situation as "grim" (*yanjun*).[66] The government still refuses to release comprehensive national soil pollution data but despite the fragmentary information and lack of detail, the data has caused widespread concern and alarm. The scale and severity of soil pollution is likely unmatched anywhere else in the world and China has virtually no technology or expertise in toxic remediation.[67]

New environmental regulations have sought to crack down on chemical dumping but they seem to have had little effect. Since 2008 new filtration plants have had to be built in special chemical industry parks to filter industrial effluents. But in 2017, Greenpeace took effluent samples from one such park in Jiangsu province. It discovered 226 different chemicals, 16 of which were deemed "definitely or probably" carcinogenic. A 2012 survey by the Institute for Nutrition and Food Safety reported that in 16 provinces 65 pesticides were detected in food.[68]

Since 2013, the government has announced grand plans for "cleaning up" the nation's air, water, and farm soil. In March 2013 the MEP proposed the Action Plan for the Prevention of Soil Pollution and in April 2015 it announced the Action Plan for Water Pollution Prevention and Control.[69] But these plans are little more than vague aspirational statements of intent, calling for distant targets but offering no detailed specifics. They're also mostly unfunded mandates. As of June 2016, the government had yet to allocate funding for these initiatives.[70] Yet even with all the money in the world, how could they really "clean up" China's water, river and lake bottoms, or polluted farmland the size of Belgium?

The Government's Inability to Clean Up Lake Tai or Any Body of Water

The incapacity of the government to remediate pollution is demonstrated by the case of Lake Tai, or Taihu, China's third-largest freshwater lake, just west of Suzhou. Lake Tai was defiled over decades by small-scale industries including tanneries, metal platers, and chemicals companies. Despite repeated orders from the late 1980s to stop polluting, and after spending billions of dollars trying to clean up the lake, the government still can't even fully suppress polluters and dumpers, much less clean the lake, and has basically given up. As Chinadialogue writes:

> In 1998, the state approved the Taihu Environmental Management Plan and, in the same year, State Council ministries and the governments of Jiangsu, Zhejiang and Shanghai started a programme to tackle the pollution. The biggest part of this was an effort in late 1998 to push the 1,035 major polluters in the area to meet emissions standards. Although the authorities claimed to have in part achieved this goal . . . fresh monitoring data clarified the situation: the pollution damaging Lake Tai's water had not stopped. In May 2008, China allocated more than 111 billion yuan (US$17.6 billion) to a plan to improve the lake's water quality from "class five"—the dirtiest category, untouchable—to "class four", and in places "class three," by 2020. But the issue remains serious. On November 1 last year [2011], China's vice minister for water resources Li Guoying admitted that water quality at over 60% of water supply points in the Taihu Basin is "below class three."[71]

Even in the US, with the most modern remediation technology available, the so-called cleanup of Superfund toxic waste sites such as old industrial plants consists mostly of just scraping up the top layers of soil and shipping them off to store in some remote storage designated "forever" site. It's prohibitively expensive and in most cases virtually impossible to remove multiple toxic chemicals from soil, let alone from river bottoms. China even hired an American company, Yonkers Environmental Protection—one of the few foreign firms licensed to do environmental remediation work in China—to try to remove cadmium from the heavily polluted soil at a closed chemical factory in Shuangqiao, Hunan province. It could not get the levels anywhere near legal limits. The best it could do was get cadmium levels down to 6.89 milligrams per kilogram whereas the government's safe level is 0.3 milligrams per kilogram. And it could only remediate a small area of land around the factory whereas the entire village and surrounding farms had cadmium levels of over 90 milligrams per kilogram.[72]

Cleanup crews have been dredging the bottom of the Hudson River in Upstate New York for decades to remove the millions of pounds of PCBs dumped into the river by General Electric's old electric capacitor plants from 1947 to 1977. And it's still not safe, even for swimming in places, let alone eating the fish. Today, 30 years after the plant shut down and cleanup efforts began, the US EPA still posts signs up and down the river warning people that eating fish from the Hudson can be dangerous. It also warns that "The river looks clean, but looks can be deceiving"; "The Hudson River is not cleaning itself"; "PCB levels in fish are not going down"; and "PCBs in the sediment are not safely buried."[73] And that's just the damage done by one company in one state.

China has hundreds of thousands of such factories and mills on hundreds of rivers and lakes across the country. The Yangtze basin alone has more than 20,000 petrochemical plants. And industrial and domestic wastes have been routinely dumped into the river untreated since the 1950s. "Ninety percent of corporate wastewater is released into rivers, whether openly or covertly, and repeated attempts to stop the practice have failed. Despite the presence of 280 sewage treatment plants in the region, less than 30 [percent] of domestic sewage is treated. Levels of heavy metals and persistent organic pollutants in some stretches of the river far exceed the maximum safe limits," reports Chinadialogue.[74] By US EPA standards, large swathes of China, including its rivers and lakes would count as Superfund toxic waste sites.

What are the Chinese going to do? Scrape off the surface of Hunan province and put it "away" somewhere? Where? Dredge the bottom of the Yangtze River, the Yellow River, and the Pearl River? And where would they dump all that muck? Tibet? Xinjiang? Mongolia? In June 2013, a *China*

Daily editorial warned that "once soil is contaminated with heavy metals, experts say it will take more than 1,000 years for it to disappear on its own."[75]

The Deliberate Adulteration of Food on a Mass Scale

Besides industry- and sewage-derived pollution, in the lawless crony-capitalist Wild West that is China today, consumers also have to contend with deliberate adulteration on a mass scale by unscrupulous producers and vendors looking to profit by selling tainted foods. It is another astonishing fact that China, the leading agricultural producer in the world and also a major food exporter, has no effective system of food safety regulation. Tang Hao, a disgusted South China Normal University professor, wrote that

> None of us can be certain that any foodstuff or drug is safe, from baby milk powder through to cooking oil. Nor can we be sure that any company—be it a backstreet workshop or a big state-owned firm—is producing safe food and drugs. Consumers were originally shocked. Now, they are simply numb. It seems the Chinese have got used to poisoning each other.[76]

Since the infant food formula scandals of 2008, China's tainted food problems have been widely reported on—contaminated milk, melamine, aluminum, and mercury; aflatoxin-tainted infant formula; contaminated bottled water and toxic toothpaste; cadmium-laced rice, pesticide-laced Chinese herbs, fake eggs, formaldehyde-laced seafood, glow-in-the-dark meat, "gutter oil," toxic food additives, contaminated wine, and chemical-laced pet food; illegal dyes, bogus vaccines, fake birth control drugs, fake HIV drugs, fake cancer drugs, lead paint-coated toys, and sulfurous drywall panels.[77] In 2008, the *China Digital Times* published a list of "50 toxic foods you need to know." After a glance at the photos, it's not hard to see why so many Chinese are moving to Vancouver. The list included such delights as "tea leaves saturated with pesticides and coloring compounds with high concentrations of lead and other metals"; "toxic stinky tofu, made with blackening chemicals or liquid made from rotten meat and flies"; "toxic dog meat, from dogs killed by baiting with rat poison"; "'gutter oil' collected from restaurant curbsides mixed with sewage from hotels or restaurants"; "toxic soy sauce, made from human hair, animal bones, blood clots and other chemicals, with concentration of carcinogens"; "toxic fungi, processed with trashed fungus products and soaked with ink and other chemicals for drying and coloring"; and "toxic popcorn, made with excessive amounts of saccharin, a sweetener that causes neural and kidney damage, and sometimes cancer."[78]

Chinese netizens joke that the food safety scandals have taught people a lot about chemistry. As one put it, "we learned of paraffin from toxic rice, learned of dichlorvos [an insecticide] from hams, learned of Sudan Red [a dye] from salted duck eggs and chili sauce, learned of formaldehyde from hotpot, learned of sulphur from tremella [jelly fungus], and . . . melamine from Sanlu brand milk."[79]

In May 2013, the *New York Times* reported that "even for China's scandal-numbed diners, inured to endless outrages about food hazards, news that lamb simmering in the pot may actually be rat tested new depths of disgust." "Is it cheaper to raise rats than sheep?" one angry citizen complained.[80] Apparently so. In recent outrages, restaurant customers are finding not just rats in their hotpot but maggots in their soup. One waiter told a shocked patron that the little white worms were "high in protein"—then swallowed one himself to prove they were safe![81] In the "zombie meat" scandal of 2015, authorities seized more than 100,000 tons of 40-year-old refrozen beef, along with chicken feet dating from the 1960s.[82]

Police go after these criminals all the time but it's a losing battle. Officials complain that "food safety crimes remain serious and are displaying new circumstances and features." The police have arrested thousands, even executing some for good measure. In 2007 the government executed Zheng Xiaoyu, the head of China's State Food and Drug Administration, for taking $850,000 in bribes for approving at least 137 medicines that had been submitted without proper testing, of which 6 were entirely fake. Chinese have been sickened and killed by fake medicines. Dozens died in Panama in 2006 from taking Chinese cough syrup laced with diethylene glycol (used in polyurethane and antifreeze). But that didn't prevent the infant formula disaster the next year, nor all the scandals since.[83] Public alarm, panic, and protests are growing too, and the endless food safety crises are driving more and more Chinese to try the restaurants in Vancouver, Los Angeles, and Sydney.[84] In 2018 a fake infant vaccine scandal—so serious that even Xi Jinping had to concede it was "appalling"—shocked a nation already deeply worried by the history of drug scandals and serial government "crackdowns" that solve nothing.[85] Hundreds of thousands of infants were injected with fake or expired vaccines. Premier Li Keqiang told the press: "We will resolutely punish lawbreakers according to the law, and resolutely and severely criticize dereliction of duty in supervision."[86] China's demoralized citizenry have heard this all before.

In April 2016 when Shanghai officials found 17,000 tubs of counterfeit milk powder bearing labels of well-known domestic brands there was another public uproar over this umpteenth milk powder scandal since 2008. Will these never stop? No, they won't. In a surprisingly frank admission in the Party mouthpiece *China Daily,* journalist Zhang Zhouxiang wrote that

> After the 2008 scandal, in which excessive melamine was found in domestically produce milk powder, authorities said they were strengthening their supervision over dairy products. This new scandal belies their words . . . Behind the large quantity of counterfeit milk powder produced there must be a complete illegal industry. Had the watchdogs performed their duty even a little, how could such an industry flourish?

How indeed? Mr. Zhang then answered his own question: "It is hard to believe such illegal activities could survive in any society with the rule of law."[87]

There you have the answer from the official *China Daily*. Generally speaking, fake milk, fake food, and fake drugs aren't serious problems in nations where the rule of law prevails (though of course these days the rule of law, and OSHA, the FDA, the EPA and their equivalents are under unprecedented assault in the US and other Western nations as wannabe authoritarians like Trump try to undo regulation in the interest of capital). Still, the only solution to China's never-ending food and drug safety crises is an independent judiciary, independent police, due process, and guaranteed punishment for violators. But that's the one solution the CCP can't accept, which is why the hapless Mr. Zhang ends his article by calling for yet another crackdown. Endless useless crackdowns but no rule of law. That's why anxious Chinese with money shop for baby formula, food, medicines, and medical care in Hong Kong, Tokyo, Auckland, Sydney, and beyond.[88] Others, sick of the smog, toxic foods, and unsafe water buy one-way tickets to the "declining West."[89]

Cadmium for the Masses, Organics for the Cadres

Unsurprisingly, China's ruling class, the senior Communist Party cadres and their crony-capitalist sidekicks, don't have to put up with such daily insults because they have access to their own *tegong* or "special supply" channels. In the early 2000s the Party established its own organic farms, tea plantations, fish farms, and pastures to raise meat and dairy products, to keep themselves well provisioned with safe food. When Barbara Demick visited the Beijing Customs Administration Vegetable Base and Country Club in Shunyi village on the outskirts of Beijing, she found what looked, from outside of the six-foot spiked fence, to be an ordinary farm, well-tended, and with a gate that admitted only select cars. A neighbor who lived across the street told her that the compound produced organic peppers, onions, beans, and cauliflowers but was "for officials only" and didn't sell to the public. Demick concluded that

> Organic gardening here is a hush-hush affair in which the cleanest, safest products are largely channeled to the rich and politically connected . . . many of the nation's best food companies don't promote or advertise. They don't want the public to know that their limited supply is sent to Communist Party officials . . . and others in the elite classes.

Gao Zhiyong, who worked for a state-run food company and wrote a book on the subject, says that "officials don't really care what the common people eat because they and their family are getting a special supply of food."[90]

Thick Black Humor: Imports and Exports with Chinese Characteristics

Repeated food scares and the inability of the government to ensure food safety has unsurprisingly driven up demand for imported foods and food crops. Imports of corn, rice, and wheat have doubled since 2010.[91] Urban Chinese scour supermarkets for imported foods. The government has bought farmland in Mozambique and Western food producers, notably, Smithfield Farms, America's largest pork producer, in the effort to bring safe foods to China where the police state controls everything but can't control its own food producers.[92] This is very bad news not only for China's basic food security but also for natural resources around the world, as China's demand for safe soybeans, corn, wheat, rice, meat, and cooking oil is leveling forests from Southeast Asia to South America.[93] But 1.4 billion Chinese cannot afford to import safe food, let alone safe water, nor can the world supply their needs.

Yet while China is importing Western powdered milk, chicken, and pork, it has also become one of the world's biggest food exporters, exporting its toxic foods to the West. In just one year (2012) the EU rejected arsenic-laced frozen calamari, pasta with maggots, parasite-infested fish, antibiotic-laced rabbit, noodles with aluminum, oyster sauce with staphylococcus, salmonella-infected ginger, radioactive spices, peanuts with toxic mold, pumpkin seeds with glass chips, cadmium-laced dried anchovies, and strawberries with norovirus.[94] The high cost of cheap.

CHINA'S TOXICS EMERGENCY

It is impossible to overstate the implications of the horrific pollution of China's water, soil, and food supplies or of the frightful toll that this is taking on the health of the Chinese people, not to mention the rest of the ecology. In 2007 Elizabeth C. Economy, author of *The River Runs Black: The Environmental Challenge to China's Future*, wrote:

> Less well documented [than air pollution] but potentially even more devastating is the health impact of China's polluted water. Today, fully 190 million Chinese are sick from drinking contaminated water. All along China's major rivers, villages report skyrocketing rates of diarrheal diseases, cancer, tumors, leukemia, and stunted growth.[95]

Economy wrote these words in 2007, long before the "airpocalypses" began in 2013, before reports began surfacing about "cancer villages," before Chai Jing's shocking 2015 documentary *Under the Dome* [*Qiongding zhi xia*]. Water and soil pollution are cumulative. With each passing year the pollution problem grows worse, as the government itself concedes. In 2016, the MEP reported that

> Efforts to tackle water pollution in China remain uneven with some areas worsening in 2016, while heavy metals and other pollutants continued to accumulate in Chinese soil . . . [Agricultural soil quality] does not allow for optimism and the problem of soil pollution for industry, companies and nearby land is prominent.[96]

The government says that it "can win the war on pollution," but there's no evidence for this. Here and there in recent years it has refurbished former industrial sites as local parks. And some farmers are trying to go "organic." But where is there unpolluted farmland in China to grow organic food crops at scale, or clean water to irrigate crops with?[97]

China's toxics emergency poses an existential threat to the nation and to the whole world.[98] When all is said and done, the only solution to the toxics crisis is to cease production of most toxic chemicals and rigorously control the few toxic chemicals we can't do without in a moderately industrialized society. That's entirely feasible. We can do without toxic pesticides, most petrochemicals, and most plastics. We can do without disposable products, the endless waste stream of electronic gadgets, and so on. We can institute the "precautionary principle" developed by scientists, doctors, and anti-toxics organizations (like Safer Chemicals Healthy Families), that would prohibit the mass production of chemicals until they are proven safe, support development of safer substitutes, invite communities to participate in decisions on chemicals, publish comprehensive safety data on all chemicals, and institute priority protection of workers and communities.[99] There are ways to stop toxic pollution. But these cannot be implemented in an economy, be it capitalist or Stalinist, where maximizing growth is the highest priority. Many of China's filthy industries are impossible to clean up in any meaningful sense and many, if not most, are dedicated to producing products that neither the Chinese nor anyone else really needs, that should never have been produced in the first place. That's going to have to change if China is ever going to abolish excessive pollution and create an "ecological civilization."

4

Cooking the Planet for What End?

"AIRPOCALYPSE NOW"

I don't want to be a human vacuum cleaner.

– Sina Weibo user, January 2013[1]

Decades of coal-powered industrialization, booming construction, and the car craze have brought China the worst smog in the world, soaring greenhouse gas emissions, and sharply rising lung cancer rates. By the 2010s China was adding two coal-fired power plants a week to what was already the world's largest fleet, with the heaviest concentrations in the industrialized northern half of the country.[2] Meanwhile, the auto industry has put tens of millions of new smog-pumpers on the roads every year, most burning extra-polluting poor-grade fuel.[3] By 2015, Beijing had five million cars and trucks on its streets. Smog blankets thicken year after year, particularly in winter when the coal-fired heaters are employed.

Below is the US EPA advisory chart for limiting exposure to airborne pollutants. The Air Quality Index (AQI) is a composite index of several airborne pollutants including PM2.5 (particulates smaller than 2.5 micrometers which easily pass into the bloodstream). The World Health Organization (WHO) recommends that exposure to PM2.5 over 24 hours be limited to no more than 25 micrograms per cubic meter of air.

Table 4.1   US EPA Air Quality Index (AQI)

0–50	Good
51–100	Moderate
101–150	Unhealthy for sensitive groups
151–200	Unhealthy
201–300	Very unhealthy
301–500	Hazardous

Source: US EPA

The AQI scale tops out at 500. In January 2013 the AQI reading in Beijing went beyond scale to 755, with the PM2.5 count hitting 866 micro-

Figure 4.1 "Who cares about the GDP if we can't live here?" A Chinese demonstrator wears a face mask alongside other demonstrators as she protests bad air quality and pushes for the closing of a large garbage incinerator in her neighborhood in Beijing on September 20, 2008. The characters on her mask say *fan chou* (oppose foul smell).

Credit: AP Images/Elizabeth Daiziel

grams per cubic meter, a record. A US Embassy staffer called it "crazy bad" in a Twitter post. Another dubbed it an "airpocalypse."[4] In October and November 2013, PM2.5 readings in Harbin, Shenyang, and other northern cities registered over 1,000 micrograms per cubic meter, with some locations higher than 1,400. As one resident of Harbin commented on Sina Weibo (China's Twitter equivalent): "You can hear the person you're talking to, but not see him." Another said that he "couldn't see the person he was holding hands with." "If this goes on any longer everyone will probably get cancer," another commented. Schools were shut, aircraft grounded, and traffic came to a standstill. With black humor, one netizen posted the following: "If you think this is a movie set for 'Silent Hill,' 'Resident Evil' or 'The Walking Dead,' you are wrong—this is Harbin."[5] In January 2015, Beijing mayor Wang Anshun said the city was "unlivable" because of its noxious smog.[6] By summer many were trying to escape the city. But not Nut Brother. In July the 34-year-old performance artist began spending four hours each day rolling a battery-powered commercial vacuum cleaner around the streets of Beijing sucking in smog and dust which he then had made into a "smog brick." Why? To prompt people to think more about "the relationship between humans and nature."[7] In November 2015 Beijing issued its first "red alert," as PM2.5 readings topped 1,000 micrograms per cubic meter.[8] Images were posted from Shenyang of neon signs "floating" in the air as the buildings on which they hung from were rendered invisible.[9] In December 2016 and January 2017, as much of northern China disappeared from satellite view under an immense blanket of smog that smothered half a billion people, hundreds of thousands of "smog refugees" fled south—some even to Australia, Indonesia, and beyond.[10]

Estimates are that airborne pollution is taking between three and five years off the lifespans of Chinese in the northern half of the country. Lung cancer is now the leading cause of death in Beijing. Pollution-induced lung diseases are now taking the lives of more than 1.2 million people per year in China. Smog-induced acid rain has reduced crop yields across northern China and devastated forests as far as Japan. Air pollution is slashing solar panel efficiency in China.[11] Pollution has also become the leading cause of social unrest, eclipsing land grabs and labor conflicts.[12] Yet as we noted in the Introduction, while the government plans to reduce coal's *share* of the

Figure 4.2 "What have you just gone through?" The nose of a CRH (China Railway High-Speed) bullet train at South Beijing Railway Station is brown with smog residues on January 2, 2017 after completing its five-hour, 1,318-kilometer run from Shanghai to Beijing, one of the smoggiest areas in China. See Josh Ye, "'What have you just gone through?': Photos of China's smog-covered high-speed trains go viral," *South China Morning Post*, January 5, 2017.

Credit: Newscom

energy mix from 69 percent to 55 percent by 2040, China's absolute level of coal consumption could grow by as much as 50 percent in the same period, in line with projected economic growth of more than 6 percent per year.[13]

WHY FOSSIL FUEL GENERATION CONTINUES
TO OUTSTRIP RENEWABLES

Still, the question remains: Even if the government insists on maintaining a growth rate above 6 percent, why can't it do this with renewables, and why can't Xi's iron-fisted police state force through the transition to solar and wind power, and suppress CO_2 emissions and smog? I suggest that the answer to this question is threefold: First, while China leads the world in solar and wind power capacity, this is growing from a tiny base compared with the fossil fuel-based power generation infrastructure that has been built up over the preceding decades. Secondly, no economy has yet solved the problem of electricity storage for utility-scale generators. Thus, the intermittent and irregular generation of solar and wind power requires that utilities both "overbuild" renewables to compensate for uneven production and also build additional fossil fuel-powered backup generators to guarantee 24/7 "base load" power generation. Thirdly, China's political economy presents additional problems due to the fragmentation and compartmentalization of the economy, the nature of intra-bureaucratic competition in this system, and the strong preference of local officials for locally available and reliable coal over often distantly produced renewables with uncertain reliability and price. Consequently, even when solar and wind power are available, many local officials and SOE bosses in China prefer not to rely on it. And, for reasons we'll explore in Chapter 5, Beijing generally cannot compel its subordinates in the localities to adopt renewables over fossil fuels.

Growth Rate vs. Mass

One often reads headlines about how much new solar or wind power capacity China has installed in recent years and these are true. But what's not always appreciated is that this increase is from a tiny base. High rates of growth in renewables capacity amount to small, even trivial percentage gains in electricity generation. Simon Göß makes this clear in Charts 4.1–4.3, below.[14] Göß notes that China's solar photovoltaic power generation grew by 21.4 terawatt-hours (TWh) in the first quarter of 2017, a record 80 percent increase over the first quarter of 2016. Even so, photovoltaic power accounted for just 1.8 percent of electricity generation in 2017. Wind power accounted for just 4.7 percent of total electricity generation in that year. The rest was produced by fossil fuels, hydropower, and nuclear energy.[15] In 2018, China added 51 percent more solar power capacity along with 20 percent more wind power capacity (Chart 4.1), bumping solar contribution up to 2–3 percent on preliminary figures, but the combined total electricity generation for both was still just 8 percent in that year (Chart 4.2).

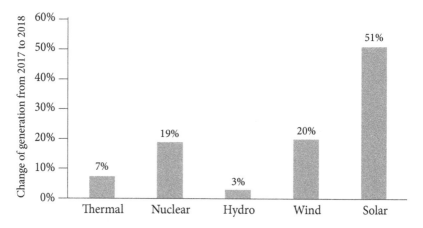

Chart 4.1   Percentage change in electricity generation from different sources in China from 2017 to 2018

Source: Simon Göß, "Overview of China's evolving energy market in 2018," *Energy Brainblog*, March 13, 2019, https://blog.energybrainpool.com/en/overview-of-chinas-evolving-energy-market-in-2018.

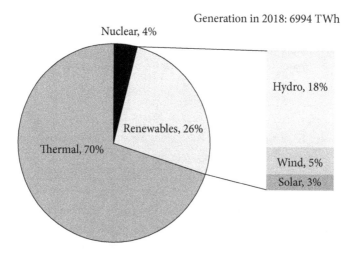

Chart 4.2   Electricity generation share by source in China, 2018

Source: Simon Göß, "Overview of China's evolving energy market in 2018."

By contrast, even though thermal power (90–95 percent coal vs. 5–10 percent natural gas) capacity grew by just 7 percent in 2018, it grew from a huge base. Thermal power generation grew by more than 320 TWh in 2018—more than double the combined total of 160 TWh generated by all renewables, including hydropower (Chart 4.3). Thus, despite the rapid growth of solar and wind power capacity, fossil fuels still accounted for 70 percent of electricity generation in 2018 (Chart 4.2). At this rate, it will be many decades before renewables outstrip fossil fuel power in China, if this ever happens at all.

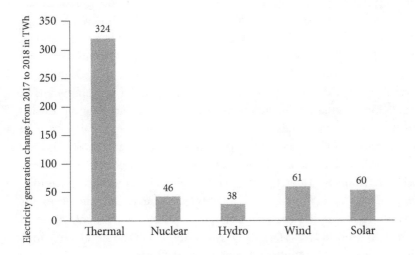

Chart 4.3 Change in electricity generation (in terawatt-hours) from different energy sources in China from 2017 to 2018

Source: Simon Göß, "Overview of China's evolving energy market in 2018."

Intermittent Generation, Lack of Storage, and the Inevitability of Curtailment

To date no one in China or anywhere else has built utility-scale battery storage (though Tesla and others are trying).[16] Without this, the problem of intermittency and power wastage or curtailment is inevitable to some degree.[17] The bigger the share of renewables the bigger the problem. In Germany wind power supplies about a quarter of electricity generation. The rest has been supplied mainly by coal-fired and nuclear power plants. But as the Merkel government has shut down nuclear power plants in the wake of the Fukushima meltdown, utilities have resorted to adding more coal-fired plants to back up renewables, largely because of public opposition to more windmills.[18] As a result, after a period in which they were falling, Germany's emissions have begun rising once again.[19]

Economic Compartmentalization and Bureaucratic Resistance to Renewable Energy

Beyond these problems, China's transition to wind and solar is also hobbled by systemic barriers built into the nature of its bureaucratic-collectivist mode of production. In 2005 the government launched its renewable energy program with a raft of renewable energy laws and regulations and generous funding to develop wind and solar power. The Renewable Energy Law (2005) and related plans stipulated that renewable energy should account for 10 percent of total energy consumption by 2010 and 20 percent by 2020 (with non-hydropower renewable generation to account for 1 percent of all grid-connected electricity by 2010 and 3 percent by 2020). Regulations mandated grid access for wind and solar farms, and provided direct subsidies and other economic incentives to their developers.[20] In China, the most abundant sunshine, strongest winds, and most powerful rivers are found in the lightly populated western and northern interior—including Xinjiang, Tibet, Qinghai, Gansu, Ningxia, Inner Mongolia, Jilin, Heilongjiang, and Yunnan—but the heaviest energy demand is in the urbanized industrialized eastern seaboard. Thus the government's plan was to develop wind and solar farms in the west and north and install ultra-high voltage power lines to transmit the power to the east.

With so much money on the table, local and provincial governments jumped into the renewable energy business wherever possible. In the ensuing renewable energy "frenzy," they built wind and solar power plants often without any grid connection, sometimes in suboptimal locations and/or with suboptimal turbines, just to get the subsidies, resulting in widespread curtailments.[21] "Overeager solar and wind farm builders have created massive amounts of new capacity that are sitting idle due to poor planning," reported Doug Young of *Renewable Energy World*.[22] By 2015–2016 solar power curtailment rates reached 30 percent across the country. In northwest China wind power curtailment rates were 48–49 percent in 2015–2016, and more than 60 percent in Xinjiang.[23] It was much the same with hydropower.[24] Grid building lagged behind wind and solar farm installations, leaving renewable energy developers no choice but to curtail power. But even as the State Grid Corporation of China installed 30,000 kilometers of ultra-high voltage transmission lines to overcome those constraints "new [wind farm] installations still outpaced grid capability, resulting in growing curtailment rates."[25] Thus paradoxically, the government is facing "over-production" of solar and wind power even as two-thirds of its electricity is still produced by coal.

What's more, even as new high-voltage lines were connected to the grid, central planners found that very often eastern coastal provinces didn't want the power. Rather than buy wind and solar power from distant locations and face higher prices, the risk of intermittent delivery, and the possibility that this supply would "squeeze out" their own coal-fired power plants, they declined the offers. When the thirteenth Five-Year Plan funded a new high-voltage line to carry hydropower from Sichuan province east to Jiangxi province, Jiangxi said it didn't want the power because it was bringing new coal-fired power plants online in 2018. Hubei likewise rejected new lines from wind farms in northwest China.[26] As a result, Beijing finds that "enthusiasm for ultra-high voltage lines is weakening" and they remain underutilized.[27]

By contrast, in Europe and North America wind and solar curtailment rates are consistently under 4 percent.[28] By 2017, China had built more than 92,000 wind turbines with more than double the generating capacity of wind farms in the US. But in that year China's wind farms accounted for just 3.3 percent of electricity generation, compared with 4.7 percent in the US.[29] What explains this difference? In Europe and North America, utilities companies address the problem of intermittency and balance between supply and demand "horizontally" by means of markets. They build power plants to meet market demand and trade electricity across regions and even countries. Electricity prices are adjusted hourly. European utilities trade across transnational grids. In North America, US and Canadian electricity trading "allow[s] for bidirectional flow of power from wind sources on both sides of the border, thus helping to address intermittency issues of renewables."[30] Such balancing and market trading has kept curtailment rates in the US and Europe down to an average of 1–4 percent.

But in China, the development of utility-scale renewable energy is not left to the market. It's dictated by central planners. China lacks a unified energy market and developed cross-regional power transmission like the US and Europe.[31] China's bureaucratically planned economy is organized vertically from central planners in Beijing down through ministries and out through the provinces, autonomous regions, prefectures, counties, and municipalities—like spokes in a wheel. Central authorities issue plans and sub-plans, set prices and quotas, allocate investment funds, issue economic incentives, and confiscate most output for planned redistribution. Responsibilities for pricing, allocation, distribution, and employment are divided between myriad bureaucracies. "Ownership" of power plants is divided between the central government, provincial governments, municipalities, and so on—each seeking to maintain its own resources, profits, and jobs, often in competition with one another. For all the market reforms of the past four decades, China's provincial economies are still highly compartmentalized with limited market exchange between them. Provinces and municipalities still strive to be self-contained much as in Mao's day in order to meet targets, and make do with rationed input allocations without having to depend on trading with neighboring provinces that have their own plans (more on this in Chapter 5)—even to the extent of erecting "market blockades" to monopolize production and trade within their own bureaucratic bailiwicks to protect local profits and jobs.[32]

In the case of electricity generation, producer prices are inflexible, fixed by the central government. "Grid operators set generation and transmission schedules up to one month in advance, and they program coal power plants to operate continuously for a week or longer. This limits their ability to accommodate hourly or daily fluctuations in renewable output. Flexibility is further limited by utilization quotas that guarantee coal plants a certain number of operating hours per year," says Peter Fairly.[33] As a result, "cross-province electricity trading and transmission face obstacle[s] . . . The provincial electricity market . . . is characterized by the self-contained system and self-balance, making the relatively closed provincial market not conducive to optimizing national electricity system planning, power source structural adjustment, cross-province power grid operation, and electricity trading."[34] *Caixin* reports that "local governments are undermining the central government's efforts to develop greener sources of electricity by squeezing production quotas for renewables and slapping extra levies on wind companies to prop up ailing coal-fired plants in their region."[35]

These tendencies have been reinforced by the economic slowdown since 2014. Southeastern provinces report that they "have little incentive to buy power from the north when they have . . . their own generation to keep local power facilities in business in the economic downturn and avoid potential losses of jobs and tax revenue."[36]

This highlights a related problem. Trading is particularly hindered in China because, since the days of Mao, localities and even individual factories have built their own captive (*zibei*, or "self-provided") coal-fired power plants.[37] Thus even out in Xinjiang, which has the most installed wind power in the country, the bulk of electricity is supplied by coal-fired plants. Given the ready availability and cheapness of coal, given its 24/7 reliability, and given the lack of electricity storage or the means to compensate for fluctuations via market trading, Xinjiang's resource-intensive industries such as mining, oil, gas extraction, and coal-chemicals plants prefer to rely on predictable and stable coal power and "export" their wind and solar power. Many provinces want to export power, but none want to risk depending on imported power, especially intermittent renewables.

Finally, local governments across northern China also prefer coal to solar and wind power in winter because they use the heat from coal boilers to heat homes and businesses. This has meant that in winter wind curtailment rates have reached 75 percent.[38] Electric boilers could in principle replace these. But again, without effective electricity storage and without trans-provincial electricity market trading, they could not guarantee consistent heating when wind or solar power are insufficient.

In summation, confronted with insurmountable technical and sociopolitical constraints on renewable energy development (the lack of electricity storage, the government's unwillingness to renounce central planning in favor of market-based sharing to even out intermittency, and the inability of the central government to compel local authorities to tear down their market blockades and obey the Renewable Energy Law's mandate that they purchase solar and wind power), Beijing finds it has no choice but to backpedal on its "renewables revolution." In the last two years it has cut subsidies for renewables by 39 percent and announced that it will end subsidies in 2021—claiming that these are no longer needed because production costs for wind and solar power plants has fallen such that they can compete with the price of coal. They have.[39] But as we've just noted, solar and wind power plants don't compete against coal power plants on price, as in capitalist economies. They compete for bureaucratically allocated subsidies and bureaucratically controlled access to the grid. As a result, as subsidies are cut, new installations of wind and solar are dropping off sharply. New solar installations hit a record 53 gigawatts in 2017 but dropped to 41 gigawatts in 2018 and 11.4 gigawatts in the first half of 2019 and are expected to grow by not more than 20–25 gigawatts per year in the foreseeable future. Energy analysts say China could and should install as much as 100 gigawatts of solar power annually, four times the current level, if it really wants to get off coal and suppress CO_2 emissions.[40] In March 2019 the government also halted big wind power projects in Xinjiang and Gansu.[41] Meanwhile, as we've noted, the government is redirecting energy investment funding into what it calls "new energy" extraction, which includes fracking of shale gas and separating methane from coal.[42] These trends do not inspire optimism for renewable energy in China.

THE QUEST FOR EXTREME POWER TO FUEL EXTREME GROWTH

As a longtime oil and gas engineer who helped develop shale fracking for the Energy Department, I can assure you that [natural] gas is not "clean." Because of leaks of methane, the main component of natural gas, the gas extracted from shale deposits is not a "bridge" to a renewable energy future—it's a gangplank to more warming and away from clean energy investments.

– Anthony R. Ingraffea[43]

Beijing's main effort to clear the skies above its smog-smothered northern cities has come not through a switch to solar or wind power so much as to another fossil fuel, "clean" natural gas. Gas offers obvious advantages. Modern natural gas power plants emit few-to-no particulates (so produce much less smog and leave no ash to dispose of) and they emit no mercury or sulphur. They emit roughly half the CO_2 per megawatt-hour of electricity as compared to coal-fired power plants. Gas-powered utilities can also run 24/7 regardless of the weather, and gas can also be transported by pipeline instead of by trains and trucks (saving more pollution). There is no doubt that the government could significantly reduce the smog over Beijing by switching to natural gas, or even to oil. After all, that's what New York did decades ago, and that dramatically reduced visible smog and particulate pollution.

Yet shifting to gas-fired power plants presents three problems: First, even if China replaced all of its coal-fired power plants with gas-fired plants, given the government's determination to maintain a GDP growth rate of at least 6 percent per year, emissions would still grow sharply because electricity generation tracks with GDP growth. Electricity generation grew by 7.7 percent in 2018 while the official GDP growth rate was 6.5 percent. From 2007 to 2017 electricity generation averaged a growth rate of 7.2 percent per year.[44] So if China's gas-powered electricity generation were to grow at, say, just 7 percent per year, less than the recent historical average, electricity generation emissions would still double by 2020 and nearly quadruple by 2040. True, those totals would only be half as large compared to coal-fired power generation. But China's CO_2 emissions are already off the charts and if we're going to prevent runaway global warming, they need to start falling sharply now, rather than just growing more slowly.[45]

Secondly, when the entire process, from drilling to distribution, is considered, many engineers and scientists think that "clean" natural gas can end up producing more climate-warming emissions than coal, because of methane "leakage." This is a huge problem in the US where there are still some reg-ulating agencies, and where communities are still free to protest leaks and demand solutions,[46] but given China's horrendous industrial safety record, the bureaucracy's instinctive preference for covering up problems instead of solving them, and given that local communities are severely repressed for protesting drilling, the worst can reasonably be assumed in China's case.

Thirdly, given the growth drivers surveyed above, the advent of "clean" natural gas would likely just encourage even more wasteful overproduction and overconstruction, in which case it will all be for naught.

The Climate Coup de Grâce: Coal-to-Gas Bases Will "Doom the Planet"

With growing public pressure to suppress the smog in China's eastern cities—especially in the thickly polluted industrial heartland of the "Jing-Jin-Ji Metropolitan Area" (encompassing Beijing, Tianjin, and Hebei)—the government might have considered shutting down its overproducing industries, power plants, and coal mines, in order to begin "degrowing" the economy. Instead, China's planners came up with a different solution—moving smog-producing industries and infrastructure out west by building dozens of huge "coal-gasification bases" in Shanxi, the Ordos Basin, Inner Mongolia, Xinjiang, and other mostly remote areas. These bases, some larger than Delaware or Connecticut, will be the largest fossil fuel projects in the world when they're completed, dwarfing Canada's tar sands. Coal-to-gas plants burn coal directly to generate electricity in situ, and convert coal to liquid fuels like "syngas" (synthetic natural gas, or SNG) and LPG (liquid petroleum gas), which are then piped or transported to cities to be burned in power plants, factories, and vehicles. But far from reducing coal use, scientists say these complexes consume so much coal-fired energy in producing SNG and LPG that they generate as much as 40 percent more CO_2 emissions than if coal were just directly burned in local power plants.[47] Instead of reducing coal smog, the response has been to simply move the sources of that smog away from Beijing and its environs. Since the first of these bases have come on-line, once pristine areas of Xinjiang now have worse air pollution than Beijing and industry-heavy Hebei province.[48] Furthermore, water-intensive coal extraction in the new coal bases in northern and western provinces threatens to seriously aggravate China's already severe water crises in those regions.[49]

The UN IPCC calculated in 2013 that if we're to keep global warming below 2°C, humanity must not add more than 880 gigatons of CO_2 emis-sions to the atmosphere before 2050. Collectively, we've already used up more than half of that "carbon budget" (see Chart 4.4 below) leaving us a remaining budget of just 349 gigatons. Scientists say that if China's planned coal bases come on-stream its CO_2 emissions will soar and China will devour the budget for the entire world by 2050—and doom the climate.[50]

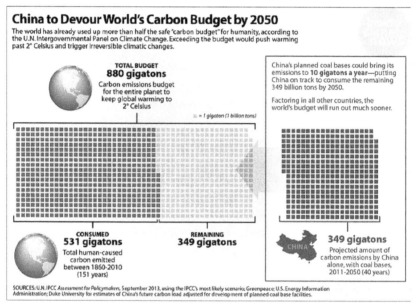

China to Devour World's Carbon Budget by 2050

The world has already used up more than half the safe "carbon budget" for humanity, according to the U.N. Intergovernmental Panel on Climate Change. Exceeding the budget would push warming past 2° Celsius and trigger irreversible climatic changes.

TOTAL BUDGET
880 gigatons
Carbon emissions budget for the entire planet to keep global warming to 2° Celsius

China's planned coal bases could bring its emissions to **10 gigatons a year**—putting China on track to consume the remaining 349 billion tons by 2050.

Factoring in all other countries, the world's budget will run out much sooner.

= 1 gigaton (1 billion tons)

CONSUMED
531 gigatons
Total human-caused carbon emitted between 1860-2010 (151 years)

REMAINING
349 gigatons

349 gigatons
Projected amount of carbon emissions by China alone, with coal bases, 2011-2050 (40 years)

SOURCES: U.N. IPCC *Assessment for Policymakers*, September 2013, using the IPCC's most likely scenario; Greenpeace; U.S. Energy Information Administration; Duke University for estimates of China's future carbon load adjusted for development of planned coal base facilities.

Chart 4.4 China to devour world's carbon budget by 2050

Credit: Paul Horn/Inside Climate News

Extreme Extractions: Fracking, "Fire Ice," Arctic Drilling

Completing its arsenal of planetary destruction, the government has also declared its intention to develop fracking wherever possible, to mine "combustible ice" (methane) from the bottom of the South China Sea, and to drill for oil under the Arctic Ocean.[51]

CHINA'S "GREEN" HYDROPOWER SOLUTION
IS WORSE THAN THE PROBLEM

China's plan to peak emissions by 2030 and to grow the non-fossil fuel share of electricity generation to 20 percent also relies heavily on the growth of hydropower, its second-largest source of energy generation after coal. China is home to half the world's 80,000 dams, more than the US, Brazil, and Canada combined.[52] Hydropower is touted as a "green" renewable energy, but China's experience shows that this reputation is undeserved when building dams results in widespread environmental damage. The twelfth Five-Year Plan saw the completion of the Three Gorges Dam in 2006, the largest hydropower project in the world, generating as much electricity as fifty million tons of coal each year. The plan called for tremendous further expansion, more than 50 additional large-scale power plants, most to be built in the southwest on the upper reaches of the Yellow River and the Yangtze, but also on the Mekong (Lancang Jiang) and Brahmaputra (Yarlung Tsangpo) rivers. By 2020, China plans to have 430 gigawatts of installed hydroelectric capacity, up from 300 gigawatts today, and more than Europe and the US combined. Advocates say the country can almost double its current capacity to 540 gigawatts by 2050.

However, China's plans have ignited a firestorm of opposition in China, as well as from environmentalists and governments in South and Southeast Asia, forcing the government to shelve some projects. Environmentalists say they should shelve them all, for several reasons.

First, dams have not reduced the need for coal-fired power plants in China. If anything, experience to date shows they increase coal consumption. That's because most of China's dams work only intermittently, like solar and wind, and so require coal backup in periods of low rainfall. The need for coal backup is likely to grow because droughts are intensifying and spreading in China as the climate warms. Drought has already forced the suspension of thousands of hydropower turbines in recent years. Declining snowfall melt spells more trouble in the coming decades. Currently, China's glaciers are all in retreat due to global warming, one-third have melted to virtually nothing, and sources of the Yangtze are drying up and upstream areas are turning to desert. As a result, the more hydropower that the government builds, the more coal backup they need to build. Beth Walker writes that "Guizhou province has built more coal-fired generating capacity than hydropower to ensure a stable supply of power in the dry season. Sichuan, Guangxi and Yunnan are doing the same."[53] There is no reason to expect this pattern to change.

Secondly, China's hubristic dam builders have a long history of ignoring scientists' warnings and charging ahead, often even without approval, to build dams on top of earthquake faults—sometimes with predictably horrific results. As it happens, most of China's new dams are slated to be built in the southwest (Sichuan province and the Tibetan Plateau), which is riddled with faults. What's more, China's dam builders have a consistent history of sloppy construction and poor maintenance. These two factors have caused appalling loss of life, mostly unreported in the West. China embarked on its first dam building spree during the Great Leap Forward, and many of those dams subsequently collapsed. Dai Qing, China's indomitable environmentalist (imprisoned for ten months in 1989 for criticizing the Three Gorges Dam) reported that by 1980, 2,796 dams had failed, killing more than 240,000 people.[54]

Mega-dams and water management systems have been the favored prestige projects of Chinese emperors for millennia. Soviet-Stalinist nation builders also used mammoth projects to build "socialism in one country" and win allies abroad—as with the Aswan Dam built by the Soviets for Egypt's Gamal Abdel Nasser. Most of China's top leaders since the 1950s have been trained as engineers. Mega-projects like dams have burnished their images and promoted their rise in the bureaucracy. Dai Qing, who herself grew up in the central Party compound of Zhongnanhai in Beijing, knows them well. Her books present withering critiques of China's dam building industrial bureaucracies.[55] In her indictment of the Three Gorges Dam project, she writes:

In China the so-called red specialists (*hongse zhuanjia*) consider themselves infallible even though the history the People's Republic is littered with grandiose technological and economic projects gone wrong, often at enormous costs to the treasury and to human life . . . At every turn—from its preference for a planned economy with a focus on iron and steel production, to its promotion of grain production, population growth, and large-scale dam construction—the Chinese leadership has made decisions which run counter to the Chinese philosophical concepts of maintaining order and balance between humankind and nature. . . .

With the promotion of a new market economy since 1978, profit once again comes first in the minds of China's leaders, and all they think about is plundering nature rather than conserving it and maintaining the balance. Adding to the problem is the fact that so many of these specialists make decisions based on blind self-interest, or on the narrow interests of their bureaucratic bailiwicks . . . the Three Gorges Project is illustrative . . . the decision to launch the project is really about meeting the personal interests of workers and their families in the various construction gangs and organizations that make up the dam-building industry in China. . . .

The best alternatives involve building smaller dams on the Yangtze River's tributaries. But alternatives were never seriously considered by the top leadership. Why? Because China is in the midst of "uncontrolled" development where a sense of moderation and restraint are completely absent. This lack of control is evident at every level of planning for the

Three Gorges project: From the "red specialists" faith in technology, to the closed decision making of autocratic leaders, and the complete disregard for the environmental effects of the project on the river valley and its residents.[56]

The 2008 Sichuan earthquake—which took 88,000 lives—has been widely blamed on the filling of the Zipingpu Dam reservoir, completed two years before (the dam was heavily damaged in the disaster). That catastrophe resulted in massive public opposition to more dam building, and China's bureaucracy is itself deeply divided because it knows very well that the failure of any of its large dams would result in the loss of potentially millions of lives. Even so, although the government has been forced to shelve some projects, at least twenty major dams are still currently under construction in the southwest.[57]

Thirdly, China's relentless dam building threatens the livelihoods and lives of hundreds of millions of people living downstream of rivers that flow from China and Tibet, as well as multiple fragile ecologies and endangered species. Chinese hydropower projects could potentially disrupt seasonal water flows and increase water scarcity, wreaking havoc on agriculture from India to Vietnam.[58] It's not completely clear how glacial melt will affect hydropower projects in China and elsewhere, but scientists think it will mean reduced water flow, and reduced and disrupted hydroelectric generation.[59] Furthermore, the industrialization of western China is blanketing the Qinghai-Tibetan Plateau glaciers with black carbon (along with pollution from South Asia). Scientists say this is accelerating glacial melting which will affect water security over vast areas of Asia and "may result in grave environmental and social problems."[60] Melting permafrost has already destabilized parts of the Tibetan Plateau, undermining highways and railways, and reducing the flow of water into the Yangtze River basin, shrinking lakes and causing droughts.[61] Not content just to dam up rivers upon which hundreds of millions of people depend, contrary to its repeated denials the Chinese government is also diverting water that would normally flow into South Asia back into China to supply its failing south–north water diversion project.[62]

China's dams also threaten biodiversity, local ecologies, local fisheries, and endangered species.[63] As David Gibson and Luan Dong write:

In southwestern China, three parallel rivers—the Nu, Lancang and Jinsha (also known as the Upper Mekong, Salween and Yangtze, respectively)—form a series of corridors that connect the tropical rainforests of Southeast

Asia to the Tibetan Plateau. These areas are some of the most biodiverse in the world, and scientists argue they have value as "climate refugia"— places worth preserving in order to allow species to retreat to cooler, more suitable climates as temperatures rise. A cascade of dams, however, has been planned for the region, threatening to submerge habitats, reduce the flow of tributary rivers and make the area less suitable for many plant and animal species.[64]

China's dam building frenzy is still at full-throttle but protest and resistance is growing from Asia to Africa and Latin America.[65]

WHAT'S IT ALL FOR?

At the end of the day, there is no sustainable way to meet the endlessly rising demand for electricity in China, or anywhere else. Replacing fossil fuel-fired electricity generation with renewables is essential if we want to maintain a habitable planet. But if China's renewable energy is just squandered by converting more and more of nature into the same endless waste stream of disposable products, redundant highways and trains, unneeded apartment blocks, ghost cities, needless "blingfrastructure," superfluous gadgets, surveillance cameras, internet servers, and vehicles then the planet will still be on the road to environmental collapse.[66] What the Chinese and the rest of the world need to do is to get off fossil fuels, downsize consumption of energy and all resources, and not use "green" energy to consume even more.[67]

The foregoing trends all raise the question, why are China's leaders determined to maintain their manic annual growth rate north of 6 percent, and produce the power to fuel this growth—the climate be damned? That's the subject of the next chapter.

5

China's Engine of Environmental Collapse

RULING-CLASS IMPERATIVES AND SYSTEMIC GROWTH DRIVERS

What is our objective in uniting with all the forces that can be united, inside and outside the Party and at home and abroad? It is to build a great socialist country . . . Therefore, once built up, China will be a great socialist country and will radically transform the situation in which for over a century it was backward, despised and wretched. Moreover, it will be able to catch up with the most powerful capitalist country in the world, the United States . . . Oughtn't we catch up? Definitely yes . . . [to] overtake the United States is not only possible, but absolutely necessary and obligatory. If we don't, the Chinese nation will be letting the nations of the world down and we will not be making much of a contribution to mankind.

– Mao Zedong, August 30, 1956[1]

We must seize every opportunity to make the country develop quickly . . . if we fail to seize it, it will be gone very soon . . . Both the central authorities and localities must take action. You cannot keep waiting but must sack, as soon as possible, those who hesitate to move, or are indifferent to, or even try to boycott reform . . . Any leader who cannot boost the economy should leave office.

– Deng Xiaoping, 1992[2]

In his address to the Nineteenth Congress of the Communist Party in October 2017 Xi Jinping didn't talk about growth so much as about turning China into an "ecological civilization" (*shengtai wenming jianshe*), controlling pollution, building a "Beautiful China," and "giving people a better life":

Man and nature form a community of life; we, as human beings, must respect nature, follow its ways, and protect it. Only by observing the laws of nature can mankind avoid costly blunders in its exploitation. Any harm we inflict on nature will eventually return to haunt us. This is a reality we have to face. . . .

We must realise that lucid waters and lush mountains are invaluable assets and act on this understanding, implement our fundamental national policy of conserving resources and protecting the environment, and cherish the environment as we cherish our own lives. We will adopt a holistic approach to conserving our mountains, rivers, forests, farmlands, lakes, and grasslands, implement the strictest possible systems for environmental protection, and develop eco-friendly growth models and ways of life. We must pursue a model of sustainable development featuring increased production, higher living standards, and healthy ecosystems. We must continue the Beautiful China initiative to create good working and living environments for our people and play our part in ensuring global ecological security . . . The modernization that we pursue is one characterised by harmonious coexistence between man and nature.[3]

To give force to his policy initiatives, Xi elevated the State Environmental Protection Agency (SEPA) to ministerial rank, becoming the Ministry of Environmental Protection (MEP), with powers equal in theory to the big industrial ministries. He further pledged that his government would "complete work on drawing 'redlines' for protecting the ecosystems, designating permanent basic cropland, and delineating boundaries for urban development . . . promote afforestation, take comprehensive steps to control desertification . . . soil erosion, strengthen wetland conservation and restoration . . . improve the system for protecting natural forests . . . [and] rigorously protect farmland."

Xi's government has taken practical steps to improve the environment. It has shut down tens of thousands of smaller private polluters (though it hasn't applied the same heavy hand to state-owned companies, the biggest polluters).[4] In 2017 it banned the import of electronic and plastic waste from the West, which had been poisoning Chinese communities for decades (though not only have Western companies not stopped producing plastics and e-waste, but China is now drowning in plastic and e-waste of its own making and Chinese recycling companies have just relocated their polluting operations to poison communities in Thailand, Malaysia, and elsewhere, so it's hard to count this as an environmental gain).[5] In the same year the government announced that it would ban the sale of internal combustion vehicles (at some unspecified date in the future) and announced plans to introduce a carbon tax (again, at some unspecified point in the future). It has drawn redlines around nature reserves that it wants to protect and initiated numerous ecological restoration projects around the country.[6] Some of these represent real environmental gains, as far as they go. But given the scale and depth of the problems we've surveyed, it's obvious that these efforts are too little, too late, and don't really address the causes and sources of toxic pollution, waste, and soaring CO_2 emissions.

One need not doubt Xi's sincerity, but this chapter argues that regardless of his intentions, he can't lead the fight against global warming and suppress pollution beyond narrow limits because he runs a politico-economic system characterized by systemic growth drivers which are, if anything, more powerful and more eco-suicidal than those of "normal" capitalism in the West, but which he is powerless to alter. These drivers are responsible for China's "blind investment," "blind growth," "blind production," out-of-control resource consumption, and wanton pollution—what Xi himself describes as "meaningless development at the cost of the environment."[7]

Xi's limitations begin with his comrades and nominal "subordinates." As I will try to demonstrate in this chapter, Xi cannot systematically compel subordinate officials to stop squandering resources and polluting the country and the planet, because, for all of his nominal authority as head of the most powerful police state in history, in reality power is widely shared throughout the 90-million-member ruling Party. This means that most of the time he can't force subordinate officials to give up their ruinous practices when to do so would undermine their economic interests.

Furthermore, I contend that for all his ecological rhetoric, Xi can't suppress these destructive practices because Xi himself is the leading driver of "meaningless growth at the expense of the environment." His overriding concern, like that of Mao and Deng Xiaoping before him, is not to build an ecological civilization but to make China rich and powerful, to restore its "greatness," to "catch up and overtake the United States" and become the world's leading superpower. Like Stalin and Khrushchev, Chinese leaders have always understood that in the context of a hostile global imperialism, economic and military parity, if not superiority, are the only guarantors of power. The Soviet Union was doomed by its failure to win the economic and arms race with the US. This lesson was not lost on Xi. As China itself became deeply enmeshed with, and dependent upon, global capitalism, it became vulnerable. Were China to fully open to Western investment, Western corporations could easily dominate, even take over, key sectors of its economy. That's why Xi is pushing back against Western companies;

enforcing import substitution at the expense of "market rationality"; subsidizing China's state-owned and state-controlled industrial "champions" to turn them into world-class competitors; building a relatively self-sufficient high-tech economy protected from Western threats; resisting Western demands that China fully open its economy to Western investment; and striving to win economic and military supremacy, or at least parity, with the US. This I posit, is the main driver and shaper of China's economic development and trajectory.

From the standpoint of the environment, the problem with this hyper-nationalist ambition is that the hyper-industrialization required to realize Xi's "China Dream" of superpower status compels him to break the "harmonious coexistence between man and nature"—in effect, to let the polluters pollute and drive CO_2 emissions off the chart. In short, I contend that Xi is largely powerless to reverse China's eco-suicidal trajectory, even as he successfully introduces important, but far from sufficient, environmental reforms. These statist, ruling-class priorities give China's hybrid bureaucratic-collectivist capitalist system a different logic and rationality, and different drivers, contradictions, and tendencies from capitalism elsewhere.

In capitalism, competition is the motor that drives growth like a perpetual motion machine. It's automatic; competition forces producers to cut costs systematically, find cheaper inputs and wider markets, bring in new technology—in short, to constantly revolutionize the instruments and processes of production on pain of failure and extinction in the marketplace. Growth is built-in and cannot be exorcised. All efforts to date to "green" capitalism—cap-and-trade, carbon taxes, the dematerialization of production, and so on—have foundered on the brutal reality that no government or industrialized economy will accept binding limits on greenhouse gas emissions because no one has yet found a way to suppress emissions without suppressing economic growth.[8]

Yet in capitalism there is one built-in, if temporary, limit to growth—profits. If companies can't make a profit, they will cease production and lay-off workers, sometimes masses of workers. Now and again, economic recession or collapse into depression brings growth to a halt, at least for a while, until sufficient value has been destroyed such that the cycle can begin all over again on an enlarged scale. Hence the business cycle. Further, in capitalist democracies, there is still some freedom to organize, so environmental organizations have been able to impose some restraint on pollution—hard-won precious gains that are now under ferocious assault across the West.

But most of this does not apply to China's largely state-owned and state-controlled economy, because its leaders are not private capitalists— at least not with respect to the state economy (though plenty of them have private businesses on the side, not to mention millions and billions of dollars stashed away in Panama and other hideaways).[9] China's leaders run a hybrid bureaucratic-collectivist capitalist economy, a system largely, though of course not entirely, exempted from the laws of capitalism.

China's SOEs do not live and die by the rules of the market. For all the market reforms since 1978, the government has not allowed a single major SOE to fail and go bankrupt, no matter how inefficient, no matter how indebted, because those industries serve a different purpose. They do not exist just to make money. They exist to fulfil the wishes of China's Communist Party leadership, especially as they contribute to import substitution and national industrialization. China's statist economy thus abides by different laws of motion, different drivers, which I shall try to elucidate here.

CHINA'S HYPER-GROWTH DRIVERS

Capitalist economies are driven by a single maximand: Profit. China's statist-bureaucratic mode of production is driven by a different maximand: Maintaining the security, power, and wealth of the Party bureaucracy. This driver is not systemic and automatic like the motor of competition in capitalism but necessitated by the historical exigencies of ruling-class reproduction. In China's state-owned economy, growth is driven by the conscious decisions of Party authorities. If the leaders choose to develop (or not to develop) an industry, it will be developed (or not). Central planning replaces market competition's role in shaping economic development and prioritizing and funding desired industries. China's leaders have been in the enviable position of having the freedom to plan their economic development more or less as they choose because of their triumphant success in turning their capitalist export bases into the workshop of the world for more than three decades—a feat no other bureaucratic-collectivist regime, notably the Soviet Union, could match. Given the growing foreign exchange surpluses of China's export earnings and positive trade balances since the 1990s (see Tables 5.1 and 5.2 in the Appendix), it has been able to lavishly fund strategic priorities, build up industrial "national champions," hothouse new high-tech and import-substitutionist industries, and spend monies to smooth out global recessionary crises (as in 2008–09). All of these policies have prompted both grudging admiration and concern about the threat of China's "state capitalism" from the Western business press.[10]

The Three "Must Dos"

Since China's leaders are state-based, they must be first and foremost nationalists. From Mao to Xi, they have sought to build their nation into a modern industrial superpower, but one which is as self-sufficient as possible in order to shield their economy from the return of foreign domination (been there, done that).[11] Thus, while introducing capitalism, the government has systematically maintained state domination of the economy and induced foreign companies to hand over technology and intellectual property in exchange for market access. It has also restricted foreign investors to limited sectors (auto manufacturing, electronics, export industries, some retail, foods, and others) in order to prevent their taking over key sectors and the commanding heights of the economy.[12] Since the turn to market reform in 1978 the Party's strategic goal of state-led economic development has obliged China's leaders to rely on three main "drivers":

Driver 1: Maximizing economic growth and self-sufficient industrialization
Driver 2: Maximizing employment generation
Driver 3: Maximizing consumption and consumerism

Beyond these, as we'll see, Reform and Opening presented a vast panorama of legal and illegal opportunities for officials all down the line to profit from driving growth at their own levels. We'll see how subordinate officials seek to maximize growth for their own reasons, independently of Beijing, often defying the central government's intentions while remaining within the law. And outside the law, we'll also see how corruption itself has become a major, if inadvertent, driver of growth, overconsumption, overconstruction and, unavoidably, pollution.

DRIVER 1: MAXIMIZING ECONOMIC GROWTH
AND SELF-SUFFICIENT INDUSTRIALIZATION

In 1982 Deng Xiaoping called on China's officials and managers to double per capita GDP to $500 by 1990, and then double it again to $1,000 by 2000, and then to keep doubling it to achieve a national GDP of one trillion dollars by the mid-twenty-first century.[13] In 1992, he pressed local officials and SOE bosses to *xia hai,* or "jump into the sea" (of commerce), and exhorted them to grow the economy or get out of the way. "Any leader who cannot boost the economy must leave office," Deng threatened. China's leaders have forced the pace of industrialization and modernization with successive Five-Year Plans, sub-plans, and related initiatives that prioritized "strategic," "key," and "pillar" industries and projected the leaders' visions of comprehensive national development: From steel, coal, and power generation in the 1950s to smart manufacturing, robotics, cloud computing, 5G internet, big data, new materials, renewable energy, hybrid vehicles, biotech, and AI today.

China's Permanent Great Leap Forward

"Let me say something first about the echoes of the Great Leap Forward, starting with some statistics showing the rapid growth of steel output in China. In 1978, the first year of the reforms, it was just over 30 million tons. Two years later, in 1980, it reached 37.12 million tons, the fifth largest steel output in the world. By 1996 it had jumped to No. 1 in the world, where it has stayed ever since. In 2008 it exceeded 500 million tons, or 32 percent of the world's total steel output, more than the next seven nations in the world combined. In 2009 China's steel output reached 600 million tons, outstripping by 30 percent the goal set by the government of 460 million tons . . . The same kind of frenzied steep production that we saw during the Great Leap Forward has taken place once more on Chinese soil."

Source: Yu Hua, *China in Ten Words* (New York: Random House, 2011), 11.

TOP-DOWN DRIVERS

The eighth and ninth Five-Year Plans (1990–2000) prioritized oil, coal, iron, and steel production, rail upgrades, road building, energy, auto manufacturing, ports and airports, telecoms, and the Three Gorges Dam. In the 1990s the government also launched its great urbanization drive—history's largest land grab, a vast state-directed enclosure movement that expropriated more than 200 million people, mostly farmers, and forced them into newly built but often shabby suburbs, often far from their jobs and families, in order to lease their lands to developers to build new industrial parks, apartment blocks, and so on. Plans are now in the works to "relocate" another 250 million people.[14]

Responding to growing labor strikes and protests over land grabs and environmental deterioration, the tenth and eleventh Five-Year Plans (2001–2010), stressed building a "harmonious socialist society" (*shehuizhuyi hexie shehui*) by addressing inequality, boosting wages, creating 45 million new jobs, and developing backward regions, mostly in the western half of the country. They funded a drive to make China a "leading manufacturer" of IT, based on "indigenous breakthroughs," and ordered SOEs to "focus on import substitution to make China's IT less reliant on the West."[15]

The twelfth Five-Year Plan (2011–2016) funded gargantuan and staggeringly unsustainable infrastructure projects (some of which we discussed in Chapter 2): It funded a major expansion of the auto industry prioritizing "strengthening R&D capability, realizing technical autonomy of key parts," and developing domestically built electric cars; it allocated funding for the construction of a national express highway system 83,000 kilometers in total length, a national high-speed rail system totaling 45,000 kilometers, and subway systems in more than twenty cities; it funded commercial aircraft development and hundreds of new airports including Beijing International Airport's Terminal 2; it increased expenditures for aerospace to launch an orbital space station and land a rover on the moon; it funded expansion of housing targeting urbanization rate to reach 52 percent; it increased spending on consumer goods industries and subsidized the development of a consumer credit industry. Wherever possible, SOEs were instructed to "promote independent brand building, improve brand value and effects, and accelerate the development of large enterprises with world-famous brands and core competencies."[16]

The energy development section of the plan called for "accelerating construction of coal-to-gas bases in Shaanxi, Inner Mongolia" and elsewhere; "creating 5 large-scale oil and gas producing areas" in the Tarim Basin and other basins; "accelerating exploration and development of offshore and deep water oil and gas fields"; "accelerating development of nuclear power in coastal provinces" to bring capacity up to 40 million kilowatts; and the expansion of hydropower, and wind and solar power. The plan budgeted for more ports and more shipbuilding, with priority given to "the development of large liquefied natural gas (LNG) and liquefied petroleum gas (LPG) vessels, ocean-going fishing vessels, and luxury liners."

The strategic emerging industries section called for "seven emerging industries" that the government hoped would become the "backbone" of China's future transition from low-end assembly to high-value manufacturing: The new-generation IT industry (internet, cloud computing, and high-end servers); biotechnology; high-end equipment manufacturing (aeronautics and astronautics, high-speed railways, marine engineering, and intelligent manufacturing); renewable energy and smart grids; new-energy cars; and new materials.[17]

Made in China 2025: Xi's China Dream of Techno-Industrial Supremacy

With the thirteenth Five-Year Plan (2016–2020), and the "Made in China 2025" plan (announced in 2015) and Belt and Road Initiative (2013), Party leaders have a master plan for techno-nationalist industrial self-sufficiency capable of powering China to global economic and military supremacy and geopolitical domination over Asia and beyond—nothing less than a "New World Order." The Made in China 2025 plan vowed to spend trillions of dollars to acquire the world's most cutting-edge technology, and to hothouse "indigenous innovation" and free the country from dependence on the West. It called for China to become industrially dominant and self-sufficient in ten industries: IT; high-end machinery and robotics; aerospace; marine equipment and ships; advanced rail transport; new-energy vehicles; electric power; agricultural machinery; new materials; and biomedical industries.[18]

In 2017, the State Council added AI to this list. With this, China's strategy envisions warp-speed expansion into, and domination of, the "fourth industrial revolution." *Bloomberg* reports that China's AI industry will be "in-line" with those of the most advanced countries by 2020, and China will be "the world's primary AI innovation center by 2030." Breathlessly, the State Council tells us:

> Artificial intelligence has become the new engine of economic development. As the core driving force of the new round of industrial transformation . . . From the macro to the micro-intelligent new demands, new technologies, new products, new industries, new formats, and new models have been created, which have triggered major changes in the economic structure, profoundly changed the way of life and thinking of human beings, and achieved an overall leap in social productivity . . . It is necessary to accelerate the in-depth application of artificial intelligence, cultivate and strengthen the artificial intelligence industry, *and inject new kinetic energy into China's economic development.*
>
> In accordance with the unified arrangements of the Party Central Committee . . . The relevant departments will carry out the deployment and implementation of the planning tasks . . . Promote the construction of artificial intelligence think tanks, support various think tanks to carry out research on major issues of artificial intelligence, and provide strong intellectual support for the development of artificial intelligence . . . let the healthy development of artificial intelligence become the consensus

of the whole society, and mobilize the enthusiasm of the whole society to participate in supporting the development of artificial intelligence.[19]

In response, officials across the country scrambled to build their own research centers for AI and "new industries," with nary a thought to whether they would sell what they made, or whether China really "needs" self-driving cars, robot grocery deliveries, or AI video spies monitoring primary school children, let alone their impact on the environment, but with every concern to milk those startup subsidies from Beijing. This is indicative of how China's "new engines"—"blind growth" and "blind investment" overproduction crazes—begin at the top, in Beijing, in the Party's bid to win bragging rights, global tech supremacy, and superpower status.

MINISTERIAL AND PROVINCIAL DRIVERS

Beyond Zhongnanhai—the leadership's command center in central Beijing—the industrial ministries, including coal, oil, steel, railroads, telecoms, state construction companies, and others, are mighty drivers of growth in their own right. They employ tens of millions and contribute billions in GDP growth and tax revenues. SOE bosses and local, provincial, and ministerial officials don't face market competition so much as they face intense bureaucratic competition for access to resources and appropriations from the center. This particularistic intra-ruling-class struggle over access to state funds also shapes the broad pattern of China's economic development, powering tendencies to redundancy, duplication, irrational investment, and waste throughout the economy. In his book on China's growing airline industry, James Fallows writes:

> Foreign reports often present these projects as carefully coordinated expressions of China's larger ambitions for a modern transportation system and to an extent they are. But there are also bitter bureaucratic and commercial rivalries between the airline and railroad interests within China, each seizing on any opportunity to argue that it reflected the wiser and more farsighted use of the country's resources.[20]

China's state-owned infrastructure builders—companies like China State Construction Engineering Corporation, China Railway Construction Corporation, China Harbor Engineering, China Road and Bridge Group, and dozens of others with their thousands of sub-contractors—run a self-perpetuating gravy train of "cost-plus" contracts. They employ so many workers and sustain so many other industries that even though the government knows that the country is already massively overbuilt, it can't stop them.

Building 363 Golden Gate Bridges in a Year

In 2016 alone China added 26,100 road bridges, including 363 "extra-large" bridges, with an average length of about one mile. San Francisco's Golden Gate Bridge is four-fifths of a mile long. Imagine building 363 Golden Gate Bridges, plus another 26,000 or so shorter bridges, in a single year.[21] That gives you some idea of the manic pace and scale of infrastructure overconstruction in China today. And that's just the bridges.

Many of these grandiose "blingfrastructure" projects are little used and have burdened local governments with huge debts they can never hope to recover from tolls. But infrastructure accounts for at least 9 percent of China's GDP (vs. 2.5 percent in the US) and millions of jobs. Given its concern with keeping those builders building (and keeping the coal miners, steel mill workers, and others whose jobs depend upon construction working), it just keeps approving more projects to build more useless bridges, expressways, airports, and ghost cities while also striving to redeploy them to infrastructure projects along the Belt and Road Initiative projects that are springing up all over Asia, Africa, Latin America, Europe, and even the US.[22] As Xi said at a bridge opening in Hunan in 2013: "It's very important to improve transport and other infrastructure so that impoverished regions can escape poverty and prosper. We must do more of this and keep supporting it." Music to the ears of bridge builders. But the *New York Times* asked a local farmer in the shadow of one such impressive but virtually unused bridge what he thought of it all. The farmer replied: "If you don't build roads, there will be no prosperity. But this is an expressway, not a second- or third-grade road. One of those might be better for us."[23] Probably, but would a mere second- or third-grade bridge impress superiors as much as the longest or highest bridge in the province, or the country? Likely not. That's why aspiring local officials find it rational to squander funds on gigantic prestige projects that are often useless to local people. As we'll see, this logic applies even to entire (and entirely redundant) cities.

LOCAL DRIVERS

Then there are the local-level drivers: Municipal, county, and provincial governments, and local state-owned industries. When Deng Xiaoping introduced market reform he cut profit-sharing deals with local officials and SOE bosses. Most SOEs were still required to fulfill their planned production targets as previously. Government planners still imposed numerous quotas and targets but gave them the right to sell over-quota output on the new free markets, to re-invest their retained profits as they saw fit, and to initiate new lines of production for the market.

GDP "Tournaments"

Local officials didn't need to be told twice. Deng's exhortations led in short order to GDP "tournaments," as local officials competed to generate higher growth rates to win promotions and more government largesse. While the eleventh Five-Year Plan set the target national GDP growth rate at 7.5 percent, all of China's 31 provinces set targets higher than this. The average target growth rate was 10.1 percent, the highest 13 percent, and the lowest 8.5 percent.[24]

Competition-driven local GDP growth has in turn helped drive the national GDP to overshoot central planners' targets as well. Since 1978, China's Five-Year Plans have never called for national growth rates higher than 8 percent per year. But that target has been routinely exceeded: In 1983–88, GDP growth averaged 11.9 percent per year, and nearly doubled the target rate when it hit 15.2 percent in 1985. For two decades (1992–2011), GDP growth averaged 10.5 percent, topping 11 and 14 percent on the crest of the boom in 2006 and 2007 (see Table 5.3 in the Appendix). In this way, China's competitive officials easily soared past Deng's national GDP target of one trillion dollars—exceeding *eleven* trillion dollars in 2016.

What's more, once they had met whatever quotas they were required to meet, if any, it didn't seem to matter what they produced. Everything counted toward GDP growth. Contrast this with Western capitalism: When Ford's Edsel, Sony's Betamax, Coca-Cola's New Coke, Harley-Davidson's "biker cologne," or Google's creepy Google Glass failed to sell, they didn't count toward any company's bottom line, or to the US GDP. But in the bizarre accounting practices of China's state-owned economy, even if a product has no use value, even if it fails to sell or rent out, it's still counted toward the GDP. So mountains of unsold steel and aluminum, virtually unused international airports in provincial towns, skyscraper office buildings devoid of tenants, empty ghost cities, useless vanity projects of all kinds—all these and more get counted toward some local official's GDP (and promotion prospects), and thus toward the national GDP.

Rational Irrationalities

What's more, the introduction of market incentives within the framework of a bureaucratic-collectivist economy not only produced GDP tournaments but they also magnified, instead of ameliorating, most of the qualitative problems that plagued Mao's bureaucratic-collectivist economy from its inception: Inefficiency, duplication, resource waste, energy waste, lack of specialization, lack of economies of scale, local protectionism, resistance to cooperation, excessive pollution, and so on. This has, in turn, further worsened China's environmental problems. Why is that?

Back in the heyday of market reform in the 1980s and 1990s, market-crusading Chinese and Western economists told us that the adoption of market reforms within the framework of state ownership and planning would make China's bureaucratic-collectivist economy work like a capitalist economy, make its "companies" behave like regular capitalist companies, without having to abandon state planning and privatize state-owned industries.[25] Many argued that market transparency would also obviate the "need" for corruption as the old black market distribution of resources in Mao's Stalinist "shortage" economy would be replaced by transparent market exchange.

The "Trapped Transition"

The problem was, as I argued in my 1989 doctoral thesis, this strategy was doomed to fail because the only way to make the state economy work like a capitalist economy would have been to *actually make it a capitalist economy*: Abandon central planning, privatize state industries, and fully commoditize the economy.[26] But to do that would have meant the end of Communist Party rule. Since the Party persistently refuses to enact real reform, to this day China's state-sector market reform project has remained permanently stalled in what Minxin Pei called a "trapped transition."[27] Instead of a broad shift to competition-induced, market-disciplined, productivity-driven growth, China's SOEs have continued with their decades-long "extensive" pattern of input-driven and debt-fueled growth, "blind production" and "blind investment" with little regard for efficiency, productivity, resource waste, and pollution, but on a vastly greater scale with horrendous consequences for global resource exhaustion and CO_2 emissions.[28]

The March of the Undead

[The lowest growth rate acceptable to the government is that needed] to ensure fairly full employment and realize reasonable increase of people's income.

— Premier Li Keqiang, 2014[29]

In 1990, Premier Li Peng decried "generally declining economic results" after twelve years of market reform in the state-owned industries:

At present, many products are . . . still heavily stockpiled, but they are still being produced by enterprises . . . Furthermore, no fundamental change has been made regarding the similarity of regional economic structures and the duplication of production and construction . . . At present, too many projects are being planned by various quarters . . . If such reckless and blind development is allowed to continue, the consequences will be serious . . . we shall continue to restrain and control the construction of [guest houses, amenities, offices and meeting-hall projects] . . . At present, some areas are practising regional blockade in the purchase and marketing of some products and supply of some raw materials . . . Practising regional blockade is tantamount to protecting the backward . . . some enterprises are pursuing false profits with actual deficits.[30]

Well, isn't that exactly what we see today: Massive overproduction of Chinese steel dumped onto world markets, huge stockpiles of aluminum ingots (even tens of thousands of them piled up in the middle of a Mexican desert in hopes of illegally sneaking them into the US as "Mexican" aluminum to beat quotas on Chinese imports),[31] redundant production and construction across the economy, and the persistence of local protectionism and "market blockades?"[32] What's changed is the scale of the waste, as China's hugely profitable capitalist SEZ export economy has enabled overproduction and gigantism on a hitherto unimagined scale. Today, China's steel capacity is greater than the combined totals for Japan, Russia, and the US, the three next-largest producers. China's cement capacity is ten times that of India, the world's second-largest producer. The government has been trying to cut overcapacity in coal, aluminum, copper, lead, zinc, autos, electric power, textiles, glass, paper, synthetic fibers, luxury housing, and other sectors for decades but the problem only grows worse.[33] Since the 1990s China's SOEs have grown enormously in size and wealth not because of their market prowess but because they're cosseted monopolies with protected markets and enjoy endless rollover loans from state banks. Thus, for all the decades of market reforms, today China's SOEs are even more bloated, overstaffed, and indebted than in Li Peng's day. The country is littered with half-dead ghost factories and SOEs kept on life support by regular intravenous injections of fresh cash. As the boss of one "zombie" cement plant told a reporter, stopping production was "not an option" because "maintaining stability" by keeping people working was a higher state priority.[34]

Rational Zombies

In 2017 *Caixin* reported that China Railways Corporation (CRC, now China State Railway Group)—operator of the world's largest rail system and China's premier state-owned industrial "champion"—was effectively bankrupt, and that wasn't even the worst of its problems:

> Despite its attempts to behave like a company, the state-owned operator is plagued by a bloated payroll of 2 million employees and the inability to quickly roll out new products to capture market demand and generate new revenue. Instead, CRC has emerged from its former status as a government entity to become a slow-moving behemoth saddled by trillions of yuan in debt, with little prospects of repaying that money anytime soon. Adding further baggage to the company is a culture lacking transparency and a series of traumatic accidents that have dogged CRC . . . Safety has also been an issue dogging the operator, especially after the 2011 high-speed train crash in southeast Zhejiang province that killed 40 people and shocked the world. The now-defunct Railways Ministry released a detailed investigation in that case. But the CRC is far less forthcoming more often. Many accidents that injured or killed rail workers were never made public before, as the ministry ran a separate judicial system. In December [2016] two accidents happened in four days in northern Henan province that killed eight workers. Many believe such incidents would have been concealed in the past, and only become public after going viral on social media . . . Falling freight traffic is also a cause for worry as demand for bulk commodities slides with China's slowing economy. At the same time, the company is saddled with 4.3 trillion yuan ($625 billion) in debt from building the nation's high-speed rail network, now 22,000 km long and set to keep growing over the next five years. Some have likened that load to a ticking time bomb, which could one day explode unless the company can develop new revenue sources.[35]

Despite this, the bosses know *for certain* that the government is never going to let their company fail, so they keep "irrationally" investing, overproducing, and overbuilding (not forgetting to build themselves more guest houses, luxury offices, and divert some cash to their offshore bank accounts). Since there's been no change in the basic property and surplus relations in the state-owned economy, marketization in the context of bureaucratic collectivism has served to amplify many of the endemic irrationalities of the old system, greatly increasing waste and pollution in the process—while also adding new market irrationalities, including entirely new industries like counterfeit goods,[36] just-in-time execution of political prisoners to supply the organ transplant tourism industry,[37] the fentanyl-export industry,[38] and more.

Inefficiency and Duplication

Every locality acts as if it's a separate country.

– State official[39]

Consider the situation provincial and municipal officials who nominally "own" the SOEs that are not directly managed by the central government. Aside from their basic salaries, these officials can only personally profit from new incentives and opportunities presented by marketization in the "mini economies" directly under their control—their province, municipality, or SOE. Generally speaking, they can't invest their profits in SOEs in some other province or in some other national economy—like capitalist investors in Hong Kong, Singapore, or New York. In this circumstance, local officials see their neighbors as competitors in a zero-sum game of competition for central disbursements, market profits, and promotions. They're incentivized to build their own more-or-less self-sufficient mini economies even if this means investing in inefficient small-scale plants with out-of-date technology producing inferior products and generating excessive pollution.[40]

When Deng cut his profit-sharing deal with local officials to give them incentives to produce for the market on the side, he hoped to get not only more growth but also a more rational, modern economy with less waste and duplication—bigger factories with up-to-date technology, greater economies of scale, wider markets, and so on. He got the extra sideline production but decentralization just reinforced inefficiencies and local protectionism.[41]

This is a function of the basic property/surplus extraction system. If local officials in Sichuan, Henan, or Yunnan want to profit from central government initiatives and subsidies to boost auto, solar, or windmill production, the way to do so is to build their own "as if they were a separate country." So instead of large-scale factories to optimize economies of scale, local officials tend to build hundreds of thousands of low-capacity, redundant, mostly small-to-medium-sized enterprises (SMEs) across the economy. Furthermore, the "weak and balkanized legal system ... permits local political authorities to pressure courts in their jurisdictions to favor local firms."[42]

For example, in the 1980s and 90s, when Beijing ramped up spending on the domestic auto industry, every locality wanted to be a Detroit. In 1978 China had 56 "small but complete" (*xiao er quan*) auto factories scattered about in almost every province producing around 200,000 low-quality "brand new antique" cars and trucks per year copied from Soviet models from the 1940s and built with outdated technology. In the 1980s and 90s Western companies set up modern, efficient, high-technology, large-scale plants in the SEZs in joint ventures with state partners to produce Audis, Toyotas, Buicks, etc. for the domestic market. Beijing hoped to graft their technology, management skills, and R&D capabilities onto its state-owned companies. But market reform largely failed to transform the state-owned domestic auto industry. Lu Zhang writes that "Despite the government's efforts to consolidate the auto industry . . . there was a continued proliferation of small and inefficient auto assembly plants in almost every province"—115 of them by 2011. "Many of these . . . had limited annual output of a few thousand or just a few hundred units and operated under the protection of local governments." Local officials still try to force the sale of these cars in their bailiwicks to keep out "foreign" imports from other provinces, much as in Mao's day. Small-scale inefficient auto plants not only waste resources, but many such plants also rely on small-scale "captive" coal-fired power plants that also pollute excessively (see below).[43]

When the Made in China 2025 initiative boosted spending for new energy vehicles (NEVs), every mayor wanted to become an electric car impresario. As of June 2018, China had no less than 487 manufacturers of electric vehicles (versus 2 in the US). With the government pushing electric cars, many companies "concluded that 'simply giving it a shot' and receiving government support [could] be a reasonable business model, even if they never put an electric car on the road."[44] Thanks to subsidies, Chinese manufacturers sold 1.25 million electric cars in 2018, 62 percent more than in 2017, putting the country on track to meet its goal of two million NEVs sold in 2020. China now accounts for more than half the electric car sales in the world. Yet like Americans, China's fashion-conscious consumers want big SUVs, not econo-boxes, and least of all China's low-quality, unreliable domestic electric cars, some of which tend to spontaneously combust.[45] So now Beijing is trying to rein in its zombie electric car factories along with its zombie gasoline-powered car factories.[46]

When the government decided in 2005 that renewable energy (hydro, wind, and solar) should account for 10 percent of electricity generating capacity by 2020, officials all over China got into the renewable energy business to get the subsidies to build capacity, whether wind or solar output were actually sufficient in their region or not, as we noted in Chapter 4. Thus, by 2010 China had more than 100 wind turbine producers and excess capacity was already near 50 percent.[47]

When the government launched its national high-speed rail system in 2008, every mayor (like mayors everywhere) wanted to link it to his own municipality in order to benefit from anticipated real estate speculation and growth, even if their small municipalities didn't warrant it. The state planning agency complained that: "Competition between cities has often . . . resulted in stations being built miles away from downtown areas and with 'ambitious edifices far too large for their respective purposes.'" In Henan province, for example, a feud between Dengzhou and Xinye resulted in a new railway station being built sixteen kilometers from Dengzhou and fourteen kilometers from Xinye. The planners warned that "smaller cities should not 'overestimate the contribution a high-speed rail project can make to economic prospects' and just blindly copy the development plans of bigger cities."[48]

In the same vein, China has more than 30 airlines (almost one for each province), and multiple wannabe "Wall Streets," "Silicon Valleys," and so on. Today every locality wants to be a tourist destination or an AI research center. But instead of large-scale, efficient, specialized plants dominating production, one more often finds enormous numbers of SMEs surrounding China's cities. As Elizabeth C. Economy writes: "In Jiangsu province, which surrounds Shanghai, roughly one such enterprise can be found per square kilometer."[49] Same with power plants, as local SOEs not infrequently build their own small-scale but "captive" power plants to ensure regular supplies of power:

> The central government has tried to consolidate energy suppliers into large-scale power plants, where environmental technologies are easier to enforce. But local governments have encouraged the proliferation of small (under 50 megawatts [MW]), inefficient, and highly polluting

coal-fired power plants to meet growing local energy needs. The smallest of these plants (12 MW) release three to eight times more particulates, consume 60 percent more coal, and are 35–60 percent more costly to operate than plants of 200 MW or more. [50]

Little wonder that China's industrial regions are blanketed in coal smog and dust.

Bias to Uneconomical Scale

As Mark DeWeaver explains, local officials with limited capital but looking to profit from particular industries often build plants of a sub-optimal scale, duplicating what their neighbors build. We see this with autos, steel plants, cement plants, oil refining, aluminum, zinc smelting, and so on. Sub-optimal plants using antiquated technology and industrial processes that in some cases dating to the nineteenth and early twentieth centuries both waste resources and generate excessive pollution. [51] DeWeaver reports that by 2004 China had a total of 280 steel mills, most of which had an annual capacity of less than 100,000 tons. This compares to capacity of about 3 million tons at even the smallest international producers. While cement companies in other countries typically produce millions of tons a year, in China most cement is still made in plants with capacity of only 50,000 tons–200,000 tons per year, and which are still using shaft kilns like in the 1960s. That the product is often of poor and uneven quality has contributed to the collapse of so many buildings and bridges. [52]

Resistance to Cooperation

Instead of cooperating with neighbors to build larger-scale, more efficient, and more modern units of production, economist Zhou Li-An reports that: "Localities are less able to cooperate than the many independent countries that have entered into bilateral and multilateral trade agreements." Thus, the use of such small-scale, archaic, and highly polluting equipment and processes remains widespread in China. [53] At the opposite extreme, DeWeaver points out that: "Localities may also strive to be in the leading position in as many sectors as possible. This can easily lead to investment in facilities that far exceed the optimal scale." So small towns build "first-tier" airports when they only have a few flights a week. Or rival officials in adjoining municipalities build airports virtually next to each other, as around Shanghai, in the race for customers. [54] Or officials build skyscrapers, superhighways, or entire subway systems in provincial towns just to burnish their image.

Thus, after four decades of market reform, the old Maoist pattern of "big and all-inclusive" and "small and all-inclusive" is still widespread in the state sector, indeed on a far larger scale.

The Rationality of "Blingfrastructure" and Gigantism

As China grew rich in the 2000s, officials high and low indulged themselves in delusions of grandeur and squandered vast sums on useless "blingfrastructure" and entire industries that the Chinese do not need and the planet cannot sustain. They've lavished money on the world's largest auto industry, what is soon to be the world's largest aviation industry, a burgeoning cruise ship industry, and a yacht industry. They lavish more money on pharaonic neo-Stalinist prestige projects to glorify the Communist Party, flatter local officials, and promote patriotism: The world's largest dam and radio telescope, fastest supercomputer and high-speed train, longest high-speed rail system and express highway system, the longest and highest bridges,[55] biggest airports, the first "quantum satellite," the highest-altitude ring road, and more.[56]

DeWeaver writes that "some 'image projects' have no discernable rationality at all aside from creating the impression that officials are getting something done." He quotes a Ministry of Industry and Information Technology vice minister who says that one of China's largest wind farms—a huge, ten-gigawatt project in Gansu province (dubbed the "Three Gorges of the land")—is a "typical image project." It sits unconnected to any grid "while the projects' turbines are being continuously blasted by sand from the Gobi Desert."[57]

GRAFT-DRIVEN GROWTH

Transparency International points out that corruption is typically a bigger problem in construction than in any other sector worldwide. That's because with large construction projects, especially infrastructure projects, every bridge, tunnel, dam, highway, and railway is to some extent unique, a custom job, unlike mass production where everything is standardized, and costs can be calculated exactly and compared with competing producers. Construction projects often require legions of sub-contractors, cost overruns are routine, and cost-plus contracts are typical. All these factors make it easy to conceal graft because auditors can't really know what the builders' actual costs should have been. In fact, many projects are "conceived solely as vehicles for corruption."[58] DeWeaver wonders if China would ever have built such a huge high-speed train network, such a lengthy express highway system, or so many other superfluous and needlessly huge projects if these weren't mainly "vehicles for corruption." In 2011 both the minister of railways, Liu Zhijin and his deputy general engineer, Zhang Shuguang, were removed, tried, and imprisoned, Liu for taking bribes totaling 2.1 billion yuan. Zhang, the "father of Chinese high-speed rail," was reported to have stashed $2.8 billion in Swiss bank accounts.[59] Now imagine this pattern across the entire economy.

Primitive Accumulation and the Great Urbanization Drive

The real estate-construction industrial complex is easily the most spectacular example not only of overconstruction, waste, needless dislocation, and pointless pollution, but also of corruption, because the whole industry is founded on "primitive accumulation"—the theft of land from its occupants. In China, ceaseless primitive accumulation is the engine of urbanization and urban renewal. In what exiled economist and journalist He Qinglian termed "the marketization of power," China's leaders effectively combined the capitalist incentive of profit maximization with the bureaucratic-collectivist monopoly of property and power to open the way for officials high and low to grow fabulously rich by dispossessing tens of millions of peasants and urban residents alike, selling long-term leases for their properties to developers at huge profits, and securing for themselves a cut of the future profits of developments in the bargain.[60]

DeWeaver wryly compares this process with the fifteenth-century enclosure movement in Britain and Ireland, which expropriated peasant freeholders, and enclosed and privatized their farms and common lands to the benefit of capitalist landlords in the centuries-long process that Marx termed "primitive accumulation":

> In today's China the tragedy is being restaged, with factories, property developments, and even Olympic Games facilities replacing sheep farms, Communist Party cadres acting the part of Renaissance nobles, and ordinary Chinese playing British peasants. The main elements of the plot are the same. First, property is transferred from weak hands to strong through the introduction of new private ownership rights. Next, large-scale forced evictions are followed by the wholesale destruction of farms and residential areas. Finally, the dispossessed farmers, like the "vagabonds" created by the enclosure movement, have no alternative but to migrate to the cities in search of work.[61]

In Britain and Ireland, this struggle lasted centuries. China's leaders have repeated this process anew in mere decades. The process began in 1986 when the government issued a decree establishing long-term leasing of state-owned land in the SEZs to attract foreign investment to build industrial parks, hotels, and so on. "In an instant," He Qingliang writes, "the frenzy to open up economic development zones spread across the entire country." Subsequent decrees through the 1990s extended the privatizations, as localities competed both to attract foreign capital and to develop peri-urban farmland.[62] Since the 1990s, municipal governments have been empowered and incentivized to expropriate millions of peasants in a perpetual drive of urban expansion. First, surrounding farms are enclosed by the city which then develops the land, building apartment blocks, shopping malls, industrial parks, and so on. Then they grab the next ring of farms further out, and then the next, and so on. This is how over the last three decades China's once-compact cities have been turned into vast semi-urban sprawls, as "cities surround the countryside."[63] This is how local mayors have filled their bedrooms with floor-to-ceiling stacks of ill-gotten 100-yuan notes. And this is how China's real estate-construction industrial complex came to be a major driver of the economy, accounting for as much as 20 percent of GDP growth since the 1990s.

Between 1990 and 2007, the government issued a series of decrees privatizing most urban housing (the apartments and houses, not the land).[64] Under the old system, urban workers' housing was virtually free. Since the 1990s, workers have been required to buy their apartments, but occupant prices were initially set well below market rate and cheap government mortgages eased the transition while the government accelerated urban housing construction. By 2005, 82 percent of housing was privatized and owner-occupied.[65] The combination of marketization, state-driven urban renewal/dispossession, and non-stop new housing construction quickly turned real estate into a speculative gold rush as the city centers of Beijing, Shanghai, and hundreds of other cities—with housing dating back to the Ming and Qing dynasties—were demolished in waves of urban renewal. Xiao-xi Hui describes the results as follows:

> In Beijing, the gated communities for the rich and upper stratum occupy the best locations of the city, and the middle class can only afford the market housing prices of the outskirts. Most of social-oriented housing neighbourhoods were less accessible and far from the city centre. The mid-low and low income groups have to live in decayed, old areas or move to the suburbs as relocatees of urban reconstruction.[66]

Furthermore, Hui notes, the privatization and marketization of urban housing stock also entailed extensive ecological damage and pollution:

> Unlimited real estate development consumed large amounts of land resources and speeded up the process of urban sprawl and suburbanisation. The built-up urban area of Beijing city rapidly sprawled from 488.28 km in 1998 . . . to 1289.3 km in 2007. Along with the urban sprawl, the daily commute between city centre and suburb hugely increased, thereby creating increasingly severe traffic jams and air pollution. Furthermore, the profit-hungry real estate development sector, in which one-time investment was much more of a deciding factor than the lifecycle cost of building, [failed to implement] ecological building technologies for energy saving.[67]

Primitive Accumulation with Chinese Characteristics

There is no doubt that when Deng Xiaoping turned China down the capitalist road in the early 1980s, many of his comrades would have loved to privatize the whole economy. After all, didn't Marx say that capitalism was a prerequisite for socialism? The problem was, there was no way they could actually privatize the economy without inviting social revolution of that kind that happened in the Soviet bloc countries. How could they divide up 200 or so huge SOEs between millions of Communist Party officials? Who would get what? How could they divide up the land and natural resources? How could they even be sure that, once privatization was in motion, the Party bureaucrats would end up as the new capitalist ruling/owning class? Given widespread and bitter resentment of the Party after the disasters of the Great Leap Forward, the Cultural Revolution, and the military intervention against the Tiananmen protests in 1989, many would have asked, why not put the Party on trial instead? In Russia, Gorbachev's privatizations eventually wiped out the Communist Party as a ruling class. Deng and his comrades were not looking to repeat that fatal error.

Instead, the Party elite settled for maintaining the predominance of state ownership and state planning, and enforced Party dictatorship (no liberalization, no multiparty democracy), while inviting Western investors and companies to help modernize the economy, after which they took "their" share of the growing wealth of the state by looting the state economy and privatizing bits and pieces around the edges (mainly smaller, non-strategic SOEs) where they could. Formally, the bulk of the state economy would remain in state hands while, privately and individually, they would extract the wealth and hide it, launder it, and invest it in private Chinese companies like Anbang or Alibaba, or ▶

funnel it out of the country via underground and Western banks, Hong Kong gangsters, and the like.

In the end, this turned out to be a brilliant strategy. While communist regimes collapsed across Europe, while Cuban and North Korean communists hung on as Stalinist antiques teetering on collapse, China's communists "rejuvenated" China, turned it into an economic powerhouse second only to the US, saved the Communist Party and enriched the "red bourgeoisie" beyond their wildest dreams, richer by far than most national capitalist classes. A tour de force, no doubt—though there remains the difficulty that this is all illegal and therefore insecure, as many, like Bo Xilai and his multimillionaire wife with her Côte d'Azur hideaway and secret Cayman Islands bank accounts, have found out.

Analytically, we can distinguish two types of corruption. The first is state-private collusion: Bribery and kickbacks for contracts, influence-pedaling, selling offices, and smuggling—the garden variety sorts of corruption one finds in most capitalist countries in varying degrees. What's different about this in China's case is its vast extent, which is due both to the country's huge size and because it takes place in a society plagued by every sort of corruption. The second is looting the state directly: Misappropriation, embezzlement, turning SOEs and state banks into ATMs for the cadres, and the massive extraction of wealth. This one sees only in a once-in-an-epoch tectonic transformation, such as the transition from feudalism to capitalism in England, or the wholesale privatization of the western states and territories of the US (after the native Americans were more or less fully wiped out and the Mexicans booted out). In such cases, vast fortunes are made in one-off land grabs of enormous proportions. China's private looting and large-scale privatization of state assets belong to this category.

Yet even with all of this, the bulk of the economy, all property, and all natural resources remain in state hands, and even where substantial assets have been privatized, there is as yet no security of private property, because there's no independent state judiciary and police to guarantee all this property. So what we have here is "privatization interruptus" so to speak: De facto but not yet de jure, and only partial at that.

China's Consuming Billion

Since the 1980s, more than 200 million mostly young ex-farmers volun-tarily left their parents' farms and migrated to China's big cities and the coastal export zones in search of jobs in construction, manufacturing, and the service economy. Besides these, according to an official tally, by 2010 the government had also forcibly evicted at least 50 million farmers and millions more urban residents to make way for government projects and private sector developments.[68] In 1978, just 20 percent of China's population were classified as urban. By 2000 this share reached 36 percent. By 2010, 50 percent.[69] But for the government, this has not been fast enough. China's leaders say that to be "modern" and to increase consumption, China needs to be a majority urban country like Japan and the US. The twelfth and thirteenth Five-Year Plans called for "accelerating the transfer of rural farmers to the cities." Xi's government wants to raise the urban population share to 70 percent by 2025—some 900 million people—by forcing 250 million Chinese to give up farming and move to newly built cities.

Why? Because as economic growth has slowed and exports have slumped since the boom years before 2008, the government wants domestic demand to take up the slack and become the main engine of economic growth. Their solution is to increase the numbers of modest consumers by turning hundreds of millions of peasant farmers into urban dwellers and mass consumers. As Ian Johnson writes, Party officials "speak knowingly of what is best for China's 1.3 billion people, where they should live and how they should earn a living." For them, urbanization and industrialization are "an objective rule in the process of modernization."[70] At least that's how officials rationalize their expropriations. In 2005, Chen Yuan—chairman of China Development Bank (the leading financier of urban reconstruction) and the "princeling" son (see Chapter 6) of Mao's chief economic planner Chen Yun—declared that urbanization was "the most important and enduring motive force in stimulating consumption and investment in China's domestic economy today."[71]

Land Grabs, Dispossession, Protests, Suicides, and Revolts

China's "socialist" government doesn't trouble to ask the citizenry if they want to be uprooted and forced to live elsewhere. Government compensation has varied from generous to nothing at all. Either way it's take it or leave it. In Huaming township, a "new town" not far from Tianjin that was widely promoted by the government as a model of successful planned urbanization, only half the peasants accepted the government offer for their farms. But as Ian Johnson discovered, the local government wouldn't take no for an answer, and used "intense pressure to force farmers out of their villages":

> It tore up roads and cut electricity and water. Even so, thousands stayed on. As a final measure, the schoolhouses—one in each village—were demolished. With no utilities and no way to educate their children, most farmers capitulated and moved to town.[72]

With non-stop infrastructure and urban construction since Mao's day, impermanence and relocation has become a way of life for better or worse for generations of Chinese.[73]

Across the country since the 1990s, land grabs like this have provoked bitter resistance: Mass protests, suicides, and violent confrontations with police.[74] In 2010, China reported more than 180,000 "mass incidents"— most of which were strikes or protests against corruption and land grabs.[75] Eviction is often gratuitously violent, in keeping with the Party's long tradition of senseless cruelty toward the people it claims to "serve." According to *South China Morning Post* correspondent Tom Miller, one government banner strung along a fence surrounding a poor Beijing neighborhood slated for clearance in 2010 read: "SEVERELY SMASH BEHAVIOR THAT DISTURBS ORDER DURING THE RESETTLEMENT PROCESS!"[76]

In September 2011, after numerous fruitless petitions to the government over land grabs, villagers in Wukan, Guangdong province (pop. 12,000) expelled all Party officials and held off government forces for nearly three months in what came to be called the "Siege of Wukan." Protesters demanded: "Give us back our farmland," and "Let us continue farming." Extensive Western press coverage prevented the government from "severely smashing" the movement for a while, though in the end, after the press was gone, it was indeed severely smashed. Land grabs, mass protests, and violent state repression have continued in Wukan, and inspired other villages to resist.[77]

Warehousing the Poor

Today, hundreds of millions of ex-peasants are being warehoused in urban ghettos with few-to-no jobs, dispersed families, and hopeless futures. Government propagandists promote dazzling visions of a vibrant urban future to these peasant urbanites, but as Ian Johnson reports from Huaming, the reality is far different:

Today, Huaming may be an example of another transformation: The ghettoization of China's new towns. Signs of social dysfunction abound. Young people, who while away their days in Internet cafes or pool halls, say that only a small fraction of them have jobs. The elderly are forced to take menial work to make ends meet. Neighborhood and family structures have been damaged. Most worrying are the suicides, which local residents say have become an all-too-familiar sign of despair.

"We're talking hundreds of millions of people who are moving into these places, but the standard of living for these relocatees has actually dropped," said Lynette Ong, a University of Toronto political scientist who has studied the resettlement areas. "On top of that is the quality of the buildings—there was a lot of corruption, and they skimped on materials" . . . Trees line the streets that lead to elementary, middle and high schools. But the new homes have cracked walls, leaking windows and elevators with rusted out floors. For farmers who were asked to surrender their ancestral lands for an apartment, the deterioration adds to a sense of having been cheated. "That was their land," said Wei Ying, a 35-year-old unemployed woman whose parents live in a poorly built unit. "You have to understand how they feel in their heart."[78]

The sense of despair and alienation surfaces in suicides—a late-night leap from a balcony, drinking of pesticide, or lying down on railroad tracks. "I have anxiety attacks because we have no income, no job, nothing," said Feng Aiju, a former farmer who moved to Huaming in 2008 against her will. She said she had spent the equivalent of $1,500—a small fortune by local standards—on antidepressants. "We never had a chance to speak; we were never asked anything. I want to go home," she said.

Adding insult to deprivation, these dispossessed farmers are often just given a bare cement shell of an apartment. They have to spend the equivalent of thousands of dollars for flooring, lighting, appliances, cabinetry, and paint. They often can't afford the high cost of electricity to run appliances, so they sit around bonfires outside instead of heating their cement apartments. Said one ex-farmer: "These buildings look modern on the outside, but they're . . . the worst quality." The ceilings leak, the windows leak, and they're "almost uninhabitable in winter."[79]

And yet for all the dislocation, there's often no economic development, nor jobs. Local officials, in competition with one another to attract outside and foreign investment, are quick to tear down villages to offer land to developers, but they don't always get the expected investment. Consequently, many such "new towns" are built on the far outskirts of cities, in desolate landscapes of demolished villages with little or no significant economic development: "Mostly, one is confronted with mile after mile of empty lots – once farmland, now lying fallow, sometimes blocked from view by endless sheet-metal fences painted with propaganda about prosperity and development," Johnson notes.[80]

Unskilled, aging, impoverished ex-farmers are not driving any consumer revolution in China. Nor are their children, wasting their days away playing video games.

"Blind Demolition": Urban Renewal with Chinese Characteristics

Out with the old, in with the new; out with the new, in with the newer.
– Wade Shepard[81]

Yet it's in urban renewal where the combination of capitalism and bureaucratic-collectivism has reached new breakthroughs in creative destruction: "Permanent primitive accumulation," one might say. China's urban homeowners, like peasant farmers, don't own the land under their houses and apartment blocks and so don't really even own their houses or condos either, since municipal governments can and do seize them at will. When municipal authorities decide to requisition someone's home, or entire neighborhoods, the government just posts notices on the buildings and presents the "homeowners" with a take-it-or-leave-it offer of compensation.[82] No public hearings, no fights over eminent domain, no legal recourse, just "get out by this date."[83] This is how mayors get rich.

But the real "miracle" in urban China is that mayors don't just get rich once off this theft. In many cities they've turned their monopoly of power and property into a perpetual motion machine of dispossession-demolition-construction-dispossession-demolition-construction *on the same piece of land*, with all the dislocation, waste (and profit) that entails. Wade Shepard, author of *Ghost Cities of China: The Story of Cities without People in the World's Most Populated Country*, writes:

Li Dexiang of Tsinghua University told the *China Daily* that "what we see nowadays is the blind demolition of relatively new buildings, some of which have only been standing for less than 10 years." Modern Chinese buildings are essentially disposable; they stand for one, two, or three decades and are then requisitioned and demolished, whereupon bigger, better and more expensive buildings will go up in their place. This fits in well with the country's broader economic structure: Houses that can last a century are not nearly as profitable as ones that can be demolished, rebuilt and sold three times over within this span of time. As 40 percent of construction land in China is created every year by the demolition of older buildings, the financial incentives for these urban upgrades is evident. Demolition, too, increases the GDP. Under this strategy there is no limit on development, as once all the available construction land is used it will be high time to start tearing down what was just built to build it again.

How brilliant is that, from the standpoint of the insatiable mayor? Not only that but:

> The Chinese have applied the economic stimulus of consumer culture to urbanization; these shiny new cities that are going up across the country are like new refrigerators which are designed to break down after a few years of use so you have to go out and buy a new one—built-in obsolescence in urban planning.[84]

Voilà—disposable cities! Who says the Chinese can't innovate? Now think about the staggering waste of resources and the coal-powered electricity generation needed to fuel this non-stop "blind demolition" and "blind construction" juggernaut in hundreds of cities across the country. And with disposable housing comes disposable people, disposable culture, and disposable communities: Universal alienation.[85]

Cities the Size of Countries for What Purpose?

Then we have Xi Jinping, who complains about "meaningless development at the cost of the environment," but in September 2017 launched construction of an entirely new "innovation city" south of Beijing—elegantly christened Xiong'an New Area. This is planned to be *three times the size* of New York.[86] Yet Xi is building this when he's already got a huge ghost city, Yujiapu, just east of Beijing, which, as we noted in Chapter 2, sits unfinished and mostly unoccupied. Xi also promises that Xiong'an will be a "smart and green city" with a "beautiful environment." That's going to be difficult to pull off. Chinadialogue reported in 2017 that Xiong'an—which is to be built on plains and marshlands 120 kilometers south of Beijing in Hebei, China's most polluted province—already "has terrible air quality . . . ranked the worst in the country in two of the past three years." Nearby Lake Baiyangdian, which is supposed to provide fresh water for this new city, is ranked Grade 5 in terms of water quality ("too polluted to touch").[87] And if the lake is unfit to drink from, 80 percent of the underground aquifers across the north China plains are, as noted in Chapter 3, so polluted as to be useless. How many tech innovators are going to want to move to this disaster? Not to mention that building a city three times the size of New York is going to require immense quantities of steel, cement, and electricity, all of which are going to bring a lot more dust and pollution to the Beijing region—and accelerate global warming at "China speed."

And if all this weren't enough, Xi's planners are also building the rails, roads, bridges to create three gigantic megalopolises with populations the size of countries: Beijing, Tianjin, and Hebei are metastasizing into one huge conurbation, an 82,000 square mile "city" now simply called "Jing-Jin-Ji." This "city" will be the size of New England and have a combined population of 130 million, larger than Japan. In the southeast, nine cities including Shenzhen and Hong Kong will be cross-laced with rails, roads and bridges and merged into another megalopolis. Shanghai will be the center of a third megalopolis encompassing the Yangtze coastal basin.[88]

DRIVER 2: MAXIMIZING EMPLOYMENT GENERATION

Secondly, the Chinese leadership must constantly think of ways of maximizing growth to generate jobs, in order to maintain near-full employment and keep the peace. By contrast, in capitalist economies, corporations don't care about the unemployed. If workers, even masses of workers, get laid off, that's not the capitalists' problem. It's not even the government's problem, except in severe downturns like the Great Depression, when they face the potential of revolt. But because the CCP was once a workers' party, and because the Party derives its legitimacy, its very raison d'être, from its status as the self-appointed representative of the working class, it cannot completely ignore the workers as capitalists can do in the West.

Under Mao, workers in state-owned industries enjoyed the famous "iron rice bowl" system of permanent employment and cradle-to-grave benefits (including state-provided housing at nominal cost, free schooling, childcare, medical care, pensions, and other subsidies). Deng wanted to dismantle this system in the 1980s but couldn't get very far because there was not yet enough of a private economy for workers to find employment outside of state industries. But as the foreign-invested and domestic private economy grew and took off in the late 1980s and 1990s, the market reformers began dismantling this system with the introduction of short-term labor contracts in 1986. In 1995 the adoption of the National Labor Law effectively smashed the iron rice bowl. In the late 1990s and early 2000s, SOEs shed some 30 million employees. With the shift to contracts, workers not only lost their guaranteed jobs but also lost their social benefits, including pensions and medical insurance.[89] The layoffs provoked growing protests and strikes in the late 1990s and 2000s.[90]

The Communist Party has been very cruel to China's workers. But it must still strive to keep them employed for fear of unrest. Since the 1990s the government has faced hundreds of mass protests across the country every day, including strikes and protests against unpaid back pay or overtime, land grabs, pollution, the siting of incinerators and chemical plants, and corruption.[91] The government cannot afford to have masses of unhappy unemployed workers milling about. That's why, in November 2013, prime minister and economic czar Li Keqiang stated that:

> Employment is the biggest thing for well-being. The government must not slacken on this for one moment . . . For us, stable growth is mainly for the sake of maintaining employment.[92]

This explains why the twelfth and thirteenth Five-Year Plans have insisted that the government will do all it can to keep unemployment below 5 percent, declaring that it will create some fifteen million new jobs each year if necessary. This is the main reason why, apart from their contribution to import-substitution industrialization, the government keeps its "zombie" steel and aluminum companies, coal mines, and construction companies in business year after year, rolling over their debts rather than letting them fail and close down, as Western capitalist economists and the business press are always admonishing them to do. China's state-owned zombies may be "irrational" in capitalist terms but since China's state-owned economy is driven by different maximands, this ceaseless "march of the undead" is supremely rational on its own terms.

DRIVER 3: MAXIMIZING CONSUMPTION AND CONSUMERISM

Third, after the collapse of communism in the Soviet Union, and the Chinese communists' own near-death experience with the Tiananmen Square protests in 1989, the Party leadership was determined to create a mass consumer economy and raise incomes in order to focus people's attention on consumption and take their minds off politics. This is why, ever since the early 1990s, successive Five-Year Plans have prioritized new consumer industries and the government has promoted one consumer craze after another —the car craze, condo craze, shopping mall craze, tourism craze, golf course craze, theme park craze, bike sharing craze, cruise boat craze, food delivery craze, online shopping craze, and so on. Tourism, mostly domestic, accounted for 11 percent of the national GDP in 2017 and the government is keen to grow this sector and to promote nationalism along with it. On every holiday, masses of Chinese workers are sent on sub-sidized group tours by their state-owned employers.

Figure 5.1   Beijing, June 11, 1989. A man leads two ponies past a huge advertising billboard promoting tourism in China just a few days after troops brutally crushed the democracy protests in and around Tiananmen Square.

Credit: Peter Charlesworth/LightRocket/Getty Images

The government has also partnered with and backed private capitalists, including Jack Ma's e-commerce giant Alibaba and other consumer-oriented industries, to promote shopping, the movie industry, video gaming, theme parks, tourism, social media, and more shopping. State banks went into the mortgage business to promote housing speculation, then created a consumer credit industry to keep consumers focused on making money to spend on new trinkets.[93] Housing privatization promoted the growth of fur-niture, home decoration, and renovation markets, spurring more growth.

Some government efforts have been duds. Xi's government wasted millions building the world's biggest Formula 1 racetrack in Shanghai in 2004, bragging that China would soon become a "Formula 1 superpower." But hardly anyone showed up to watch so the track is all but closed.[94] Xi also virtually ordered the country to take up soccer. But in China's hypercom-petitive society, neither children nor parents see much point in spending afternoons kicking a ball around a field, while China's workers, for their part, don't seem so inclined to become glued-to-the-television sports fans like their colleagues in the West.[95] But consumerism has certainly been a smash hit for Xi and the CCP. China's leading retail festival, "Singles' Day," grossed more than America's Black Friday and Cyber Monday combined in 2017 (of course). After centuries of privation and decades of Maoist austerity, it seems the Chinese have gone in for consumerism with a vengeance. As many say, "It's our turn now."[96]

COMMAND WITHOUT CONTROL

Centralized enforcement . . . is arguably ineffective in addressing China's long-standing problem of weak environmental policy implementation.

– Xuehua Zhang

I don't dare open my mouth out of fear that [the polluters] will see that I have no teeth.

– Ding Yan, director of the MEP's
Vehicular Pollution Research Institute

The foregoing overview summarized the built-in drivers of excessive growth, overproduction, overconstruction, pollution, and so forth in China. As we've seen, when it comes to production and construction, China's government gets things done like no other nation on Earth, and at "China speed." But when it comes to suppressing overproduction, overconstruction, pollution, or transitioning to solar and wind power, strangely, the government's commands often fall on deaf ears, be they ignored or defied.[97]

For example, in 2013, as the skies above northern China's cities darkened with sulfurous smoke belching from the smokestacks of steel plants and coal-fired power plants, the Party organ *Beijing Review* complained that "blackened skies have become the norm, an outcome of over-expansion in China's iron and steel industry." In response to the "airpocalypse," the State Council ordered the steel industry to "cut 15 million tons of capacity per year," or 80 million tons by 2017, to comply with its anti-pollution guidelines.[98] Yet while Beijing was demanding cuts, officials in Hebei—China's largest steelmaking province, which accounts for more than one-fourth of national output (and which also has seven of China's ten worst-polluted cities, including Beijing)—were pushing to *increase* output by another 60 million tons in 2013–14. Hebei Iron and Steel Co. chairman Wang Yifang told the *Wall Street Journal* that his company, China's second-largest steel mill by output, had no plans to cut production. "The goal to reduce output is the government's plan," he said, "we don't have such a plan and will act according to market demand."[99] And market demand was growing because

China's booming residential and commercial construction and auto industries—two other sectors the government was trying to restrain—demanded ever more steel, cement, aluminum, and sheet glass to go with it. Thus, China's steel output has continued its relentless growth from 130 million tons in 2000 to 831 million tons in 2017.[100] Steel production capacity has grown even more sharply.[101] China's overproduction has driven global steel prices down by 70 percent since 2011 as the market has been swamped with cheap steel.

But what's most interesting is that Wang Yifang—a *Communist Party member* and chairman of a *state-owned* company headquartered just 165 miles southwest of Beijing—says that he doesn't care what Beijing's plan is. He has his own plan. Imagine a division chief of a major US corporation saying he doesn't care what the CEO's orders are. They don't apply to him; he has his own agenda. How long would he keep his job?

In the winter of 2016–17, Beijing sent a team of environmental inspectors to see how effectively local officials were implementing orders to clean up urban environments in three of China's largest cities. Here's what they found:[102]

Beijing

- The city planned to clean up nineteen heavily polluted waterways last year but work on only one was completed.
- Three mining companies continue to operate near the Miyun Reservoir, one of the city's main sources of drinking water, even after they were ordered to close in 2008.
- None of the fourteen planned facilities to deal with waste from sewage-treatment plants was built . . . resulting in 630,000 tons of waste being dumped in temporary sites near residential areas.
- The city's upmarket Shuyi district failed to meet its goal for reducing PM2.5 particulate matter in the air for two consecutive years from 2014.

Shanghai

- Only 10 of 50 sewage-treatment plants met the required standards. These 10 were small plants that accounted for just 4 percent of the city's sewage-handling capacity.
- Forty-six landfill sites built before 2008 didn't have facilities to treat wastewater.

- Water quality in the city's Baoshan district has continued to deteriorate since 2013; all sixteen samples taken from local waterways were heavily polluted.

Chongqing

- Thirty-nine of the 54 sewage-treatment facilities that the city government promised to build between 2011 and 2015 were still under construction.
- The city gave the green light to build 98 large chemical plants near the Yangtze River, including 62 that would handle hazardous materials, threatening water quality.

Inspectors upbraided city officials for dodging responsibility, but they had no power to actually punish them, or force them to comply with orders from above. In recent years, government inspectors and regulators have shut down thousands of small-scale privately-owned industrial polluters, at least temporarily. But they have little or no power against state- and municipality-owned polluters.

Well, why is it that in a "command and control" economy, ministerial officials, provincial governors, local officials, and SOE bosses can routinely defy Beijing's orders? The answer, I suggest, is to be found in the collectivist nature of China's ruling class and in the congruent and contradictory interests of leaders and subordinate officials.

COLLECTIVE RULING CLASS, DISPERSED POWER

Xi Jinping sits at the apex of the most powerful police state in history. Yet for all his nominal authority, in reality power is shared widely throughout the 90-million-member Party. Beijing can't systematically enforce its writ against resistance from below because it can't systematically fire insubordinate bureaucrats. They're not just employees like in capitalism. They're Communist Party cadres, members of the same ruling class as the leaders in Beijing, and so they are not powerless themselves. They have their own particular interests to defend against central authorities, and they often have ample means to resist orders from above.

Of course, formally, all Party officials are ranked in the hierarchical nomenklatura system which assigns rank, responsibilities, duties, salaries, housing assignments, privileges, and so on. Cadres have bosses, and their bosses have bosses. But since there's no rule of law in China, formal rank and position are not the only determinant of one's power and influence. As they say in China, "without the rule of law there is only the rule of men." This means that in this formally hierarchical system, the day-to-day reality is that all relations are intensely personal, governed by what the Chinese call *guanxi* (connections or relations). If you've got good *guanxi* with higher-ups, especially all the way to Beijing, and a solid base of supporters below, then you can feign compliance, ignore orders from above, and keep making money on your polluting factory, buy off your superiors, pay your taxes, and carry on.[103] Beijing is generally loathe to force the shutdown of SOEs, or even private businesses, because it's concerned with maximizing growth and employment. This means that very often Beijing cannot force officials to give up their polluting practices when to do so would undermine their economic interests. That's why officials can, and very often do, ignore or defy Beijing with impunity.

That's why Wang Yifang and officials like him don't worry much about Beijing's orders to cut back. Company bosses and local mayors, dependent on polluting companies for jobs and local revenue, routinely resist Beijing's demands by feigning compliance and dragging their feet. They shut down polluting industries when the inspectors are coming, then reopen them after they've left. They close down outmoded mills only to open new replacements with even greater capacity.[104] Since the government began requiring localities to monitor and report emissions levels in 2013, emissions data fakery has become rampant.[105] Officials stuff cotton in emissions monitors to get cleaner readings, even send trucks outfitted with "mist canons" to spray water vapor around air quality monitoring stations to fool the sensors. Emissions inspectors have been locked out by SOE management;[106] even in Beijing itself.[107] MEP officials are bribed.[108] Greenpeace and government studies have shown that because of systematic underreporting, pollution in Beijing and other cities has been "much worse than acknowledged."[109] Such bureaucratic-obstructionist practices are so universal and long established that they've given rise to a raft of popular aphorisms: "Xi Jinping is master of nothing"; "Orders don't leave Zhongnanhai"; "Above are orders, below are counter-orders"; "Complying in public but opposing in private"; "Wait and see, glancing left and right."[110]

In her stunning documentary *Under the Dome* Chai Jing asks Ding Yan, the director of the MEP's Vehicular Pollution Research Institute about why his agency doesn't compel China's vehicle manufactures to stop selling trucks with stickers certifying that they meet the highest emissions standards, when in fact they only meet the lowest standards. "If you [the MEP] assert you have legal authority, no one can deny that, so why not just execute the law?" Chai asks. Ding's reply is that, regardless of the law, his agency had no real power to enforce it: "I don't dare open my mouth out of fear that they will see that I have no teeth."[111]

NATIONALIST LEADERS MUST PROTECT INDUSTRIAL "CHAMPIONS" AT THE EXPENSE OF THE ENVIRONMENT

Since Xi Jinping can't rely on independent regulatory agencies, courts, and the police to enforce environmental regulations, then, like leaders before him, his only option has been to resort to harassment campaigns, like his "war on pollution" and "war on corruption."[112] But this approach has been largely ineffectual. Beijing issues big directives, sends inspectors around, and fines the polluting companies. But fines are just for show, idle threats, useless against the state's own industries. As often as not local government partners just pay the fines, or block regulators from shutting down the polluters, even block them from investigating, or let the regulators shut them down but then let the companies reopen under a new name. Factory bosses have even been known to detain MEP inspectors against their will in order to prevent shutdowns of their coal-fired power plants![113]

Likewise, central "interventions" by Beijing have had little success. Scholarly studies of "local protectionism" (*difang baohuzhuyi*) show that when key enforcement powers have been delegated to local environmental protection bureaus (EPBs) which are all funded and managed by local governments, this "has led to local protectionism which promotes local economic growth at the expense of damaging the local environments and thus leads to enforcement failure." But when the central government recentralizes control and intervenes directly to enforce its environmental rules, the result is much the same. According to Xuehua Zhang: "Direct MEP enforcement has usually been in the form of campaigns that have generated notable but short-term effects" and "centralized enforcement is arguably ineffective in addressing China's long-standing problem of weak environmental policy implementation."[114] In recent years, Beijing has tried to enforce compliance by adding environmental protection to the list of criteria for local official advancement. But here too, studies have shown that GDP, jobs, local investment, and revenue generation still take precedence.[115]

The fact that subordinate officials can defy central government orders to reduce overproduction and pollution is problem enough. But this is compounded by the fact that Xi himself still refuses to subordinate growth to environmental protection. For all his talk about building an "ecological civilization" and "balancing green mountains and gold mountains," Xi goes for the gold every time—and I would say he cannot do otherwise. Given his superpower ambitions, his need to grow his national champions, the threat of labor strikes at the slightest slowdown, his need to grow domestic consumption and consumerism to distract the masses, the mountains of local debt for which growth is their only salvation, and now, the threat of trade wars with the US, Xi has no choice but to keep the engines of growth at full throttle in the effort to achieve that GDP growth target, and thus to keep on producing surplus steel, ghost cities, and all the pollution that inevitably results from this hypergrowth.[116]

To these ends, he must protect his SOEs. Thus in their 2017 study of central–local relations, Sarah Eaton and Genia Kosta found that the central government systematically protects its SOE polluters:

> Officials in the central bureaucracy, principally SASAC (State-Owned Assets Supervision and Administration Commission—the nominal owner/manager of government-owned enterprises), provide a measure of shelter for chronic polluters within SASAC's ranks by incentivizing senior SOE managers to look upon the achievement of traditional industrial policy goals such as profitability, scale, market share and efficiency—and not compliance with environmental regulations—as the *sine qua non* of a positive enterprise performance evaluation and possible promotion for managers themselves.[117]

It must protect them because the central government's foremost concern is to build up its "national champions" to compete with the West:

> As subjects of a long-standing industrial policy programme that aims at creating global players in key sectors, central SOEs face tacit, yet nonetheless strong, incentives to shirk on environmental rules that would harm their economic performance . . . [Enterprise groups] are relentlessly called upon to "go bigger and go stronger" . . . via scaling up and striving to attain global standards of competitiveness . . . maintaining and increasing the value of state assets.[118]

ALL CARROT AND NO STICK PROMOTES BLIND GROWTH

The foregoing has important implications for SOE behavior. Virtually all of China's SOEs of any significant size are included within the state-planned economy. So long as their SOEs are in-plan, and particularly if they've been designated "strategic," "pillar," or "key" industries—such as coal, oil, autos, aerospace, biotech, high-speed rail, electric vehicles, pharmaceuticals, or some other priority—SOE managers can assume that they will never be forced out of business regardless of their economic performance; and they have not been. As a result, SOE managers have the best of both worlds—they have every incentive to borrow and spend, especially on capital construction (including the palatial offices, guest houses, etc.), but they face little or no threat of discipline for excess or failure. Given the profit-sharing arrangement between the center and the SOEs, for bosses it's capitalism when the SOE is making money but socialism when it needs a government bailout. This is why, for all the government's vows to rationalize, China's SOEs refuse to cut back. Despite Beijing's orders to halve production, even with Trump's 25-percent tariff, China's steel producers broke records in 2018, up 6.6 percent, and up another 8.3 percent in 2019.[119] Producers can sell this on the world market at a loss if necessary, confident that the state will nonetheless continue lending them the money to keep rolling on. And "China Inc." seems willing, like many strategic-thinking Western corporations before it, to take the losses in order to dominate world markets. For example, cheap Chinese steel is the battering ram that's wiping out the last of the British steel industry, hastening the deindustrialization of the UK and its subordination to Chinese state capitalism.[120]

Thus, given the central government's concern with building its "national champions," to "go bigger and go stronger" it comes as no surprise that despite its formal elevation from agency to ministry, the MEP under Xi Jinping remains very much a second-class ministry. It is severely underfunded and understaffed, it lacks properly trained inspectors and effective monitoring equipment, it has no real enforcement powers against SOEs, and its local regulators are often subordinate to the officials they're supposed to regulate. Consequently, it is regularly ignored, as Chai Jing discovered.[121]

6

Guanxi and the Game of Thrones: Wealth, Property, and Insecurity in a Lawless System

BEIJING'S GAME OF THRONES

> When the top is corrupt, this is how it will be all the way down.
>
> – Dai Qing

The environmental destruction wrought by China's communist-capitalist economic system is approached only by the social rot of Communist Party corruption. China's ruling class consists of the upper ranks of the Party nomenklatura—the few dozen or perhaps few hundred families at the pinnacle of power.[1] Since the victory of the revolution in 1949, China has been run by a political-military-bureaucratic aristocracy, the top leaders of which have traditionally resided behind the walls of Zhongnanhai.[2] Today the state-owned economy is run by their children, and will soon be run by their grandchildren.

After Mao's death in 1976, the inner circle of the ruling "red families" was headed by the so-called "Eight Immortals": Deng Xiaoping, Chen Yun, Wang Zhen, Li Xiannian, Peng Zhen, Song Renqiong, Yang Shangkun, and Bo Yibo.[3] As these elders retired and died off they entrusted the reins of power to their children, the so-called "princelings" (*taizidang*).[4] Since the bad old days when Mao and his Gang of Four dispatched their rivals to rot in dungeons (or in the case of Mao's one-time number two, Lin Biao, purportedly shot his plane out of the sky to prevent his escape to the Soviet Union), the Party had made every effort to present a public façade of leadership, unity, and discipline, and to portray its internal workings as "regularized" with "collective leadership," ensured in part by the ten-year rotations of presidents and premiers, and the mandatory retirement of senior officials at 65. Nothing could be further from the truth however, as we saw in spring 2018 when the Party dropped this pretense to grant Xi Jinping unlimited tenure.

126

Today, as in Mao's day, the reality is that the internal political machinations of the Communist Party are treacherous and fratricidal. From Mao's purges of "capitalist roaders" (including Deng Xiaoping), to Deng's own purge of the Maoist Gang of Four and Xi Jinping's 2014 show trial of rival Bo Xilai (the son of Bo Yibo) and the subsequent takedowns of powerful opponents in the "oil faction" and the secret police (led by former domestic security chief Zhou Yongkang), the Party's internal political dramas differ little from the power struggles of the Corleones, Barzinis, and Straccis of *The Godfather*, the bloody feudal wars of the Starks, Tullys, and Boltons in *Game of Thrones*, or the Triads, Tongs, and Green Gangs of pre-revolutionary China.[5]

How could it be otherwise? In the absence of the rule of law, with no security of person or private property, without elections to choose government representatives, without constitutional procedures to regularize succession to office, and without an independent judiciary, attorneys general, and police, arbitrary state power and generalized insecurity condition every aspect of life in China—*especially* within the Party itself. Life in the Party is not so different from life in the mafia. There is no lasting security.[6] At the highest levels, life is a constant, treacherous, and highly dangerous war between crime families over top offices and treasure, while the claim of the paramount leader *du jour* to the red throne in Zhongnanhai is never completely secure.[7] All the way down, ministerial, provincial, municipal, and local officials find themselves locked in perpetual competition over central appropriations, subsidies, and profits, often in the context of broader familial and factional conflict.

As we noted in the previous chapter, in such an environment, every cadre's security and chances for promotion depend above all on building networks of *guanxi* with patrons above and supporters below. These relationships are typically based on family, kinship, and, beyond that circle, political factions and business partnerships. Kerry Brown describes the taxonomy and complexity of these relationships among the Party elite in *The New Emperors: Power and the Princelings in China*. Brown, like some other scholars, objects that *guanxi* has become so overused as to verge on the meaningless. After all, he says, "what society doesn't put a premium on connections?"[8] True enough. Isn't that why many of the world's wealthy—Xi included—spend small fortunes sending their children to Ivy League schools? But what's different about "connections" in China is that in an environment of generalized insecurity and capricious, arbitrary, and unpredictable rule by powerful superiors, good *guanxi* is the surest protection, the best insurance that a cadre can buy—though it's never an absolute guarantee against arbitrary dismissal, seizure of assets, arrest, imprisonment, or worse. It's also the most reliable means they have of winning promotions, lucrative appointments, and opportunities for graft and corruption. In other words, while connections are important in capitalist societies, in China's political economy *guanxi* is *all* important.

The key to solidifying those networks is sharing the loot from corruption with superiors and subordinates to build networks of supporters from the localities all the way up to central authorities in Beijing. As Michael Oksenberg has observed, "all attuned bureaucrats . . . [are] intense 'Pekingologists,' constantly charting how their man is doing in the Party pecking order."[9] In Minxin Pei's words: "If your patrons do not protect you, you're toast . . . Corruption is the glue that keeps the party stuck together."[10]

Xi is widely portrayed as the most powerful Chinese leader since Deng Xiaoping. But he also is keenly aware of the precarious position of all Chinese leaders. Since launching his war on corruption in 2012, he has made countless enemies, high and low. According to foreign intelligence reports he has even survived several assassination attempts.[11]

Xi came into power in 2012 on a campaign vowing to "kill tigers and swat flies" (to discipline both senior officials and the rank and file). He had previously been tapped to replace the disgraced mayor of Shanghai, Chen Liangyu, on the strength of his anti-corruption campaigns in Zhejiang province, where he once told an anti-graft conference: "Rein in your spouses, children, relatives and friends and staff, and vow not to use power for personal gain."[12] But Xi and his family are as corrupt as the rest.

According to exiled dissident author Yu Jie, *The Godfather* was Xi's political study guide. "The Communist Party is China's biggest Mafia, and the party boss Xi Jinping is the Godfather of China," he said. As if to confirm Yu's thesis, when he tried to publish his 2014 book *Xi Jinping: China's Godfather* in Hong Kong, one of the publishers was subsequently arrested in Shenzhen and "disappeared." After a second prospective publisher received a threatening call from Beijing he immediately dropped the project.[13] Yu Jie's second book, *Xi Jinping's Nightmare*, originally slated for publication in January 2016, was withdrawn after more kidnappings, and after Beijing forced kidnapped booksellers to confess their "crimes" on national television in 2015.[14]

Surplus Extraction, Gangster Capitalism, and the Necessity of Corruption

China's economy mirrors its politics. The Party-state has grown fabulously wealthy from vast rivers of cash flowing into government coffers from state-owned industries and services (mostly monopolies), tax receipts from foreign-invested and private industries in China, interest on US treasury bonds, returns on investments in Western companies, mineral resources, properties, thousands of overseas construction projects, overseas companies the government has bought, and loans to foreign governments.[15] But the question is, how is this wealth divided up amongst China's ruling class, the gang of 90 million cadres, or even the few hundred top crime families?

In capitalist economies like the US, the distribution of wealth and the security of property is completely formalized and regularized: Private property, in the form of land, means of production, housing, cash, stocks and bonds, and so on, are all secured by the rule of law, with independent courts, judiciary, and police to back it up. Contracts can be enforced in courts. Corporate stock is mostly held by mutual funds, investment banks, and pension funds on behalf of individual investors who receive dividends and other profits of stock ownership. Returns on investment are divided between profits for shareholders, salaries for corporate officers, wages for workers, and rents to landlords, all according to contracts. Wealth is evidenced by possession of stock certificates, deeds to properties, bank savings accounts, and similar legal proof. This is all so normal, accepted, and unquestioned as to be unremarkable.

China has none of this. Cadres don't individually own SOEs, they don't own shares in SOEs, they don't own any property in China—not even the apartments and villas that they live in, or the limousines that they're chauffeured around in. The state owns the land, natural resources, most of the economy, its offshore investments, foreign exchange holdings, and so on, and the Party owns the state *collectively*. They're not capitalists living off the profits of investments, at least not with respect to the state economy. No cadre, no matter what rank, has any legal right to the vast wealth held in the name of the government. Cadres are Party members and government employees, legally entitled to no more than ordinary salaries and benefits, which are stipulated according to their rank in the nomenklatura. These benefits include allocations of housing, cars and drivers, medical care, education, vacations, and various other perks, according to a system that was copied from the Soviet Union in the early 1950s.[16] Official salaries are not published, but researchers have gleaned that they are among the lowest in the world. In January 2015, *China Daily* reported that Party officials had given themselves a raise, the first since 2006. Xi Jinping's basic yearly salary rose to 136,620 yuan ($19,517). The lowest ranked civil servants saw their pay nearly double to 15,840 yuan ($2,262).[17]

But everyone knows that these salaries are meaningless. Indeed, Feifei Wang has written that

> For politburo members . . . their salary is a joke, everyone knows they have other income. First of all, they don't need to pay for anything. Everything they need: Clothing, food, transportation, housing . . . is paid for by the state. They live in the best houses, with many vacation houses all over the country, they ride the best cars with chauffeurs and bodyguards, food is prepared by the best cooks with material grown from the best local organic farms, clothing is handcrafted and if they do buy brand-name clothing, the state will reimburse the expense. All in all, there's absolutely no place they can possibly spend their salary.[18]

Top Party cadres have gotten gloriously rich out of Reform and Opening, as tell-all books on the lives of high-ranking cadres, trials of corrupt officials, revelations about secret offshore bank accounts, records of foreign property purchases, and headline exposés have confirmed.[19] The *New York Times* calculated that Premier Wen Jiabao—whose annual salary was thought to have been around $15,000—was worth at least $2.7 billion when he retired in 2012, nearly all of it secreted under the names of his relatives and associates ("white gloves" as they're called in China).[20] His mother, a retired school teacher, likely had no idea that properties in her name were worth $190 million. The *Times* reported that

> Unlike most new businesses in China, the family's ventures sometimes received financial backing from state-owned companies, including China Mobile, one of the country's biggest phone operators, the documents show. At other times, the ventures won support from some of Asia's richest tycoons . . . Wen's relatives accumulated shares in banks, jewelers, tourist resorts, telecommunications companies and infrastructure projects, sometimes by using offshore entities . . . The holdings include a villa development project in Beijing; a tire factory in northern China; a company that helped build some of Beijing's Olympic stadiums, including the well-known "Bird's Nest"; and Ping An Insurance, one of the world's biggest financial services companies.[21]

The *Times* described how Wen's younger brother got rich from government contracts awarded under his tenure, how relatives and friends made fortunes investing in companies like Ping An Insurance before its stock market listing (thanks to Wen's control over IPO listings), how his son used state monies as startup capital for his private tech company and an investment bank, and how Wen's relatives teamed up with real estate developers trading government control over land and permits in return for setting up investment vehicles benefiting the Wen family.[22] In China, they call this the "one family, two systems" strategy—parents in government, children in business. The parents loot the state and set their children up in business.[23]

As Xi climbed the Party ranks his extended family developed lucrative sources of income in minerals, real estate, and telecoms equipment. By 2012 when he took office, his family was already reportedly worth at least $376 million, again with virtually all of it under the names of his close relatives and associates.[24] Xi's promise to "crack down on the business ties of officials" is risible in light of the Panama Papers disclosures, which revealed that family members of at least eight current and former members of the Politburo Standing Committee—including Xi's wife, older sister, and brother-in-law Deng Jiagui, along with former Party chief Li Peng's daughter Li Xiaolin (the vice president of state-owned China Power Investment Corporation)—had all socked away tens and hundreds of millions of dollars in just this one little secret haven.[25] And they're not alone; 90 percent of China's 1,000 richest people tracked by the Hurun China Rich List are members of the CCP.[26]

MORAL HAZARDS AND THE MARKETIZATION OF POWER

When Deng ditched Maoism in the 1980s and told the Chinese people that now it was "glorious to get rich,"[27] he faced an immediate political and moral dilemma: Reform and Opening presented the personally penniless but functionally all-powerful CCP cadres with a once-in-an-epoch opportunity to grab the brass ring, to get rich, *really* rich and *fast*. The Party-state owned all land, resources, and industries, controlled the banks, investment funds, pension funds, foreign trade and currency exchange, the courts, police, and military—everything. The problem was, officials were legally entitled only to their government salaries. They didn't personally own anything. They were supposed to promote capitalism but weren't supposed to become capitalists themselves unless they first quit the Party. Their *families* could go into business, but it would not do for high officials of the party of the proletariat to be seen living in mansions with pools and servants, tooling about in Ferraris and Bentleys, partying on yachts along the Shanghai Bund, and jetting off on private jets like Michael Bloomberg. You don't see that in China. The Mao suits and military garb are gone, replaced by conservative Western business suits. In Beijing, top officials live in considerable comfort, but in government-owned apartments and compounds, not in private mansions. They're rich beyond measure, but as guilty, embarrassed leaders of the Chinese *Communist* Party, they're reluctant to flaunt it. Just the opposite. They hide it. Even before Xi's 2013 ban on extravagant feasting and conspicuous consumption, cadres kept a low profile compared with their peers in the West.

Since they had no individual legal claims to the government's growing wealth, the only ways they could privately take "their share" of the state's growing treasure were all illegal: Graft, bribery, kickbacks, smuggling, influence pedaling, selling offices, misappropriation, embezzlement, profiteering, asset stripping, privatization of state companies at huge discounts, and so on. The very people who stood to gain the most from the coming market boom were supposed to refrain from self-dealing.

Risky, but how could they resist? After all, in the transition to "socialism with Chinese characteristics," hadn't Deng himself said that "some would have to get rich first"? And didn't Deng see to it that his own children were first at the public trough when he set some of them up in state-backed real estate development companies? Far from resisting, the cadres led the way in what exiled economist and journalist He Qinglian called "the marketization of power."[28] China's notoriously lazy officials, so inept at industrial efficiency, productivity, and financial discipline, have proven endlessly inventive and uncharacteristically industrious when it comes to devising new means to loot the state and stay one step ahead of corruption investigators.

Even so, the breadth and brazenness of corruption grew slowly at first. According to writer and activist Bao Tong: "A bottle of Moutai, two cartons of Chungwa cigarettes—corruption was no more than that at the beginning . . . Now an enterprise worth 10 billion yuan can be purchased with 1 billion. This would have been appalling to people back then." Yet by the 1990s the daughter of one top Politburo official was able to buy an entire luxury goods company for just one dollar, from a Chinese capitalist anxious to curry favor with her father, this while she was still just a teenage student at Stanford University.[29]

In Mao's day, when China was poor, there wasn't much to steal and sporting a Rolex would get you a stretch in prison as a capitalist roader, or worse. Even Mao and his wife Jiang Qing, cloistered in Zhongnanhai, lived surprisingly modestly, less comfortably than many middle-class American families of the era, and they certainly didn't have Panamanian bank accounts. With Reform and Opening however, the cadres made up for lost time.

In the first phase of market reform, from 1978 to 1989, the opportunities for graft were limited. This was before the country grew rich on exports, before commodification had gone very far, before the government had created the land market to promote the housing boom, and before privatization of many SOEs. Corruption consisted mostly of bribery, nepotism, smuggling, "borrowing" money from state funds and not returning it, feasting on the state's tab, and profiteering by reselling state goods on the free market. Banqueting and other modes of communal consumption were (and remain) favorite ways to "eat from the big pot." Yan Sun writes that "feasting fever is driven by a calculation to escape anticorruption regulations: Dining and wining do not violate any laws and nobody is pocketing any money personally."[30] Government institutions and enterprises spent vast sums, more than 100 billion yuan a year, on extravagant banqueting.[31] This in turn supported China's high-end restaurants and catering services. The same logic applied to building luxury office buildings like the one pictured in Chapter 2, and walled-off collective housing compounds, and importing fleets of Mercedes-Benz "company" limos. Extravagant but not exactly theft, not illegal privatization, and hard to pin on individuals when the whole work unit indulged.

Perry Link says that in the late 1980s "the mode of corruption that provoked the most resentment was *guandao* ('official profiteering')"—reselling state goods on the free market. In 1985, in an effort to bring prices more in line with markets, the government instituted a system of dual-track pricing for some commodities and products. The result was more corruption, as cadres with access to state-priced raw materials and commodities from planned production profiteered off resale at higher market prices. As Link says: "This kind of corruption was born of China's transitional economy in the mid-1980s, in which Soviet-style central planning and a market economy were awkwardly juxtaposed. It especially drew people's ire not only because it involved millions of yuan but also because access to *guandao* was limited to very high officials and their families—the very ones whose morality, in Chinese tradition, is supposed to guide the country."[32] Opening up the country to the West and dispensing with Maoist austerity also gave the police, the military and regional governments in coastal provinces incentives to get into the smuggling of televisions, cars, and luxury goods for the cadres to spend their ill-gotten wealth on. In the first phase of reform, the top economic crimes prosecuted by the government were bribery, embezzlement, and *guandao*.[33] Even so, the scale of corruption in the 1980s paled by comparison with what was to come.

"My Daddy's Rich and My Lamborghini's Good-Looking"

In the second phase of reforms, from the early 1990s to Xi Jinping's accession in 2012, the government radically expanded and accelerated marketization, which in turn, vastly expanded opportunities and incentives for corruption.[34] Among the most important reforms, in 1990 the government created a market for land by permitting the sale of long-term leases (40–70 years) for residential and commercial construction and use (although all land remained the property of the state).[35] In 1994 it expanded these rights by granting local governments the right to keep the receipts of land lease sales. These once-in-an-epoch institutional changes opened up a vast new sector for plunder and incentivized corruption across the country.[36] From central ministries down to the counties, officials at every level could become instant millionaires, and eventually billionaires, by kicking millions of people off their land in order to sell leases to developers. This in turn set off the building boom that has powered economic growth for the past three decades. During the 1990s, the government also freed up many prices and encouraged its state-owned industries to produce for the market beyond their quotas, as we noted in Chapter 5. This eliminated most *guandao* as a means of profiteering but incentivized local officials to skim industrial profits that had been confiscated by the state in Mao's economy. As we'll discuss below, in the mid-1990s the government also privatized thousands of smaller non-strategic SOEs in textiles, garments, and so on, which well-placed local officials were able to pick up at a fraction of their worth. Then in 2000 the government began pushing its SOEs to "go out" in the world in search of new markets for natural resources and exports—offering still more opportunities to skim state profits and secure offshore nooks in which to hide them.

As China grew rich the opportunities for officials to get gloriously rich through corruption grew exponentially, while the buffet of benefits spread before them grew to include not just lavish state-provided housing, but foreign vacation villas, state-funded travel, and plenty of foreign currency for shopping sprees on BMWs, French fine wines, Rolexes, Louis Vuitton handbags, and Ferraris and Lamborghinis for their "rich second generation" kids (*fu er dai*). Since China's leaders live in considerable luxury on the state's tab, and since they still cannot really spend and really live in the open like their peers in the West, they've mostly opted to stash their loot in secret bank accounts in the Caribbean tax havens and overseas properties. Having acquired cliff-top mansions in Vancouver, tower condos in Manhattan, or waterfront estates in Sydney and Miami, they can then send their wives and children there to live the good life till daddy can join them later.[37]

GANGSTERS, "BANKSTERS," AND THE ARMY THAT MAKES MONEY

At the top, princelings are often the heads of giant conglomerates owning dozens or even hundreds of individual SOEs. This gives them access to vast income streams and ample opportunities for plunder. In his study of the 50 corruption cases that received the most press attention in China, Minxin Pei found that the largest SOEs were also the most corrupt, presumably because of the huge amounts of money involved—commonly tens of millions of yuan. And while the amounts stolen were relatively small in the early years, Pei concluded that graft had "risen to astronomical amounts in the late 2000s."[38]

Even China's leaders complain that the state's banks have been turned into "ATMs for officials and official businessmen."[39] As one SOE boss put it: "It doesn't matter who owns the money, it only matters who gets to use it."[40] As individuals, they loot according to their rank, the opportunities available to them by their position in the economy, and their *guanxi*. The *Financial Times* Beijing bureau chief Richard McGregor quotes a businessman jailed on corruption charges who said: "Every official has three lives. Their public life, their private life, and their secret life."[41]

Corruption flourished on a previously unimagined scale in the boom years of the 1990s–2010s, as China's ruling class began taking their cues from the New York "banksters" who were then becoming their partners and backers. High officials embezzled tens and hundreds of millions of dollars from state banks, SOEs, and ministries. They siphoned off state monies to invest in private companies, private investments, and foreign properties.[42] They privatized state enterprises, and looted pension funds and state charities.[43] They profited from illegal arms sales, smuggling, large-scale kidnapping, and the trade in children.[44] They bought and sold offices.[45] They made vast fortunes in real estate. They took cuts from listing Chinese companies on the New York Stock Exchange in partnership with Wall Street banks. And they smuggled vast amounts of money out of the country to stash in secret offshore bank accounts.[46]

Princelings and Privatization

In all this the princelings have led the way. Since none of them had a dime to their name in 1978 at the outset of Reform and Opening, the only means by which they could capitalize on the transition to the market were by selling influence, taking bribes and kickbacks from businessmen, privatizing and stripping assets from state firms, and other illegal activities.[47] According to an extensive investigative report by *Bloomberg*, princelings looted their state companies and "borrowed" state monies to set up private businesses for themselves and their children. They also bought up and privatized state businesses for a pittance.[48]

In the 1980s, Deng Xiaoping, Chen Yun, and the other aging revolutionary leaders entrusted their children to run the new market-oriented state conglomerates. Wang Jun, son of Wang Zhen, was tapped to head China's sovereign wealth fund CITIC (China International Trust and Investment Corporation)[49] and joined Deng's son-in-law He Ping atop newly formed China Poly Group, a vast conglomerate with interests in arms, African oil, and property. Another of Deng's sons-in-law, Wu Jianchang, was appointed head of numerous metals companies and then became, conveniently, head of the Ministry of Metallurgical Industry. His son, Deng's grandson, Zhuo Su, was appointed head of a company that bought into an Australian iron ore business. In 2011, just three princelings—Wang Jun, He Ping, and Chen Yuan—headed state-owned companies with combined assets of about $1.6 trillion, equivalent to more than a fifth of China's annual economic output in that year.[50]

Chen Yuan was installed as head of the giant state-owned China Development Bank, which manages assets of more than $1 trillion. His sister, Chen Xiaodan worked at Morgan Stanley in New York before setting up her own private equity firm, and worked with China Development Bank to support Chinese firms investing abroad in Europe and elsewhere.[51] Wang Zhi, Wang Zhen's third son, "borrowed" 300,000 yuan from his employer, the Ministry of Electronics, to set up his own company building personal computers, eventually partnering with Bill Gates to develop a Chinese version of the Windows operating system. Deng's daughter Deng Rong and her brother Deng Zhifang were among the first to go into real estate during the building boom of the 1990s, a time in which peasants' land was being seized to sell off to developers of housing, malls, hotels, golf courses, and resorts. As Yang Dali of the University of Chicago put it: "The entire country was in business—the Party, the military, the courts, the prosecutor's office, the police . . . Insiders could get rich very quickly."[52]

They also used state funds to buy properties in Europe and the US, and to pay for European and American private schools and colleges for their kids. Lots of cadres spent state monies on setting up and maintaining their mistresses.[53] Minxin Pei points out that mistresses often play an important economic role as fronts for handling investments and buying real estate. They act as custodians, hiding ill-gotten cadre wealth like the cadres' wives and children do.[54]

Opportunities for getting rich are of course greatest at the top—in the central ministries and SOE headquarters. In October 2014, one high-level cadre in the National Energy Commission who was caught up in Xi's anti-corruption sweep was found to have stashed away 200 million yuan ($28.5 million) in banknotes in one of his apartments. It filled whole rooms and weighed more than 2.3 tons.[55] But the looting goes on all down the line from Beijing to the lowest county and village levels. In the same year *China Daily* reported that Gu Junshan, a mere lieutenant general with a salary of less than $1,000 per month, managed to buy dozens of apartments in central Beijing and build himself a mansion in Puyang, Henan province, modeled on the Forbidden City. The "General's Mansion," as locals called it, contained gold wash basins, a gold statue of Mao Zedong, and all manner of luxuries. Gu, a logistics officer with less than a high school education, profited from handling military business operations and land deals. Logistics is the job to get.[56] *Caixin* reported the case of a manager of a water supply company in a small city in Hebei province who was found with 37 kilograms of gold and 120 million yuan ($17 million) in cash stashed in his home, plus documents showing ownership of 68 properties. What was notable about this case was that, as the *South China Morning Post* reported, "he was such a minor official." The case became known by the shorthand "little official, giant corruption."[57]

Officials still can't privately appropriate major SOEs but they've found ingenious ways to privatize their wealth and assets, sometimes financially gutting them and leaving a shell. X. L. Ding shows how, in the 1990s, SOE managers stripped billions of dollars in assets from state-owned industries, while privatizing their best assets to companies owned by close relatives and associates—"one manager, two businesses." They milked SOEs, forcing them to borrow and borrow again from the central government to stay in operation; they faked invoices to overbill the state to the profit of the privates; they diverted the best customers and contracts to their subcontractors; and so on. The practice is so pervasive that the Chinese have a pithy expression for it: "The mama is poor but her kids are rich" (*mu qiong zi fu*). Over the decades, Ding notes, this systematic looting of state companies has been a major cause of SOE indebtedness and poor performance.[58]

Likewise, the policy of "grasping the big and letting go of the small" (*zhuada fangxiao*) opened the gate to privatization of thousands of small- and medium-sized non-major and non-strategic enterprises during the late

1990s. Officials devalued state companies and sold them off to their relatives and business partners, at huge losses to the state and huge profits to themselves. They enabled privatizers to borrow state funds to finance the SOE sales so privatizers could buy a company without having to invest any of their own money, inflated the value of the SOE to borrow more than they needed from state banks to finance the sale, then pocketed the difference, falsely reported the extent of foreign capital participation in order to prepare an exit for capital, and routinely gave shares in private companies to senior officials who thus "become large shareholders overnight at little or no cost to themselves." They even gifted entire companies to senior officials in return for their protection.[59]

With reams of fake and inflated invoices, fabricated paperwork of every sort, and layers of shell companies, one can only imagine the difficulties investigators from the Central Commission for Discipline Inspection (CCDI) face when trying to figure out which officials are crooked. Even so, in Wuxi, Jiangsu province, 56 managers were caught in 1996 swindling the state with "one manager, two businesses" scams. Imagine how many more such crooks there must be across the whole country.[60] And that's just one scam.

Wang Jun was well-positioned to plunge into the arms business. Together with He Ping, they set up China Poly Group, which today makes hundreds of millions of dollars manufacturing weapons and selling them to Iran, Burma, and Pakistan. It has since expanded into coal mines, an auction house, joint ventures to build roads in Sudan, villas for expats in Beijing, entertainment, and property development. In the 1980s and 1990s the People's Liberation Army (PLA) reinterpreted its motto—"Serve the People"—by opening up hotels and tourism ventures, and converting military factories to produce pianos, appliances, televisions, motorcycles, and small passenger aircraft, with profits split between the officer corps and the central government. *The Economist* dubbed it "the army that makes money."[61]

By the 1990s the PLA had so forsaken its mission in the interests of getting gloriously rich that national security was in peril. In 1998 the government very publicly ordered it to get out of private business. The PLA has ignored that order. Tai Ming Cheung has given us a delicious and rather shocking book about the astonishing scale of the army's "military-business complex."[62] Today the PLA remains very much in business and its officers are among the most conspicuous of corrupted officials. Xi's government has prosecuted more than three dozen generals for economic crimes in military construction projects, logistics, real estate development, and other fields. As Minxin Pei writes: "The rot has even spread to the highest level of the Chinese military command. The two most senior PLA command-ers, former Politburo members and vice chairmen of the Central Military Affairs Commission, Guo Boxiong and Xu Caihou, were both arrested in 2014–2015 for accepting huge bribes in return for promoting subordin-ates." Xu had accumulated so much cash that it reportedly required twelve trucks to haul it all away.[63] More generals were arrested for corruption in 2016, including one whose wife—a fellow officer—was also charged.[64] Commander Zhang Yang avoided arrest and interrogation by hanging himself in his home in November 2017.

Fang Fenghui, a PLA general and member of the Central Military Commission arrested in 2018, was indicted for bribes, kickbacks, and other offenses. Fang helped enforce Xi's drastic reorganization of the army and had vowed unwavering support for his drive against corruption. Yet, *Liberation Army Daily* said that Fang's "ideas and convictions had been shaken, he abandoned the mission of the party and degenerated politically, becoming economically rapacious."[65]

Communist Gangsters and Capitalist Banksters

By the 2010s corruption scandals finally reached all the way to the top, hugely embarrassing the Communist Party leadership. In October 2012, the *New York Times* published the devastating exposé on the wealth of Premier Wen Jiabao's family, that shook the regime and got the *Times* website shut down and its reporters shut out of the country for a time. In just a decade as Premier, as we noted above, Wen's close family had managed to amass assets worth close to three billion dollars through a series of partnerships and investment vehicles in the insurance sector, precious stones trading, banking, tourism, telecoms, infrastructure, and real estate.

Wen's wife, Zhang Peili—the "Diamond Queen"—was a geologist and former regulator in the Ministry of Geology, then head of the state-owned China Mineral and Gem Corporation. The *Times* reported that she "began investing the state company's money in start-ups . . . setting up business ventures with friends and relatives" including Beijing Diamond, a big retailer, and Sino-Diamond, a venture financed by state-owned China Mineral and Gem Corporation, which she also headed. That company "had business ties with a state-owned company headed by another brother, Zhang Jiankun." After Wen became prime minister, she sold off some of her diamond investments and moved into real estate and finance.

Their Harvard-educated daughter, Wen Ruchun (also known as Lily Chang), worked on Wall Street for Lehman Brothers and other banks, then set up her own consulting company, Fullmark Consultants, which claimed to have "introduced and secured" for JPMorgan Chase the underwriting deal on the $5 billion initial public offering (IPO) for state-run China Railway Group. JPMorgan Chase paid Fullmark, which had only one other employee apart from Wen, $900,000 annually. The deal would eventually be put under investigation for violating the US Foreign Corrupt Practices Act, which specifically forbids hiring princelings and the like to win contracts in China or anywhere else.[66]

Wen Ruchen's brother Winston Wen's dealmaking, the *Times* reports, "has been extensive and lucrative, even by the standards of his princeling peers." He partnered with state-owned China Mobile to invest in startups. He and his wife have stakes in companies in the tech industry and electricity generation, and in government-backed online payment platform Union Mobile Pay. Wen built a $150 million private school in the Beijing suburbs and in 2005 he founded New Horizon Capital, the third-biggest hedge fund in China, with more than $2.5 billion under management. Wen later handed off day-to-day management of New Horizon to become CEO of China Satellite Communications Corporation, a state-owned company that supplies China's space program. Wen's younger brother, Wen Jiahong, controls $200 million in assets, including wastewater treatment and recycling businesses, also built on state contracts awarded since his father's elevation to the premiership.

The Wen family, like the other Immortals and princelings, got rich by, among other means, granting private entrepreneurs access to land, resources, and shares in state-owned industries in exchange for setting up private companies. According to the *New York Times*, billionaires and Western Banks "have been instrumental in getting multimillion-dollar ventures off the ground and, at crucial times, helping the members of the Wen family set up investment vehicles to profit from them."

In all these, Wen Jiabao was careful to see that nothing was listed in his own name and little in the names of his wife, son, and daughter. The *Times* says that 80 percent of the assets the paper identified and verified as owned by the Wen family are in the names of relatives outside of the immediate family—Wen's mother, his younger brother, sisters-in-law, and so on. As a businessman who set up companies with Wen's wife said that "Ms. Zhang always stayed in the background. That's how it worked."

When China's princelings partner with Wall Street "banksters," it's hard to judge which are the bigger crooks, but they're certainly a perfect match. "Everybody is involved in stuff like that. It's pervasive," said economist Andy Xie.[67] Besides Wen Ruchen, other examples include the grandson of President Jiang Zemin, who worked for Goldman Sachs, and the daughter-in-law of former Party chief Zhao Ziyang, who worked at Bank of America and Merrill Lynch. The daughter of former finance minister Xiang Huaicheng works for PricewaterhouseCoopers. In 2006, the son-in-law of Wu Bangguo, then a Politburo Standing Committee member, helped Merrill Lynch land the contract for the $22 billion stock market listing of China's biggest bank, Industrial and Commercial Bank of China (ICBC). JPMorgan Chase had previously hired Tang Xiaoning, the son of Tang Shuangning, chairman of state-controlled financial conglomerate China Everbright Group. According to the *New York Times*, "after the younger Tang joined JPMorgan Chase, the bank won several important assignments from Everbright, including advising a subsidiary on a stock offering."[68] The *Times* reported in 2012 that China's top insurance regulator asked JPMorgan Chase CEO Jamie Dimon to hire an unnamed family friend, just coincidentally, when JPMorgan Chase was seeking "a string of deals" with Chinese insurance companies. In one of those, a deal to underwrite a $297 million IPO offering for China Taiping Capital Ltd., an email revealed that JPMorgan Chase had a plan: "Hire the direct niece of [the company's] chairman," as her "link to [the] IPO is very direct." JPMorgan Chase got many of the deals but, needless to say, those coups were "unrelated" to any hiring of officials relatives and friends, and no one "is accused of wrongdoing."[69] No paper trail. Always in the background. That's how it works.

The rot has become so pervasive and so deeply entrenched throughout society that in January 2018 Xi conceded that while his five-year war on corruption had "disciplined or prosecuted more than 1.5 million cadres, including some in the highest ranks of the party and military," corruption was still pervasive and in many areas and the Party was even losing control to "triads and corrupt officials." He warned: "Officials are colluding with local criminal gangsters who, in turn, have effectively sabotaged the ruling Communist Party's grass-roots regime."[70] According to Minxin Pei, "an imperfect gauge of the extent of the rot" in the state is the large number of senior police officers who have been arrested and sentenced not only for corruption, but for murder and protection of organized crime.[71] Market reform presented crime bosses with opportunities to make huge fortunes in real estate, mining, construction, transportation, and the buying and selling of offices—far beyond what they make in their traditional businesses of gambling, prostitution, and drug trafficking. All that requires police protection. "Fortunately for the aspiring mafia bosses," Pei adds, "recruiting willing accomplices from the ranks of [police officials] has turned out to be much less challenging than they might have feared because these officials are subject to the same economic incentives that have made corruption endemic."[72] Despite repeated crackdowns by the government over decades, gangster-communist mafias now control local governments all over China. In more than half of China's provinces the government call these cases "collapse-style corruption" (*tafangshi fubai*) whereby large numbers of successive Party chiefs, mayors, and other key officials all participate to "transform the local party-state into local mafia states," effectively subverting the authority of the CCP.[73]

In concluding his January meeting with CCDI officials, Xi Jinping urged cadres to be "always politically reliable, loyal to the party, be of one mind and one heart with the central leadership, listen to the party's instructions and fulfill their responsibilities at all times and under all circumstances." Good luck on that Xi.

Get Rich and Get Out

1,000 "naked officials" found in Guangdong.
　　　　　　　　　　　　　　– The *China Digital Times*, June 8, 2014

According to He Qingliang, "the ship named China is sinking [but] the power elite has long prepared a retreat for its family members. When it is no longer possible to be a CCP cadre, it will be time for a comfortable retirement abroad."[74] It has been estimated that princelings and other high-ranking cadres and their cronies funneled nearly $4 trillion in unreported assets out of the country between 2000 and 2011.[75] That would be equal to China's entire GDP in 2007. In the wake of China's 2015 stock market crash, another billion dollars fled the country.[76]

Credit Suisse, PricewaterhouseCoopers, and UBS—Western companies with deep professional experience in sheltering tax evaders—have set up secret companies and accounts for at least 21,000 Chinese nationals, including for Wen Jiabao's son, Wen Yunsong. High cadres, their relatives, and other rich guys fly suitcases of money to North America, Australia, the Caribbean, and other friendly destinations.[77]

Typically, corrupt cadres first send their families and their ill-gotten gains overseas. These so-called "naked officials" are left with nothing at home, till the day when they themselves can get out.[78] In February 2014, it was reported that more than 45,000 Chinese *millionaires* had queued up in Vancouver, British Columbia to get investor residence visas in return for five-year interest-free loans to the Canadian government. In the US, 80 percent of the government's EB-5 Immigrant Investor Program visas are going to wealthy mainland Chinese; in Australia it's 90 percent. According to the *Guardian*, at least eighteen princelings own or run entities registered in the British Virgin Islands, Cayman Islands, Liberia, and other secret offshore tax havens. These include Deng Jiagui, real estate magnate and brother-in-law of Xi Jinping; Liu Chunhang, state banking regulator, former Morgan Stanley employee and son-in-law of Wen Jiabao; Wen Yunsong; Fu Liang, investor in yacht clubs and golf courses, and the son of former mayor of Beijing Peng Zhen; Li Xiaolin; Hu Yushi, CEO of a steel company and cousin of Hu Jintao; Wu Jiangchang, husband of Deng Xiaoping's daughter Deng Lin; Su Zhijun, CEO of a Hong Kong logistics company and grandson of one of China's most senior revolutionary commanders, Su Yu, and so on.[79]

Disgraced mayor of Chongqing Bo Xilai was in a class by himself. Bo revived Maoist operas while his wife, Gu Kailai controlled a web of businesses from Beijing to Hong Kong and the Caribbean that was worth at least $126 million. She and her sisters put many of their assets offshore, in places like the British Virgin Islands.[80]

Greater China accounted for nearly one-third of the clients of Panama Papers law firm Mossack Fonseca (33,000 individuals and entities from the mainland, 26,000 from Hong Kong). Among those named were Deng Jiagui; family members of two current Politburo Standing Committee members; Li Xiaolin; Wen Yunsong and Wen Ruchun; and relatives of Hu Yaobang, Deng Xiaoping, and Hu Jintao, among others.[81]

From "Serve the People" to "Greed is Good"

Bastards, I don't recognize them as my sons.

– General Wang Zhen[82]

After seizing power in 1949, the "Eight Immortals" were ensconced in reasonable comfort, if not extravagance, behind the walls of Zhongnanhai. In the Mao era they dressed like everyone else, in ill-fitting Mao suits or military uniforms. As the CCP grew rich in the 1990s and 2000s, the old guard traded their Mao suits for Western business suits but eschewed personal display of conspicuous consumption. It's been a different story with their children and grandchildren. The second generation had privileged childhoods with tutors in Zhongnanhai. Most of them attended college in Beijing, then went abroad to graduate school in the US and Europe in the first wave of post-Mao study-abroad students in the 1980s. (Xi, the son of the revolutionary leader Xi Zhongxun, was exiled to the countryside in 1966 at age thirteen during the Cultural Revolution so didn't finish middle school and never attended high school, but he was admitted to Beijing's Tsinghua University in 1975, where he studied chemical engineering as a "worker-peasant-soldier student." He never studied overseas.)

The third generation, growing up in the conspicuously capitalist China of the 1980s and 1990s, are even further removed from the "revolutionary values" of their grandparents. Most of these, now in their 30s and 40s, were sent abroad to fancy boarding schools and then to elite colleges in Europe and the US. Xi's daughter went to Harvard as an undergraduate. Bo Xilai's son Bo Guagua boarded at Harrow in the UK, then went on to study at Oxford, Harvard, and Columbia universities. The princelings often took jobs with Wall Street banks before returning to China. "Their lifestyle," *Bloomberg* notes, "tracks that of the global affluent class—people who were their schoolmates in Swiss, British and U.S. boarding schools."[83] After such upbringings, it's hardly surprising that these descendants share the same values as the Wall Street bankers that so many of them worked with: "Greed is good." With his partying and his Porsches, celebrity playboy Bo Guagua was a huge embarrassment to his father's goofy campaign to bring back the old-time Maoist religion in Chongqing (replete with songs extolling clean living, hard work, and selfless austerity). Such retro-Maoism did not comport with his wife's Côte d'Azur lifestyle either.

When he was lying in a hospital bed in 1990, Wang Zhen told a visitor that he felt betrayed by his own children. Decades after he had risked his life fighting for an egalitarian utopia, his children were only interested in getting rich: "Turtle eggs," he said to the visiting well-wisher, using a slang term for bastards, "I don't recognize them as my sons."[84] Even some of the princelings themselves are offended by the greed and cavorting of their peers. "My generation and the next generation made no contribution to China's revolution, independence and liberation" said Song Kehuang, businessman and son of Song Renqiong. "Now, some people use their parents' positions to scoop up hundreds of millions of yuan. Of course the public is angry. Their anger is justified."[85]

THE CORRUPTION OF CIVIL SOCIETY AND THE "DEFICIT OF HUMANITY"

Break the law big time, make a big fortune; break the law small time, make a small fortune; never break the law, never make a fortune.

– Popular saying[86]

Living in China . . . you have to be always on guard against others, as pits of fraud are everywhere.

– Shanghai netizen[87]

Communist Party corruption is appalling. But worse, Chinese society has become deeply corrupted and demoralized as a result. Whereas in the 1980s China's activist youth were idealistic, passionate protestors for democracy, today many of China's millennial generation have lost all hope for change. Seduced by capitalism and consumerism, they have become cynical and indifferent toward politics, human rights, and the environment, and insouciant toward the CCP's lies and repression.[88] Others are just giving up and emigrating. "When the top is corrupt, this is how it will be all the way down," said Dai Qing.[89] With the spectacle of China's political leadership by "communist" princeling-billionaires, corruption pervades the entire society, warps social morality, and encourages cynicism, amorality, and nihilism. As Dai Qing told an interviewer in 2010:

> The traditional Chinese ethic is gone from this society. These days, everyone is chasing money. Everyone wants a career as a public official because it's the gateway to becoming rich. In today's China, with belief in neither traditional values nor the rule of law, money means everything to almost everyone.[90]

Public incivility is rife in China today.[91] Government and academic institutions, the judiciary and police, SOEs, private companies, school admissions, university life, scientific research, medical care—corruption pervades them all, unavoidably. The internet is rife with scams, frauds, identity theft, and worse. Criminal gangs run local governments; the kidnapping of women and children is a significant "industry"; society is flooded with every imaginable kind of fakery; violent attacks on school children are not infrequent; school teachers steal food from their charges to profit themselves; doctors rip off and brutalize patients, and patient families commonly attack and even kill doctors. The list goes on.[92]

Corrupting Education

Decades ago, when things were nowhere near as abhorrent as they are today, Perry Link explained how corruption in government institutions and academia was unavoidable. His interviewees—professors and other intellectuals—told him that "nothing can get done without it." Corruption is structurally built into Chinese institutions which are all controlled by the Party. Party secretaries still have power, they are the last say in matters of a worker's rank, salary, job description, promotion, as well as other matters such as housing and access to schools. So most people are brought into it whether they intend so or not. What's more, "if a leader is too clean, he loses out."[93] In such an atmosphere, one academic told Link that "keeping good 'relations' with people becomes much more important than doing one's work well. Only the relations, not the work, count when it comes to promotions and welfare." The director of one of China's provincial academies of science told Link that "fully half the people on her academy's permanent payroll simply should not be there. They were not suited to do their jobs. They had gotten there through 'back door' connections with Party officials in the academy."[94] China's science research, practice, and teaching suffer accordingly. According to one graduate student: "The leaders want only two things from scientists: Technology and face. They want us to build and run machines to make China look 'modern'; they also want some big, glory-producing projects like a proton accelerator, which few countries have . . . What do [high officials] know about physics?"[95] The pressure to please Party officials instead of doing science encourages scientists and engineers to chase after patents to rack up numbers to please the higher-ups, even if these inventions are trivial or even faked.[96] It encourages rampant scientific fraud.[97] Moreover, chasing after scientific glory to compete with the US has resulted in China squandering money on useless projects, such as the world's biggest radio telescope, which, lacking scientists of the caliber needed to run it, has been turned into a theme park.[98]

Worse than that is the long-standing "policy of keeping the populace ignorant" (*yumin zhengce*) through the dumbing down of education, even as they build dozens of new universities. One historian told Link that:

> Our leaders' view is that they know the truth. The purpose of education is to share that truth with the masses, but even education of this sort is not terribly important. What is important is that the masses be properly led. There is no need for people to think for themselves—in fact, independent thought, as they see it, can lead to chaos and trouble.[99]

Corrupting the Legal System

Under Mao, there was no legal system, no judiciary worth the name. Since the 1980s, in part to steer growing protests into legal channels and in part to settle contract disputes in the new market economy, the government has built a legal infrastructure, a large body of criminal and civil law, set up courts, trained lawyers, established regulatory agencies, and so on. But this hardly matters because, like everything else in China, the judiciary is completely corrupt and subordinate to the Party.[100] In her book on the demolition and reconstruction of Shanghai, Qin Shao points out that in 1990 the government introduced what in principle was a very good law—the Administration Litigation Law (ALL)—which allowed citizens to sue corrupt officials. But in practice residents fighting arbitrary seizure and destruction of their homes in Shanghai almost never won:

> One reason for ALL's ineffectiveness is a lack of judicial independence. District judges answer to the same district Party bosses who adminis-trate demolition and are responsible for the abuse in the first place. No judge in his right mind would rule against the bosses even if the evidence overwhelmingly indicates that he should. Another reason . . . is that the government and the courts take it for granted that economic growth trumps everything else, including justice. In some cases, the government has banned class-action lawsuits against illegal land-taking. [Courts] openly permitted the use of force against residents.[101]

He Qingliang explains how would-be litigants face not just corrupt judges but find that even their own lawyers are often corrupt. As such, the out-come of civil legal cases often depends on "connections" to the judges. It is a common occurrence to hear lawyers promoting their services by telling cli-ents how intimate they are with a certain judge. Collusion between lawyers and judges in a lawsuit is far from unusual. There are even cases where the same lawyers act as the representative of both the plaintiff and defendant. "Public opinion holds the legal profession in very low esteem," says He.[102]

Minxin Pei writes that "the rot of collusive corruption" has spread to key institutions of the Party-state—the CCDI, police, judiciary, and regulatory agencies dealing with environmental protection, work safety, and food and drugs.[103] Municipalities have been "struck by mega-corruption scandals." The judiciary is "ravaged by crony capitalism." While judicial graft is not as lucrative as other fields and "some senior judges can be bought for a mere 10,000 yuan, others reaped millions of yuan in bribes."[104]

Corrupting Medical Practice

The privatization of medical care in the 1990s and 2000s resulted in the crass commercialization of medical practice and services. An emphasis on profits, a culture of "gift giving" and a lack of professional ethics produced an atmosphere of frustration, anger, and mistrust. During the Mao era, doctor–patient relationships were relatively harmonious. Money was scarce and resources were few, for all. But after decades of market liberalization in which hospitals sought to generate revenue by shaping treatment according to commercial rather than medical concerns, trust is gone.[105]

China's hospitals operate like profit centers. *Hongbao* or "red envelopes"—bribes—are normally essential. China's shabby medical insurance system is so inadequate, often covering only basic needs, that millions of families are driven into poverty to pay bills. Desperate people have even been known to sell an organ to save a loved one. Drugs are routinely overprescribed and overpriced, as pharmaceutical companies hand out bags of cash in kickbacks to get their drugs prescribed.[106] Unnecessary surgeries are common. Emergencies are used by doctors and hospitals to extract exorbitant fees. Patients complain that when they ask how much a procedure will cost the answer is often "how much can you afford?" Patients are mistreated by fake doctors, even fake hospitals.[107] Sina Weibo is filled with complaints about corrupt doctors and hospitals—accounts of bribes, appointment scalpers, and sexual abuse by doctors. In one case, a female patient was forced to pay additional money in the middle of her surgery![108] A University of Hong Kong sociologist commented that "you have to 'buy' a doctor's effort to save the life of a person . . . The main aim is to get the physicians to perform the surgery to the best of their ability. It's what surgeons are supposed to do, of course." At the same time "doctors often joke that they are afraid to sit in offices with their backs to the door in case they're stabbed." But it's no joke. Medical staff are physically attacked by patients or their relatives at a rate of once every two weeks (per hospital), according to the China Hospital Association. Some have even been killed by patients who have been abused or lost loved ones in hospitals.[109] Patients, relatives, doctors, "everyone feels the deficit of humanity" in China's hyper-marketized medical practice.[110]

In the 1980s, Western academic, corporate, and business media apologists for capitalism assured us that the introduction of market reform in China would do away with or at least ameliorate corruption. Many even said that marketization would entrain democratization. Instead, China got the worst of both worlds. The combination of capitalism and bureaucratic collectivism ramped up corruption, poisoning society and rendering any future transition to democracy all the more difficult.

LOSING THE ENDLESS "WAR ON CORRUPTION"

Don't go back on your old ways when our backs are turned . . . we will come back and catch you off guard.

– Wang Qishan, head of the CCDI

Given pervasive cadre corruption and rampant lawlessness, one scholar found that the government's new "social credit" monitoring system, which has been widely criticized in the West as a dystopian nightmare of high-tech police-state control is often welcomed by ordinary Chinese desperate for an effective police and judicial system to put an end to the lawlessness that conditions their lives. Anthropologist Xinyuan Wang interviewed some 500 Shanghai residents and found that in a system in which the punishments for fraud, scams, food safety violations, pharmaceutical scandals, and similar offences are not enough to deter re-offending, criminals "commit crimes in one province and set up business in another the next day, with few consequences." Many hope that the new social credit blacklisting and high-tech tracking of offenders will deter such crimes.[111] Perhaps in some cases. But I don't see why the social credit system should be any less corrupt than policing in general in China. Just because offenders can be systematically tracked doesn't mean they can't bribe their way out of jail or work their *guanxi* to avoid severe punishment.

There's a real and obvious solution to the foregoing problems: Abolish Party-state ownership of the economy in favor of social ownership, abolish one-party rule in favor of multi-party democracy, and firmly establish the rule of law through an independent judiciary and police. That was more or less what the incredibly brave human rights lawyer Yu Wensheng (already imprisoned and tortured in 2014) called for in his provocative open letter to the Communist Party, published on October 18, 2017, the day that the Nineteenth Party Congress convened. Yu called on Party delegates to remove Xi Jinping from the seat of General Secretary of the CCP in order to allow political reform and a free and democratic China to develop.[112] Instead, the government revoked his law license and then disappeared him into some gulag as it has done with so many other dissidents since Xi took over.

"Killing the Chickens to Scare the Monkeys"

By January 2018, Xi's anti-corruption campaign had netted more than 120 high-ranking officials including Politburo members, generals, ministry heads, SOE chairmen, governors, mayors, prosecutors, bank regulators, and even the nation's top cop.[113] Hundreds of others had fled the country.[114] But as many have pointed out, the anti-corruption fight is more about knocking out competitors than about rooting out corruption. While he very publicly swatted competing "mega-tigers" *(chaoji laohu)* like Bo Xilai and Zhou Yongkang, Xi has conspicuously failed to catch blatantly corrupt tigers right under his nose. Novelist Murong Xuecun writes that "the anticorruption push is more of a Stalinist purge than a genuine attempt to clean up the government." He notes that in Xi's former fiefs in Fujian and Zhejiang provinces, "not one official above the deputy provincial level has been arrested on suspicion of corruption. Recently the question was raised on the internet: Why have no 'big tigers' been found in Fujian and Zhejiang? The message was almost immediately deleted."[115]

Yet for all the campaigns, corruption only seems to grow worse year after year, to judge by the increasing numbers of prosecutions and the ever-more shocking amounts of money involved. And why would it not? Without the rule of law, independent judiciary and police, Xi's only weapon, like Mao before him, is to try to terrorize the cadres by sending down CCDI inspection teams to punish local transgressors—"killing the chickens to scare the monkeys" as the Chinese say. Yet opportunities for getting rich quick have grown as fast as the economy. And for all the drama in the press, the reality is that, as Minxin Pei says, "the detection risk is low."[116] Besides, for most corruption cases the consequences are not nearly so dire as the lurid headlines imply, especially for the most elite, the biggest Communist Party gangsters.[117] The Party is a cesspool of corruption from top to bottom: Every princeling, every ministry, every province, every locality, the army, the courts, the police, the hospitals, schools and universities, and the Chinese Communist Youth League—even the CCDI itself.[118]

Public opinion polls show that the population thinks that most, if not all, officials are corrupt. According to polls taken in 2014, 53 percent of those interviewed believed that corruption among central government officials was "somewhat common." Almost 17 percent believed that "almost all" central officials were corrupt. When asked about local officials, the sorts of officials with which people are most familiar, 61 percent thought that local official corruption was "somewhat common." Almost a quarter, 24 percent, said that they believed that "almost all" local officials were corrupt.[119] Yet the numbers of those investigated and punished for corruption are miniscule in comparison. In January 2015 the government reported that in the previous year more than 71,000 cadres were "investigated for violating Party regulations." Of these only 23,000 "received Party or administrative penalties." Most received censures. Some were sent to prison and none were reported executed in that year. Twenty-three thousand "disciplined" out of 90 million CCP members. Not bad odds. In his analysis of the 260 most-egregious, most-reported cases of official corruption, Minxin Pei shows that just 41 individuals received life sentences and only 6 were given a death sentence (all of which were eventually commuted to life in prison). Thousands of common criminals are executed every year in China, but the Party is more lenient with its own.[120]

Given the foregoing, it's hardly surprisingly that many punished officials bounce back, like child molesters in the Catholic Church. As Wang Guixiu, a professor at the Central Party School said: "Whenever there's a problem exposed, the public needs an explanation . . . so 'removal' is often used. It gives the public the illusion that officials have been held accountable, but it won't have a real impact on their political careers." Li Hanyu, vice president of the Guizhou Higher People's Court, and who led a study of accountability in 2008, said that: "The system is essentially just decoration and can easily be used as a weapon in power struggles."[121]

Debauched and dissolute as it is, the CCDI can't arrest the entire Party. Xi needs those millions of officials to run his economy and government, and in any case most are well-enough connected to avoid his terrorists. What normally happens is that after the terror passes and the CCDI teams return to Beijing, it's back to business as usual. After wrapping up a second round of inspections in ten provinces in 2014, Wang Qishan, then head of the CCDI, warned officials: "Don't go back to your old ways when our backs are turned . . . we will come back and catch you off guard."[122] But really, what can the poor CCDI do? By October, Wang was complaining that "we have stepped up the anti-graft campaign but some Party cadres are still undeterred. Some have become even more corrupt." Wang responded by vowing to "ramp up inspections of the lower tiers of government."[123] Good luck on that.

Part of Wang's problem is that he can't trust the police to systematically enforce anti-corruption measures because the police themselves are notoriously corrupt. Even his own corruption investigators can't be trusted. More than 7,900 CCDI investigators have themselves been placed under investigation for corruption and punished since 2012. Not only that but with rumors swirling over the summer of 2017 about the Wang family's own corruption—including their having funneled substantial assets to the US, establishing a so-called "one family common interest group," and founding a multi-billion dollar charity in New York to launder and transfer money abroad—Wang might himself have been an obvious target for prosecution.

The rumors around Wang parallel those around Meng Hongwei, China's top cop and president of Interpol, who mysteriously vanished in September 2018 and was sentenced in January 2020 to thirteen years in prison for "wantonly and lavishly spending state funds to satisfy his family's luxurious lifestyle."[124] But Wang had better *guanxi* (he is from a prominent princeling family and has long been close to Xi Jinping). After "retiring" as corruption chief in October 2017 to get out of the media spotlight, he was promoted the next year to become Xi's number two, China's vice president.[125]

Geremie Barmé says that most of the offspring of China's revolutionary founders—the so-called "second red generation" whose ranks include Xi Jinping and Bo Xilai—have largely escaped serious punishment:

> In the murky corridors of Communist power, an impressive number of party gentry progeny, or the offspring of the Mao-era nomenklatura, have been implicated in corrupt practices . . . But word has it that, like the well-connected elites of other climes, they've enjoyed a "soft landing": Being discretely relocated, shunted into delicate retirement or quietly "redeployed."[126]

The Logic of Luxury Prisons

"Soft" is the word for it: Bo Xilai's assets were seized but his rank, status, and *guanxi* entitled him to confinement in Qincheng prison in the wooded hills north of Beijing. Qincheng is not on any official map in China but it is complete with "pavilions, trees and grass reminiscent of a Chinese garden," according to a recent report in the *South China Morning Post*. No orange jumpsuits either. The *Post* reports, citing former residents, that "inmates at the facility—which has housed almost all the high-ranking politicians jailed in China since the 1960s—are given large private cells equipped with soft beds, sofas, desks and an ensuite bathroom."[127] "It's like a five-star hotel," said Bao Tong, a former secretary to the Politburo Standing Committee who spent seven years in the prison for opposing the crackdown on the Tiananmen Square protests. Dai Qing, who spent ten months in the prison for supporting the Tiananmen protestors, described her cell as about twenty square meters in size, "with high ceilings . . . and even a bathroom," while prison guards treated her with "warmth and care." "The head of the prison let me put on better clothes before I left," she recalled of one occasion when she was let out to visit a sick relative, "he reminded me of my old school headmaster."

Prisoners can choose their clothes, drink milk for breakfast and eat selections of soups and meat dishes for lunch and dinner. Some of the prison chefs used to work in one of Beijing's top hotels and prepare food to "ministry chief level," according to a report by the *Beijing Times*.

Chen Zeming, an academic who spent a few months there, again for supporting Tiananmen activists, told the *Post* that "Qincheng gives the best treatment of any prison in China . . . Bo Xilai won't be mistreated." Bao Tong added that top officials are often released on medical parole years before the end of their terms, often without public notice, to live out their days under house arrest. "After two years, they will say Bo is ill and he will be released, and will live next to a lake, or by the sea," he said.[128] Gu Kailai, who was given a death sentence (later commuted to life in prison) for murdering her British business partner Neil Heywood in 2011, has apparently been ensconced in acceptably luxurious conditions at Yancheng prison in Hebei province.[129]

China may be the only country with a fleet of luxury prisons to house its erring officials. Yet from the standpoint of the ruling class, such indulgences can be seen as eminently sensible and prudent because, who knows? In the next episode of "Beijing Game of Thrones" it could be Xi himself who ends up in handcuffs, like his father before him. That said, China's luxury prisons for high cadres are still prisons. And the prisoners are forced to confess, to "turn over" and "become conscious" of their errors if they want to get out. In her memoir Dai Qing recalled that former security and military officials had committed suicide in Qincheng.[130]

Pursued with too much vigor, Xi's anti-corruption campaign against senior officials risks not only unsettling elite stability but destroying what's left of the Party's credibility. As a retired princeling military officer said about an earlier campaign against graft in the army: "You can't do it too much, otherwise the Party comes out too black, and the leaders won't like it."[131] By carrying his campaign right into the Politburo itself, even displaying high-level corrupt officials for all to see on television docudramas, Xi is blackening the Party's reputation like never before. Since he can't opt for the obvious solution, "the anti-graft fight is never ending."[132]

7
Grabbing the Emergency Brake

UNINHABITABLE CHINA

Of all the threats and problems that Xi faces, the most urgent is the relentless heating of the planet driven by the industrialized nations and led by China. In July 2018 temperature records were broken around the world.[1] Year after year scientists are stunned by how much faster the planet is heating compared with what their computer models had predicted only a few years previously. Nathaniel Rich writes that

> The world has warmed more than one degree Celsius since the Industrial Revolution. The Paris climate agreement—the nonbinding, unenforceable and already unheeded treaty signed on Earth Day in 2016—hoped to restrict warming to two degrees. The odds of succeeding, according to a recent study based on current emissions trends, are only one in 20. If by some miracle we are able to limit warming to two degrees, we will only have to negotiate the extinction of the world's tropical reefs, sea-level rise of several meters and the abandonment of the Persian Gulf. The climate scientist James Hansen has called two-degree warming "a prescription for long-term disaster." *Long-term disaster is now the best-case scenario.* Three-degree warming is a prescription for short-term disaster: Forests in the Arctic and the loss of most coastal cities. Robert Watson, a former director of the United Nations Intergovernmental Panel on Climate Change, has argued that three-degree warming is the realistic minimum. Four degrees: Europe in permanent drought; vast areas of China, India and Bangladesh claimed by desert; Polynesia swallowed by the sea; the Colorado River thinned to a trickle; the American Southwest largely uninhabitable. The prospect of a five-degree warming has prompted scientists to warn of the end of human civilization.[2]

Shanghai and Shenzhen—the most advanced engines of the Chinese economy—have an average elevation above sea level of just four meters. Scientists tell us that Shanghai is the world's most vulnerable major city

Figure 7.1 Artist's rendering of Shanghai after a 4ºC rise in temperature.
Source: "New report and maps: Rising seas threaten land home to half a billion,"
Climate Central, November 8, 2015, http://sealevel.climatecentral.org/news/
global-mapping-choices.
Courtesy of *Climate Central*.

in terms of serious flooding risk.[3] With just 3°C of warming they will be
underwater, along with the rest of China's coastal cities, where 43 percent
of the population currently lives.[4] Of course you will read nothing like this
in the totalitarian press in China because the Party has set a goal of 6–7
percent GDP growth for the coming decades, and the climate be damned.

But climate collapse is coming to China, and fast. Unprecedented heat
waves smashed records across the country in July 2018. In coastal Zhejiang
province temperatures hit 34°C, forcing construction workers to down
tools because the steel became too hot to touch.[5]

A 2018 MIT study determined that unless drastic measures are taken
to limit climate-changing emissions "the North China Plain, China's most
populous and agriculturally important region, where 400 million people
currently live . . . is going to be the hottest spot [on Earth] for deadly heat
waves," and could become virtually uninhabitable before the end of the
century."[6] The study found that

The risk of deadly heat waves is significantly increased because of inten-
sive irrigation in [the North China Plain]—a region whose role in that
country is comparable to that of the Midwest in the U.S. That increased
vulnerability to heat arises because the irrigation exposes more water to

evaporation, leading to higher humidity in the air than would otherwise be present and exacerbating the physiological stresses of the temperature.

The study is the third in a set; the previous two projected increases of deadly heat waves in the Persian Gulf area and in South Asia. While the earlier studies found serious looming risks, the new findings show that the North China Plain, or NCP, faces the greatest risks to human life from rising temperatures of any location on Earth:

> Although the Persian Gulf study found some even greater temperature extremes, those were confined to the area over the water of the Gulf itself, not over the land. In the case of the North China Plain, "this is where people live" . . . and signs of that future have already begun: There has been a substantial increase in extreme heat waves in the NCP already in the last 50 years . . . Warming in this region over that period has been nearly double the global average—0.24 degrees Celsius per decade versus 0.13. In 2013, extreme heat waves in the region persisted for up to 50 days, and maximum temperatures topped 38°C in places. Major heat waves occurred in 2006 and 2013, breaking records. Shanghai, East China's largest city, broke a 141-year temperature record in 2013, and dozens died.[7]

From Greece to Portugal, Britain, California, Japan, Greenland, and Sweden, never has so much of the planet been simultaneously on fire as in July 2018.[8] Hundreds died from the heat and fires in California, Quebec, Sweden, and Japan. And all this was with just one degree of warming.[9] With summer temperatures rising close to the ability of humans to disperse heat, even in full shade, scientists tell us we could see the first mass die-offs of humans in China, the Middle East, and South Asia in the coming decades.[10] Another new study concludes that we're now at risk of entering what scientists call "Hothouse Earth" conditions as our growing emissions trigger unstoppable "feedbacks," such as the release of vast quantities of methane buried in Arctic ocean bottoms, which would send temperatures soaring 4–5°C above pre-industrial levels and raise sea levels 10–60 meters higher than today.[11]

XI'S FAILED "WAR ON POLLUTION"

After decades of breakneck industrialization and uncontrolled pollution had darkened China's skies, ruined water courses, and incited large and sometimes violent anti-pollution protests, in 2013 Xi Jinping declared "war on pollution."[12] In September the State Council rolled out its long-awaited Atmospheric Pollution Prevention Action Plan, which pledged to reduce PM2.5 levels in "Jing-Jin-Ji" by 25 percent, in the Yangtze River Delta by 20 percent, and in the Pearl River Delta by 15 percent. It pledged to reduce reliance on coal by prohibiting new coal-fired power plants, reducing coal's contribution to the energy consumption mix to 65 percent by 2017, and replace coal-fired power plants with natural-gas and non-fossil fuel energy. The plan also promised to "strictly" limit the number of vehicles in China's big cities.[13] In his March 2014 address to the National People's Congress, Li Keqiang said that "pollution is nature's red-light warning against the model of inefficient and blind development." He pledged to spend 10 billion yuan to create a smog-fighting fund and said the government would soon launch a "comprehensive clean water plan and program to remove contaminates form the soil."[14]

Six years on, Xi has won some skirmishes, suppressing visible smog in Beijing and Shanghai mainly by relocating dirty industries elsewhere, but he's losing the war on CO2 emissions, ozone pollution, and water and soil pollution.

The Cycle of Crackdowns and Backdowns

In the 2000s and early 2010s the government temporarily suppressed smog in Beijing for big events—like the 2008 Olympic Games and the Asia Pacific Economic Cooperation (APEC) summit in 2014—by banning cars and forcing shutdowns of coal-fired boilers, factories, and cement plants in the capital region. But when the events were over and the engines fired back up the "APEC blue skies" disappeared and smog came back, often worse than before as industries sought to make up for lost production and revenues.[15] Despite Li's pledges, headline-grabbing winter "airpocalypses" over Beijing worsened year by year from 2013 through 2017. Medical authorities declared that living in China's northern cities was "as deadly as smoking."[16] In December 2016, red alerts were announced in 25 cities. Airports and highways were closed due to limited visibility, and, as we noted in Chapter 4, "smog refugees" were fleeing south.[17]

Xi's efforts to suppress pollution have been undermined by subordinate officials who resist Beijing's orders.[18] Chai Jing's *Under the Dome* underlined the chronic inability of the central government to suppress pollution and regulate its own industries. Inspection teams sent out in April 2017 to assess anti-pollution performance in the city of Tianjin and six other provinces found 31,457 pollution problems, which resulted in 8,687 companies receiving punishments, 4,660 officials being held accountable, and 405 people being detained. Just as in Mao's day, Chinese bureaucrats still tally numbers of punishments imposed to indicate progress instead of assessing qualitative change. Inspectors found that in some areas pollution had worsened as a result of their decisions. "Despite tough requirements from the central government to cut air pollution" local officials built coal-fired power plants, "failed to build infrastructure to manage waste," and dumped hundreds of thousands of tons of untreated sewage into rivers. "Inspectors found that air and water quality had deteriorated in many places in the seven areas inspected, and governments failed to take effective measure to control the trend."[19] Local officials were even embezzling their smog-fighting funds to spend on entertainment and renovating their office buildings.[20] Ultimately, however, the central government's overriding concern with maximizing economic growth is the main driver of pollution. So while Xi can roll out crackdowns now and again, he can't go too far and in particular he can't be too hard on his state-owned companies because this will slow economic growth, increase unemployment, dash his hopes for a domestic consumer driven economy, and undermine his drive to build up industrial self-sufficiency.[21] This fundamental contradiction is the source of the government's perennial cycle of anti-pollution crackdowns and backdowns.

A Blue Sky in Beijing?

In the fall of 2017, Xi's aggressive campaign to shut down smokestack industries and suppress coal-fired heating, along with windy weather and a boost in the use of natural gas for heating and cooking (up by 19 percent in 2017),[22] reduced the smog enough that the government could claim that, for the first time ever, all 28 northern cities targeted for smog reduction had met their October–December targets, with PM2.5 readings down an average of 34 percent from 2016. Beijing's average dropped 54 percent and Shijiazhuang's fell by 55 percent. The official press crowed that China was "winning the war" on pollution. The *Wall Street Journal* hailed the "advantages" of Xi's dictatorship: "The shift shows what an autocratic government can do to overcome resistance from businesses and other local interests that stymied past efforts to meet a goal deemed critical."[23]

The autocrat's victory was short-lived. In late December and January 2017–18 the smog returned over north China. The capital was engulfed in "hazardous" level smog, with AQI readings over 500 in the last days of December.[24] Beijing recorded only 16 "blue-sky" days in March 2018, compared with 21 in March 2017, prompting officials "to worry that China's war on pollution might have reached a 'strategic stalemate.'"[25] In January 2018, Greenpeace reported that while the Beijing region managed record improvements in November–December 2017, average national emissions over the year fell by just 4.5 percent—"the smallest yearly improvement since the start of the National Action Plan in 2013."[26] Greenpeace also concluded that about three-quarters of the smog reduction in December could have been accounted for by unusually high winds that dispersed the smog.[27] Pollution was not so much suppressed as dispersed to other cities and provinces where production was not constrained by Beijing's winter limits.[28] Shanghai residents complained that the government was cleaning up Beijing by "pushing pollution south."[29]

Xi's ban on coal burning seems to have been mainly directed against households and private businesses rather than large SOEs.[30] Overachieving local officials ripped coal stoves out of peoples' homes, often without providing functioning natural gas replacement heaters, leaving millions shivering until the government rescinded its order after protests and resistance. Yet state-owned industries were running full-tilt.[31] "You have reduction in emissions from households. But at the same time you have increased these emissions from heavy industry. [The trends] have been going in opposite directions," Lauri Myllyvirta said.[32] From March when the six-month pollution-suppression measures were lifted, production ramped up across the north and the smog surged again, with 30 northern cities on orange alert and AQI levels rising beyond 500 again in Beijing.[33]

There was no let-up in 2019. With his economy in freefall, Xi could hardly afford to shut down polluting industries.[34] The government reported that 30 of the 39 most smog-prone cities across northern China had failed to meet their (modest) winter smog reduction target of 3 percent over the six months through March 2019. Instead PM2.5 readings climbed 13 percent. In heavily industrialized Jing-Jin-Ji, PM2.5 levels rose 24 percent. In the first quarter of 2019, PM2.5 levels in 337 major cities across the country rose 1.9 percent over 2018. In Jing-Jin-Ji they rose 8.4 percent and more than 9 percent in Shanxi and Shaanxi provinces.[35]

Besides the smog, studies by Peking University and Greenpeace found that concentrations of "ground-level ozone" rose 40 percent or more between 2014 and 2017, "despite countrywide efforts to tackle air pollution." They hit new records in 2018. Ozone is formed in chemical reactions between nitrogen oxides and volatile organic compounds in the presence of sunlight, so ozone levels typically peak in summer months. The largest sources of "volatile organic compound" emissions in China are industry and transport while the largest emitters of nitrogen oxides are power plants, industry, and transport. Both industrial output and oil demand have been rising in 2018, largely due to a construction surge resulting from stimulus policies.[36] Rising ozone levels are reducing farm yields, negatively affecting human immune systems and, Greenpeace reports, adding 180,000 premature deaths to the million or more who die from PM2.5-laden smog annually.[37] Pollution-related lung cancer rates are still climbing.[38] Air pollution accounts for about 1.6 million premature deaths per year, and this figure is growing.[39]

Greenpeace expressed particular alarm at the sharp rise in coal consumption by new "coal-to-chemicals" plants—which Myllyvirta has called the "dirtiest industry you've never heard of" (discussed in Chapter 4). Coal use in this filthy sector jumped by 60 percent from 2016 to 2018 and "another 30% increase in coal use is expected from 2018–2020."[40] In March 2019, minister of ecology and environment Li Ganjie said that while the country's air had improved somewhat, "the air pollution situation remains 'grim' and the hardest challenges still need to be tackled."[41] In sum, despite managing a few more blue-sky days in Beijing, Xi's war on air pollution is failing.[42]

Losing the War Against Water and Soil Pollution

Xi's war against water and soil pollution has barely begun, but it is already lost. When he launched his war on pollution in 2013, the MEP vowed to step up enforcement. Here and there it has won some improvements. China Water Risk (CWR) reports that "the overall quality of China's main river basins has gradually improved since 2016." But not enough. In his yearly work report to the National People's Congress in April 2017, MEP chief Chen Jining tersely reported that "improvements in water quality are uneven, with some bodies of water worsening"; agricultural land soil quality "does not allow for optimism"; and "the problem of soil pollution for industry, companies and nearby land is prominent."[43] In June 2018, CWR reported that "China's groundwater quality has been gradually deteriorating for the past several years . . . the proportion of groundwater stations with a 'good' and 'excellent' quality fell drastically from 31.9% to 10.9%; while the proportion of groundwater stations with 'bad' and 'very bad' quality rose from 66.8% to 86.2%." In September 2019, it reported that "rampant industrial pollution" was rendering much of the Yangtze River's water "unusable." In the Shanghai region, 18 percent of river water was deemed to be Grade 5 ("untouchable").[44] With chemical dumping still out of control, the government is launching yet another campaign to terrorize local officials.[45]

As with air pollution, the government has promulgated big "action plans" to address water and soil pollution: The Water Pollution Prevention and Control Action Plan (2015) and the Soil Pollution Prevention and Control Action Plan (2016).[46] But these are largely aspirational, with targets like bringing 93 percent of drinking water to a Grade 3 level or higher by 2020 and making 90 percent of polluted farmland safe for human use by 2020. The government has published no comprehensive database of what needs to be done, and where. It has detailed no methodology. It lacks cleanup technology and trained staff for detoxifying farm soil, and river and lake bottoms. It has published no schedule and has put forward no realistic budgets.[47]

Caixin, China's leading business magazine, noted that while the soil pollution plan stipulates that "remediation costs should be paid by polluters," it offers no explanation for how this will be achieved, especially considering that the biggest polluters are state-owned companies.[48] Even if China's toxic farmlands, rivers, and lakes could be cleaned, the price tag would be astronomical. The government has not, so far as we know, undertaken any comprehensive study of the problem, or costed its remediation. Even so, it "appears unprepared to foot the bill," according to Zhou Chen of *Caixin*:

> Beijing allocated only 9 billion yuan [$1.4 billion] for soil remediation projects in 2016 . . . [By comparison], the United States spends about US$15 billion a year on soil remediation through its nearly 36-year-old Superfund cleanup project overseen by the U.S. Environmental Protection Agency.[49]

The US EPA currently has about 1,300 Superfund sites on its National Priorities List. Even with the best of technology, cleanup has dragged on for decades and toxics cannot be fully extracted. Thus, trout caught in Torch Lake, Michigan are not safe to eat, groundwater in Baldwin, Florida is not safe to drink, and six acres of Bridgewater, Massachusetts are not safe to live on, even though these former Superfund sites are now considered "clean" by the EPA.[50]

As we noted in Chapter 3, China's toxic soil crisis is many orders of magnitude worse than that of the United States. In many cases there is no possible remediation. It's virtually impossible to remove chemicals, heavy metals, dioxins, and other toxics from polluted soil, let alone river and lake bottoms or underground aquifers in the US, China or anywhere else. These can only be cordoned off and left, possibly for centuries, if not forever.

Given the daunting scale of the problem, government paralysis is understandable, if unforgivable. With air pollution, the solution is comparatively easy—turn off the coal-fired power plants, shut down the toxic incinerators, park the cars and trucks, and ground the planes. That's more or less what was done in December 2017, and it worked until they started everything back up again. But with water and soil pollution, what can be done? Recall Li Gengxuan's corn field. Where would all that tainted soil be dumped? How can the toxic muck on the bottoms of nearly every Chinese river and lake be removed? Where would they dump that? How can aquifers hundreds and thousands of feet below the surface of Beijing be cleaned? If New York's Hudson River is still not safe for fishing or swimming after three decades of river-bottom scraping to remove dioxins and other toxics from a single General Electric factory in Upstate New York, imagine the state of China's water courses, which have been deluged with all manner of toxic industrial chemicals and untreated sewage from thousands of such factories, hundreds of cities, and legions of unregulated private waste services, along with farm fertilizer and pesticide runoff, for seven decades. The Chinese government spent more than $100 billion on rural water cleanup projects from 2005–2010. Yet the MEP conceded that in 43 percent of the locations it's monitoring, the water is still not even fit for human contact.[51]

The horrific fact is much of China's farmland and many of its water courses are irreversibly defiled. Its leaders know this. The bill for China's decades of quick and dirty industrialization has come due and the government can't afford to pay it. Instead of undertaking the Sisyphean task of attempting to detoxify China's farms and fresh water reserves or putting a stop to the industrial dumping by firmly shutting down those polluters, Beijing wants to maintain its hyper growth, hyper polluting industrialization drive while importing clean water from southwestern China via its south–north water transfer project and by piping in fresh water from Lake Baikal in Russia. Hydrologists and ecologists have warned that these huge boondoggles will not only fail to solve the problem, they will make it worse.[52]

An "Ecological Civilization" with a 6.5 Percent Growth Rate?

Xi's problem is that there is just no way to grow an industrialized economy without growing CO_2 emissions and other pollutants because many industries, from mining and metallurgy to chemicals, plastics, manufacturing, and transportation, are just intrinsically polluting. There's no way to magically "dematerialize" production such that we can grow our economies forever without growing resource consumption and pollution. There's no way to "green" them beyond narrow limits. The only way to suppress their pollution is to suppress those industries. That's why, year after year, decade after decade, UN climate summits collapse in failure and acrimony. No industrial nation will accept caps on pollution because they all know that caps on emissions would mean caps on growth, and growth must take priority or companies will fail and recession or worse will result. After promising to crackdown on polluters "with an iron fist" in 2014, in the face of a prolonged economic slowdown, Li Keqiang recently announced an "employment first" policy, which, in typical CCP double talk, stated that "[we should] allow enterprises a grace period for complying with environmental requirements and avoid simply shutting down factories . . . [yet] we will also resolutely oppose relaxing environmental regulations."[53]

EMERGENCY INDUSTRIAL PHASEOUTS AND RETRENCHMENTS

China's economic growth is driven by all the things it says it wants to get rid of.
— Christopher Balding, Peking University HSBC Business School

It's time to panic. I want you to act as if the house is on fire, because it is.
— Greta Thunberg, addressing the
EU Parliament in April 2019

Climate scientists led by NASA's James Hansen have been warning us since the 1980s that if we do not rapidly suppress CO2 emissions, tripping points will be breached and global warming will soar beyond any human power to restrain it.[54] Yet as we've noted, far from slowing, emissions have relentlessly increased, even accelerated, since the 1990s as China joined the world economy. When atmospheric concentrations of CO2 surpassed 400 parts per million in May 2013, climate scientists declared that we faced a "climate emergency." Mainstream institutions issued reports that would have been dismissed as alarmist in the 1990s. The IEA said that "the current state of affairs is unacceptable," energy-related CO2 emissions are at "historic highs," and emission trends are "perfectly in line with a temperature increase of 6 degrees Celsius, which would have devastating consequences for the planet."[55] British climate scientist Kevin Anderson declared that

> *We face an unavoidably radical future.* We either continue with rising emissions and reap the radical repercussions of severe climate change, or we acknowledge that we have a choice and pursue radical emission reductions: No longer is there a non-radical option. Moreover, low-carbon supply technologies cannot deliver the necessary rate of emission reductions—they need to be complemented with rapid, deep and early reductions in energy consumption.[56]

In 2014, the World Bank warned that 1.5°C of warming was "already locked in" and said that unless leaders took "strong, early action" the world was on course to a catastrophic warming of 4°C or more before the end of the century.

Estimates vary for how deep and how fast we need to cut. Hansen and others calculated that to have a chance of keeping the global temperature rise below 2°C, the worst polluters would have to suppress fossil fuel emissions by around 6 percent per year.[57] Anderson estimated that wealthy countries would need to cut their emissions by at least 10 percent every year. But those estimates were in 2013. Seven years have elapsed since then, CO2 emissions have continued growing and CO2 concentrations in the atmosphere have risen. The more years that pass with no cuts, the deeper and faster those eventual cuts will have to be if we're to save ourselves. Yvo de Boer, former executive secretary of the United Nations Framework Convention on Climate Change (UNFCCC), once remarked that "the only way" we can achieve the goal of limiting global warming to 2°C would be to "shut down the whole global economy."[58]

We can't shut down the whole world economy. But Greta Thunberg is right, it's time to panic. When the house is on fire, the first thing to do is douse the flames, stop the burning. This means shutting down the coal-fired power plants, park the cars and trucks, ground the planes. Create an emergency plan to deal with the climate emergency. Because if we don't shut down and retrench the worst polluting industrial sectors, Mother Nature will do it for us, civilization will collapse, and we'll face extinction.[59]

Preventing Planetary Collapse Requires
Degrowth Strategies from Industrial Nations

Most climate scientists are loathe to talk about the economic and political implications of their scientific conclusions, preferring to stick to the
science and keep their heads down. Conservative Canadian and Australian
governments have fired thousands of climate scientists. Presidents Bush
and Trump have hammered American climate scientists. Hansen is one
nail who won't be hammered down: He quit his NASA job to protest and
got himself arrested in front of the White House, bringing attention to the
urgency of the crisis and the campaign for a carbon tax.

At the nineteenth session of the Conference of the Parties (COP 19) of
the UNFCCC in Warsaw in 2013, British climate scientists Kevin Anderson
and Alice Bows-Larkin drew attention to the economic implications of
the science—namely that deep cuts in CO_2 emissions can only be won by
deep cuts in economic output. The time had come, they told negotiators,
to face the reality that continued economic growth is incompatible with
keeping temperature increases below 2°C.[60] In calling for "de-growth" in the
industrialized nations (albeit "temporary" and partially offset by allowing
for modest growth in the developing world), Anderson and Bows-Larkin
broke with the pro-growth religion that has dominated climate negotiations
from the beginning. For this they were sharply rebuked by pro-growth politicians at the conference. But they were correct.

Preventing the Fall of the Communist Party
Requires Hyper-Growth Strategies

After years of refusing to commit to any reduction in greenhouse gas emissions on the excuse that China is a developing nation, in November 2014
presidents Obama and Xi jointly committed their countries to reduce emissions. But as a nationalist industrializer in the May Fourth tradition, Xi's
higher priority is to make China a "rich and powerful socialist country"
by 2050.[61] So even if he wrings greater efficiencies out of his industries and
increases the share of electricity produced by renewables to the target of 20
percent from the present 13 percent, these pitiful gains cannot offset the
immense growth in emissions that will result from relentless GDP growth,
as we've noted. Xi can radically suppress China's emissions, or he can build
a rich and powerful Chinese superpower for another decade or more until
collapse. He can't do both.

Historically, China's emissions have roughly tracked its GDP growth rate.[62] In the pre-WTO era (1980–2002), China's emissions from fossil fuel combustion and cement production grew at an average annual rate of 8 percent while its GDP grew by an average of 10 percent per year. From 2002 to 2007, as FDI surged and the economy boomed, China's emissions grew by 13 percent per year, while its GDP grew at 12 percent.[63] Since the 2008 financial crisis, China's economic growth has dropped to 10 percent in 2008 and then below 7 percent per year since 2015, half of its peak in the mid-2000s. In 2018, China's emissions grew by just under 5 percent in 2018, as we noted, 2 percent under the government's reported 6.6 percent GDP gain, if the economy grew at all in that year.[64] Given this historical correspondence—and absent some miracle of decoupling growth from emissions which no other economy has yet managed—the doubling and tripling of China's GDP could double or triple China's CO_2 emissions.

Xi's Designed-to-Fail Carbon Tax

As we noted, China plans to introduce a carbon tax to reduce emissions. But in truth this is just "Potemkin environmentalism." Carbon taxes are not designed to suppress fossil fuel consumption. They're designed to delay or avoid cutting fossil fuel production. If governments really want to suppress fossil fuel consumption they could simply order cuts in production and re-impose rationing like the US government did during the Second World War. But that was a short-term five-year emergency for the US and one that focused on all-out efforts to *boost* oil production and channel it to the military, whereas what we need to do today is to enforce deep and permanent cuts in fossil fuel production until we mostly phase them out. But no capitalist government is going to impose any such draconian cuts because this would slam economic growth, bankrupt most of the world's biggest corporations and plunge the world into depression.

Carbon taxes are thus the perfect pretend solution because they don't impose any cap on output, the cost can be passed on to consumers, and companies can pose as good carbon tax-paying citizens even as fossil fuel production continues to rise. That's why Exxon Mobil, Shell, BP, and other oil giants are practically clamoring for carbon taxes. They're not looking to put themselves out of business.[65] As Myllyvirta and Fergus Green write: "China's much-hyped national carbon tax trading scheme (ETS) . . . will not feature an overall cap on carbon dioxide (CO_2) emissions. Rather it will be a CO_2 *intensity* trading scheme."[66] Reducing intensity without firmly capping emissions gives Beijing the perfect cover to maintain its suicidal hyper-growth-driven emissions.

What's more, in China the whole charade is manifestly fake. Since the government that's imposing the carbon taxes also owns nearly all the polluting mines, cement plants, power plants, steel and aluminum mills, trains, auto plants, airlines, shipping companies, power-hungry data centers, and so on, it would just be taxing itself. If the government wants to keep those companies producing the cement, coal, steel, aluminum, robots, solar panels, wind turbines, electric cars, and telecoms equipment to fulfil its Five-Year Plans and keep its workers working, not to mention building the big data servers to arm its police state, building its Made in China 2025 high-tech industries, building the highways, rails, ships and ports, power plants, and telecoms across Asia on the "New Silk Road"—then it's going to have to "lend" its polluting companies the money to pay the carbon taxes so they can fulfill their planned targets.

In theory Xi could easily impose fossil fuel rationing to suppress consumption since he doesn't have to bother with legislators, environmental reports, courts, or class-action suits. But he's not. Instead, he's doubling down on fossil fuels: His state-owned companies are pumping fossil fuels as fast as they can—tapping African oil fields, piping liquified natural gas (LNG) in from Central Asia, building an LNG terminal in Siberia, drilling in the South China Sea, scouring ocean bottoms for combustible "fire ice," staking claims to drill for oil and gas in the Arctic, ramping up domestic coal production, and building coal plants in dozens of other countries.[67] China is now the world's largest importer of both oil and natural gas.[68] Instead of cutting back on steel production as the government promised it would do in 2015, it is currently at an all-time high in China. The same is true for aluminum.[69] Production of these metals consumes mountains of coal. As economist Christopher Balding observed: "China's economic growth is driven by all the things it says it wants to get rid of."[70]

Xi's Coal-Powered Electric Car "Solution"

We need to kill the automobile age before it kills us.

– George Monbiot[71]

We also noted that China's government plans to ban the sale of fossil fuel-powered cars to ease urban pollution.[72] Elon Musk has opened a Tesla factory in Shanghai. Xi and Musk have been widely applauded for these initiatives. Switching to electric cars could be a gain for the environment, but not necessarily. In China's case, it could actually worsen pollution. First, electric cars are only as clean as their power source. If China's electric grid were powered entirely by renewables then this would be an unequivocal gain for the environment. But Chinese government projections, as well as those by BP and the IEA, indicate that fossil fuels, mainly coal, will be providing the bulk of China's electricity generation through at least 2050.[73] In that case, China would be better off sticking with gasoline-powered cars. In the most optimistic scenario, China National Petroleum projects that coal, oil and gas, and renewables will each provide one third of China's energy mix by 2050. Right now, as we noted in Chapter 4, coal provides 70 percent of electricity generation. Given the trends we've reviewed—the growing investments in coal and local bureaucratic resistance to adopting wind and solar—cutting that share in half in thirty years is going to be tough. What's more, if China's energy generation grows in line with its GDP (electricity consumption actually grew by 8.5 percent in 2018, two points faster than the GDP), the absolute volume of coal-fired generation would increase six-fold from its present level by 2050, even if coal is reduced to one-third of total output. In that case Tesla will need to build electric boats in Shanghai, instead of cars.

Secondly, increasing coal-powered generation to power electric cars will worsen China's already severe public health problems, including lung cancer. Coal combustion produces not only high levels of particulate matter, including PM2.5, but also emits many other toxics like mercury.[74] Any increase in coal-fired power generation is going to be a public health disaster. The coal industry needs to be rapidly phased out not ramped up to power electric cars.

Thirdly, producing billions of batteries and related equipment to power billions of electric cars is hardly a "green" process. Production of the necessary nickel, lithium, cobalt, and rare-earth elements are massively polluting processes.[75] Production of batteries in China, as we noted in Chapter 3, is another nightmare. Pollution from discarded batteries poses yet another concern.

Lastly, the auto industry in China, as in every capitalist country, is built on the principle of designed-in and fashion-driven obsolescence and repetitive consumption. Even if all of China's cars were entirely powered by solar and wind, they would still be responsible for enormous pollution, including CO_2 emissions. Lifetime studies show that when all the factors that go into producing cars are taken into account—extracting the metal ores and producing the steel, aluminum, rubber, plastics, metal plating, glass, upholstery, and paint—the upshot is that "the embodied emissions of a car typically rival the exhaust pipe emissions over its entire lifetime."[76] As it happens, the embodied emissions of electric cars are considerably greater than those of gasoline-powered cars. A study by the Union of Concerned Scientists found that battery electric vehicles (BEVs) release significantly more emissions (15 percent more for a mid-size Nissan Leaf, 68 percent more for the full-size Tesla S) during their production phase than comparable gasoline vehicles, mostly due to the necessary materials and fabrication processes of the lithium-ion batteries.[77] If production emissions equal tailpipe emissions, then the only way to suppress emissions from the auto industry is to make fewer cars. But ever since the 1920s, the auto industry has been based on obsolescence as it ritually pushes "new" but trivially different models every year. The resource waste of all this needless disposability and pointless resource overconsumption is staggeringly unsustainable, in addition to the greenhouse gas emissions.[78] China's government may not be capitalist in name, but nevertheless, it wants to push consumerism and manufacturing jobs, so it buys into this capitalist logic of perpetual and repetitive waste production.

In short, there is no tech solution to auto pollution. The solution to vehicle-generated smog and CO_2 emissions is not so much to replace fossil fuel-powered cars with electric cars, as to redesign our entire transportation systems in order to drastically reduce the production of vehicles (gasoline-powered or electric), take most of the existing cars off the roads, reconsolidate cities, expand public transit, encourage shared vehicles, and bring back bicycles—like an updated version of the bike-bus-train system China had in the 1980s and early 1990s, before the auto craze took off. In other words, "we need to kill the automobile age before it kills us." To the extent that we need cars, and of course we will still need some, we need to make them small, simple, and durable energy-sippers that are endlessly re-buildable and upgradeable—something like the old Volkswagen Beetles that have a virtually infinite working lifespan.[79]

PLANNED DEINDUSTRIALIZATION OR
UNPLANNED ENVIRONMENTAL COLLAPSE?

Marx says that revolutions are the locomotives of world history. But the situation may be quite different. Perhaps revolutions are not the train ride, but the human race grabbing for the emergency brake.
– Walter Benjamin[80]

It goes without saying that the Chinese have every right to modernize, industrialize, and improve their material standard of living. But they don't

How Green is my Coal-Powered High-Speed Train?

The problem of coal as fuel source applies equally to China's renowned high-speed trains. Trains are among the most energy-efficient modes of transportation, so in principle building more lines could help decarbonize China. Indeed, high-speed train travel is reducing demand for short-distance air travel in China. This would be an environmental boon if the country's high-speed trains were all powered by solar and wind energy, but they're not. As we noted earlier, 70 percent of China's electricity is currently supplied by thermal power plants (95 percent coal, 5 percent gas) while solar and wind power account for about 8 percent. So as far as pollution goes, those high-speed trains may as well be hauled along by Mao's vintage steam locomotives. "Studies show that some of China's high-speed lines have relatively large carbon footprints and are chronically underutilized. As China continues to pump money into an ever-expanding rail empire, these projects tell a cautionary tale," says Lili Pike of Chinadialogue. Researchers comparing China's most-traveled high-speed lines with those of Japan, Taiwan, France, and Germany found that even on the busiest line, the Beijing–Shanghai route, China's electric trains have larger carbon footprints than all but the Hannover–Würzburg line in Germany.

And that's the best-case scenario. In what she terms the "white elephant problem" Pike notes that "far from the densely urbanized corridor between Shanghai and Beijing, high-speed rail projects in sparsely populated regions of western and northern China are more tales of caution than low-carbon success." In January 2019, Beijing Transportation University professor Zhao Jian wrote that except for the Beijing–Guangzhou line, China's high-speed train lines are "largely underutilized." That's why China's high-speed trains average, at best, half the utilization rate as those in Japan. Yet as we noted, the thirteenth Five-Year Plan set out plans to add another 30,000 kilometers of high-speed rail lines, disproportionately allocated to the country's western provinces.

What's worse is that while the glory-seeking Communist Party is squandering money on its pet fetish, "high-speed rail's less glamorous cousin, freight rail, has been neglected." Only 17 percent of freight moves by rail now, whereas in 2005, before the high-speed trains were built, 50 percent did. The emissions intensity of freight rail is ten times that of trucks. This means that in China, high-speed trains are dirty twice over, because they're powered by coal and because they've diverted freight traffic to dirty diesel-powered trucks. That's why professor Zhao says that "at present, I don't think any more [high-speed rail] should be built … What should be built now is conventional [passenger and freight] rail. It has a lot of space for growth."

Source: Lili Pike, "How green is China's high-speed rail?" *Chinadialogue*, April 5, 2019, www.chinadialogue.net/article/show/single/en/11174-How-green-is-China-s-high-speed-rail-.

need a "China Dream" of ever-growing consumerism like the capitalist West.[81] They don't need a *higher standard* of living, based on consuming ever-more stuff like Americans. They need a *better mode* of living—clean air, water, and farm soil; safe, nutritious, untainted, and unadulterated food; safe medicines; a shorter working day. They need democracy, independent regulators, courts, and police. They need safe, good-quality housing that doesn't collapse. They need a public transportation system centered on urban bicycles and public transit instead of private cars and ring roads. They need good public schools and universities that encourage free intellectual inquiry, so they don't have to send their children abroad to get a decent education. They need quality socialized medical care instead of the bribe-for-service predatory health care system that they've had to endure since medical care was privatized in the 1990s.[82] We all need to live better by consuming less and consuming rationally, fairly, and sustainably. Given the planet's desperate shape today, the only way humanity is going to survive this century is if developed and developing countries "contract and converge" our resource consumption around a sustainable global average that will permit all the world's peoples to live in acceptable material comfort and dignity while setting aside resources for future generations and also leaving enough for the other life forms with which we share this small blue planet.[83]

Grabbing the Emergency Brake

In October 2018, IPCC climate scientists painted a stark portrait of how quickly the planet is heating up and called on governments to take immediate steps to suppress emissions:

> If emissions continue at [the] current rate, [the] atmosphere will warm by as much as 2.7 [degrees] Fahrenheit, or 1.5 [degrees] Celsius, above preindustrial levels by between 2030 and 2052. Further, warming is more extreme further inland of large water bodies. [To keep temperatures from rising beyond 1.5°C] anthropogenic CO_2 [must] decline by about 45% worldwide from 2010 levels by 2030 . . . [This] would require rapid and far-reaching transitions in energy, land, urban and infrastructure (including transport and buildings), and industrial systems . . . These systems transitions are unprecedented in terms of scale . . . and imply deep emissions reductions in all sectors, a wide portfolio of mitigation options and a significant upswing in those options.[84]

Given the manifest failure of carbon taxes and the like to suppress emissions (because they were designed to fail),[85] the only way we can make the sorts of deep emissions cuts that are needed is for the governments of industrialized nations to declare states of emergency and organize rationally planned, democratically managed industrial drawdowns, shutdowns, and retrenchments. The US, Europe, and Japan would need to shut down and/or drastically curtail fossil fuels and petrochemicals; abolish harmful unsustainable industries, from pesticides to disposable products and the military; drastically curtail auto production and restructure the auto industry; ration air travel and eliminate most air freight; cut back on construction; and rethink and reduce tourism. These countries would need to accelerate the transition to renewable energy; reconsolidate cities; rationalize transportation to replace cars wherever possible with public transportation; encourage shared vehicles; and promote bicycling. It isn't necessary to go back to living in log cabins, only to produce less, consume less, and live differently; minimize instead of maximize resource consumption; "contract and converge" overdeveloped and underdeveloped economies around a sustainable and hopefully satisfactory medium level of consumption; share limited resources; and set aside resources for future generations and other species.

In China's case, such an industrial retreat, reprioritization, and restructuring would likely have to include at least the following:

- *Energy generation*
  Given China's huge dependence upon coal, a priority would be to shut down all non-essential coal-fired power plants. China needs to abandon the hideously polluting coal-to-gas projects, curtail coal-based industries like steel and aluminum production, and curb electricity wasted on pointless manufacturing, Orwellian surveillance systems, useless advertising, and excessive urban illumination. They need to rapidly transition to renewable sources of electricity generation, but with the goal of producing much less electricity overall, closer to what was produced in the early 1990s before the overproduction and overconstruction booms took off. As noted, experts say that China already produces more electricity than it needs, and wastes vast amounts. The US and other developed countries should be obliged to provide extensive technical and material assistance to facilitate this wholesale transition to renewables since the West is responsible for this whole setup.

- *Autos*
  The auto industry would need to be drastically cut back. Transportation is China's second-largest source of CO_2 emissions after electricity generation. Urban transportation should shift to back to bicycles, buses, trains, and subways—basically a modernized and expanded version of what the Chinese had before the auto craze took off. But the air will be cleaner, transportation will be faster, people will be healthier, and resources will be conserved.

- *Aviation, rail, and shipping industries*
  China would need to curtail if not abolish air freight (save for necessities like emergency medical supplies), sharply reduce and ration air travel, and stop promoting unsustainable tourism.[86] It should abandon further expansion of the high-speed rail network, as Chinese experts have recommended. It needs to shut down most of the shipbuilding industry, the bulk of which is geared to building container ships to be filled with unsustainable products and bulk carriers to import the raw coal, iron ore, lumber, and oil needed to produce more unsustainable products.[87] The Chinese, along with Americans and Europeans, need to abolish the cruise ship industry. Cruise ships are by far the biggest per capita polluter in the history of travel. One large cruise liner puts out more, and filthier, emissions in a day than five million cars (the equivalent of all the cars in Beijing). The coastal provinces of China, the Los Angeles basin, and Mediterranean Europe are smothered under layers of bunker fuel fumes from ships.[88]

- *Disposables*
  The Chinese need to abolish production of disposable products, from plastic junk to fast fashion, iPhones, IKEA furniture, and ritual "new model" cars. There's just no way to have sustainable economies in China or anywhere if we don't stop making disposable, designed-to-be-obsolesced, repetitive-consumption products.[89] We need to restructure our economies to produce for need not profit, and make what we do need as durable, long-lasting, re-buildable, upgradeable, recyclable, and shareable as possible.

- *Chemicals*
  China needs an emergency shutdown of non-essential polluting chemical industries. Greenpeace was right when it said that the only solution to many toxic chemicals is the "elimination of their use at the source." They need to be abolished wherever possible and replaced with non-toxics, while those which we do need for critical applica-

tions need to be rigorously controlled by independent regulators. Toxic chemical pollution is, as noted, an existential crisis for China (and the world), one that grows worse with every passing day as the dumping continues.[90] Since China's chemical industries were largely offshored from the US and other industrialized nations, here again the West should be obliged to help China remove and/or contain those toxics.

- *Construction*
  China's construction industry needs to be drastically curtailed. The country is already overbuilt and the population is declining. China, like the US, needs to reconsolidate its cities to shorten commutes, revive communities and street life, turn more land back to nature, and construct buildings that last for centuries instead of decades.[91]

- *Urbanization*
  The urbanization drive needs to be abandoned. Urban life has its attractions, but urbanites consume several times the energy and natural resources, and generate far more pollution, than rural farm families. Besides, most of the hundreds of millions of Chinese families who were "relocated" to the cities by the government in the last three decades did not go voluntarily. Ex-farmers who wish to return to the land should be permitted to do so and supported where possible. There's no law of nature that says farm families must live in poverty. Family farmers with adequate land and technology can market their own produce and do very well, even under capitalism.[92] China's farmers are poor because the Communist Party has been underpaying them in order to fund its industrialization drive for seven decades. The best way to raise rural living standards and improve the health of farmers is give them security in their farms, pay them fair prices for their produce, and help them return to organic farming.[93] And the best way to feed China is for it to grow most of its own food, not to burn down the Amazon rainforest to grow food to feed Chinese workers producing disposable products for export to Americans.

- *Environmental remediation and restoration of public health*
  Chinese environmental and health experts have called for a comprehensive integrated plan to address the nation's environmental and public health issues. Again, a significant share of the costs of this remediation should also be borne by the Western nations whose companies callously contributed to this pollution by offshoring their dirtiest industries to China.

- *A national public works jobs program*
  If China is going to have to shut down and curtail so many industries to brake the drive to ecological collapse, then it is going to have to create new jobs for all those displaced workers. Hundreds of millions of Chinese workers are employed producing unsustainable products and building unsustainable cities. That's a big problem. But unbreathable air, undrinkable water, unsafe food, polluted farmland, cancer, rising temperatures, and rising seas along coastal China are bigger problems. There's just no way around this very inconvenient truth: The producing of unsustainable products and services in China and in all the industrialized nations has to stop, stopping it will disemploy hundreds of millions of workers, and non-destructive, low-carbon jobs have to be found or created for them. In China, there is no shortage of socially and environmentally useful work to do: Environmental remediation, re-forestation, transitioning to organic farming, transitioning to renewable energy, expanding and improving health care, rebuilding and expanding public social services, rebuilding the social safety net, responsibly caring for China's ageing population, and much else.

Needless to say, this sounds extreme. But given the science, I don't see what alternative we have. If we don't quickly suppress emissions, Australia's present will be the world's future. On the positive side, since so much of China's overproduction, overconstruction, and resource waste is completely unnecessary, what sounds like a program for extreme austerity would be just the opposite—liberation, a way to step off the consumerism treadmill and transition a "better mode of life," an opportunity for China's citizens to build the "ecological civilization" that Xi talks about but sabotages every day with his policies and practices.

8

The Next Chinese Revolution

THE COMMUNIST PARTY'S EXISTENTIAL POLITICAL CRISIS

Why is a powerful country like China so afraid of a beauty queen?
– Anastasia Lin[1]

Pan Yue was certainly prescient. The Chinese "miracle" has come to an end because the environment can no longer keep pace. The question is, can the Chinese find a way to grab the emergency brake and wrench this locomotive of destruction to a halt? One thing seems certain: The locomotive is not going to be stopped so long as the Communist Party has its grip on the controls. The CCP is locked in a death spiral. It can't rein in ravenous resource consumption and suicidal pollution because, as a nationalist superpower-aspirant, it needs to maximize growth to "catch up with and overtake the USA," maximize jobs to keep the peace, provide more bread and circuses to distract the masses, and build the glitziest "blingfrastructure" to wow the masses and the world with the "Amazing China" that it has built. The Communist Party doesn't do subtlety or understatement. Given these drivers, I just don't see how China's spiral to ecological collapse can be reversed by anything short of social revolution—one way or another.

The Party leadership presents itself as all-powerful, unassailable, monolithic, confident, and self-assured. It's anything but. The Party is paranoid, terrified of independent thought and the slightest public disagreement, frightened of any personal or institutional autonomy, and shocked by the results of the explosive growth of capitalism that it has unleashed. It is strategically and ideologically bankrupt, demoralized and weakened by Xi's relentless anti-corruption campaign and fracturing as wealthy cadres flee the country and send their families abroad.[2]

For a government that presents itself as a superior model for the world, a deserving successor to the US and the "declining West,"[3] its outwardly unflappable president is surprisingly thin-skinned, bristling at the slightest criticism, let alone mockery—more like Trump than Deng Xiaoping. Xi is terrified not just of beauty queens but Mongolian historians, Uighur professors, Tibetan linguists, the *New York Times*, the *Wall Street Journal*, Google, Instagram, Youtube, Facebook, Twitter, Western movies, artists, democracy advocates, workers, trade unionists, environmental activists, human rights attorneys, Liu Xiaobo (even after his death) and his wife Liu Xia, Christian ministers, Hong Kong booksellers and high school students, Marxist university students, Maoist study groups, the NBA, Turkish soccer stars, and so many other real and imagined threats.[4] In his current state of extreme paranoia, no perceived threat is too insignificant. Like the exasperated journalist Liang Xiangyi who rolled her eyes in disgust at another reporter's unctuous and gushing question to a high official in the Great Hall of the People in Beijing during the March 2018 National People's Congress. Captured by China's national news broadcaster, CCTV, the moment went viral and the government responded by yanking her media accreditation, taking down her Sina Weibo page, and erasing her name from the internet.[5] In recent years Xi's censors have banned cartoonists, hip-hop, video games, the bawdy humor app Neihan Duanzi, Winnie the Pooh, Peppa the Pig, the letter "N," celebrity gossip, Stephen Colbert, and Saturday Night Live.[6]

Chinese women too are posing a threat, like the so-called "Feminist Five."[7] The #MeToo movement particularly worries the powers that be. As one commentator said: "The leadership has understood from the beginning that the movement has shades of anti-authoritarianism and they're afraid the allegations will spread to officials."[8]

In totalitarian self-parody worthy of Armando Iannucci's *The Death of Stalin*, Beijing recently banned exports of black clothing to Hong Kong as the color is favored by protesters.[9] Today, China's leaders face unprecedented threats—and not least from those black-clad protesters in Hong Kong.

Economic Slowdown Fractures the Social Contract

Since the Tiananmen Square protests of 1989, the implicit social contract between the Communist Party and Chinese society has been that "we'll keep the economy booming, provide jobs and consumer goods, and you won't come back to Tiananmen with your protest signs." That strategy worked pretty well for three decades. But the glory days of 10 percent annual GDP growth rates look to be in the rear-view mirror. In 2018, China experienced its slowest economic growth in three decades—a claimed 6.5 percent increase, although many economists think that the true rate was less than half that. The stock market was down by 25 percent for 2018. Factory activity dropped sharply in the second half of the year. Defaults are soaring. The downturn only intensified in 2019.

China's economy has been slowing since 2012, long before Trump's tariffs were imposed. Blame the rapidly ageing population, the shrinking work-force, the falling birth rate (in 2018 it was the lowest since 1961, a year of famine, and 2019 was the lowest since 1949), the slowing global economy, and ever-mounting local debt. In the 1980s and 1990s, China's economic growth was powered by its seemingly bottomless pool of young migrant workers. By 2012, the working-age population had begun to shrink, the inevitable result of the one-child policy that was enacted in 1979. The country now faces a graying population and a dwindling workforce to support it in the decades ahead.[10] The ultra-low labor costs that attracted the world's low-end assembly work to China are an artifact of the past too. As we noted in Chapter 1, striking workers have pushed wages up in export bases like Shenzhen and Shanghai, such that today they match or exceed those of most emerging market economies, making China a less attractive destination for foreign companies.[11]

Layoffs have increased as thousands of low-end assembly factories in the Pearl River Delta migrate to Vietnam, Cambodia, and beyond. The slowdown not only brought layoffs among factory workers but also among educated white-collar workers, even at big tech companies like the online retailer JD.com and Didi Chuxing, China's answer to Uber.[12] Retail sales have slumped across the board. Car sales, smartphone sales, and e-commerce sales all plummeted by double digits in 2018, and the slide has deepened through 2019.[13] Economic stagnation, layoffs, the deflating housing market, falling yuan, and rising inflation are all tearing at the social contract.[14]

Trade surpluses that ran as much as 10 percent per year in the boom years of the mid-2000s funded the renovation and rise of China. The country's trade surplus with the US is still growing, up 11 percent in 2018, a new record, but its global trade surpluses are approaching zero. China recorded its first quarterly trade deficit in 17 years in 2018, and again in 2019.[15] The World Bank, Morgan Stanley, and others predict that trade deficits are going to be a regular feature of China's economy from 2019.[16] That's going to leave Xi with less cash to splash on his Made in China 2025 industrial policy and Belt and Road Initiative.[17]

The government hopes that rising domestic consumption would displace exports and infrastructure as economic drivers, and it has promoted the expansion of consumer credit to that end. But China's 400 million middle-class consumers are now more indebted than Americans or Japanese, and, fearing for the future, people are saving, not spending.[18] Young Chinese whose only experience has been sustained economic growth now face declining job opportunities, stagnant wages, and higher costs of living. As such, they're skipping not just new smartphones, cars, and trips abroad but even marriage and families.[19]

With growth decelerating and without domestic consumption to fill the gap, Xi has once more had to forego suppressing debt and open the spigots to build more unneeded infrastructure, fast-tracking coal-fired power plants, skyscrapers, empty highways, and bridges to nowhere—"more of the things Xi said he wanted to stop building."[20] Useless, but if Xi can't maintain growth, jobs, and consumption, he's going to need more cops.

Strikes and Protests

Labor strife has increased decade after decade, along with growing protests over land grabs, pollution, the siting of chemical plants, incinerators, and coal-fired power plants. Environmental protests frequently involve thousands of people and are often violent.[21] China Labour Bulletin counted 1,700 industrial strikes in 2018, up from 1,200 the year before. In April 2018, the "Changsha Tower Crane Operators Federation" organized a mass strike across dozens of cities on Labor Day (May 1); 10,000 crane operators went on strike in Chengdu alone. This nearly nationwide strike by a spontaneously organized autonomous union—redolent of Poland's Solidarity trade union in 1980—got Beijing's attention; it responded by sending in the police to crush the strike and arrest the leaders. Nevertheless, labor historian Wang Jiangsong has argued that the strike should be "considered the beginning of a historical inflection point in China."[22]

By June truck drivers were striking and army veterans were marching.[23] If the economy continues its downward trajectory, expect more of the above.[24] The Shanghai Municipal Government, desperate to prevent mass layoffs, reportedly ordered not only state companies but even some private companies to keep paying their workers the minimum monthly wage of 2,500 yuan, even though their workforce was totally idled. The salaries of some state employees have been slashed by a third.[25]

In another first for the Xi Jinping era, in spring 2018 incredibly brave students from Peking, Nanjing, and Renmin universities led the formation of a student-worker coalition to back the efforts of workers at Shenzhen Jasic Technology, a manufacturer of welding machines, to form an independent trade union to fight company practices which included weeks of compulsory work without days off, wage theft, and illegal penalties. Solidarity spread nationwide, with independent unions forming in other cities.[26] Adding to Xi's headaches, #MeToo activists joined with labor unionists to broaden the struggle for equality, justice, and labor rights.[27]

Figure 8.1   Jasic Workers Support Group, August 2018. The banners read (front row, from left to right): "Nankai University support group," "Return to us Mengyu, return to us our comrades of the support group, return to us our workers!" "Nanjing University of Chinese Medicine support group"; (back row, from left to right) "Peking University support group," "Beijing University of Language and Culture support group," "Renmin University of China support group."

Credit: Photo and caption courtesy of Jenny Chan and Jasic Workers Support Group © 2018.

Figure 8.2   Nearly 50 members of the Jasic Workers Support Group pose for a group photo on August 20, 2018. From Shenzhen to Huizhou, workers and student supporters were surveilled and tailed by local police and national security officials. Despite growing pressure, they delivered public speeches to draw support from all over the country. They also raised funds to meet the urgent needs of the families of workers at Shenzhen Jasic Technology. In response, on August 24, some 200 policemen in riot gear stormed their rental apartment to arrest them. Worse yet, universities, in collaboration with the Party-state, began to take aim at the students who had been leading the Jasic campaigns since the summer. Marxist university student organizations were either completely dissolved or thoroughly reorganized by the end of the fall semester. As of early February 2019, the Chinese New Year, 55 people—including Jasic Technology workers, students, graduates, supporters, and non-governmental labor activists—were still being detained or had gone missing.

Credit: Jasic Workers Support Group © 2018. Photo and caption courtesy of Jenny Chan.

For "Marxist" Xi Jinping, the students' red banners, their portraits of Mao and Marx were all too much. He crushed the strike in August, arresting dozens of workers and students and throwing them in prison, where most remain. Recognizing that this was a fight that the Party could not afford to lose, Xi again went after Marxist study groups at Peking University in February 2019, arresting student members.[28] More were seized in May.[29] But this repression is only manufacturing enemies among the educated leftist youth that Xi very much needs, and who might have supported the Party in the past, but no more. As the economic downturn continues through 2019, labor unrest and arrests have increased. Whereas in the past the authorities tolerated non-violent labor activism so long as it was strictly geared to job-related issues, now there is "zero tolerance for dissent," according to labor scholar Elaine Hui. In the eighteen months leading up to December 2019, 140 workers, activists, and student supporters were arrested.[30]

From Tech Theft to Concentration Camps, Xi Turns the World Against China

For all his cracking down on corruption at home, Mr. Xi envisions China as a nation of patriotic thieves.

– Yi-Zheng Lian[31]

Since Mao met Richard Nixon in 1972, China's leaders have sought to build good relations with the West. That strategy suffered a blow in 1989, though as the economy boomed and East–West trade surged over the last three decades, hopes grew anew that political change would eventually follow. Those hopes were dashed again when tough guy Xi Jinping took over in 2012 and launched his campaign against "Western values"—fining Western companies and jailing some executives, ramping up tech and intellectual property (IP) theft, imprisoning democracy campaigners and human rights lawyers, installing his surveillance state, and projecting the same aggression and repression abroad as at home. China was losing friends long before Trump came along with his trade war. Obama tried to restrain the PLA's cyberthieves, but Trump is the first, and so far the only, Western leader to have publicly called out the Party's criminal operations for what they are. Regarding state-backed Huawei's program of paying bonuses to its employees for stealing technology and intellectual property from Western companies that they work for, Yi-Zheng Lian, professor of economics at Yamanashi Gakuin University wrote that

Mr. Xi's government has also damaged both China's international reputation and its own moral fabric by encouraging Chinese citizens and entities worldwide to engage in acts of moral turpitude . . . Such a policy is encouraged, even arguably mandatory, under China's 2017 National Intelligence Law. For all his cracking down on corruption at home, Mr. Xi envisions China as a nation of patriotic thieves.[32]

Despite Trump's tariffs, Xi has refused to cave on demands that China stop forced tech transfer, tech and IP theft, stop subsidizing and protecting SOEs against foreign competition, and open up his home market. Xi is happy to buy more soybeans, pigs, microchips, and jetliners but he can't cave on those core demands because they're key to his whole economic setup. His Stalinist state-owned sector is a poor innovator and without domestic IP protection his private sector isn't much better. That's why you don't see any counterparts to Bill Gates, Steve Jobs, or Elon Musk in China. What rational capitalist would risk investing millions today when all their IP could be stolen tomorrow? China's billionaire capitalists like Alibaba's Jack Ma or Huawei's Ren Zhengfei are big and rich because their companies are cosseted, state-funded, state-protected monopolies or near monopolies, not because they're great innovators.[33] China's leaders have been trying to spur "indigenous innovation" for decades with little to show for it.[34] Since Xi's economy has been unable, so far, to invent the advanced technology it needs, the government has been critically dependent upon importing that from the West since Reform and Opening in 1978, largely by forced transfer, and tech and IP theft.[35] (Indeed, Xi's party ideologues reject the very notion that anyone should own intellectual property and firmly defend China's "right" to steal it.)[36] Trump's trade war has only aggravated Xi's systemic problems. Since 2018 growing American and European concerns about Chinese takeovers caused them to curb Chinese investments in Western tech companies, which have dropped sharply in the US since 2018. The US and Europe also blocked further purchases of high-tech companies like Syngenta and Kuka Robotics.[37] As those doors close, they leave Xi with few options but to double down on tech theft, especially cybertheft, which he's doing.[38]

Tariffs or no tariffs, the damage is done and it's as much political as economic.[39] As the extent and depth of the Chinese government's perfidy has become more broadly understood, Trump's trade war became bipartisan in the US, and international.[40] Even the US Chamber of Commerce, which up until a year ago was attacking Trump's tariffs, now says that its members have had enough and back them.[41] Even the Russians are protesting Chinese tech theft.[42]

For a president who tells the world "not to fear China's peaceful rise," Xi finds countless ways to make the world fear China's rise: Locking up and torturing millions of Uighurs in concentration camps and committing cultural genocide to erase their language, history, mosques, and even their cemeteries;[43] committing cultural genocide in Tibet; seizing the South China Sea and plundering fish and petroleum from Vietnamese and Philippine waters; threatening to invade Taiwan; bullying and threatening the US, Canada, Australia, New Zealand, Germany, Sweden, Denmark, and other countries;[44] kidnapping Canadians, Hong Kong booksellers, and Uighur students; shackling vulnerable trade partners in debt traps; defying international law, treaties, and the world court; and attacking Western scholars. Most recently, Xi personally threatened a gruesome death to the "splitters" in Taiwan and Hong Kong in pungent prose: "Their bodies [will be] smashed and bones ground to powder."[45]

Yet Xi's sociopathic behavior is stunningly self-defeating. He's not only turning the world against China but turning many Chinese against his thuggery and lawlessness, while giving ammunition to his enemies in the Party. With tariffs hammering China's growth, stocks, and the yuan in the spring of 2018, state media was ordered to stop mentioning Made in China 2025, rescind the hype about China's tech supremacy, and dial back the cult of Xi Jinping (at least for a while).[46] Xi's humiliation prompted invidious comparisons between his triumphalist braggadocio and Deng Xiaoping's slogan, "Hide your capabilities, bide your time" (*taoguang yanghui*).[47] There's even talk about the "specter of collapse."[48] With China's own citizens too terrified to openly oppose the government, some are whispering that "only Trump can save China." According to Zhu Ning, an economist at Tsinghua University, "the trade war is a good thing. It gives us hope when we're hopeless."[49]

HONG KONG'S THREAT TO THE COMMUNIST PARTY

If Xi didn't have enough problems he also faces an existential crisis in Hong Kong, the only city in China where people are free to speak their mind. Under the terms of the "Basic Law"—Hong Kong's mini-constitution—residents enjoy most of the freedoms found in Western capitalist democracies: The right to vote and stand for election to public office (Article 26); the right to "freedom of speech, of the press and of publication; freedom of association, of assembly, of procession and of demonstration; the right and freedom to form and join trade unions, and to strike" (Article 27); the right to "freedom of person" including protection against "arbitrary or unlawful arrest, detention or imprisonment" and security against "arbitrary or unlawful search of, or intrusion into, a resident's home or other premises" (Articles 28 and 29); freedom of movement within the Special Administrative Region, freedom of conscience, freedom of religion, and freedom of occupation (Articles 31–33). It also guarantees that Hong Kong "shall be vested with independent judicial power, including right of final adjudication" (Article 19).[50]

Further, while the city's chief executive "shall be selected by election or through consultations held locally and appointed by the Central People's Government" (an arrangement that has enabled Beijing to appoint party loyalists to the post since 1997),[51] Article 45 explicitly promises that "the ultimate aim is the selection of the chief executive by universal suffrage upon nomination by a broadly representative nominating committee in accordance with democratic procedures." Article 68 extends this same promise to the election of city legislators.

However, and perhaps most importantly, Article 158 gives Beijing the power to *interpret* the Basic Law, a power which it has frequently wielded by issuing "decisions" countermanding its initial intent.[52]

China's Berlin

The Basic Law was a compromise worked out between Britain and Deng Xiaoping in 1984, when China was still mostly an agrarian economy. Deng was willing to grant Hong Kong "a high degree of autonomy," let it keep its bourgeois freedoms and limited political democracy, with a promise that "the socialist system and policies" would not be practiced in Hong Kong and that "the previous capitalist system and way of life" would "remain unchanged for 50 years" (Article 5), because of his certainty that in 2047 China would take over the city and demolish those rights, freedoms, and institutions.

But Deng's successors have grown impatient to extinguish those freedoms and fold the "two systems" into the one that they own, because they fear that Hongkongers, imbued with Western ideas about freedom, democracy, and rule of law could spread those subversive ideas to the mainland. That's why, in August 2019, China's ambassador to the US, Cui Tiankai, said that "currently, the biggest peril for 'One Country Two Systems' comes from ill-intentioned forces, both inside and outside Hong Kong, who seek to turn the SAR [Hong Kong Special Administrative Region] into a bridgehead to attack the mainland's system and spark chaos across China."[53] Long before Xi began threatening to smash the bodies of separatists, Beijing had already reneged on its promises and taken increasingly brazen steps to erode those rights and freedoms. This is what the huge protests and street battles are all about; this is what millions of Hongkongers have been protesting with boundless energy and marvelous creativity for more than two decades.[54]

Thus, in July 2012, in defiance of the Party's promise in Article 5 not to impose its "socialist system," Beijing tried to force its "moral and national" school curriculum into Hong Kong schools. Course material extolled the benefits of one-party rule and equated multi-party democracy with chaos. Tens of thousands of mostly high school students protested this attempt to introduce crude brainwashing, led by the then fifteen-year-old Joshua Wong and his Scholarism student organization. In late August, 100,000 protesters laid siege to the government headquarters for ten days until the government backed down and dropped the proposal. In November 2019, Xi vowed to try again, calling for a new push to introduce "love the country, love the Communist Party" patriotic brainwashing in Hong Kong schools.[55]

In October 2015, in defiance of Articles 27 and 28, mainland agents kidnapped five Hong Kong booksellers and imprisoned them on the mainland for selling tell-all books about the corrupt and scandalous lives of Party grandees, including Xi's relations. In 2017, Party-linked gangsters reportedly abducted a democracy activist and tortured him.[56]

In 2016 six newly elected members of Hong Kong's Legislative Council (LegCo) were ousted because they refused to "solemnly swear" that they loved China as much as they loved Hong Kong.[57] The Hong Kong government has barred others from running for office, including Agnes Chow, a prominent student leader during the 2014 protests in Hong Kong, and most recently Joshua Wong in October 2019—again ignoring the right to free speech and imposing political tests of fealty to Beijing and the Communist Party, contrary to Article 27.[58]

In March 2019, Hong Kong's chief executive, Carrie Lam, proposed an extradition bill which would have given Beijing the right to extradite anyone to the mainland without a court order and without due process— precisely the arbitrary arrest, detention, and imprisonment prohibited by the Basic Law. The bill would have "sealed . . . the death of the 'one country, two systems' principle," said Joshua Wong.[59] Lam's proposal ignited what has become the largest and longest-sustained resistance movement against Beijing's totalitarianism, and one that quickly broadened to include universal suffrage and other democratic demands. Tens of thousands marched on April 28 to protest the law. On June 6, 3,000 lawyers marched in black to protest the extradition law. On June 9, one million turned out to protest, and on June 16, nearly two million. Mass protests have followed every weekend, involving trades unions, lawyers, civil servants, doctors and hospital staff, accountants, "gray hairs" (retirees), teachers, and students. On July 21, after hundreds of thousands protested in various parts of the city, some were violently beaten by white-shirted gangs while the police looked on.[60] On August 5 a general strike shut down the airport, schools, and many businesses. On August 18 an estimated 1.7 million protesters paraded through the city to Victoria Park. On September 2, thousands of university and secondary students boycotted classes. The same day, Lam apologized for causing "unforgiveable havoc"; two days later, on September 4, she formally withdrew the extradition bill. That was an important concession, but too little too late. Democracy protesters insist on "five demands, not one less"—the other four being the establishment of an independent inquiry into police violence; the retraction of the protests' designation as a "riot" (a charge which can bring a ten-year prison sentence) and amnesty for arrested protesters; the resignation of Lam; and direct elections.

By the fall of 2019 the protesters had fought the Hong Kong government to a standstill. In August, Beijing threatened to send in the army and even distributed a training video of Chinese soldiers practicing shooting black-clad Hong Kong protesters.[61] Xi obviously has the power to crush Hong Kong. But then what? With its nuclear arsenal the US could have easily "won" its war in Vietnam too, but the cost would have been unbearable. That's Xi's dilemma today. Crushing Hong Kong would invite devastating world opprobrium, global anti-China boycotts, the collapse of tourism, the flight of Western businesses, and the end of Xi's dream of superpower status. It's far from certain that he could even subdue a city of 7.5 million, most of whom revile his bloodstained Party. Graffiti sprayed on walls all over Hong Kong reads: "CHINAZI—IF WE BURN YOU BURN WITH US!"[62] Xi knows all this, which is why for all his bombast he's something of a "paper tiger" for now, though the Party has other weapons.

The Specter of Democracy Contagion

In Taiwan, we don't worship our president, we criticize our president.
– Miao Poya, pro-independence member
of the Taipei City Council[63]

This interregnum gives Hong Kong's valiant democracy activists space and time to mobilize and build connections with resisting workers and anti-totalitarians inside and outside of China,[64] to build a united front for democracy with Taiwan, and to turn Hong Kong into that "bridgehead to attack the mainland's system."

On November 24, 2019, during a thirteen-day student occupation of Hong Kong Polytechnic University in which thousands of mostly high-school students battled the cops with bricks, bows and arrows, and Molotov cocktails, Hong Kong went ahead with its scheduled district council election. This election was for one of the lowliest elected offices in the city, responsible for community issues like bus stops and traffic lights. Voter turnout is typically low, but this time it was a record 70 percent, delivering a stunning electoral victory for pro-democracy parties, who captured 389 of 452 seats, up from only 124 prior to the election. Pro-China parties were humiliated, hanging on to just 56 seats, down from 300. "There has been a very deep awakening of the Hong Kong people," said Alan Leong, chairman of the Civic Party, one of the largest pro-democracy parties in Hong Kong.[65] Beijing was blindsided and left speechless. Its media suddenly fell silent. Like dictators everywhere, Xi and his Party believed their own propaganda, so much so that state newspapers had already prepared headlines for the morning editions trumpeting the victory of the "silent majority" of Hongkongers who "love the Communist Party" but who, it turned out, do not exist.

Beijing ignored the election results and state media played endlessly looping videos of what it termed "rioters," "terrorists," and "enemies of the people" battling the police at Polytechnic University. Once again, *People's Daily* declared, protests show how "democracy fuels chaos." State media denounced the protesters for "paralyzing traffic, storming government offices, vandalizing public property, setting fires, attacking the police ... and turning Hong Kong ... into the base camp of violent radicals and weapon factories."[66] One might expect that all this trashing and violence would turn the people of Hong Kong against the protesters. No doubt, many oppose the violence. But apparently many more support the protesters. On December 8, 800,000 people turned out in a vast show of public support for those "violent" "enemies of the people" in another deafening rebuke to Lam and the CCP.[67]

Beijing says that the protests were instigated and funded by the "black hands" of the CIA. But the democracy movement didn't need CIA help. From the start, thousands of Hong Kong citizens from all walks of life spontaneously came together in a multi-class, intergenerational expression of solidarity to build an impressive behind-the-scenes provisioning network bringing the young protesters food, money, and supplies including prepaid travel cards, respirators, helmets, disguises, and of course umbrellas. Since June they have raised more than $10 million in small donations to pay legal fees and medical bills. They buy plane tickets to Taiwan for those who fear long prison terms. They organize fleets of late-night "school buses"—private cars chauffeured by parents and adult supporters—to evade the police and ferry protesters safely back home after street battles. "Aunties" and "uncles" stand between protesters and police to try to defuse tensions. Lawyers volunteer to help get protesters out of jail. Doctors set up first aid stations to treat injuries.[68]

On December 22, 2019 more than 1,000 Hongkongers turned out waving the blue flag of "East Turkestan" in solidarity with Xinjiang Uighurs, the first pro-Uighur protest on Chinese soil and exactly the sort of bridgehead that Xi fears.[69] Also in December, angry employees at Huawei's factories in Shenzhen took to social media in early December to express their outrage when an engineer who quit the company after 13 years was arrested and jailed for 251 days after demanding his accumulated benefits. The uproar forced a court to release him and awarded $15,000 in compensation. In tens of thousands of viral posts on Sina Weibo, employees drew parallels between their struggle and the situation in Hong Kong. They repurposed the Hongkongers' five demands by calling for an independent inquiry into the actions of Huawei and the Shenzhen police, universal suffrage, and other demands. Millions of people in China read those posts before censors took them down.[70]

Xi's thuggish crackdowns on Hong Kong democracy protesters and threats against Taiwan have had precisely the opposite of their intended effect: They've deepened, broadened and empowered democratic forces in Hong Kong, forging them into a genuine mass anti-CCP movement. And they've galvanized support for Taiwan's pro-independence president Tsai Ing-wen. Even the China-friendly Kuomintang (KMT) party now opposes reunification, effectively dooming the prospects for any kind of Hong Kong-style "one country, two systems" outcome in Taiwan.[71] In August, the government scoffed at Xi's threats and offered refuge and political amnesty to fleeing Hong Kong protesters.[72] With the democracy contagion beginning to "spark chaos" on the mainland itself, a worse set of outcomes for the CCP could hardly be imagined.

At the end of the day, the only guarantee of democracy in Hong Kong is democracy in China. True, there's no evidence of any such movement at the moment. But why did Xi's ambassador say that the Hong Kong democracy movement is the "biggest peril" his Party faces if there isn't something to it? And if the mainland Chinese "love and cherish the Communist Party" like Xi claims, why doesn't he trust them? Why does he need to surveil their every waking moment and lock them all up behind his "Great Firewall"?[73] What's he afraid of?

IS THE COMMUNIST PARTY CRACKING UP?

The people don't need freedom. These years are the best of all.
  – Lyrics from "The People Don't Need Freedom" by Li Zhi[74]

Everyone feels they are in danger. . . . How do we make progress, how can we produce innovations in this environment?
  – Professor You Shengdong (fired from Xiamen University in 2018 for criticizing Party propaganda slogans)[75]

There is no university in China that has freedom of thought or academic independence. Thought control has been one of the critical parts of the Communist Party's governance . . . Art should serve politics; intellectuals should serve the party. This has always been the rule. It has never been changed, and it will never be changed.
  – Professor Peidong Sun, Fudan University[76]

In March 2018, a triumphant Xi was at the top of his game. His personal cult had reached its apogee as the Party "legislature" jettisoned term limits, permitting him to rule for life, and inscribed his featherbrained "thoughts" in the constitution, alongside the sacred scribblings of Chairman Mao. But having centralized all power in his hands and having asserted that all correct ideas came from him and him alone, he was increasingly vulnerable should problems arise. They were not long in coming. The ZTE affair in April was a stunning setback, deflating Xi's balloon and exposing the pretentions of his high-tech self-sufficiency rhetoric.[77] Trump's first round of tariffs on July 6, 2018 blindsided the Party leadership. Later that month, revelations came out about tainted vaccines that were produced by multiple manufacturers and given to hundreds of thousands of children—the third big drug scandal since 2010, despite repeated crackdowns on corruption and incompetent regulators. Infuriated parents protested across the country forcing Xi himself to publicly order yet another crackdown.[78] By summer the country seemed adrift, public trust had been shattered yet again, and discontent had begun to surface. On July 4, a young woman in Shanghai streamed a live video of herself dousing a poster of Xi with black ink in protest against his "authoritarian tyranny." That got her arrested and sent to a psychiatric hospital, confirming her thesis.[79]

The Monolith Fractures and the "Supremo" Comes Under Attack

Who's going to be the first to stick their head above the parapet?

– Zhang Lifan[80]

In late July, Xu Zhangrun, a professor of constitutional law at Beijing's prestigious Tsinghua University, published a scorching, erudite, and sarcastic jeremiad against Xi entitled "Imminent fears, immediate hopes."[81] Capturing the zeitgeist of revolt against Xi's Orwellian China, Xu accused "the Supremo" of returning China to "KGB-style control" and Maoist totalitarianism. "After 40 years of reform, suddenly we are back in the ancien régime," he said. He attacked "the gunpowder stench of militant ideology," the renewed push to "Put Politics in Command," and the "renewed imposition of Thought Reform." After decades in which it seemed that "the Totalitarian was transitioning towards the Authoritarian," Xu said, "we have seen things moving in the opposite direction, ergo the widespread anxiety that we may all be witnessing a 'Thorough-Going Return to Totalitarian Politics'. . . . Without Intellectual Freedom . . . what hope is there for people to explore the unknown, for the advancement of scholarship or for intellectual creativity?" What indeed? Xu urged the Communist Party Congress to reinstate the two-term limit on the presidency, end the cult of Xi, rehabilitate those punished for the Tiananmen Square protests in 1989, and move the country toward a constitution-based rule of law. Xu's bombshell brought a few more heads above the parapet.[82] Xi responded with a vintage retro-Maoist "struggle campaign" of thought reform against insufficiently patriotic intellectuals.[83] But as Xu said, "people cannot be duped like the hapless and uncomplaining subjects of yesteryear." In March 2019 Xu was suspended and "placed under investigation," which normally means he will be tried (or not) and fired or even sent to prison. Xu responded to his suspension two days later with another defiant essay entitled "I will not submit, I will not be cowed."[84]

In December 2019 Xi took the final step of formally outlawing critical thinking and free speech in schools and universities. The Ministry of Education announced articles of amendment to the charter of Shanghai's prestigious Fudan University—long considered one of the country's most liberal academic institutions—that stripped out all references to "freedom of thought" (*sixiang ziyou*). The amendments placed absolute adherence to

Communist Party rule over academic independence.[85] This triggered a rare and risky protest by students, who gathered in a cafeteria to sing the school anthem, the lyrics of which include references to "academic independence" and "freedom of thought."[86] In place of those, the charter revision substituted references to "serving the governance of the Communist Party" and "dedication to patriotism," according to a notice posted on the website of the Ministry of Education.[87] Taking its cue from Xi's Qin dynasty-era totalitarian anti-intellectualism, the ministry also ordered all primary and secondary schools to "firmly cleanse" their libraries of reading material deemed illegal, improper, or outdated, in order to "create a healthy and safe environment for education." Thus, after a 2,000-year hiatus, Chinese librarians are once again burning books. In October, employees of a county public library in Gansu province set fire to 65 "illegal publications" in front of the library.[88] For good measure, Xi is also shutting the last independent bookstores in China.[89]

Xi's trying hard but he can't lock the whole population up in psychiatric hospitals and concentration camps. He's already spending more on internal "stability maintenance costs" than he spends on the military.[90] But these iron-fisted crackdowns just underscore his weaknesses, and the harder he cracks down the worse his problems become. The more he cracks down on popular culture and the internet, dumbs down schools, and invades and polices students' personal lives, the more he's driving generations of young people—the youth he needs most—away from the Communist Party. The more he cracks down on political deviation and freedom of thought, burns books, and shutters think tanks and bookstores, the more his paralyzed cadres, industrial managers, and scientists fear taking any initiative that could come back to haunt them.[91] It's hard to see how this is going to help his "indigenous innovation" drive, without which he won't be able to achieve his "China Dream" of superpower status. It didn't work for Stalin and Khrushchev either.

With all the enemies Xi has made in the Party, the knives are out and he can't trust anyone.[92] In November, an anonymous official sent a tranche of 403 pages of internal documents detailing China's torture program in Xinjiang to the *New York Times*. The papers included secret speeches given by Xi that outlined the program of imprisonment, torture, brainwashing, and family separation which has involved millions of Uighurs, Kazaks, and other ethnic minorities. The leaked papers are a shocking condemnation of Xi, smuggled out by one of his own "to prevent him from escaping culpability" and discredit him on the world stage. A few days later, another disloyal official leaked a copy of the operations manual for running the mass detention camps in Xinjiang and exposed the mechanics of the region's Orwellian system of mass surveillance and "predictive policing."[93] More than enough to get Xi arrested and tried in the Hague for crimes against humanity—if the world had any more prosecutors like Baltasar Garzon.[94]

Long before his latest crises, his social base of graft-soaked Party cadres and crony capitalists could see the writing on the wall and were heading for the exits. Surveys show that China's rich have been getting out, buying homes and sending their kids to school in the "declining West." (Trump notwithstanding, the US was still their top destination in 2018.) China Merchants Bank found that by 2013, "among those mainland business owners who possess over 100 million [yuan] (about $16 million), 27 percent have already emigrated, while another 47 percent are considering emigrating." The 2018 Hurun China Rich List found that 37 percent of those it surveyed were considering emigration.[95] From Los Angeles to Melbourne, locals are being priced out of housing markets as Chinese buy up foreign homes as investments and safe havens. In Vancouver alone in 2014 more than 45,000 Chinese millionaires queued up to apply for green card residence permits in return for five-year interest free loans of $800,000 to the government, prompting public outrage that forced the Canadian government to shut the program down.[96] Chinese spent $40 billion on overseas home purchases in 2017, defying new laws against taking money out of the country.[97] Money has been leaving China at a record rate in 2019 as the government is trying to staunch the flow to prevent the sort of financial panic that sapped its reserves by hundreds of billions of dollars in 2015.[98]

If Xi's "Amazing China" is "on the rise" and destined to replace the "declining West" as the "new model for the world," as his media trumpets every day, one would expect that lots of people would want to move there. Just the opposite. Xi should be asking himself, "why do so many want out?"[99] This has to be the first ruling class in history that's abandoning its own "miracle economy" en masse. And it's not just the rich. Smog, food safety concerns, vaccine scandals, a rigid educational system, Party-controlled school curricula, toxic school food, toxic schools,[100] corruption, police-state censorship, lack of freedom, and arbitrary state power are driving more and more middle-class Chinese to join the exodus.[101] Mandarin is almost a second language in my neighborhood of Chelsea in Manhattan. Ex-PRC Chinese have long been the fastest-growing immigrant population in New York State, and Chinese have been the largest immigrant group in the US since 2013.

CAPITALISM OR ECOSOCIALISM?

No doubt many in China yearn for a transition to a capitalist democracy like in Taiwan or the US. Who wouldn't? That's what Hongkongers are fighting for today. That was the thrust of Lu Xiaobo's "Charter 08" manifesto, which called for freedom, democracy, constitutional rule, rule of law, human rights, independent regulators, an independent judiciary, equal opportunity, and an open educational system—but also for privatization of state assets, market competition, and the institution and guarantee of private property.[102]

But capitalism, democratic capitalism, or even "green capitalism" is no solution for China's environmental crisis, because around the world democratic capitalism and green capitalism are racing China off the cliff to extinction. Corporations aren't necessarily evil, though plenty of them are very evil. They just can't help themselves. They're doing what they're supposed to do because their legal and fiduciary responsibility is to maximize profits for their owners. Under capitalism, profit maximization is an iron rule that trumps all else. But this means that so long as most of the world economy is based on private ownership and competitive production for market we're doomed to collective suicide. No amount of tinkering with the market can brake the drive to global environmental and ecological collapse. We can't shop our way to sustainability because the problems we face cannot be solved by individual choices in the marketplace. They require collective democratic control over the economy to prioritize the needs of society and the environment. And they require national and international economic planning to reorganize the economy and redeploy labor and resources to these ends. If humanity is to save itself, we have no choice but to cashier both Western capitalism and China's communist capitalism and replace them both with some form of mostly publicly owned, and democratically planned and managed ecosocialist economy.[103]

Synchronized Revolutions in China and the United States?

The great sci-fi master, ecosocialist, and enduring optimist Kim Stanley Robinson concludes his near-future thriller *Red Moon* with simultaneous uprisings by millions of Chinese workers in Beijing and millions of Americans in Washington DC. That's certainly what the world needs right now. Improbable? Of course. But if we're going to prevent global climate collapse we need wholesale system change, especially in China and the US; one way or another, and we can't wait till 2047.[104] I'm not suggesting that revolution is the only solution for China. Taiwan transitioned from dictatorship to capitalist democracy without a revolution. So did South Korea. "Velvet" revolutions brought down the Soviet regimes in Eastern Europe with almost no bloodshed after 1989. Some have imagined an elite-led transition to capitalist democracy in China rather than a popular revolution.[105] Who knows? We can't predict such things. But one way or another, the CCP is headed for the dustbin of history. The East German Stalinists never saw it coming either. Yet however it falls, my contention here is that transitioning to capitalist democracy is not enough to save China or the world from climate collapse because no capitalism, green or otherwise, can accept the drastic changes we need to make to save ourselves. The solution for China, and for the rest of the world, is ecosocialist democracy not capitalist democracy.

China's Long Struggle for Democracy

Some are asking: Can the Hong Kong protesters win? My answer is that if they persist, they cannot lose. This is a struggle over human values—freedom, justice, dignity—and in that realm the Hong Kong people have already won. Yes, if they give up, then the machine will take over. But while a brutal dictatorship might outlast them, it can never "win." It is human nature to have ideals and to put them into action. A dictatorship cannot change those facts. Its defeat is only a matter of time.

– Ai Weiwei[106]

It always seems impossible until it's done.

– Nelson Mandela

The struggle for democracy has a long history in China.[107] From the May Fourth Movement that championed "Mr. Science and Mr. Democracy" to the workers' revolution of the 1920s, the Democracy Wall movement of 1978, the Tiananmen Square protests of 1989, the Charter 08 petition, and the Hong Kong protestors' call for "revolution in our time"—the long history of popular struggles in modern China have all shared the common objective of democratization. The most radical of those have envisioned democratization of the economy as well as politics. Therein lies China's best hope.

Will the Chinese People Stand Up?

Will it be the crane operators, the trade war, the collapse of farming on the North China Plain, or the Hong Kong democracy movement? Xi would like the world to believe that China's masses are deliriously happy in their hermetically sealed Communist Party theme park, surrounded and protected by the "Great Firewall" from the evil "spiritual pollution" of "Western" ideas like trades unions, elections, democracy, and freedom of thought. He wants the world to believe that the last remaining roadblocks in the way of China's "inevitable rise" to world supremacy are imposed by the jealous West, in particular Trump, who wants to "hold China back." But Xi doesn't need Trump's help holding China back. From the famines caused by Mao's Great Leap Forward to the crackdown on protesters in Tiananmen Square, from the Sichuan school building collapses to the Xinjiang prison camps, from north China's "airpocalyptic" smog to Xi's war on democracy in Hong Kong, the Communist Party has capably held China's masses back for seven decades all by itself. The Communist Party's nationalist obsession with overtaking the West and reclaiming the imagined "glory" of China's feudal era is not going to stop the looming ecological collapse. As this book has tried to show, the Party's concern with maximizing growth at any cost and its lust for grandiose prestige projects, needless industries, and one-upping the West have turned China into the leading driver of planetary collapse. Xi can keep his pedal to the metal driving China and the world off the cliff to collapse, or he can slam on the brakes, shut down China's engines of environmental destruction, and build that ecological civilization. He can't do both.

On October 29, 2019 climate scientists published new research showing that on present trends, global warming is going to "all but erase" Shanghai, Shenzhen, and "most of the world's great coastal cities by 2050"—barely *thirty years* from now. There won't be any "great rejuvenation" and glory for the Communist Party when Shanghai and Shenzhen are underwater, when China's glaciers melt and its rivers dry up, when farming collapses across the North China Plain. There will be famine and collapse, untold human suffering, and ecological apocalypse.[108]

The Party can't solve the country's environmental crisis—the worst crisis it has ever created. Only the initiative of China's immensely creative, talented, and industrious but long-suppressed citizens, freed from the police-state shackles that hold them back, can open the way for them to join with others around the world struggling to "grab the emergency brake," to create an emergency plan to save our planet, and to create a global ecological civilization.

When Mao Zedong proclaimed the establishment of the People's Republic from the balcony of the Tiananmen Gate of the Forbidden City on October 1, 1949, he declared that "The Chinese people have stood up." At the end of

Under the Dome, Chai Jing does something few Chinese dare to do publicly: She calls on her fellow citizens to take action, to report violations of environmental laws, to stand up and demand change. "It's tens of millions of ordinary people," she says, "one day they say 'no.' I'm not satisfied. I don't want to wait. I'm not going to shirk the responsibility. I'm going to stand up and do something. I'm going to do it right now. At this moment. At this place."[109]

It's time the Chinese people stood up again. The fate of their nation and the fate of the planet depend greatly on them.

Appendix

Table 5.1   Net inflows to China of foreign direct investment, 1982–2018 [billions of US dollars]

Year	US dollars	Year	US dollars
1982	430	2001	47,053
1983	636	2002	53,074
1984	1,258	2003	57,901
1985	1,659	2004	68,117
1986	1,875	2005	104,109
1987	2,314	2006	124,082
1988	3,194	2007	156,249
1989	3,393	2008	171,535
1990	3,487	2009	131,057
1991	4,366	2010	243,703
1992	11,156	2011	280,072
1993	27,515	2012	241,214
1994	33,787	2013	290,298
1995	35,849	2014	268,097
1996	40,180	2015	242,489
1997	44,237	2016	174,750
1998	43,751	2017	166,084
1999	38,753,	2018	203,492
2000	42,095		

Balance of payments, current US dollars
Source: The World Bank

Table 5.2   China's current account balance, 1982–2018 [billions of US dollars]

Year	US dollars	Year	US dollars
1982	4.37	2001	28.084
1983	2.475	2002	37.383
1984	−32,000,000	2003	35.821
1985	−12.592	2004	51.174
1986	−7.589	2005	124.627
1987	291	2006	208.919
1988	−4.06	2007	308.036
1989	−4.92	2008	348.838
1990	10.668	2009	220.13
1991	11.601	2010	223.024
1992	4.998	2011	181.904
1993	−11.497	2012	231.845
1994	7.611	2013	235.38
1995	11.958	2014	221.229
1996	17.551	2015	357.871
1997	42.824	2016	255.737
1998	43.837	2017	217.01
1999	30.641	2018	102.921
2000	28.874		

Balance of payments, current US dollars
Source: The World Bank

Table 5.3   China's GDP, 1978–2018

Year	Growth Rate (%)	GDP (US dollars, selected years)	Year	Growth Rate (%)	GDP (US dollars, selected years)
1978	11.7	149,541,000	1999	7.1	
1979	7.6		2000	8	
1980	7.8		2001	8.3	
1981	5.2		2002	9.1	
1982	9.1		2003	10	
1983	10.9		2004	10.1	
1984	15.2		2005	9.9	
1985	13.5		2006	11.1	
1986	8.8		2007	14.2	
1987	11.6		2008	9.6	4,594,000,000
1988	11.3	312,354,000	2009	9.2	
1989	4.1		2010	10.6	
1990	3.8		2011	9.5	
1991	9.2		2012	7.7	
1992	14.2		2013	7.7	
1993	13.5		2014	7.3	
1994	12.6		2015	6.9	
1995	10.5		2016	6.7	
1996	9.6		2017	6.9	
1997	8.8		2018	6.5	13,608,000,000
1998	7.8	1,029,000,000			

Current US dollars
Source: The World Bank

Table 6.1   China's foreign exchange reserves, 1978–2019 [billion of US dollars, end-year]

Year	US dollars	Year	US dollars
1977	2.3	1999	146.2
1978	1.6	2000	165.6
1979	2.2	2001	212.2
1980	2.5	2002	286.4
1981	5.1	2003	403.3
1982	11.3	2004	609.9
1983	15.0	2005	818.9
1984	17.4	2006	1,066.3
1985	12.7	2007	1,528.2
1986	11.5	2008	1,946.0
1987	16.3	2009	2,399.2
1988	18.5	2010	2,847.3
1989	18.0	2011	3,181.1
1990	29.6	2012	3,311.6
1991	43.7	2013	3,821.3
1992	20.6	2014	3,843.0
1993	22.4	2015	3,330.4
1994	52.9	2016	3,010.5
1995	75.4	2017	3,140.0
1996	107.0	2018	3,070.0
1997	142.8	2019	3,186.3
1998	149.2		

Source: State Administration of Foreign Exchange of the People's Republic of China and People's Bank of China

References

All hyperlinks accessed before December 31, 2019.

PREFACE

1. China's CO2 emissions in 2018 totaled 13,442 million metric tons of CO2 equivalent, while the emissions from the US, India, Russia, Japan, and Germany in that year totaled 13,700 million metric tons; Climate Action Tracker, "Climate Action Tracker global emissions time series: China" (2018), https://climateactiontracker.org/countries/china.

INTRODUCTION

1. Nectar Gan, "Xi Jinping Thought—the Communist Party's tighter grip on China in 16 characters," *South China Morning Post*, October 25, 2017, www.scmp.com/news/china/policies-politics/article/2116836/xi-jinping-thought-communist-partys-tighter-grip-china; Chris Buckley and Steven C. Meyers, "China's leader says Party must control 'all tasks' and Asian markets slump," *New York Times*, December 18, 2018, www.nytimes.com/2018/12/18/world/asia/xi-jinping-speech-china.html.
2. Richard Smith, "China's communist-capitalist ecological apocalypse," *Real-World Economics Review*, no. 71 (May 2015): 19–63, www.paecon.net/PAEReview/issue71/Smith71.pdf.
3. Climate Action Tracker, "Climate Action Tracker global emissions time series: US" (2018), https://climateactiontracker.org/countries/usa; "Climate Action Tracker global emissions time series: China" (2018). The measuring of CO2 emissions is fraught with uncertainties, and is made even more difficult in China's case because climate scientists are dependent upon government figures of uncertain veracity. For example, in 2015 researchers discovered that for years China had been burning up to 17 percent more coal than it had previously disclosed. Since there's no way to directly measure CO2 emissions from millions of sources, emissions estimates are based mainly on reported or estimated quantities of fossil fuels burned. As China's reported figures are problematic, estimates sometimes vary. See Jan Ivar Korsbakken et al., "Uncertainties around reductions in China's coal use and CO2 emissions," *Nature Climate Change*, March 28, 2016, www.nature.com/articles/nclimate2963; Chris Buckley, "China burns much more coal that reported, complicating climate talks," *New York Times*, November 3, 2015.
4. "Climate Action Tracker global emissions time series: US" (2018).
5. "Climate Action Tracker global emissions time series: EU" (2018), https://climateactiontracker.org/countries/eu.

6. Lauri Myllyvirta and Emma Howard, "'Globally significant': China's emissions keep on rising," *Greenpeace*, September 21, 2018, https://unearthed.greenpeace.org/2018/09/21/china-emissions-rise-2018.

7. Jess Shankleman, "Xi at Davos urges Trump to stay in 'hard won' Paris climate deal," *Bloomberg*, January 16, 2017, www.bloomberg.com/news/articles/2017-01-16/climate-experts-see-xi-touting-clean-energy-leadership-at-davos; Sam Geall, "Clear waters and green mountains: Will Xi Jinping take the lead on climate change?" *Lowy Institute*, November 16, 2017, www.lowyinstitute.org/publications/clear-waters-and-green-mountains-will-xi-jinping-take-lead-climate-change.

8. United Nations Intergovernmental Panel on Climate Change (UN IPCC), "Global warming of 1.5°C" (October 2018), https://report.ipcc.ch/sr15/pdf/sr15_spm_final.pdf.

9. United Nations (UN), "Adoption of the Paris Agreement" (December 2015), 2, https://unfccc.int/resource/docs/2015/cop21/eng/l09r01.pdf.

10. See the interactive charts in Brad Plumer and Nadja Popovich, "Here's how far the world is from meeting its climate goals," *New York Times*, November 6, 2017, www.nytimes.com/interactive/2017/11/06/climate/world-emissions-goals-far-off-course.html. See also "Climate Action Tracker global emissions time series: US" (2018).

11. Pep Cannadell et al., "Carbon emissions will reach 37 billion tonnes in 2018, a record high," *Phys.org*, December 6, 2018, https://phys.org/news/2018-12-carbon-emissions-billion-tonnes-high.html; Brady Dennis and Chris Mooney, "'We are in trouble': Global carbon emissions reached a record high in 2018," *Washington Post*, December 5, 2018, www.washingtonpost.com/energy-environment/2018/12/05/we-are-trouble-global-carbon-emissions-reached-new-record-high; Li Jing, "Global carbon emissions rise in 2017, driven by China," *Climate Home News*, November 13, 2017, www.climatechangenews.com/2017/11/13/global-emissions-expected-rise-2017-say-researchers.

12. "Climate Action Tracker global emissions time series: China" (2018).

13. Li is quoted in Wu Yixiu, "Is coal power winning the U.S.-China trade war?" *Chinadialogue*, October 12, 2019, www.chinadialogue.net/article/show/single/en/11642-Is-coal-power-winning-the-US-China-trade-war-; Michael Forsythe, "China cancels 103 coal plants, mindful of smog and wasted capacity," *New York Times*, January 18, 2017; Michael Lelyveld, "China adds coal capacity despite pledge to cut," *Radio Free Asia*, April 15, 2019, www.rfa.org/english/commentaries/energy_watch/china-adds-coal-capacity-despite-pledge-to-cut-04152019103742.html; Christine Shearer et al., "Tsunami warning: Can China's central authorities stop a massive surge in new coal plants caused by provincial overpermitting?" (CoalSwarm, September 2018), https://endcoal.org/wp-content/uploads/2018/09/TsunamiWarningEnglish.pdf; Adam Vaughan, "Satellite images show 'runaway' expansion of coal power in China," *Guardian*, September 26, 2018, www.theguardian.com/world/2018/sep/26/satellite-images-show-runaway-expansion-of-coal-power-in-china; Michael J. Coren and Daniel Wolfe, "China's provinces are secretly building coal plants in defiance of the national government," *Quartz*, September 30, 2018, https://qz.com/1404934/chinas-provinces-are-secretly-building-coal-plants-in-defiance-of-the-national-government; "China's top coal province defies Beijing, allows new coke projects: Ministry," *Reuters*, May 6, 2019, www.reuters.com/article/us-china-economy-pollution/chinas-top-coal-province-defies-beijing-allows-new-coke-projects-

ministry-idUSKCN1SC163; Lauri Myllyvirta, "China's power industry calls for hundreds of new coal power plants by 2030," *Greenpeace*, March 28, 2019, https://unearthed.greenpeace.org/2019/03/28/china-new-coal-plants-2030-climate.

14. Wu Yixiu, "Is coal power winning?" See also Wu Wenyuan, "China's 'clean coal' power: A viable model or cautionary tale?" *Chinadialogue*, June 27, 2017.

15. Feng Hao, "China's coal consumption is on the rise," *Chinadialogue*, March 1, 2019,www.chinadialogue.net/article/show/single/en/11107-China-s-coal-consumption-on-the-rise; Ren Qiuyu and Zhang Zizhu, "China's renewed embrace of coal bucks global trend," *Caixin*, April 2, 2019, www.caixinglobal.com/2019-04-02/chinas-renewed-embrace-of-coal-power-bucks-global-trend-101400065.html.

16. Christine Shearer et al., "Out of step: China is driving the continued growth of the global coal fleet" (Global Energy Monitor, November 2019), https://endcoal.org/wp-content/uploads/2019/11/Out-of-Step-English-final.pdf; "China's unbridled export of coal power seen as imperiling climate goals," *Japan Times*, December 6, 2018,www.japantimes.co.jp/news/2018/12/06/business/chinas-unbridled-export-coal-power-seen-imperiling-climate-goals; Beth Walker, "China stokes coal growth," *Chinadialogue*, September 23, 2016; Jonathan Watts, "Belt and Road summit puts spotlight on Chinese coal funding," *Guardian*, April 25, 2019, www.theguardian.com/world/2019/apr/25/belt-and-road-summit-puts-spotlight-on-chinese-coal-funding.

17. "Hope for global solar boom turning to bust as China underwhelms," *Bloomberg*, November 1, 2019, www.bloomberg.com/news/articles/2019-11-01/china-seen-missing-its-2019-solar-target-after-policy-delay.

18. Lauri Myllyvirta, "China's CO2 emissions surged in 2018 despite clean energy gains," *Greenpeace*, February 28, 2019, https://unearthed.greenpeace.org/2019/02/28/china-coal-renewable-energy-2018-data-trends; Zach Boren, "Dramatic surge in China carbon emissions signals climate danger," *Greenpeace*, May 30, 2018, https://unearthed.greenpeace.org/2018/05/30/china-co2-carbon-climate-emissions-rise-in-2018.

19. The growth rate estimate of 4.7 percent was within a range of variation from +2 percent to +7.4 percent; Corinne Le Quéré et al., "Global carbon budget 2018," *Earth Systems Science Data*, vol. 10, no. 4 (December 2018): 2141–2194, www.earth-syst-sci-data.net/10/2141/2018. Kendra Pierre-Louis, "Greenhouse emissions accelerate like a 'speeding freight train' in 2018," *New York Times*, December 5, 2018; R. B. Jackson et al., "Global energy growth is outpacing decarbonization," *Environmental Research Letters*, vol. 13, no. 12 (December 2018), https://iopscience.iop.org/article/10.1088/1748-9326/aaf303; Glen Peters et al., "Guest post: China's CO2 emissions grew slower than expected in 2018," *Carbon Brief*, March 5, 2018, www.carbonbrief.org/guest-post-chinas-co2-emissions-grew-slower-than-expected-in-2018.

20. Lauri Myllyvirta, "Guest post: Why China's CO2 emissions grew by 4 percent during the first half of 2019," *Carbon Brief*, September 5, 2019, www.carbonbrief.org/guest-post-why-chinas-co2-emissions-grew-4-during-first-half-of-2019.

21. United Nations Environment Program (UNEP), "Emissions gap report 2019" (November 2019), https://wedocs.unep.org/bitstream/handle/20.500.11822/30797/EGR2019.pdf; "China avoids calls for bold action as climate warnings escalate," *Bloomberg*, November 27, 2019, www.bloomberg.com/news/articles/2019-11-27/amid-rising-climate-alarms-china-keeps-calm-and-carries-on.

22. Data sourced from International Monetary Fund (IMF) World Economic Outlook (WEO) database, October 2018 edition. Even comparing the two countries in GDP purchasing power parity (PPP) terms, China's per capita GDP PPP in 2018 was still only one-third that of the US. See "China vs. United States—a GDP comparison," *MGM Research*, December 21, 2018, https://mgmresearch. com/china-vs-united-states-a-gdp-comparison.

23. British Petroleum (BP), "BP Statistical Review of World Energy 2018" (June 2018), www.bp.com/content/dam/bp/business-sites/en/global/corporate/pdfs/energy-economics/statistical-review/bp-stats-review-2018-full-report.pdf; Alister Doyle, "China to surpass US as top cause of global warming," *Reuters*, April 13, 2015, https://uk.reuters.com/article/climatechange-china-idUKL5N0XA1JD20150413; Robert Rapier, "China emits more CO2 emissions than the US and EU combined," *Forbes*, July 1, 2018, www.forbes.com/sites/rrapier/2018/07/01/china-emits-more-carbon-dioxide-than-the-u-s-and-eu-combined.

24. It's also been said in China's defense that its extraordinary emissions are in part attributable to the dirty industries offshored to China from the West. This is true but when China's exports of embodied CO2 are balanced against its imports of embodied CO2 (meat, soybeans, microchips, Boeing airplanes, and so on), only 14 percent of China's CO2 emissions can be attributed to production for export. See Hanna Ritchie and Max Rosner, "CO2 and greenhouse gas emissions," *Our World in Data*, May 2017, https://ourworldindata.org/co2-and-other-greenhouse-gas-emissions.

25. Environmental Investigation Agency (EIA), "Blowing it: Illegal production and use of banned CFC-11 in China's foam blowing industry" (July 2018), https://eia-international.org/wp-content/uploads/Blowing-It-final.pdf; "High-flying whodunit: Someone in East Asia is cheating on the 1987 Montreal ozone treaty, pumping out huge amounts of banned CFC gas," *South China Morning Post*, May 17, 2018, www.scmp.com/news/world/article/2146529/high-flying-whodunit-someone-east-asia-cheating-1987-ozone-treaty-pumping; Feng Hao, "Ozone-depleting substances test China's commitment to global treaty," *Chinadialogue*, August 22, 2018, www.chinadialogue.net/article/show/single/en/10785-Ozone-depleting-substances-test-China-s-commitment-to-global-treaty.

26. Silvio Marcacci, "Cheap renewables keep pushing fossil fuels further away from profitability—despite Trump's efforts," *Forbes*, January 23, 2018, www.forbes.com/sites/energyinnovation/2018/01/23/cheap-renewables-keep-pushing-fossil-fuels-further-away-from-profitability-despite-trumps-efforts.

27. Chris Mooney, "California, 17 other states sue Trump administration to defend Obama-era climate rules for vehicles," *Washington Post*, May 1, 2018, www.washingtonpost.com/news/energy-environment/wp/2018/05/01/california-17-other-states-sue-trump-administration-to-defend-obama-era-vehicle-efficiency-rules.

28. See William Laurance, "The dark legacy of China's drive for global resources," *Yale Environment 360*, March 28, 2017, https://e360.yale.edu/features/the-dark-legacy-of-chinas-drive-for-global-resources; Giles Hosch, "China ranked worst country in new illegal fishing index," *Chinadialogue*, April 16, 2019, https://chinadialogueocean.net/7568-china-ranked-worst-country-in-new-illegal-fishing-index; Isabella Kaminski, "Ghana's fish stocks decimated by illegal fishing," *Chinadialogue*, October 12, 2018, https://chinadialogueocean.net/4731-ghanas-

fish-stocks-decimated-by-illegal-fishing; Environmental Justice Foundation (EJF), "China's hidden fleet in West Africa: A spotlight on illegal practices within Ghana's industrial trawl sector" (October 2018), https://ejfoundation.org//resources/downloads/China-hidden-fleet-briefing-v2.pdf.

29. Craig Simons, *The Devouring Dragon: How China's Rise Threatens Our Natural World* (New York: St. Martin's Press, 2013), 73.

30. William Laurance, "China's appetite for wood taking a heavy toll on forests," *Yale Environment 360*, November 17, 2011, https://e360.yale.edu/features/chinas_appetite_for_wood_takes_a_heavy_toll_on_forests; Thais Lazzeri, "Chinese demand for beef raises deforestation risk," *Diálogo Chino*, March 27, 2019, https://dialogochino.net/25355-chinese-demand-for-brazilian-beef-raises-deforestation-risk.

31. Eileen Guo, "Chinese consumers' crazy rich demand for rosewood propels drive toward its extinction," *South China Morning Post*, September 29, 2018, www.scmp.com/news/china/society/article/2164603/chinese-consumers-crazy-rich-demand-rosewood-propels-drive-toward.

32. Steven Lee Myers, "Ravaging faraway forests while protecting trees at home," *New York Times*, April 10, 2019; Zhang Chun, "Rapid decline of China's wetlands threatens mass extinction of rare birds," *Chinadialogue*, October 20, 2015, www.chinadialogue.net/article/show/single/en/8253-Rapid-decline-of-China-s-wetlands-threatens-mass-extinction-for-rare-birds.

33. Laurance, "China's appetite."

34. Rachael Bale, "Poached for its horn, this rare bird struggles to survive," *National Geographic*, September 2018, www.nationalgeographic.com/magazine/2018/09/helmeted-hornbill-bird-ivory-illegal-wildlife-trade; Simons, *Devouring Dragon*; Kate Whitehead, "Saving rhinos: South Africa's fight against Chinese demand for horns that's pushing species to extinction," *South China Morning Post*, May 26, 2018, www.scmp.com/magazines/post-magazine/long-reads/article/2147778/saving-rhinos-africas-fight-against-chinese; Aron White, "EIA: China's tiger farms are a threat to the species," *Chinadialogue*, June 15, 2017, www.chinadialogue.net/article/show/single/en/9849-EIA-China-s-tiger-farms-are-a-threat-to-the-species; Vivienne L. Williams, "Tiger-bone trade could threaten lions," *Nature*, July 15, 2015, www.nature.com/articles/523290a; Zhang Qifeng et al., "Eating habits in South China driving endangered animals to extinction," *Chinadialogue*, December 18, 2012, www.chinadialogue.net/article/show/single/en/5506-Eating-habits-in-south-China-driving-endangered-animals-to-extinction-; Feng Yongfeng, "Market trade is fueling the killing of migratory birds in Northern China," *Chinadialogue*, December 10, 2012, www.chinadialogue.net/article/show/single/en/5465-market-trade-is-fuelling-the-killing-of-migratory-birds-in-northern-china; Tiffany May, "Seizure of 14 tons of Pangolin scales in Singapore sets a dismal record," *New York Times*, April 8, 2019; Stephen Nash, "Vietnam's empty forests," *New York Times Magazine*, April 1, 2019; Jonathan Watts, "Taking wildlife off the menu," *Chinadialogue*, June 4, 2009; "Last female Yangtze giant softshell turtle dies," *China Daily*, April 14, 2019; Sebastian Strangio, "Rich Chinese are literally eating this exotic mammal to extinction," *PRI.org*, October 20, 2014, www.pri.org/stories/2014-10-20/rich-chinese-are-literally-eating-exotic-mammal-extinction.

35. Zhu Dongjun, "Newly-aired documentary film presents an amazing, confident China," *People's Daily*, March 5, 2018, http://en.people.cn/n3/2018/0305/c90000-9433087.html. See also Tianyu M. Fang, "'Amazing China,' a documentary extolling

Xi Jinping, is the movie that officials want people to love," *SupChina*, March 16, 2018, https://supchina.com/2018/03/16/amazing-china-a-documentary-extolling-xi-jinping.

36. Javier C. Hernandez, "China reverses ban on rhino and tiger parts in medicine, worrying activists," *New York Times*, October 29, 2018; "Only in emergency: China waters down its ban on the use of tiger and rhino parts," *The Economist*, November 3, 2018, www.economist.com/china/2018/11/03/china-waters-down-its-ban-on-the-use-of-tiger-and-rhino-parts; "State-sponsored quackery: China is ramping up its promotion of its ancient medical arts," *The Economist*, September 2, 2017.

37. Robert Wilson, "America versus China: The new reality of global energy," *Energy Collective*, May 12, 2014, www.energycentral.com/c/ec/america-versus-china-new-reality-global-energy.

38. Joseph Kahn, "China quick to execute drug official," *New York Times*, July 11, 2007.

39. "Chinese local governments are planning enough housing for 3.4 billion people by 2030," *Shanghaiist*, July 19, 2016, http://shanghaiist.com/2016/07/19/too_many_houses.php; "New 'ghost cities' typify out-of-control planning," *Chinadialogue*, November 15, 2015, www.chinadialogue.net/article/show/single/en/8239-new-ghost-cities-typify-out-of-control-planning.

40. See Xi Jinping, "Pushing China's development of an ecological civilization to a new stage," *Qiushi Journal* (English edition), vol. 11, no. 2, issue no. 39 (April–June 2019), http://english.qstheory.cn/2019-09/17/c_1124932126.htm. I have previously argued that this is inconceivable with a 6.5 percent growth rate in Richard Smith, "China's drivers and planetary ecological collapse," *Real-World Economics Review*, no. 82 (December 2017): 2–28, www.paecon.net/PAEReview/issue82/Smith82.pdf.

41. For an outline of my own views on the essential characteristics and requirements of an ecosocialist political economy see Richard Smith, "Six theses on saving the planet," *Next System Project*, November 3, 2016, https://thenextsystem.org/six-theses-on-saving-the-planet. I also proposed a strategy of decarbonization centered on nationalization of the fossil-fuel industrial complex in the US that could begin under capitalism but would require a transition to some form of ecosocialism to succeed in Richard Smith, "An ecosocialist path to limiting global temperature rise to 1.5°C," *Real-World Economics Review*, no. 87 (March 2019): 149–180, www.paecon.net/PAEReview/issue87/Smith87.pdf.

CHAPTER 1

1. Alexandra Harney, *The China Price: The True Cost of Chinese Competitive Advantage* (London: Penguin, 2008), 3.

2. Jim Yardley, "Where growth and dysfunction have no boundaries," *New York Times*, June 9, 2011; Vikas Bajaj, "A high-tech titan plagued by potholes: Dearth of civil engineers is stifling India's economy," *New York Times*, August 26, 2010; Gardiner Harris and Vikas Bajaj, "As power is restored in India, the 'blame game' over blackouts heats up," *New York Times*, August 2, 2012; Geeta Anand, "India graduates millions but too few are fit to hire," *Wall Street Journal*, April 5, 2011; Preetkia Rana, "IKEA's India bet hits thicket of rules," *Wall Street Journal*, February 24, 2016.

3. Hari Kumar and Kai Schultz, "In rotten, teetering towers, garbage is piling up in India," *New York Times*, June 11, 2018.

4. Iain Marlow, "The world's fastest-growing economy has the world's most toxic air," *Bloomberg*, October 21, 2018, www.bloomberg.com/news/features/2018-10-21/the-world-s-fastest-growing-economy-has-the-world-s-most-toxic-air.

5. It is certainly true that the hundreds of millions of workers who migrated to China's SEZs and accepted Industrial Revolution-era wages did so voluntarily to escape the even deeper (state-induced) poverty of rural life. The world over young people have been leaving the countryside for the attractions and life-changing possibilities of urban life for centuries. That said, nowhere else in the twenty-first century do we find industrial working conditions so harsh that desperate workers jump out of windows or from the roofs of buildings in despair at the hopelessness of their plight or commit mass suicides by drinking pesticide. You don't see that anywhere except in "socialist" China.

6. Jack Nicas, "A tiny screw shows why iPhones won't be 'Assembled in U.S.A.'" *New York Times*, January 28, 2019, www.nytimes.com/2019/01/28/technology/iphones-apple-china-made.html

7. The Vietnamese Communist Party's efforts to reproduce China's cheap and dirty industrial model are already running into unexpected mass resistance against pollution. See Nguyen Dong, "Da Nang suspends steel factories after days of pollution protests," *VNExpress*, March 1, 2018, https://e.vnexpress.net/news/news/da-nang-suspends-steel-factories-after-days-of-pollution-protests-3717013.html; "Vietnamese protestors to maintain blockade of polluting textile factory," *Radio Free Asia*, September 22, 2017, www.rfa.org/english/news/vietnam/vietnamese-protesters-to-maintain-blockade-of-polluting-textile-factory-09222017144849.html.

8. Harney, *China Price*, 8–11.

9. Keith Bradsher, "Courting factories in India," *New York Times*, October 15, 2015; Raymond Zhong and Saptarishi Duta, "India suffers as workers abandon cities," *Wall Street Journal*, April 14, 2014; "Millions strike in India over government labour reforms," *Al Jazeera*, September 2, 2015, www.aljazeera.com/news/2015/09/millions-strike-india-government-labour-reforms-150902121919088.html.

10. Hao Ren, *China on Strike: Narratives of Workers' Resistance* (New York: Haymarket, 2016), Introduction.

11. Yaxue Cao, "Chinese authorities orchestrate surprise raid of labor NGOs in Guangdong, arresting leaders," *China Change*, December 10, 2015, https://chinachange.org/2015/12/10/chinese-authorities-orchestrate-surprise-raid-of-labor-ngos-in-guangdong-arresting-leaders; "China must release detained crane workers on strike & would-be May 1st protesters," *Chinese Human Rights Defenders*, May 3, 2018, www.nchrd.org/2018/05/china-must-release-detained-crane-workers-on-strike-would-be-may-1st-protesters; Elaine Hui, "Effort to form union in China meets ferocious repression," *Labor Notes*, September 25, 2018, www.labornotes.org/2018/09/effort-form-union-china-meets-ferocious-repression; Mimi Lau, "Chinese labour rights activists detained as authorities try to shut down silicosis campaign," *South China Morning Post*, March 22, 2019, www.scmp.com/news/china/politics/article/3002732/chinese-labour-rights-activists-detained-authorities-try-shut.

12. Harney, *China Price*, 8–9.

13. "Made in China?" *The Economist*, May 12, 2015, www.economist.com/leaders/2015/03/12/made-in-china.

14. Vaclav Smil, *Making the Modern World: Materials and Dematerialization* (Chichester, UK: John Wiley & Sons 2014), 90.

15. "The poetry and brief life of a Foxconn worker: Xu Lizhi (1990–2014)," *Chuang*, October 29, 2014, http://chuangcn.org/2014/10/the-poetry-and-brief-life-of-a-foxconn-worker-xu-lizhi-1990-2014. Xu jumped to his death in September 2014 from the roof of a building near the Foxconn factory in Shenzhen where he worked.

16. In addition to Harney's *China Price* see Anita Chan, *China's Workers Under Assault: The Exploitation of Labor in a Globalizing Economy* (Armonk, NY: M.E. Sharpe, 2001); Ching Kwan Lee, *Against the Law: Labor Protests in China's Rustbelt and Sunbelt* (Berkeley: UC Press, 2007); Hsiao-Hung Pai, *Scattered Sand: The Story of China's Rural Migrants* (London: Verso, 2012); Pun Ngai, *Migrant Labor in China* (New York: Polity Press, 2016); Jack Linchuan Qiu, *Goodbye iSlave: A Manifesto of Digital Abolition* (Urbana: University of Illinois Press, 2016); China Labour Bulletin; China Labor Watch.

17. Mark Duell, "Forced to stand for 24 hours, suicide prevention nets, toxin exposure and explosions—inside the Chinese factories making iPads for Apple," *Daily Mail*, January 27, 2012, www.dailymail.co.uk/news/article-2092277/Apple-Poor-working-conditions-inside-Chinese-factories-making-iPads.html.

18. Foxconn Technology Group, "Corporate social and environmental responsibility annual report 2012" (2013), 4, http://ser.foxconn.com/javascript/pdfjs/web/viewer.html?file=/upload/CserReports/42470921-ed8f-4e16-8021-81c8cb9a 813b_.pdf. According to Jenny Chan (personal communication), Foxconn's number of employees now hovers around one million, with robots replacing humans.

19. Jenny Chan, Mark Selden, and Pun Ngai, *Dying for an iPhone: Apple, Foxconn and the Lives of China's Workers* (Pluto Press, 2020).

20. See for example Michael Blanding and Heather White, "How China is screwing over its poisoned factory workers," *Wired*, April 6, 2015, www.wired.com/2015/04/inside-chinese-factories.

21. "Revolt of the iSlaves—more labour unrest at China's Foxconn factories," *Libcom. org*, October 17, 2012, https://libcom.org/news/revolts-islaves---more-labor-unrest-chinas-foxconn-factories-fall-2012-17102012; "China: Labour activist jailed for four and a half years for publishing account of Tiananmen crackdown," *Amnesty International*, July 7, 2017, www.amnesty.org/en/latest/news/2017/07/china-labour-activist-jailed-for-account-of-tiananmen-crackdown; Andrew Jacobs, "China to investigate death of labor activist," *New York Times*, June 15, 2012.

22. This is not only true of the notoriously militarized Foxconn factories, but elsewhere too. See Robert Foyle Hunwick, "Desperate Chinese turn to mass suicide," *USA Today*, May 15, 2015, www.usatoday.com/story/news/world/2015/05/20/globalpost-chinese-suicides/27642891; Nectar Gan, "Chinese taxi drivers attempt mass suicide in Beijing during vehicle leasing protest," *South China Morning Post*, April 4, 2015, www.scmp.com/news/china/article/1756065/suicide-bid-more-30-chinese-taxi-drivers-beijing-protest-over-vehicle.

23. Jenny Chan, "A suicide survivor: The life of a Chinese worker," *New Technology, Work and Employment*, vol. 28, no. 2 (2013): 91.

24. Ibid., 92. See also *Complicit* (2017), directed by Heather White and Lynn Zhang, available at http://complicitfilm.org.

25. Qiu, *Goodbye iSlave*, 74.

26. Jenny Chan et al., "Interns or workers? China's student labor regime," *Asia-Pacific Journal*, September 7, 2015, https://apjjf.org/-Jenny-Chan/4372. China is one of the handful of nations where independent trade unions are illegal, and strikes and picketing are unprotected; see International Trade Union Confederation (ITUC), "ITUC global rights index: The world's worst countries for workers 2015" (2015), www.ituc-csi.org/IMG/pdf/survey_global_rights_index_2015_en.pdf. On the difficulties workers face in trying to quit see Qiu, *Goodbye iSlave*, 64–67; Chan, "A suicide survivor."

27. David Barboza, "A manufacturing model tough to export," *New York Times*, September 20, 2017. Foxconn has set up manufacturing plants in Southeast Asia, India, and other countries in response to both local content rules and Trump's trade war. But these lack the scale and police state "advantages" of China.

28. Geoffrey Crothall, "China's labour movement in transition," *Chinoiresie*, August 13, 2018, www.chinoiresie.info/chinas-labour-movement-in-transition. See also the crowdsourced map of labor unrest "China Strikes—mapping labor unrest cross China" at https://chinastrikes.crowdmap.com.

29. Jenny Chan, "Intern labor in China," *Rural China*, vol. 14 (2017): 82–100; David Barboza and Charles Duhigg, "Foxconn said to use forced student labor to make iPhones," *New York Times*, September 10, 2012; Eva Dou, "China tech factories turn to student labor," *Wall Street Journal*, September 24, 2014, www.wsj.com/articles/chinas-tech-factories-turn-to-student-labor-1411572448; Zhuang Pinghui, "University in China apologises after students forced to do internships at Foxconn," *South China Morning Post*, July 21, 2017, www.scmp.com/news/china/society/article/2103529/university-china-apologises-after-students-forced-do-internships; Tom Hancock, Yuan Yang, and Nian Liu, "Illegal student labour fuels JD.com 'Singles Day' sale," *Financial Times*, November 21, 2018, http://polyucrdn.eksx.com/userfiles/file/Jenny%20Chan%20Illegal%20student%20labour%20FT%2021%20NOV%202018.pdf.

30. Will Steffen et al., "The trajectory of the Anthropocene: The great acceleration," *The Anthropocene Review*, vol. 2, no. 1 (2015): 81–98, http://journals.sagepub.com/doi/pdf/10.1177/2053019614564785.

31. Joseph Kahn and Mark Landler, "China grabs West's smoke-spewing factories," *New York Times*, December 21, 2007; William J. Kelly and Chip Jacobs, *The People's Republic of Chemicals* (Los Angeles: Vireo, 2014).

32. Basel Action Network (BAN) et al., "Exporting harm: The high-tech trashing of Asia" (February 25, 2012), https://noharm-uscanada.org/sites/default/files/documents-files/84/Exporting_Harm_Trashing_Asia.pdf; "China's electronic waste village" *Time*, 2006, http://content.time.com/time/photogallery/0,29307,1870162,00.html.

33. Jemima Kelly, "When fast fashion jumps on the eco-wagon," *Financial Times*, November 7, 2019, https://ftalphaville.ft.com/2019/11/06/1573073449000/When-fast-fashion-jumps-on-the-eco-wagon.

34. Stephanie Vatz, "Why America stopped making its own clothes," *KQED*, May 24, 2013, www.kqed.org/lowdown/7939/madeinamerica.

35. Deborah Drew and Genevieve Yehounme, "The apparel industry's environmental impact in six graphics," *Planet Aid*, August 23, 2017, www.planetaid.org/blog/the-apparel-industrys-environmental-impact-in-six-graphics.

36. Araz Hachadourian, "The 150-mile wardrobe: A solution for one of the world's most polluting industries," *Truthout*, December 21, 2017, www.truth-out.org/news/item/42979-the-150-mile-wardrobe-a-solution-for-one-of-the-world-s-most-polluting-industries.

37. Elizabeth L. Cline, "Wear clothes? That's a problem," *New York Times*, November 4, 2019.

38. Ibid.

39. Leah Messinger, "How your clothes are poisoning our oceans and food supply," *Guardian*, June 20, 2016, www.theguardian.com/environment/2016/jun/20/microfibers-plastic-pollution-oceans-patagonia-synthetic-clothes-microbeads.

40. Elizabeth L. Cline, *Overdressed: The Shockingly High Cost of Cheap Fashion* (New York: Penguin, 2012), 3, 124–125; "Fabric and your carbon footprint," *O Ecotextiles*, March 10, 2013, http://oecotextiles.wordpress.com/2013/10/03/fabric-and-your-carbon-footprint.

41. Alison Moodie, "Can Apple's $1.5bn green bond inspire more environmental investments?" *Guardian*, March 20, 2016, www.theguardian.com/sustainable-business/2016/mar/20/apple-green-bond-environment-energy-toyota-climate-change.

42. Vincent Lai, a program director for Fixers Collective, a New York-based club that repairs devices and promotes anti-consumerism (by which he means the idea that it makes sense to take care of what you have rather than incessantly buying new stuff), says that in the early years of pads and smartphones, when those devices were sluggish and limited in abilities, it made sense to upgrade frequently. But now "a five-year old computer is completely fine. . . . We're starting to hit that same plateau with phones now"; Brian X. Chen, "Upgrade? Why not love the gadget you've got?" *New York Times*, April 21, 2016.

43. Emma Foehringer Merchant, "Lithium-ion battery production is surging, but at what cost?" *Green Tech Media*, September 20, 2017, www.greentechmedia.com/articles/read/lithium-ion-battery-production-is-surging-but-at-what-cost; Max Opray, "Nickel mining: The hidden environmental cost of electric cars," *Guardian*, August 24, 2017, www.theguardian.com/sustainable-business/2017/aug/24/nickel-mining-hidden-environmental-cost-electric-cars-batteries.

44. Niu Yue, "China no. 1 dumper of plastic into ocean," *China Daily*, February 19, 2015. See also Charles Moore, *Plastic Ocean: How a Sea Captain's Chance Discovery Launched a Determined Quest to Save the Oceans* (New York: Avery, 2011); Edward Humes, *Garbology: Our Dirty Love Affair with Trash* (New York: Avery, 2012).

45. Kiera Butler, "Earth to IKEA, what that Poäng chair really costs," *Mother Jones*, May/June 2009.

46. One company, Fairphone, is trying; see www.fairphone.com. See also "The repair manifesto," available at www.ifixit.com/manifesto.

47. For more on this problem see Richard Smith, "Essay 2 (2010): Beyond growth or beyond capitalism?" in *Green Capitalism: The God That Failed* (World Economic Association Press, 2016), 38–46.

CHAPTER 2

1. Above quotations are from Ariana Enjung Cha, "Solar energy firms leave waste behind in China," *Washington Post*, March 9, 2008.

2. See for example Erin Chan, "Gas leak at Chinese drug company leaves villagers vomiting and gasping for breath," *South China Morning Post*, June 14, 2018, www.scmp.com/news/china/society/article/2150862/gas-leak-chinese-drugs-factory-leaves-villagers-vomiting-and; "Chinese birth defects soar due to pollution: Report," *Reuters*, October 29, 2007, www.reuters.com/article/environment-china-birth-dc-idUSPEK15525020071029; Jim Yardley, "Rules ignored, toxic sludge sinks Chinese village," *New York Times*, September 4, 2006; Catherine Wong, "China pollution scandal: Air, water in school near toxic site normal, say officials," *South China Morning Post*, April 27, 2016, www.scmp.com/news/china/policies-politics/article/1938925/china-pollution-scandal-air-water-school-near-toxic; "China targets perfunctory officials in fight against pollution," *South China Morning Post*, June 22, 2018, www.scmp.com/news/china/policies-politics/article/2151993/china-targets-perfunctory-officials-fight-against; Zheng Jinran, "Lax anti-pollution efforts highlighted," *China Daily*, February 8, 2017; He Huifeng, "At least five more people detained over Huizhou incinerator protest," *South China Morning Post*, September 15, 2014, www.scmp.com/article/1593055/least-five-more-people-detained-over-huizhou-incinerator-protest.

3. Noah Smith, "Get used to it, America: You're no longer no. 1," *Bloomberg*, December 18, 2018.

4. See "The rise of state capitalism," and "The visible hand," *The Economist*, January 21, 2012.

5. "The Chinese miracle will end soon," *Der Spiegel*, March 7, 2005, www.spiegel.de/speigel/0,1515,345694.html. SEPA was renamed the Ministry of Environmental Protection (MEP) in 2018, then renamed again as the Ministry of Ecology and Environment (MEE) in 2018.

6. Elizabeth C. Economy and Michael Levi, *By All Means Necessary: How China's Resource Quest is Changing the World* (Oxford: Oxford University Press 2014), Chapters 3, 4.

7. Ibid.; James West et al., *Resource Efficiency: Economics and Outlook for China* (New York: United Nations Publications, 2013), 7; Chuin-Wei Yap, "China iron-ore imports are set to rise," *Wall Street Journal*, February 25, 2014.

8. Simons, *Devouring Dragon*, 9, and Chapters 7 and 8.

9. Tamara Stark and Sze Pang Cheung, "Sharing the blame: Global consumption and China's role in ancient forest destruction" (Greenpeace, March 2006) cited in Simons, *Devouring Dragon*, 249, Footnote 16.

10. Cited in Simons, *Devouring Dragon*, 128. See also Laurance, "China's appetite."

11. William Laurance, "China's growing footprint on the globe threatens to trample the natural world," *The Conversation*, December 5, 2017, https://theconversation.com/chinas-growing-footprint-on-the-globe-threatens-to-trample-the-natural-world-88312.

12. Simons, *Devouring Dragon*, 129.

13. Ibid., 132.

14. Economy and Levi, *By All Means Necessary*, 64–65, 154–163.

15. Despite profligate resource consumption and environmental destruction perhaps not many more than 300 million of China's 1.4 billion people enjoy a "middle-class" consumerist lifestyle today. It's difficult to equate the many factors that comprise a middle-class lifestyle in China vs. the US, but in *The Chinese Dream: The Rise of the World's Largest Middle Class and What it Means to You* (Bestseller Press, 2010) Helen Wang uses this definition: "Urban professionals and

entrepreneurs from all walks of life, who have college degrees and earn an annual income from $10,000 to $60,000." According to Wang, "over three hundred million people, or about 25 percent of China's population, met these criteria in 2010." The Chinese National Bureau of Statistics categorizes a middle-class household as one with an annual income ranging between $3,640 and $36,400; see "China's middle class in 5 simple questions," *China Briefing*, February 13, 2019, www.china-briefing.com/news/chinas-middle-class-5-questions-answered. Based on data from 2015, the Pew Research Center determined the following breakdown of income classes:

Table 2.2   China's population by income/class, 2015

Class	Share of pop. (%)	Income per day (per year)	Total
Upper	0.78	>$50	10,686,000
Upper-middle	9.65	$20–50 ($7,300–$18,250 per year)	132,205,000
Lower-middle	29.06	$10–20 ($3,650–$7,300 per year)	398,122,000
Low	59.58	$2–10 ($730–$3,650 per year)	816,246,000
Poor	0.93	>$2 ($730 per year)	1,274,000

Data: Pew Research Center, cited in "How well-off is China's middle class?" *China Power*, December 3, 2018, https://chinapower.csis.org/china-middle-class.

By this account, China's middle classes comprise 531 million people, 39 percent of the population. Counting people who make $10–$20 per day ($3,600–$7,200 per year) as "middle class"—even in China—seems a stretch. Even so, this still leaves the "low-income" 816 million living on an average of $7.60 per day and the desperately poor 1.3 million living on less than $2 per day. In other words, 60 percent of China's population lives on less than $10 per day, and another nearly 400,000 live on $10–$20 per day. Furthermore, because Deng's market reformers broke the "iron rice bowl" of state benefits in the 1990s, forcing Chinese workers to pay privately for services that used to be subsidized or provided free of charge by the government under Mao (schooling, childcare, medical care, housing, and pensions), the income gains of market reform have been offset by the higher costs of living resulting from those same reforms. Largely because of this, millions of peasants and laid-off workers have fallen into deeper poverty. The World Bank reported that the income of the poorest 10 percent of China's 1.3 billion people fell absolutely by 2.4 percent between 2001 and 2003, to less than $83 per year. And this was during a period when the economy was growing by 10 percent per year and the income of the richest 10 percent grew by 16 percent; see Terry Sicular, "The challenge of high inequality in China," *Inequality in Focus*, vol. 2, no. 2 (August 2013): 2, Figure 2, www.worldbank.org/content/dam/Worldbank/document/Poverty%20documents/Inequality-In-Focus-0813.pdf. All this raises an important question with respect to the subject of this book. If China has consumed so many domestic and global resources to raise less than one-fourth of its population to the middle class, how many planets' worth of resources would it take to elevate the other three-fourths of the Chinese population to the Western consumerist lifestyle?

16. Environmental Investigation Agency (EIA), "Vanishing point: Criminality, corruption and the devastation of Tanzania's elephants" (2014), 22, https://eia-

international.org/wp-content/uploads/EIA-Vanishing-Point-lo-res1.pdf;   Dan Levin, "Report implicates Chinese officials in smuggled Tanzanian ivory," *New York Times*, November 6, 2014; Li Lianxing, Zhao Huanxin, and Beth Walker, "Monga—Myanmar's gateway for pangolin smuggling into China," *Chinadialogue*, January 4, 2016, www.chinadialogue.net/article/show/single/en/8774-Mongla-Myanmar-s-gateway-for-pangolin-smuggling-into-China;   Damian   Kayya, "Investigation: How illegal timber from Cameroon's rainforest could be landing in China's ports," *Greenpeace*, March 21, 2016, http://energydesk.greenpeace. org/2016/03/21/investigation-how-illegal-timber-from-cameroons-rainforest-could-be-landing-in-chinas-ports.

17. Li Jing, "China's industrial growth 'a threat to resources,'" *South China Morning Post*, August 3, 2013, www.scmp.com/news/china/article/1294075/chinas-transformation-industrial-powerhouse-eating-away-resources.

18. Brian Wingfield, "China's power problem," *Forbes*, July 7, 2007.

19. World Bank, "Water productivity, total (constant 2010 US$ GDP per cubic meter of total freshwater withdrawal)," https://data.worldbank.org/indicator/ER.GDP. FWTL.M3.KD.

20. For their arguments see Richard Smith, "The Chinese road to capitalism," *New Left Review*, no. 199 (May–June 1993): 55–57.

21. See for example Lauri Myllyvirta, "China keeps building coal plants despite new overcapacity policy," *Greenpeace*, July 12, 2016, https://unearthed.greenpeace. org/2016/07/13/china-keeps-building-coal-plants-despite-new-overcapacity-policy; Lucy Hornby, "Greenpeace warns over China's excess power capacity," *Financial Times*, July 12, 2016, www.ft.com/content/565a872a-480e-11e6-8d68-72e9211e86ab; Roger Harrabin, "China embarked on wind power frenzy, says IEA," *BBC News*, September 20, 2016, www.bbc.com/news/science-environment-37409069.

22. Smil, *Making the Modern World*, 91–92. The Chinese are not just damming rivers and paving over farms but paving over their coastline too. According to a recent report, most of China's eastern seaboard has been paved over or walled up, as ports, industrial parks, and urban expansion push up and down the coast, much of it behind some 18,000 kilometers of sea walls that have been built to protect these developments (what critics have dubbed the "new great wall" of China). In recent decades, the report found, China has developed more than half of the coastal wetlands in its temperate northern regions and nearly 75 percent of the mangrove forests and 80 percent of coral reefs along its southern coast, with dire consequences for wildlife and diversity. More than 60 percent of coastal shoals and wetlands that existed in the 1950s have disappeared, 23 percent of them just in the years between 2003 and 2013, and China's swelling cities want to pave over still more. Paving over China's coastal wetlands, estuaries, salt flats, reefs, and shoals is not only wiping out coastal fisheries and diminishing biodiversity, but is also imperiling the migratory birds for whom China's wetlands are "irreplaceable and integral parts of the East Asian-Australian Flyway," providing critical breeding, staging, and over-wintering sites for 246 species, including 22 that are listed as globally threatened, the report found. Cui Zheng, "Coastal sprawl and a last stand for wetlands," *Caixin*, December 19, 2014, http://english.caixin. com/2014-12-19/100765285.html; Tom Philpott, "China is turning its fish breeding grounds into smartphone factories," *Mother Jones*, October 21, 2015,

www.motherjones.com/tom-philpott/2015/10/china-paving-over-wetlands-alarming-rate-imperiling-its-fisheries.

23. Smil, *Making the Modern World*, 55.
24. Available at www.twitter.com/laurimyllyvirta, April 13, 2019.
25. Feng Hao, "Efforts to cut steel capacity not working," *Chinadialogue*, March 2, 2017, www.chinadialogue.net/article/show/single/en/9642-Efforts-to-cut-steel-capacity-not-working.
26. The State Council of the People's Republic of China, "Guowuyuan guanyu jiakuai peiyu he fazhan zhanlüexing xinxing chanye de jueding" [State Council decision on accelerating the development of strategic emerging industries] (October 2010), www.gov.cn/zwgk/2010-10/18/content_1724848.htm; The State Council of the People's Republic of China, "Guowuyuan guanyu yinfa 'Shi'erwu' guojia zhanlüexing xinxing chanye fazhan guihua de tongzhi" [State Council twelfth Five-Year Plan on the development of strategic emerging industries] (July 2012), www.gov.cn/zwgk/2012-07/20/content_2187770.htm; Ministry of Finance (MOF) and National Development and Reform Commission (NDRC) of the People's Republic of China, "Guanyu yinfa 'zhanlüexing xinxing chanye fazhan zhuanxiang zijin guanli zhanxing banfa' de tongzhi" [Interim measures for the administration of special funds for strategic emerging industries] (December 2012), http://jjs.mof.gov.cn/zhengwuxinxi/zhengcefagui/201301/t20130124_729883.html.
27. State Council, "Twelfth Five-Year Plan," Chapter 9, Sections 1 and 2.
28. Sarah Zheng, "China now has over 300 million vehicles," *South China Morning Post*, April 19, 2017, www.scmp.com/news/china/economy/article/2088876/chinas-more-300-million-vehicles-drive-pollution-congestion; M. Wang et al., "Projections of Chinese motor vehicle growth, oil demand, and CO2 emissions through 2050" (Argonne National Laboratory, December 2006), 36, Table 10, https://greet.es.anl.gov/files/rwdz78ca; "China auto sales top the world again, hit 28.8 million in 2017," *People's Daily*, January 22, 2018, http://en.people.cn/n3/2018/0122/c90000-9418252.html.
29. United States Environmental Protection Agency (EPA), "Sources of greenhouse gas emissions" (2017), www.epa.gov/ghgemissions/sources-greenhouse-gas-emissions.
30. See for example the following headline: Stefan Nicola, "Cars become biggest driver of greenhouse gas increases," *Bloomberg*, April 9, 2014.
31. Lester R. Brown et al., *State of the World 1990* (New York: Norton, 1990), Chapter 7; Lester R. Brown et al., *State of the World 1991* (New York: Norton, 1991), Chapter 4.
32. See for example Shai Oster, "China traffic jam could last weeks," *Wall Street Journal*, August 24, 2010.
33. Liu Qin, "Cars the main culprit for Beijing's smog: Government figures," *Chinadialogue*, April 2, 2015, www.chinadialogue.net/blog/7829-Cars-the-main-culprit-for-Beijing-s-smog-govt-figures/en; Zhang Chun, "Beijing's car controls not enough to beat the smog," *Chinadialogue*, February 2, 2016, www.chinadialogue.net/article/show/single/en/8567-Beijing-s-car-controls-not-enough-to-beat-the-smog.
34. Richard Smith, "New problems for old: The institution of capitalist economic and environmental irrationality in China," *Democracy and Nature*, vol. 5, no. 2 (1999): 249–274. Lee Schipper and Wei-Shiuen Ng explore numerous externalities of the

automobilization of China in World Resources Institute, "Rapid motorization of China: Environmental and social challenges" (October 2004), http://cleanairinitiative.org/portal/system/files/60209_china.pdf.

35. Hua Wang, "Policy reforms and foreign direct investment: The case of the Chinese automobile industry," *Journal of Economics and Business*, vol. 6, no. 1 (2003): 288.

36. For more on this, see Richard Smith, "Creative destruction: Capitalist development and China's environment," *New Left Review*, no. 222 (March–April 1997): 1–41.

37. Next up is skiing, see Suzi Steiger, "Skiing: Potential 'remains mostly untapped,'" *China Daily*, May 3, 2019. On the other hand, see Neil MacFarquhar, "Chinese tourists flock to Lake Baikal, Siberia. Local Russians growl," *New York Times*, May 3, 2019.

38. Tom Lasseter, "Empty highways," *McClatchy News*, August 24, 2006, http://blogs.mcclatchydc.com/china/2006/08/empty_highways.html.

39. Liu Rong, "China's top 10 unique bridges, highways and roads," *People's Daily*, August 19, 2015, http://en.people.cn/n/2015/0819/c90000-8938180.html.

40. Fang Tian, "Over half of China's glaciers could vanish in 50 years," *People's Daily*, July 19, 2017, http://en.people.cn/n3/2017/0719/c90000-9243785.html; Liu Qin, "Cross-border cooperation needed to reduce Himalayan glacier loss," *Chinadialogue*, October 18, 2016, www.chinadialogue.net/article/show/single/en/9318-Cross-border-cooperation-needed-to-reduce-Himalayan-glacier-loss.

41. Qi Xiaome et al., "Empty high-speed rail stations face reckoning," *Caixin*, August 8, 2018, www.caixinglobal.com/2018-08-09/empty-high-speed-rail-stations-face-reckoning-101313020.html.

42. Sun Wenjing, "Government throwing money away on bullet trains, expert says," *Caixin*, July 10, 2014, http://english.caixin.com/2014-07-10/100702343.html.

43. "The lure of speed," *The Economist*, January 14, 2017, 36.

44. Wang is quoted in Tania Branigan, "Riding Beijing's subway end to end: 88km of queues and crushes on 20p ticket," *Guardian*, September 10, 2014, www.theguardian.com/cities/2014/sep/10/-sp-beijing-subway-china-metro-queues-ticket-investment.

45. Kevin Lim, "'Meaningful probability' of a China hard landing: Roubini," *Reuters*, June 13, 2011.

46. Frank Tang, "Full speed ahead for China's fast rail network with $112 billion investment," *South China Morning Post*, January 3, 2018, www.scmp.com/news/china/economy/article/2126548/full-speed-ahead-chinas-fast-rail-network-us112-billion.

47. "China to spend over $1 trillion on planes over next 20 years: Boeing," *Reuters*, September 6, 2017, www.reuters.com/article/us-china-aviation-boeing/china-to-spend-over-1-trillion-on-planes-over-next-20-years-boeing-idUSKCN1BH0T2; James Fallows, *China Airborne* (New York: Vintage, 2012), 28–29; David Barboza, "Airports in China hew to an unswerving flight path," *New York Times*, April 3, 2013; "China plan seeks to bolster airports, locally-produced airplanes," *Bloomberg*, January 21, 2013, www.bloomberg.com/news/2013-01-21/china-plan-seeks-to-bolster-airports-locally-produced-airplanes.html.

48. "Analysis: Aviation could consumer a quarter of 1.5C carbon budget by 2050," *Carbon Brief*, August 8, 2016, www.carbonbrief.org/aviation-consume-quarter-carbon-budget; Hiroko Tabuchi, "'Worse than anyone expected': Air travel emissions vastly outpace predictions," *New York Times*, September 20, 2019.

49. UN IPCC, "Aviation and the global atmosphere: A special report of the Intergovernmental Panel on Climate Change" (1999), www.grida.no/climate/ipcc/aviation/index.htm; George Monbiot, *Heat: How We Can Stop the Planet Burning* (Cambridge, UK: Penguin, 2007), 174.

50. Monbiot, *Heat*, 182; and sources cited therein.

51. Lisa Baertlein, "Amazon's rising air shipments fly in the face of climate plan," *Reuters,* November 6, 2019, www.reuters.com/article/us-amazon-com-airplanes-analysis/amazons-rising-air-shipments-fly-in-the-face-of-climate-plan-idUSKBN1XG2FP.

52. Daisy Dunne, "Tourism responsible for 8% of global greenhouse emissions, study finds," *Carbon Brief,* May 7, 2018, www.carbonbrief.org/tourism-responsible-for-8-of-global-greenhouse-gas-emissions-study-finds; Gavin Haines and Oliver Smith, "Our desire to see the world is killing it—here's what you can do to help," *Telegraph,* May 8, 2018, www.telegraph.co.uk/travel/comment/tourism-carbon-emissions-how-to-help.

53. William Wilkes, "Airlines were supposed to fix the pollution problem. It's just getting worse," *Bloomberg,* March 10, 2019, www.bloomberg.com/news/articles/2019-03-10/airline-pollution-is-soaring-and-nobody-knows-how-to-fix-it.

54. Jasper Becker, *City of Heavenly Tranquility: Beijing in the History of China* (Oxford: Oxford University Press, 2008), Chapters 17 and 18; Qin Shao, *Shanghai Gone: Domicide and Defiance in a Chinese Megacity* (New York: Rowman & Littlefield, 2013); Tom Miller, *China's Urban Billion: The Story Behind the Biggest Migration in Human History* (London: Zed, 2012), 25–30.

55. Lin Jinbing, "Looking up: Chinese cities race to build skyscrapers," *Caixin*, April 8, 2015, www.caixinglobal.com/2015-04-08/looking-up-chinese-cities-race-to-build-skyscrapers-101012552.html; Esther Fung, "Towering prospect: China seeks tenants," *Wall Street Journal*, January 8, 2014.

56. "Years later, CCTV may finally be moving into its headquarters," *Wall Street Journal*, October 20, 2014, https://blogs.wsj.com/chinarealtime/2014/10/20/years-later-cctv-may-finally-be-moving-into-its-headquarters.

57. Mamta Badkar, "An eerie tour of the abandoned Chinese amusement park that's finally being torn down," *Business Insider*, May 10, 2013, www.businessinsider.com/chinas-abandoned-wonderland-photos-2013-5; Alice Yan, "Disney, Ocean World, Legoland . . . why is Shanghai building so many theme parks?" *South China Morning Post*, June 16, 2017, www.scmp.com/news/china/society/article/2098603/its-happy-birthday-shanghai-disney-competitions-lining-crash.

58. Mandy Zuo, "Stop concreting over prime farmland, China's big cities told," *South China Morning Post*, November 9, 2014; Cui Zheng, "Scientists issue warning over development of coastal wetlands," *Caixin*, November 25, 2014.

59. Luna Lin, "Blindly expanding cities is like spreading out big pancakes," *Chinadialogue*, August 30, 2013, www.chinadialogue.net/blog/6321-Blindly-expanding-Chinese-cities-is-like-spreading-out-big-pancakes-/en.

60. Wade Shepard, *Ghost Cities of China: The Story of Cities Without People in the World's Most Populated Country* (London: Zed Press, 2015), 34–38.

61. Douglas Heaven, "The eerie cities where nobody lives," *BBC News*, February 24, 2017, www.bbc.com/future/slideshow-gallery/20170224-the-eerie-cities-where-nobody-lives; Darmon Richter, "Welcome to Ordos: The world's largest 'ghost city' [China]," *The Bohemian Blog*, February 13, 2014, www.thebohemianblog.

com/2014/02/welcome-to-ordos-world-largest-ghost-city-china.html; Holly Krambeck, "Rise of the Chinese ghost town," *World Bank Blog*, July 12, 2010, https://blogs.worldbank.org/transport/rise-of-the-chinese-ghost-town; "China's real estate bubble," *CBS News*, August 11, 2013, www.cbsnews.com/news/chinas-real-estate-bubble-11-08-2013; *Unborn Cities* (2016), directed by Kai Caemmener, available at http://kaimichael.com/unborncities; "China's empty cities," www.youtube.com/watch?v=V3XfpYxHKCo; George Steinmetz, "Let a hundred McMansions bloom," *New York Times Magazine*, September 21, 2014.

62. Laura Mallonee, "The unreal, eerie emptiness of China's 'ghost cities,'" *Wired*, February 4, 2016, www.wired.com/2016/02/kai-caemmerer-unborn-cities.

63. Melia Robinson, "Surreal photos of China's failed 'city of the future,'" *Business Insider*, May 5, 2017, www.businessinsider.com/ordos-china-ghost-town-2017-5.

64. Dominique Fong, "China's ghost towns haunt its economy," *Wall Street Journal*, June 16–17, 2018; Mamta Badkar, "China's most famous ghost city got even worse in the last 4 years," *Business Insider*, June 9, 2014, www.businessinsider.com/chinas-ghost-cities-in-2014-2014-6; Kiyo Dörrer, "What's become of China's ghost cities?" *Deutsche Welle*, December 25, 2016, www.dw.com/en/what-has-become-of-chinas-ghost-cities/a-36525007.

65. Alexandra Stevenson and Cao Li, "'China's Manhattan' borrowed heavily. The people have yet to arrive," *New York Times*, April 10, 2019, www.nytimes.com/2019/04/10/business/china-economy-debt-tianjin.html. Simon Rabinovitch, "Wall St. wannabe points to China's growth risks," *Financial Post*, March 4, 2011, https://business.financialpost.com/investing/wall-st-wannabe-points-to-chinas-growth-risks.

66. Rob Schmitz, "China's economic boom leaves a trail of ghost cities," *Marketplace*, June 2, 2014, www.marketplace.org/2014/06/02/world/live-stage/chinas-economic-boom-leaves-trail-ghost-cities.

67. Tom Miller, "Time for a reality check on China's ghost cities," *Chinadialogue*, October 8, 2013, www.chinadialogue.net/article/show/single/en/6402-Time-for-a-reality-check-on-China-s-ghost-cities.

68. Hughes, "New 'ghost cities' typify out-of-control planning"; Tom Philips, "China goes west: A ghost city in the sand comes to life," *Guardian*, March 21, 2017, www.theguardian.com/cities/2017/mar/21/china-west-ghost-city-comes-to-life-lanzhou-new-area.

69. Giles Sabrie, "Caofeidian, the Chinese eco-city that became a ghost-town—in pictures," *Guardian*, July 23, 2014, www.theguardian.com/cities/gallery/2014/jul/23/caofeidian-chinese-eco-city-ghost-town-in-pictures. See also Jonathan Kaiman, "China's 'eco-cities': empty of hospitals, shopping centers and people," *Guardian*, April 14, 2014, www.theguardian.com/cities/2014/apr/14/china-tianjin-eco-city-empty-hospitals-people.

70. Huang Youqin, "Lack of affordable housing threatens China's urban dream," *Chinadialogue*, September 20, 2013, www.chinadialogue.net/article/show/single/en/6365-Lack-of-affordable-housing-threatens-China-s-urban-dream.

71. "Beijing has built thousands of cheap apartments no one wants," *Bloomberg*, December 12, 2019, www.bloomberg.com/news/articles/2019-12-12/beijing-has-built-thousands-of-cheap-apartments-no-one-wants.

72. See Yefei Chen, "Chasing ghosts, where is China's next wave of empty 'new towns'?" *South China Morning Post*, February 13, 2015, http://multimedia.scmp.com/china-ghost-towns/; Steven Lee Myers et al., "China's looming crisis: A

shrinking population," *New York Times*, January 17, 2019, www.nytimes.com/interactive/2019/01/17/world/asia/china-population-crisis.html.

73. Alexandra Stevenson and Cao Li, "Rising towers, sinking fortunes," *New York Times*, December 31, 2018; Vincent Fernando, "There are now enough vacant properties in China to house over half of America," *Business Insider*, September 8, 2010, www.businessinsider.com/there-are-now-enough-vacant-properties-in-china-to-house-over-half-of-america-2010-9; Dinny McMahon, "China's ghost cities and their multibillion-dollar debt are raising concerns," *Australian Financial Review*, April 6, 2018, www.afr.com/news/world/asia/chinas-ghost-cities-and-their-multibilliondollar-debt-20180404-hoybjz.

74. Nik Martin and Jose Qian, "Sudden drop in Chinese property prices leaves speculators reeling," *Deutsche Welle*, October 26, 2018, www.dw.com/en/sudden-drop-in-chinese-property-prices-leaves-speculators-reeling/a-46056805.

75. "13 officials suspended over 'White House' building scandal," *China Daily*, July 22, 2007. For a tour see Bianca Bosker, *Original Copies: Architectural Mimicry in Contemporary China* (Honolulu: University of Hawaii Press, 2013).

76. Chris Buckley, "As China vows austerity, giant brass fish devours $11 million," *New York Times*, October 12, 2013. See also "Top 12 strange Chinese buildings," www.youtube.com/watch?v=8jVrFxqeLCE.

77. See "Top 10 weirdest buildings in China," *China Daily*, August 30, 2013, http://usa.chinadaily.com.cn/china/2013-08/30/content_16933404_10.htm.

78. "China puts up a 6-floor building in 1 day (24 hours)," www.youtube.com/watch?v=txhSY41G9Gw; "Building a 15 story hotel in 6 days," www.youtube.com/watch?v=PNv13fY_3jY; "China builds a 57-story building in 19 days," www.youtube.com/watch?v=N6f_saywomM; "'China speed' amazes world," *People's Daily*, November 30, 2015, http://en.people.cn/n/2015/1130/c90000-8983488.html.

79. Smil, *Making the Modern World*, 91–92. On pages 55–56, Smil discusses the general problem of concrete's vulnerability to premature deterioration and relatively short lifespan, which in many instances is likely to be measured in decades rather than centuries:

> Concrete is not a highly durable material and it deteriorates for many reasons (exposure to moisture, freezing in cold climates, bacterial and algal growth in warm humid regions, acid deposition in polluted urban areas, vibration, reactions with carbonates, chlorides, and sulfates, and so on). Given the rate of post-1990 global concretization, it is inevitable that the post-2030 world will face an unprecedented burden of concrete deterioration. This challenge will be particularly daunting in China . . . where the combination of poor concrete quality, damaging natural environment, intensive pollutants, and heavy use of concrete structures will lead to premature deterioration of tens of billions of tons of the material that has been poured into buildings, road, bridges, dams, ports, and other structures during the past generation. Because maintenance and repair of deteriorating concrete have been inadequate, the future replacement costs of the material will run into trillions of dollars.

80. Zarathustra, "China's crumbling infrastructure model," *Macrobusiness*, July 28, 2012, www.macrobusiness.com.au/2011/07/is-chinas-growth-model-a-trainwreck. Keith Bradsher, "Collapse of new bridge underscores worries about China infrastructure," *New York Times*, August 24, 2012.

81. Wade Shepard, "Half the houses will be demolished in 20 years: On the disposable cities of China," *City Metric,* October 21, 2015, www.citymetric.com/skylines/half-houses-will-be-demolished-within-20-years-disposable-cities-china-1470.

82. Zheng Fengtian, "Weak buildings threaten life," *China Daily,* April 11–14, 2014.

83. Frank Langfitt, "Chinese blame failing bridges on corruption," *NPR,* August 29, 2012, www.npr.org/2012/08/29/160231137/chinese-blame-failed-infrastructure-on-corruption.

84. Edward Wong, "China admits building flaws in quake," *New York Times,* September 4, 2008.

85. "Ai Weiwei—the Sichuan earthquake & 90 tons of steel," *Public Delivery,* June 26, 2019, https://publicdelivery.org/ai-weiwei-straight.

86. *Disturbing the Peace* (2009), directed by Ai Weiwei; "What is Ai Weiwei doing with 9000 children's backpacks?" *Public Delivery,* August 14, 2013, https://publicdelivery.org/ai-weiwei-remembering-haus-der-kunst-muenchen-2009.

87. Mimi Lau, "Dying for China's economic miracle: Migrant workers ravaged by lung disease, fighting to pay for their funerals," *South China Morning Post,* October 10, 2018, www.scmp.com/news/china/politics/article/2167706/dying-chinas-economic-miracle-migrant-workers-ravaged-lung.

88. US Congressional Commission on China, "Coal mine safety in China: Can the accident rate be reduced?" (2005), 1.

89. David Barboza, "Explosion at Apple supplier caused by dust," *New York Times,* May 24, 2011; Andrew Jacobs, "Explosion kills dozens at eastern China plant," *New York Times,* August 2, 2014; "Death toll from China oil pipeline blast rises to 52, 11 missing," *Xinhua,* November 24, 2013, http://news.xinhuanet.com/english/china/2013-11/24/c_132913391.htm; "Power plant explosion in China kills over 20," *RT News,* August 11, 2018, www.rt.com/news/355517-china-chemical-blast-dead; Austin Ramzy and Javier C. Hernandez, "Explosion at chemical plant kills 64; employees detained," *New York Times,* March 22, 2019.

90. Gerry Shih, "After China's deadly chemical disaster, a shattered region weighs the cost of the rush to 'get rich,'" *Washington Post,* March 31, 2019.

91. "Seven killed in China plant explosion, second deadly blast this month," *Reuters,* March 31, 2019, www.reuters.com/article/us-china-blast-idUSKCN1RC0AC.

92. Shih, "After China's deadly chemical disaster."

93. US figures from US Bureau of Labor Statistics. In October 2003, China's government reported that 95,612 workers were killed on the job in the first nine months of that year, "a slight decrease compared with the same period in 2002." See Fu Jing, "Accidents kill 95,612 in 9 months," *China Daily,* October 24, 2003. For reporting on the 127,000 deaths in 2005 see Li Fangchao, "More time needed to improve work safety," *China Daily,* December 22, 2006; Fu Jing, "Officials punished for mine disasters," *China Daily,* December 24, 2005.

94. "Exposing the cover-up," *China Daily,* January 11, 2010. China Labour Bulletin, an independent organization that monitors and promotes workers' rights in China reports that "it is much more cost-effective for coal mine operators to buy off the families . . . than risk closure by reporting an accident," leaving many deaths overlooked. Quoted in Michelle Phillips, "In China, workplace deaths a small cost," *Washington Times,* August 8, 2010.

95. On workplace conditions see Duell, "Forced to stand for 24 hours." See also Charles Duhigg and David Barboza, "In China, human costs are built into an iPad," *New York Times,* January 26, 2012.

96. IHLO (Hong Kong) et al., "Breathless for blue jeans: Health hazards in China's denim factories" (June 2013), www.setem.org/media/pdfs/Breathless.pdf; Charles Kernaghan, "Made in China: The role of US companies in denying human rights and worker rights" (National Labor Committee, 2000); Charles Kernaghan, "Behind the label: 'Made in China'" (National Labor Committee, 1998); Anita Chan, *China's Workers Under Assault* (Armonk: M.E. Sharpe 2001); Michael Blanding and Heather White, "How China is screwing over its poisoned factory workers," *Wired*, April 6, 2015, www.wired.com/2015/04/inside-chinese-factories.

97. Gerry Shih, "They built a Chinese boomtown. It left them dying of lung disease with nowhere to turn," *Washington Post*, December 15, 2019, www.washingtonpost.com/world/asia_pacific/they-built-a-chinese-boomtown-it-left-them-dying-of-lung-disease-with-nowhere-to-turn/2019/12/15/4f070e54-0010-11ea-8341-cc3dce52e7de_story.html.

98. Ibid.

99. Quoted in Hugh Williamson, "China's toy industry tinderbox," *Multinational Monitor*, vol. 14, no. 9 (September 1, 1994).

100. Justin Yifu Lin, "Why continued growth in China is a win for the world," transcript of address given at the Wharton School, November 27, 2012, http://knowledge.wharton.upenn.edu/article/TheEconomist-justin-yifu-lin-why-continued-growth-in-china-is-a-win-for-the-world.

101. Quoted in Li Jing, "China's industrial growth 'a threat to resources,'" *South China Morning Post*, August 3, 2013, www.scmp.com/news/china/article/1294075/chinas-transformation-industrial-powerhouse-eating-away-resources, emphasis added.

102. Ibid.

CHAPTER 3

1. He Guangwei, "China's dirty secret: The boom poisoned its soil and crops," *Yale Environment 360*, June 30, 2014, https://e360.yale.edu/features/chinas_dirty_pollution_secret_the_boom_poisoned_its_soil_and_crops.

2. Javier C. Hernández, "'No such thing as justice' in chemical pollution fight in China," *New York Times*, June 13, 2017.

3. He Guangwei, "In China's heartland, a toxic trail leads from factories to fields to food," *Yale Environment 360*, July 7, 2014, https://e360.yale.edu/features/chinas_toxic_trail_leads_from_factories_to_food; Kelly and Jacobs, *People's Republic of Chemicals*, 124, 131, and Chapter 7.

4. "Film: How China became the world's rubbish dump," *Chinadialogue*, May 1, 2014, www.chinadialogue.net/books/6947-Film-How-China-became-the-world-s-rubbish-dump/en.

5. Yan Shuang, "Beijng air laden with arsenic, other heavy metals," *China Times*, April 24, 2013, www.globaltimes.cn/content/777053.shtml; Jake Bleiberg, "China's toxic waste problem is just as bad as its notorious air pollution," *Vice News*, March 8, 2016, https://news.vice.com/article/chinas-toxic-waste-problem-is-just-as-bad-as-its-notorious-air-pollution; Tom Phillips, "China's toxic school: Officials struggle to contain uproar over sick students," *Guardian*, April 19, 2016, www.theguardian.com/world/2016/apr/19/chinas-toxic-school-officials-struggle-to-hold-back-uproar-over-sick-students; Chien-min Chung, "China's

electronic waste village, a photo essay," *Time,* 2009, http://content.time.com/time/photogallery/0,29307,1870162_1822148,00.html.

6. Since the 1990s the government has spent billions of dollars in efforts to clean up Lake Tai west of Shanghai. China's third largest lake, Lake Tai was once a scenic wonder and the source of the Suzhou and Huangpu rivers, but today it is massively polluted by decades of heedless dumping from thousands of shoreline chemical plants, metal-platers, tanneries, and the like, as well as fertilizer and pesticide runoff. Scientists doubt that it can ever be restored to its former glory, or even be good enough to provide safe drinking water for nearby communities. See Liang Guorui and He Hanfu, "Long struggle for a cleaner Lake Tai," *Chinadialogue,* February 12, 2012, www.chinadialogue.net/article/4767-Long-struggle-for-a-cleaner-Lake-Tai-; Andrew Jacobs, "Despite persecution, guardian of Lake Tai spotlights China's polluters," *New York Times,* November 23, 2014.

7. Edward Wong, "As pollution worsens in China, solutions succumb to infighting," *New York Times,* March 21, 2013.

8. Chris Buckley and Vanessa Piao, "Rural water, not city smog, may be China's pollution nightmare," *New York Times,* April 11, 2016.

9. See for example "9 biggest water pollution disasters in China (since 2010)," *Global Times,* April 15, 2014, www.globaltimes.cn/content/854711.shtml. See also Judith Shapiro's summary in *China's Environmental Challenges* (Malden, Mass: Polity Press, 2012), 50–54. In 2006 the Associated Press reported that China's Songhua River, in addition to being "the site of a massive chemical spill that halted water supplies for tens of millions of people," had also been hit by more than 130 water pollution accidents over the preceding eleven months; "China's Songha River suffering near-daily chemical spills," *China Digital Times,* September 11, 2006, http://chinadigitaltimes.net/2006/09/official-chinas-songhua-river-suffering-near-daily-chemical-spills-ap. See also Li Guang et al., "The denim capital of the world: So polluted you can't give the houses away," *Chinadialogue,* August 13, 2013, www.chinadialogue.net/article/show/single/en/6283-The-denim-capital-of-the-world-so-polluted-you-can-t-give-the-houses-away; "River contaminated with cadmium in South China," *Xinhua,* January 21, 2012, http://en.people.cn/90882/7711357.html.

10. Ten years previously, a pollution tide killed fish and sickened thousands of people. By 2001 the government claimed to have shut down polluters and declared the cleanup a success. But the Huai River basin is now a symbol of the failure of environmental regulation in China. After spending more than $8 billion over a decade to clean up the area, the State Environmental Protection Administration concluded in 2004 that "some areas were more polluted than before"; Jim Yardley, "Rivers run black, and Chinese die of cancer," *New York Times,* September 12, 2004; An Baijie, "Polluted river flows with carcinogens," *China Daily,* August 8, 2013.

11. Yang Jian, "China river pollution 'a threat to people's lives,'" *Shanghai Daily,* February 17, 2012, http://en.people.cn/90882/7732438.html.

12. Ma Jun, *China's Water Crisis* (Norwalk, CT: EastBridge, 2004), vii; "One third of fish species in Yellow River believed extinct," *People's Daily,* January 16, 2007, http://en.people.cn/200701/16/eng20070116_341792.html.

13. Ma Jun, *China's Water Crisis,* 16.

14. Sun Xiaohua, "Pollution takes heavy toll on Yangtze," *China Daily*, April 16, 2007; Wu Jin, "Experts: Yangze ecology collapses," October 23, 2013, *China.org.cn*, www.china.org.cn/environment/2013-10/23/content_30377118.htm.

15. Shai Oster, "Why Chinese dam is forcing yet another mass exodus," *Wall Street Journal*, November 6, 2007; Courtney Verrill, "13 striking photos show how polluted China's water has become," *Business Insider*, March 25, 2016, www.businessinsider.in/13-striking-photos-that-show-how-polluted-Chinas-water-has-become/articleshow/51544220.cms.

16. For images see "Stash of trash at the Three Gorges Dam," *Caixin*, July 23, 2010, http://english.caixin.com/2010-07-23/100163671_2.html.

17. "Floating trash threatens Three Gorges Dam," *China Daily*, January 31, 2015.

18. "City water vulnerable to 'cancerous' river," *Xinhua*, May 30, 2006, http://chinadigitaltimes.net/2006/05/city-water-vulnerable-to-cancerous-river-xinhua-news-agency.

19. Han Wei, "Officials failing to stop textile factories dumping waste in Qiantang River," *Chinadialogue* January 8, 2013, www.chinadialogue.net/article/show/single/en/5589-Officials-failing-to-stop-textile-factories-dumping-waste-in-Qiantang-River. Shanghai sits between the Qiantang and Yangtze rivers.

20. Greenpeace, "Toxic threads: Putting pollution on parade" (2012), www.greenpeace.org/international/Global/international/publications/toxics/Water%202012/ToxicThreads02.pdf.

21. PFOA was the subject of the 2019 film *Dark Waters* starring Mark Ruffalo, about DuPont's dumping of chemical waste in a West Virginia river. It was based on Nathaniel Rich, "The lawyer who became Dupont's worst nightmare, *New York Times Magazine,* January 6, 2016.

22. Greenpeace, "Toxic threads," 18.

23. Ibid., 20, italics added.

24. Nicola Davidson, "Rivers of blood: The dead pigs rotting in China's water supply," *Guardian*, March 28, 2013, www.theguardian.com/world/2013/mar/29/dead-pigs-china-water-supply; "Upper Yangtze ecology 'collapses,'" *China Digital Times*, October 2013, http://chinadigitaltimes.net/2013/10/upper-yangtze-ecology-collapses.

25. Wu Jiao, "Sea waters 'heavily polluted,'" *China Daily,* January 13, 2007. Beth Walker, "Most of China's coastal waters heavily polluted," *Chinadialogue*, March 11, 2015, www.chinadialogue.net/blog/7777-Most-of-China-s-coastal-waters-heavily-polluted-/en. For a similar account from further up the coast see "Bohai sea drowns in discharged waste," *China Digital Times*, September 14, 2011, http://chinadigitaltimes.net/2011/09/bohai-sea-drowns-in-discharged-waste.

26. Cecilia Torajada and Asit K. Biswas, "The problem of water management," *China Daily*, March 5, 2013; Gong Jing and Liu Hongqiao, "Half of China's urban drinking water fails to meet standards," *Chinadialogue*, June 6, 2013, www.chinadialogue.net/article/show/single/en/6074-Half-of-China-s-urban-drinking-water-fails-to-meet-standards.

27. Chen Jia, "Birth defects soar due to pollution," *China Daily*, January 31, 2009, www.chinadaily.com.cn/china/2009-01/31/content_7433211.htm; "China birth defects soar due to pollution: Report," *Reuters*, October 29, 2007, www.reuters.com/article/environment-china-birth-dc-idUSPEK15525020071029.

28. Chen Xia, "80% of underground water undrinkable in China," *China.org.cn*, April 11, 2016, www.china.org.cn/environment/2016-04/11/content_38218704.htm. Buckley and Piao, "Rural water."

29. "Beijing reservoir unfit even for irrigation," *Chinadialogue*, November 29, 2006, www.chinadialogue.net/blog/586-Beijing-reservoir-unfit-even-for-irrigation/en; "Reservoir that supplies Beijing could contain unsafe levels of lead: Study," *Chinadialogue*, July 24, 2015, www.chinadialogue.net/blog/8088-Reservoir-that-supplies-Beijing-could-contain-unsafe-levels-of-lead-study/en. On pollution, overpumping, and other stresses on deep aquifers in northern China see Matt Currell, "The shrinking depths below," *Chinadialogue*, March 19, 2012, www.chinadialogue.net/article/4814-The-shrinking-depths-below. See also Zhang Chun, "One tenth of groundwater deserves top grade, admit Chinese officials," *Chinadialogue*, June 13, 2013, www.chinadialogue.net/blog/6092-One-tenth-of-groundwater-deserves-top-grade-admit-Chinese-officials/en.

30. Chris Buckley and Vanessa Piao, "China says 80% of tested wells had water too polluted to drink, *New York Times*, April 12, 2016; Zhou Chen and Zhang Yan, "China's tainted soil initiative lacks pay plan," *Chinadialogue,* June 2, 2016, www.chinadialogue.net/article/show/single/en/9028-China-s-tainted-soil-initiative-lacks-pay-plan.

31. Lu Hongqiao, "China set to miss safe rural drinking water targets," *Chinadialogue*, March 5, 2015, www.chinadialogue.net/article/show/single/en/7762-China-set-to-miss-safe-rural-drinking-water-targets; Huang Hao, "Village water supplies in China hit by scarcity and contamination," *Chinadialogue*, March 5, 2014, www.chinadialogue.net/article/show/single/en/7209-Village-water-supplies-in-China-hit-by-scarcity-and-contamination.

32. Abigail Barnes, "China's bottled water: The next health crisis?" *Chinadialogue*, July 22, 2014, www.chinadialogue.net/article/show/single/en/7152-China-s-bottled-water-the-next-health-crisis-.

33. See Hongqiao Liu, "Bottled water in China—boom or bust?" (China Water Risk, September 2015), www.chinawaterrisk.org/wp-content/uploads/2015/09/CWR-Bottled-Water-In-China-Boom-Or-Bust-Sep-2015-ENG.pdf; Hongqiao Liu, "China's bottled water industry poses new threat to precious resources," *Chinadialogue*, January 21, 2016, www.chinadialogue.net/article/show/single/en/8550-China-s-bottled-water-industry-poses-new-threat-to-precious-resources.

34. "Nearly half of Chinese provinces miss water targets, 85% of Shanghai's river water not fit for human contact," *Greenpeace*, January 6, 2017, www.greenpeace.org/eastasia/press/releases/toxics/2017/Nearly-half-of-Chinese-provinces-miss-water-targets-85-of-Shanghais-river-water-not-fit-for-human-contact; Deng Tingting, "In China, the water you drink is as dangerous as the air you breathe," *Guardian*, June 2, 2017, www.theguardian.com/global-development-professionals-network/2017/jun/02/china-water-dangerous-pollution-greenpeace. China has never issued a specific drinking water source quality standard. It categorizes "surface water" on a scale between one and five (see below). But water quality is monitored (or inadequately monitored) by multiple overlapping agencies such that there is no clear standard to measure quality. To meet particular class standards, surface water quality must meet numerous toxicological indicators but different agencies and different cities use tables of indicators from as few as 80 to over 300, so ratings are often inconsistent. Here's a

common list: Grade 1—unpolluted, safe for drinking; Grade 2—light pollution, safe for drinking; Grade 3—moderate pollution, acceptable for drinking after treatment (filtering/purification); Grade 4—polluted, not fit for human contact; Grade 5—seriously polluted, not fit for any use. See Hongqiao Liu, "Who is responsible for China's water?" *Chinadialogue,* April 10, 2015, www.chinadialogue. net/article/show/single/en/7839-Who-is-responsible-for-China-s-water-.

35. Ibid.

36. See *Beijing Besieged by Waste* (2011), directed by Wang Jiuliang, www.youtube. com/watch?v=IL5vMHcIJQk.

37. Chen Yifang, "Towers of trash pile up at China's unregulated landfills," *Caixin,* June 12, 2015, http://english.caixin.com/2015-06-12/100818731.html. For photos see "Lethal trash," *Caixin,* June 25, 2013, http://english.caixin.com/2013-06-25/100545919.htm.

38. Chen Yifang, "Towers." See also Roma Eisenstark, "China's rural dumping ground," *Caixin,* May 29, 2015, http://english.caixin.com/2013-08-08/100566999. html.

39. "Grim video shows huge waves of industrial waste that have left scores of missing in China," *Vice News,* December 21, 2015, https://news.vice.com/article/grim-video-shows-huge-waves-of-industrial-waste-that-have-left-scores-missing-in-china; "Huge rubbish pile threatens to contaminate China lake," *Financial Times,* July 11, 2016, https://next.ft.com/content/9145393a-474a-11e6-8d68-72e9211e 86ab.

40. Li You, "China's largest dump fills up 20 years ahead of schedule," *Sixth Tone,* November 13, 2019, www.sixthtone.com/news/1004838/China's%20Largest%20 Dump%20Fills%20Up%2020%20Years%20Ahead%20of%20Schedule.

41. Hannah Ellis-Peterson, "Deluge of electronic waste turning Thailand into 'world's rubbish dump,'" *Guardian,* June 28, 2018, www.theguardian.com/world/2018/ jun/28/deluge-of-electronic-waste-turning-thailand-into-worlds-rubbish-dump; Hannah Beech and Ryn Jirenuwat, "The price of old laptops: Toxic fumes in Thailand's lungs," *New York Times,* December 8, 2019, www.nytimes.com/ 2019/12/08/world/asia/e-waste-thailand-southeast-asia.html.

42. Raymond Zhong and Carolyn Zhang, "Food delivery apps are drowning China in plastic," *New York Times,* May 28, 2019.

43. Li Jing, "China produces about a third of waste polluting the world's oceans, says report," *South China Morning Post,* February 13, 2015, www.scmp.com/ article/1711744/china-produces-about-third-plastic-waste-polluting-worlds-oceans-says-report.

44. Zhong and Zhang, "Food delivery apps are drowning China in plastic."

45. Zhuang Pinghui, "Thousands protest in central China over waste incineration plant," *South China Morning Post,* July 5, 2019, www.scmp.com/news/china/ society/article/3017386/thousands-protest-central-china-over-waste-incineration-plant; "Thousands protest waste incinerator plans in Guangdong town," *South China Morning Post,* September 13, 2014, www.scmp.com/news/ china/article/1591751/thousands-protesters-march-against-trash-incinerator-plans-guangdong-town; Nectar Gan, "Chinese protest against incinerator plant turns violent," *South China Morning Post,* July 3, 2016, www.scmp.com/news/ china/policies-politics/article/1984955/chinese-protest-against-incinerator-plant-turns-violent.

46. Yuan Suwen and Li Rongde, "Burning unsorted garbage could cost Beijing billions in health care costs," *Caixin,* March 24, 2017, www.caixinglobal. com/2017-03-24/burning-unsorted-garbage-could-cost-beijing-billions-in-health-care-costs-101069583.html.

47. Anna Baptista, "Garbage in, garbage out: Incinerating trash is not an effective way to protect the climate or reduce waste," *The Conversation,* February 27, 2018, https://theconversation.com/garbage-in-garbage-out-incinerating-trash-is-not-an-effective-way-to-protect-the-climate-or-reduce-waste-84182; David Klein, "Humans make more trash than the Earth can handle. Blame capitalism," *Los Angeles Time*s, June 1, 2018, www.latimes.com/opinion/readersreact/la-ol-le-trash-recycling-capitalism-20180601-story.html.

48. Gong Jing, "What's coming out of China's taps?" *Chinadialogue,* June 7, 2012, www.chinadialogue.net/article/show/single/en/4962-What-s-coming-out-of-China-s-taps-.

49. Investigators have found that only around a third of China's wastewater treatment plants operate as planned. The rest run at below capacity, "while in some cities water treatment levels are zero"; Cui Zheng, "Seas of sewage," *Caixin*, October 12, 2012, http://english.caixin.com/2012-10-12/100446374.html.

50. Cui Zheng and Liu Zhiyi, "China's urban sludge dilemma: Sinking in stink," *Caixin,* August 8, 2013, http://english.caixin.com/2013-08-08/100566999. html?p2.

51. Cui and Liu, "China's urban sludge"; Yang Dazheng, "China deluged by toxic sludge," *Chinadialogue*, July 17, 2016, www.chinadialogue.net/article/show/single/en/5115-China-deluged-by-toxic-sludge.

52. The State Council of the People's Republic of China, "Law of the People's Republic of China on prevention and control of water pollution" (August 23, 2014), http://english.www.gov.cn/archive/laws_regulations/2014/08/23/content_281474983 042375.htm.

53. Zhang Yang, "Dumping toxins in a cloudy legal environment," *Caixin*, April 26, 2016, http://english.caixin.com/2016-04-26/100936798.html.

54. Kelly and Jacobs, *People's Republic of Chemicals*, 165, and Chapters 6–12. See also the comments of industrial managers in Steven Zhang, "What Chinese factory bosses really think about environmental protection," *Chinadialogue*, August 27, 2013,www.chinadialogue.net/article/show/single/en/6317-What-Chinese-factory-bosses-really-think-about-environmental-protection.

55. Zhang, "Dumping toxins."

56. Ibid.

57. Xu Nan, "Poisoned groundwater sparks media storm in China," *Chinadialogue*, February 2, 2013, www.chinadialogue.net/blog/5749-Poisoned-groundwater-sparks-media-storm-in-China/en; Gao Shengke, "Pumping pollution into China's groundwater," *Chinadialogue*, May 29, 2014, www.chinadialogue.net/article/show/single/en/7011-Pumping-pollution-into-China-s-groundwater.

58. Under the Mao-era imperative to relentlessly maximize output, China's farmers have applied four times as much fertilizer and three times as much pesticide as the global average. China is the world's largest consumer of agricultural chemicals, using more than 30 percent of global fertilizers and pesticides on 9 percent of the world's arable land. As a result, half of China's lakes and reservoirs, many rivers, and the country's coastal waters suffer from eutrophication, while "the heavy use of agrochemicals has led to a severe deterioration of arable and poses a serious

threat to domestic grain output." Since China's farmers don't own their farms and are only rewarded for maximizing output, "farmers usually only care about crop output and income. They seldom consider the soil damage and potential risks to human health from overusing fertilizers," according to Li Shilin, the director of a technical station in Anhui province. Decades of heavy application of agrochemicals has boosted output but now China's farmlands are said to be in poor shape, with soil too hard and too thin to support deep planting and high-yield crops and too fragile to withstand natural disasters. See Jin Zhu, "Heavy use of chemicals threatens grain output," *China Daily*, July 18, 2011; Narissa Hannink, "Overuse of fertilizers and pesticides in China linked to farm size," *Stanford Earth*, June 17, 2018, https://earth.stanford.edu/news/overuse-fertilizers-and-pesticides-china-linked-farm-size.

59. Chris Buckley, "Rice tainted with cadmium is discovered in southern China," *New York Times*, May 21, 2013. See also Hongqiao Liu, "The polluted legacy of China's largest rice-growing region," *Chinadialogue*, May 30, 2014, www.chinadialogue. net/article/show/single/en/7008-The-polluted-legacy-of-China-s-largest-rice-growing-province.

60. He Guangwei, "In China's heartland, a toxic trail leads from factories to fields to food." So far as we know, the Chinese government has not conducted extensive national testing for cadmium and for other toxic contaminants, but there is concern that such pollution is very widespread. See Liu, "The polluted legacy." On farmland poisoned with cadmium and other heavy metals from sewerage-laced irrigation water see Hongqiao Liu, "The poison eaters of Gansu province," *Caixin*, March 1, 2013, http://english.caixin.com/2013-03-01/100496199.html.

61. Nadya Ivanova, "Toxic water: Across much of China, huge harvests irrigated with industrial and agricultural runoff," *Circle of Blue*, January 18, 2013, www. circleofblue.org/2013/world/toxic-water-across-much-of-china-huge-harvests-irrigated-with-industrial-and-agricultural-runoff.

62. He Guangwei, "In China's heartland, a toxic trail leads from factories to fields to food."

63. See Sam Geall and Elizabeth Hilton, "Culture of secrecy behind China's pollution crisis," and Angel Hsu and Andrew Moffat, "China's soil pollution crisis still buried in mystery," in Chinadialogue, "Pollution and health in China: Confronting the human crisis" (September 2014), 73–74, 77–79, https://s3.amazonaws.com/ cd.live/uploads/content/file_en/7289/chinadialogue_health_journal.pdf.

64. Liu, "The polluted legacy"; Zheng Yesheng and Qian Yihong, *Shendu youhuan— dangdai Zhongguo de kechixu fazhan wenti* [Grave Concerns: Problems of Sustainable Development for China] (Beijing: Zhongguo chubanshe, 1998), 8–10.

65. "China says more than 3m hectares of land too polluted to farm," *South China Morning Post*, December 30, 2013. On the horrific state of China's farm soils, see the following three-part investigative series by He Guangwei: "Special report: The victims of China's soil pollution crisis," *Chinadialogue*, June 30, 2014, www. chinadialogue.net/article/show/single/en/7073-Special-report-The-victims-of-China-s-soil-pollution-crisis; "Special report: The legacy of Hunan's polluted soils," *Chinadialogue*, July 7, 2014, www.chinadialogue.net/article/show/single/ en/7076-Special-report-the-legacy-of-Hunan-s-polluted-soils; "China faces long battle to clean up its polluted soil," *Chinadialogue*, July 14, 2016, www. chinadialogue.net/article/show/single/en/7079-China-faces-long-battle-to-clean-up-its-polluted-soil.

66. Ministry of Environmental Protection and Ministry of Land and Natural Resources of the People's Republic of China, "Quanguo turang wuran zhuangkuang diaocha gongbao" [Nationwide survey of soil pollution bulletin] (April 2014), www.mep.gov.cn/gkml/hbb/qt/201404/t20140417_270670.htm. See also Xinhua, "More than 40% of China's arable land degraded," *China Daily*, November 5, 2014.

67. Zheng Chun, "China 'lacks experience' to clean up its polluted soil," *Chinadialogue*, April 14, 2014, www.chinadialogue.net/article/show/single/en/6897-China-lacks-experience-to-clean-up-its-polluted-soil; He Guangwei, "China faces long battle."

68. "The bad earth: The most neglected threat to public health in China is toxic soil," *The Economist*, June 8, 2017, www.economist.com/briefing/2017/06/08/the-most-neglected-threat-to-public-health-in-china-is-toxic-soil.

69. Lu Qin, "China unveils landmark plan to curb water pollution," *Chinadialogue*, April 16, 2015, www.thethirdpole.net/en/2015/04/19/china-unveils-landmark-plan-to-curb-water-pollution.

70. Kong Lingyu, "Government announces grand plans for cleaning up nation's pollution," *Caixin*, May 1, 2015, http://english.caixin.com/2015-05-01/100805752.html; Zhang Yan and Zhou Chen, "China's tainted soil initiative lacks pay plan," *Chinadialogue*, June 20, 2016, www.chinadialogue.net/article/show/single/en/9028-China-s-tainted-soil-initiative-lacks-pay-plan.

71. Liang and He, "Long struggle"; "Rubbish dumped on edge of Lake Tai puts drinking water of millions at risk," *South China Morning Post*, July 11, 2016, www.scmp.com/news/china/policies-politics/article/1988592/rubbish-dumped-edge-lake-tai-puts-drinking-water.

72. See He Guangwei, "China faces long battle."

73. US EPA, "Just the facts—cleaning up Hudson River PCBs" (February 2016), www3.epa.gov/hudson/just_facts_08_04.htm.

74. Zhang Jinping et al., "The waters of life may turn to poison," *Chinadialogue*, March 22, 2007, www.chinadialogue.net/article/show/single/en/869--The-waters-of-life-may-turn-to-poison-.

75. "Soil contamination," *China Daily*, June 14, 2013.

76. Tang Hao, "China's food scares show the system is bust," *Chinadialogue*, August 31, 2012, www.chinadialogue.net/article/show/single/en/5142-China-s-food-scares-show-the-system-is-bust.

77. Laurie Burkitt, "Chinese inspectors find milk with carcinogens," *Wall Street Journal*, December 28, 2011; Zhou Wenting, "Toxic metals common in kids' goods," *China Daily*, December 8, 2011; Gong Jing and Liu Hongqiao, "Confronting China's cadmium-laced rice crisis," *Caixin*, June 5, 2013; "Alarm as over 150 pig carcasses found in China's Gan River," *South China Morning Post*, March 19, 2012, www.scmp.com/news/china/article/1452448/renewed-alarm-over-150-pig-carcasses-found-chinas-gan-river. (The Gan River in Jiangxi province supplies drinking water to the provincial capital, Nanchang.) "Chinese herbs tainted by toxic pesticides, says Greenpeace," *South China Morning Post*, June 24, 2013; Olivia Rosenman, "Baby formula is contaminated with aluminum," *South China Morning Post*, October 11, 2013; Barbara Demick, "China wrestles with food safety problems (including phosphorescent glow-in-the-dark pork)," *Los Angeles Times*, June 26, 2011; Jonathan Watts, "Made in China: Tainted food, fake drugs and dodgy paint," *Guardian*, July 5, 2007, www.theguardian.com/business/2007/jul/05/china.internationalnews1. On carcinogens found in baby

formula see "China's Hunan Ava Dairy recalls tainted infant formula," *Reuters*, July 23, 2012, www.reuters.com/article/2012/07/23/us-china-dairy-idUSBRE 86MoE820120723.

78. See "Netizen: List of toxic foods you need to know," *China Digital Times*, September 29, 2008, http://chinadigitaltimes.net/2008/09/list-of-toxic-foods-you-got-to-know. For more examples see Zhou Qing, *What Kind of God: A Survey of the Current Safety of China's Food*, trans. by Flora Drew (Reportage Literature, 2004), and "Conversation: Zhou Qing: punished to save them," PEN AMERICA (September 12, 2011), https://pen.org/zhou-qing-punished-to-save-them/. On regulatory failure see Guanqi Zhou, "The regulatory regime of food safety in China: A systemic not accidental failure" (PhD. diss., Unversity of Adelaide, May 2016), https://digital.library.adelaide.edu.au/dspace/bitstream/. 2440/100197/2/02whole.pdf.

79. Alice Yan, "Apologies won't fix the sorry state of food safety," *South China Morning Post*, April 30, 2011.

80. Chris Buckley, "Rat meat sold as lamb highlights fear in China," *New York Times*, May 3, 2013, emphasis added.

81. Phoebe Zhang, "Rat in hotpot shocks pregnant woman, shuts down restaurant in eastern China," *South China Morning Post*, September 10, 2018, www.scmp.com/news/china/society/article/2163524/rat-hotpot-shocks-pregnant-woman-shuts-down-restaurant-eastern.

82. "China pledges to trace origin and crackdown on trade in smuggled, frozen 'zombie meat,'" *South China Morning Post*, July 13, 2015, www.scmp.com/news/china/society/article/1838304/china-pledges-trace-origin-and-crackdown-trade-smuggled-frozen.

83. Joseph Kahn, "China quick to execute drug official," *New York Times*, July 11, 2007. See also Gordon Fairclough, "China boosts food-safety oversight, toughens penalties," *Wall Street Journal*, March 2, 2009; Gordon Fairclough, "China sentences two to death in milk scandal," *Wall Street Journal*, January 23, 2009. More executions would follow, but to little effect. See Sharon LaFraniere, "Two executed in China for selling tainted milk," *New York Times*, November 25, 2009; James Areddy, "More tainted-milk cases are highlighted in China," *New York Times,* January 26, 2010; Sharon LaFraniere, "In China, fear of fake eggs and 'recycled' buns," *New York Times*, May 8, 2011; Laurie Burkitt, "Hundreds in China fall ill: Additive suspected," *Wall Street Journal*, April 26, 2011; Zhou Wenting, "Hundreds captured for illegal additive," *China Daily*, August 30, 2011; Christopher Weaver, "How fake cancer drugs entered the U.S." *Wall Street Journal*, July 20, 2012. So inevitably comes another crackdown, again without apparent effect. See Colum Murphy, "China food-safety crackdown," *Wall Street Journal*, December 28, 2012; Lin Yunshi, "Official fired over milk scandal gets top job in agriculture ministry," Caixin, July 20, 2015, www.caixinglobal.com/2015-07-20/official-fired-over-milk-scandal-gets-top-job-in-agriculture-ministry-101012322.html.

84. Polls show that public concern about food safety has risen sharply in recent years. In 2008 only 12 percent of people rated food safety as "a very big problem." By 2013 this had risen to 38 percent, just behind concerns about air pollution (47 percent in 2013 vs. 31 percent in 2008) and water pollution (40 percent in 2013 vs. 28 percent in 2008). The safety of medicines was seen as a very big problem by 27 percent of respondents in 2013 (9 percent in 2008). Pew Research,

"Environmental concerns on the rise in China" (September 2013), www. pewglobal.org/2013/09/19/environmental-concerns-on-the-rise-in-china.

85. Jinshan Hong et al., "Chinese parents panic over infant vaccine safety," *Bloomberg*, July 30, 2018, www.bloomberg.com/news/articles/2018-07-30/china-s-vaccine-scandal-revives-safety-concerns-as-parents-panic.

86. Michael Walsh and Ning Pan, "Chinese rabies vaccine scandal sparks outrage among authorities and public," *ABC News*, July 23, 2018, www.abc.net.au/news/2018-07-23/chinese-vaccine-scandal-sparks-outrage/10025352.

87. "Milk powder scandal result of lax supervision," *China Daily*, April 8, 2016. This was more than a decade after the first big infant formula scandal, and after repeated "crackdowns."

88. Edward Wong, "Chinese search for infant formula goes global," *New York Times*, July 25, 2013.

89. Bill Birtles, "If China's on the rise, why do many want out?" *ABC News*, September 9, 2018, www.abc.net.au/news/2018-09-09/if-china-is-on-the-rise-why-do-many-want-to-leave/10214604.

90. "In China, what you eat tells who you are," *Los Angeles Times*, September 16, 2011.

91. Wang Yue, "Polluted farmlands leads to Chinese food security fears," *Chinadialogue*, January 7, 2014, www.chinadialogue.net/article/show/single/en/6636-China-forced-to-import-food-as-its-environment-declines.

92. Tom Philpott, "Why China wants US-grown pork chops," *Mother Jones*, July 30, 2013.

93. Wang Yue, "Polluted farmland leads to Chinese food security fears," *Chinadialogue*, July 1, 2014, www.chinadialogue.net/article/show/single/en/6636-Polluted-farmland-leads-to-Chinese-food-security-fears; Tom Lefitt, "What are the ecological costs of China's food imports?" *Chinadialogue*, September 10, 2010, www.chinadialogue.net/article/show/single/en/5154-What-are-the-ecological-costs-of-China-s-future-food-imports-; Beth Hoffman, "How increased meat consumption in China changes landscapes around the globe," *Forbes*, March 26, 2014; John Dearing, "China's polluted soil and water will drive up world food prices," *Chinadialogue*, March 3, 2015, www.chinadialogue.net/article/show/single/en/7768-China-s-polluted-soil-and-water-will-drive-up-world-food-prices.

94. "You get what you pay for: The hidden price of food from China," *Der Spiegel*, October 17, 2012, www.spiegel.de/international/world/europe-worries-about-health-hazards-of-cheap-food-from-china-a-861406.html; Mark McDonald, "Maggots in the pasta: Europe screens tainted Chinese food," *New York Times*, October 21, 2012.

95. Elizabeth C. Economy, "The great leap backwards: The costs of China's environmental crisis," *Foreign Affairs*, vol. 86, no. 5 (September–October 2007): 38–59.

96. "China's environment ministry finds patchy progress on water and soil pollution," *Reuters*, April 24, 2017, www.reuters.com/article/us-china-pollution/chinas-environment-ministry-finds-patchy-progress-on-water-and-soil-pollution-idUSKBN17R02V.

97. See for example Zheng Jinran, "Land laid waste by coal is reborn as cultural garden," *China Daily*, October 31, 2017; Wang Xiaodong, "Green growth: Organic farms boom across China as awareness of health and concern for environment increases," *China Daily*, July 14–16, 2017; Zhang Youting, "Supplier ensures

organic products are authentic," *China Daily*, July 14–16, 2017. But given rampant fraud, and the lack of expertise, technology, and facilities to do extensive testing of foods, soils, and water, why should consumers trust this supplier's word? There might be the odd unpolluted farm here and there, but at scale to feed hundreds of millions of people? That's not possible in China today. As Zhang Youting writes, "a big challenge for the organic industry in China is lack of trust from consumers. . . . Some producers may also not be able to find the right [organic] pesticides, which brings risk of faking." Indeed. With China's rivers, lakes, and aquifers severely polluted, would-be "organic" farmers face extremely difficult if not insurmountable barriers.

98. Luna Lin, "China's water pollution will be more difficult to fix than its dirty air," *Chinadialogue*, February 17, 2014, www.chinadialogue.net/blog/6726-China-s-water-pollution-will-be-more-difficult-to-fix-than-its-dirty-air-/en; Zhang Chun, "China 'lacks experience' to clean up its polluted soil," *Chinadialogue*, April 14, 2014, www.chinadialogue.net/article/show/single/en/6897-China-lacks-experience-to-clean-up-its-polluted-soil; He Guangwei, "The soil pollution crisis in China: A cleanup presents daunting challenge," *Yale Environment 360*, July 14, 2014, https://e360.yale.edu/features/the_soil_pollution_crisis_in_china_a_cleanup_presents_daunting

99. See the discussion of these in Smith, "Essay 2 (2010): Beyond growth or beyond capitalism?" 38–46.

CHAPTER 4

1. Quoted in David Pierson, "China's smog taints economy, health," *Los Angeles Times*, January 26, 2013.

2. Lauri Myllyvirta, "China keeps building coal plants despite new overcapacity," *Greenpeace*, July 12, 2016, https://unearthed.greenpeace.org/2016/07/13/china-keeps-building-coal-plants-despite-new-overcapacity-policy.

3. On the consequences of low-grade fuel see "Where does Beijing's pollution come from?" *China File*, February 3, 2013, www.chinafile.com/multimedia/infographics/where-does-beijings-pollution-come.

4. Edward Wong, "On a scale of 0–500, Beijing's air quality tops 'crazy bad,'" *New York Times*, January 12, 2013.

5. Mia Li, "'Airpocalypse' hits Harbin, closing schools," *New York Times*, October 21, 2013,https://sinosphere.blogs.nytimes.com/2013/10/21/air-pollution-hits-harbin-in-northeast-china-closing-schools-and-roads.

6. Jonathan Kaiman, "Beijing smog makes city unlivable says mayor," *Guardian*, January 28, 2015, www.theguardian.com/world/2015/jan/28/beijing-smog-unliveable-mayor-wang-anshun-china.

7. Zheping Huang, "A Chinese artist vacuumed up Beijing's smog for 100 days and made a brick from what he collected," *Quartz*, December 1, 2015, https://qz.com/562319/a-chinese-artist-vacuumed-up-beijings-smog-for-100-days-and-made-a-brick-from-what-he-collected.

8. "Beijing issues first ever red alert," *Chinadialogue*, December 12, 2015, www.chinadialogue.net/blog/8419-Beijing-issues-first-ever-red-alert-on-smog/en.

9. "China decries Shenyang pollution called 'worst ever' by activists," *BBC News*, November 10, 2015, www.bbc.com/news/world-asia-china-34773556; Tom

Philips, "Smog refugees flee Chinese cities as 'airpocalypse' blights half a billion," *Guardian*, December 21, 2016, www.theguardian.com/world/2016/dec/21/smog-refugees-flee-chinese-cities-as-airpocalypse-blights-half-a-billion.

10. Eva Li, "Heavy smog continues to choke China heartland," *South China Morning Post*, January 3, 2017, 2016, www.scmp.com/news/china/society/article/2058770/heavy-smog-continues-choke-chinas-heartland; Eva Li, "Drone footage showing extent of smog-stricken Beijing's traffic jams leaves viewers gasping," *South China Morning Post*, January 3, 2017, www.scmp.com/news/china/society/article/2058926/drone-footage-beijing-smog-traffic-jams-leaves-internet-viewers; Zhuang Pinghui, "Beijing's 'smog refugees' flee the capital for cleaner air down south," *South China Morning Post*, December 19, 2016, www.scmp.com/news/china/society/article/2055739/beijings-smog-refugees-flee-capital-cleaner-air-down-south; "Chinese flee smog to go on 'lung cleaning breaks' overseas," *South China Morning Post*, January 9, 2017, www.scmp.com/news/china/society/article/2060477/chinese-flee-smog-go-lung-cleansing-breaks-overseas.

11. "Beijing air laden with arsenic, other heavy metals," *China File*, April 30, 2013, www.chinafile.com/links/Beijing-Air-Laden-Arsenic-Other-Heavy-Metals; Feng Hao, "Dirty air takes shine off solar power," *Chinadialogue*, October 20, 2017, www.chinadialogue.net/article/show/single/en/10157-Dirty-air-takes-shine-off-solar-power.

12. "Chinese anger over pollution becomes main cause of social unrest," *Bloomberg*, March 6, 2013, www.bloomberg.com/news/articles/2013-03-06/pollution-passes-land-grievances-as-main-spark-of-china-protests; Liu Qin, "Shanghai residents throng streets in 'unprecedented' anti-PX protest," *Chinadialogue*, July 2, 2017, www.chinadialogue.net/article/show/single/en/8009-Shanghai-residents-throng-streets-in-unprecedented-anti-PX-protest.

13. Lily Kuo, "China's nightmare scenario: By 2025 air quality could be much much worse," *Quartz*, March 11, 2013, http://qz.com/61694/chinas-nightmare-scenario-by-2025-air-quality-could-be-much-much-worse; Wang Yue, "China unlikely to reduce coal use in the next decade," *Chinadialogue*, February 10, 2014, www.chinadialogue.net/blog/6718-China-unlikely-to-reduce-coal-use-in-the-next-decade/esn.

14. Simon Göß, "Overview of China's evolving energy market in 2018," *Energy Brainblog*, March 13, 2019, https://blog.energybrainpool.com/en/overview-of-chinas-evolving-energy-market-in-2018.

15. Simon Göß, "China's electricity system in 2017: Record PV expansion," *Energy Brainblog*, February 8, 2018, https://blog.energybrainpool.com/en/chinas-electricity-system-in-2017-record-pv-expansion; and Göß, personal communication, December 10, 2019.

16. "Introducing Megapack: Utility-scale energy storage," *Tesla.com*, July 29, 2019, www.tesla.com/blog/introducing-megapack-utility-scale-energy-storage.

17. Xi Lu et al., "Challenges faced by China compared with the U.S. in developing wind power," *Nature Energy* vol. 1, article no. 16061 (2016), www.nature.com/articles/nenergy201661.

18. Jo Harper, "German wind power blown off course," *Deutsche Welle*, November 21, 2019, www.dw.com/en/german-wind-power-blown-off-course/a-51341340.

19. Richard Martin, "Germany runs up against the limits of renewables," *MIT Technology Review*, May 24, 2016, www.technologyreview.com/s/601514/germany-runs-up-against-the-limits-of-renewables.

20. Feng Wang et al. "China's renewable energy policy: Commitments and challenges," *Energy Policy* 38 (2010), 1873-1874, www.ourenergypolicy.org/wp-content/uploads/2014/07/China.pdf.

21. Roger Harribin, "China embarked on wind power frenzy, says IEA," *BBC News*, September 20, 2016, www.bbc.com/news/science-environment-37409069; Joern Huenteler et al., "Why is China's wind power generation not living up to its potential?" *Environmental Research Letters*, 13.4, March 19, 2018, https://iopscience.iop.org/article/10.1088/1748-9326/aaadeb.

22. Doug Young, "Reports point to failure of China's EV, green power policies," *Renewable Energy World*, September 9, 2016, www.renewableenergyworld.com/articles/2016/09/reports-point-to-failure-of-china-s-ev-green-power-policies.html.

23. "2016 detailed electricity statistics," *China Energy Portal*, January 20, 2017, https://chinaenergyportal.org/en/2016-detailed-electricity-statistics; Guoliang Luo, "Why the wind curtailment of northwest China remains high," *Sustainability*, no. 10 (February 2020): 2-4; Qi Ye et al., "Wind curtailment in China and lessons from the United States" (Brookings-Tsinghua Center for Public Policy, March 2018), 11, www.brookings.edu/research/wind-curtailment-in-china-and-lessons-from-the-united-states; Dave Elliot, "Green power curtailment in China," *Physicsworld*, July 17, 2019, https://physicsworld.com/a/green-power-curtailment-in-china; Javier C. Hernandez, "It can power a small nation. But this wind farm in China is mostly idle," *New York Times*, January 15, 2017; Kate Gordon and Anders Hove, "How China wastes its renewable energy," *Wall Street Journal*, September 13, 2016, https://blogs.wsj.com/experts/2016/09/13/how-china-wastes-its-renewable-energy.

24. Darrin Magee, "Hydropower boom in China and along Asia's rivers outpaces electricity demand," *Chinadialogue*, April 28, 2017, www.chinadialogue.net/article/show/single/en/9760-Hydropower-boom-in-China-and-along-Asia-s-rivers-outpaces-electricity-demand.

25. Coco Liu, "Facing grid constraints, China puts a chill on new wind energy projects," *Inside Climate News*, March 28, 2016, https://insideclimatenews.org/news/28032016/china-wind-energy-projects-suspends-clean-energy-climate-change.

26. Edmund Downie, "Sparks fly over ultra-high voltage power lines," *Chinadialogue*, January 29, 2018, www.chinadialogue.net/article/show/single/en/10376-Sparks-fly-over-ultra-high-voltage-power-lines.

27. Ibid.

28. Qi Ye, "Wind curtailment in China," 5; Luo, "Why wind curtailment remains high," 4.

29. Hernandez, "It can power a small nation."

30. Center for Strategic and International Studies (CSIS), "Mapping the U.S-Canada Energy Relationship" (May 2018). Luo, "Why curtailment remains high," 3-4.

31. Luo, "Why curtailment remains high," 13; Wang, "China's renewable energy policy," 1873–1875.

32. Luo, "Why curtailment remains high," 20–23; Qi Ye, "Wind curtailment in China," 9–10.

33. Peter Fairly, "Wind battles coal for access to China's grid," *IEEE Spectrum*, September 20, 2016, https://spectrum.ieee.org/energy/renewables/wind-battles-coal-for-access-to-chinas-grid.

34. Luo, "Why curtailment remains high," 6, see also 12–13, 17–18.
35. Zhang Yan, "Coal addiction spells trouble for wind power producers," *Caixin*, April 29, 2016, www.caixinglobal.com/2016-04-29/coal-addiction-spells-trouble-for-wind-power-producers-101011708.html.
36. Qi Ye, "Wind curtailment in China," 9.
37. Xiong Congru et al., "Xinjiang zi bei dianchang 'jingpen shi' fazhan cang fengxian" [The 'blowout' surge of captive coal-fired power plants conceals a risk for Xinjiang], *Jingji cankao* [Economic Information Daily], February 2, 2017, http://dz.jjckb.cn/www/pages/webpage2009/html/2017-02/20/node_7.htm; Qi Ye, "Wind curtailment in China," 12; Luo, "Why curtailment remains high," 13–14; Huw Slater, "Coal power and privilege: China's problems with industry-owned generators," *Chinadialogue,* September 5, 2017, www.chinadialogue.net/article/show/single/en/10040-Coal-power-and-privilege-China-s-problem-with-industry-owned-generators.
38. Qi Ye, "Wind curtailment in China," 13–14.
39. Josh Gabbatiss, "Solar is now 'cheaper than grid electricity' in every Chinese city, study finds," *Carbon Brief*, December 8, 2019, www.carbonbrief.org/solar-now-cheaper-than-grid-electricity-in-every-chinese-city-study-finds.
40. "China solar installations to slow as subsidy cuts bite: Executive," *Reuters*, September 5, 2019, www.reuters.com/article/us-china-solar/china-solar-installations-to-slow-as-subsidy-cuts-bite-executive-idUSKCN1VR08R; Liu Bin, "China solar industry struggles through sudden subsidy cuts," *Climate Home News*, October 15, 2018, www.climatechangenews.com/2018/08/15/china-solar-industry-struggles-sudden-subsidy-cuts.
41. Yin Yijin, "Wind power projects halted in northwest China," *Sixth Tone*, March 12, 2019, www.sixthtone.com/news/1003666/wind-power-projects-halted-in-northwest-china.
42. Michael Standaert, "Why China's renewable energy transition is losing momentum," *Yale Environment 360*, September 26, 2019, https://e360.yale.edu/features/why-chinas-renewable-energy-transition-is-losing-momentum.
43. "Gangplank to a warm future," *New York Times*, July 28, 2013, www.nytimes.com/2013/07/29/opinion/gangplank-to-a-warm-future.html.
44. BP, "BP Statistical Review of World Energy 2019" (2019), www.bp.com/content/dam/bp/business-sites/en/global/corporate/pdfs/energy-economics/statistical-review/bp-stats-review-2019-china-insights.pdf.
45. Brad Plumer and Nadja Popovich, "Here's how far the world is from meeting its climate goals," *New York Times,* November 6, 2017.
46. "Control methane now, greenhouse gas expert warns," *ScienceDaily*, May 14, 2014, www.sciencedaily.com/releases/2014/05/140514165251.htm; Justin Gillis, "Should we have to choose between two evils: Carbon dioxide vs. methane?" *New York Times,* July 7, 2014; Sabrina Shankman, "Oil and gas fields leak far more methane than EPA reports," *Inside Climate News*, June 21, 2018, https://insideclimatenews.org/news/21062018/methane-leaks-oil-gas-climate-change-risks-natural-gas-slcp-global-warming-pollution-science-edf-study.
47. Zach Boren, "China: CO2 emissions from coal-to-chemical industry set to soar," *Greenpeace*, April 25, 2017, https://unearthed.greenpeace.org/2017/04/25/china-coal-to-chemical-carbon-emissions; Yue Qin et al., "Air quality, health, and climate implications of China's synthetic natural gas development," *Proceedings of the National Academy of Science*, vol. 114, no. 19 (May 2017): 4887–4892, https://

doi.org/10.1073/pnas.1703167114; Matthew Brown, "Converting coal would help China's smog at climate's expense," *Phys.org*, April 24, 2017, https://phys.org/news/2017-04-coal-china-smog-climate-expense.html; Edward Wong, "China invests in region rich in oil, coal, and also strife," *New York Times*, December 20, 2014; Zhang Chun, "Critics line up against coal-to-gas power in China," *Chinadialogue*, August 15, 2014, www.chinadialogue.net/article/show/single/en/7223-Critics-line-up-against-coal-to-gas-power-in-China.

48. Li Jing, "Where in China can you find the worst air pollution? You might be surprised . . ." *South China Morning Post*, April 20, 2016, www.scmp.com/news/china/policies-politics/article/1937381/where-china-can-you-find-worst-air-pollution-you-might; Liu Qin, "China's far west poised to overtake Hebei in a 'most polluted' list," *Chinadialogue*, June 15, 2016, www.chinadialogue.net/article/show/single/en/9017-China-s-far-west-poised-to-overtake-Hebei-in-a-most-polluted-list.

49. "China's coal expansion may spark water crisis, warns Greenpeace," *Guardian*, August 15, 2012. See also the accompanying documentary photos by Lu Guang: "China's mega coal power bases exacerbate water crisis—in pictures," *Guardian*, August 21, 2012, www.theguardian.com/environment/gallery/2012/aug/21/china-mega-coal-water-crisis-in-pictures.

50. William J. Kelly, "China's plan to clean up air in cities will doom the climate, scientists say," *InsideClimate News*, February 13, 2014, http://insideclimate news.org/news/20140213/chinas-plan-clean-air-cities-will-doom-climate-scientists-say.

51. See Sophie Beach, "China's fracking boom and the fate of the planet," *China Digital Times*, September 19, 2014, http://chinadigitaltimes.net/2014/09/chinas-fracking-boom-fate-planet. Western companies are not so sure Chinese conditions are suitable for fracking; Huang Kaixi et al., "BP bows out of fracking in China," *Caixin*, April 12, 2019, www.caixinglobal.com/2019-04-12/bp-bows-out-of-fracking-in-china-101403590.html; "China succeeds in mining combustible ice in South China Sea," *People's Daily*, May 18, 2017, http://en.people.cn/n3/2017/0518/c90000-9217345.html; "Chinese rig starts drilling in Russian Arctic," *Eye on the Arctic*, August 1, 2017, www.rcinet.ca/eye-on-the-arctic/2017/08/01/drilling-starts-on-chinese-rig-in-russian-arctic; Mia Bennett, "China's Belt and Road Initiative moves into the Arctic," *Cryopolitics*, June 27, 2017, www.cryopolitics.com/2017/06/27/chinas-belt-and-road-initiative-moves-into-the-arctic.

52. Beth Walker and Liu Qin, "The hidden cost of China's shift to hydropower," *The Diplomat*, July 29, 2015, https://thediplomat.com/2015/07/the-hidden-costs-of-chinas-shift-to-hydropower.

53. "China's shift from coal to hydro comes at a heavy price," *Chinadialogue*, July 27, 2015, www.chinadialogue.net/article/show/single/en/8093-China-s-shift-from-coal-to-hydro-comes-at-a-heavy-price.

54. Dai Qing, *The River Dragon Has Come!* (London: M. E. Sharpe, 1998), Chapter 3.

55. Dai Qing, *River Dragon*, and *Yangte! Yangtze!* (London: Earthscan, 1994).

56. Dai Qing, *River Dragon*, 9–12.

57. Zhang Chun, "China needs redlines to protect its rivers from hydropower craze," *Chinadialogue*, January 1, 2014, www.chinadialogue.net/blog/6682-China-needs-red-lines-to-protect-its-rivers-from-hydropower-craze/en; David Stanway, "Dam nation: China's crackdown spares big state hydropower projects," *South China*

Morning Post, September 4, 2018, www.scmp.com/magazines/post-magazine/long-reads/article/2162523/dam-nation-china-crackdown-spares-big-state.

58. Richard Bernstein, "China's Mekong plans threaten disaster for countries downstream," *Foreign Policy,* September 27, 2017, https://foreignpolicy.com/2017/09/27/chinas-mekong-plans-threaten-disaster-for-countries-downstream.

59. "When the glaciers go: Hydroelectric vulnerability and climate change, *The Climate Examiner,* April 21, 2016, http://theclimateexaminer.ca/2016/04/21/when-the-glaciers-go-hydroelectric-vulnerability-and-climate-change.

60. Chaoliu Li, "Sources of black carbon to the Himalayan-Tibetan Plateau glaciers," *Nature Communications,* August 23, 2016, www.ncbi.nlm.nih.gov/pmc/articles/PMC4996979. See also Liu Qin, "Cross-border cooperation needed to reduce Himalayan glacier loss," *Chinadialogue,* October 18, 2016, www.chinadialogue.net/article/show/single/en/9318-Cross-border-cooperation-needed-to-reduce-Himalayan-glacier-loss; "Pollution from China grounds flights in Tibet," *Telegraph,* December 20, 2013, www.telegraph.co.uk/news/worldnews/asia/tibet/10529581/Pollution-from-China-grounds-flights-in-Tibet.html.

61. Beth Walker, "Melting permafrost reduces Yangtze River flow," *Chinadialogue,* January 27, 2012, www.chinadialogue.net/blog/4745-Melting-permafrost-reduces-Yangtze-River-flow/en.

62. Fan Xiao, "The 'madcap' scheme to divert the Brahmaputra," *Chinadialogue,* January 17, 2018, www.chinadialogue.net/blog/10350-The-madcap-scheme-to-divert-the-Brahmaputra/en.

63. Tom Fawthrop, "Leaked report warns Cambodia's biggest dam could 'literally kill' the Mekong river," *Guardian,* May 16, 2018, www.theguardian.com/environment/2018/may/16/leaked-report-warns-cambodias-biggest-dam-could-literally-kill-mekong-river; Wan Rong, "Dam-building threatens endangered green peacock," *Chinadialogue,* April 24, 2017, www.chinadialogue.net/blog/9747-Dam-building-threatens-endangered-green-peacock/en.

64. David Tyler Gibson and Luan Dong, "The environmental impact of China's dam rush," *Chinadialogue,* April 7, 2014, www.chinadialogue.net/blog/6859-The-environmental-impact-of-China-s-dam-rush/en.

65. "Violent protests over development of the Pubugou dam, China," *Environmental Justice Atlas,* February 2, 2018, https://ejatlas.org/conflict/the-pubugou-dam-development-controversy; Peter Bosshard, "Grassroots protests against Chinese dams in Africa," *International Rivers,* February 23, 2011, www.internationalrivers.org/blogs/227/grassroots-protests-against-chinese-dams-in-africa; Hans Nicholas Jong, "Indonesian activists protest China-funded dam in orangutan habitat," *Mongabay,* May 9, 2018, https://news.mongabay.com/2018/05/chinas-plan-to-build-dam-in-rarest-apes-habitat-in-sumatra-condemned; "10 Reasons why climate initiatives should not include large hydropower projects," *International Rivers,* December 3, 2015, www.internationalrivers.org/node/9204; Kraisak Choonhavan, "Vietnam demands halt to Mekong dams," *Chinadialogue,* June 10, 2014, www.chinadialogue.net/article/show/single/en/7032-Vietnam-demands-halt-to-Mekong-dams.

66. See for example Bibek Bhandari, "China's internet industry causing 'significant' carbon emissions," *Sixth Tone,* September 9, 2019, www.sixthtone.com/news/1004537/China's%20Internet%20Industry%20Causing%20'Significant'%20Carbon%20Emissions.

67. See for example Liu Qin, "Shopping festivals deliver disaster for environment," *Chinadialogue*, January 4, 2018, www.chinadialogue.net/article/show/single/en/10331-Shopping-festivals-deliver-disaster-for-environment; Chen Ronggang, "The mountains of takeout trash choking China's cities," *Sixth Tone*, October 15, 2017,www.sixthtone.com/news/1001003/the-mountains-of-takeout-trash-choking-chinas-cities; Zhang Chun, "Downsizing China's consumer dream could bring huge carbon cuts, report says," *Chinadialogue*, July 6, 2016, www.chinadialogue.net/article/show/single/en/9073-Downsizing-China-s-consumer-dream-could-bring-huge-carbon-cuts-report-says; Feng Hao, "China's Belt and Road Initiative still pushing coal," *Chinadialogue*, May 12, 2017, www.chinadialogue.net/article/show/single/en/9785-China-s-Belt-and-Road-Initiative-still-pushing-coal.

CHAPTER 5

1. Mao Zedong, "Strengthen party unity and carry forward party traditions," *Marxists.org*, August 30, 1956, www.marxists.org/reference/archive/mao/selected-works/volume-5/mswv5_53.htm.

2. Quoted in Michael E. Marti, *China and the Legacy of Deng Xiaoping* (Washington DC: Brassey's, 2001), 94, see also 87, 92, 104.

3. "Full text of Xi Jinping's report at the 19th CPC National Congress," *Xinhua*, http://news.xinhuanet.com/english/special/2017-11/03/c_136725942.htm. See also State Council of the People's Republic of China, "Zhonggong zhongyang guowuyuan yinfa 'Shengtai wenming tizhi gaige zongti fang'an,'" [State Council of the Communist Party Central Committee publishes "Overall plan for the reform of ecological civilization system"] (September 21, 2015), www.gov.cn/guowuyuan/2015-09/21/content_2936327.htm.

4. David Stanway, "A pollution crackdown compounds slowdown woes in China's heartland," *Reuters*, May 23, 2019, www.reuters.com/article/us-china-economy-henan-pollution-insight/a-pollution-crackdown-compounds-slowdown-woes-in-chinas-heartland-idUSKCN1SU025.

5. Laura Parker, "China's ban on trash imports shifts waste crisis to Southeast Asia," *National Geographic,* November 16, 2018, www.nationalgeographic.com/environment/2018/11/china-ban-plastic-trash-imports-shifts-waste-crisis-southeast-asia-malaysia; Stephen Leahy, "China's booming middle class drives Asia's toxic e-waste mountains," *Guardian*, January 16, 2017, www.theguardian.com/environment/2017/jan/16/chinas-booming-middle-class-drives-asias-toxic-e-waste-mountains.

6. See for example "Land laid waste by coal is reborn as cultural garden," *China Daily*, October 31, 2017; Wuhan's Daijia Lake reborn from decades as ash heap mountain," *China Daily*, June 8–10, 2018.

7. "President highlights importance of protecting the environment," *People's Daily*, April 21, 2017, http://en.people.cn/n3/2017/0421/c90000-9206085.html.

8. Smith, *Green Capitalism*.

9. Stuart Lau, "Chinese dominate list of people and firms hiding money in tax havens, Panama Papers reveal," *South China Morning Post*, May 10, 2016, www.scmp.com/news/hong-kong/article/1943463/chinese-dominate-list-people-and-firms-hiding-money-tax-havens-panama; Patti Waldmeir and Tom Mitchell, "Panama Papers: Top officials tied to offshore companies," *CNBC News*, April

7, 2016, www.cnbc.com/2016/04/07/panama-papers-top-china-leaders-tied-to-offshore-companies.html.

10. "The rise of state capitalism," *The Economist,* January 21, 2012, www.economist. com/leaders/2012/01/21/the-rise-of-state-capitalism; "Not just tilting at windmills," *The Economist,* October 6, 2012, www.economist.com/leaders/2012/ 10/06/not-just-tilting-at-windmills; Michael Wines, "China fortifies state businesses to fuel growth," *New York Times,* August 30, 2010.

11. See for example Keith Bradsher and Paul Mozur, "China has a plan to be nearly self-sufficient by 2025. Global rivals call it unfair," *New York Times,* March 8, 2017.

12. See for example Tom Mitchell, "The door to China's real investment riches remains locked," *Financial Times,* March 31, 2015, www.ft.com/content/719b1134-d763-11e4-94b1-00144feab7de; Jack Marshall, "China's walled-off promise," *Wall Street Journal,* June 20, 2017.

13. Marti, *China and the Legacy,* 183.

14. Ian Jonhson, "China's great uprooting," *New York Times,* June 15, 2013, www. nytimes.com/2013/06/16/world/asia/chinas-great-uprooting-moving-250-million-into-cities.html; Miller, *China's Urban Billion;* Tom Hancock, "China drive to relocate millions of rural poor runs into trouble," *Financial Times,* June 13, 2017.

15. Cindy Fan, "China's eleventh Five-Year Plan (2006–2010): From 'getting rich first' to 'common prosperity'" *Eurasian Geography and Economics,* vol. 47, no. 6 (2006): 708–723.

16. "China's twelfth Five-Year Plan (2011–2015)—the full English version," *China Direct,* May 11, 2011, http://cbi.typepad.com/china_direct/2011/05/chinas-twelfth-five-new-plan-the-full-english-version.html; State Council, "Guowuyuan guanyu jiakuai peiyu he fazhan zhanlüexing xinxing chanye de jueding."

17. "China's twelfth Five-Year Plan (2011–2015)—the full English version."

18. See the Made in China 2025 website at http://english.gov.cn/2016special/ madeinchina2025. Li Keqiang, "Innovation a solid foundation for competitiveness," transcript of address to the National Science and Technology Awards Conference in January 2017, *China Daily,* January 11, 2017; Jost Wübbeke et al., "Made in China 2025: The making of a high-tech superpower and consequences for industrial countries" (Mercator Institute for Chinese Studies, December 2016); Bradsher and Mozur, "China has a plan to be nearly self-sufficient by 2025."

19. State Council of the People's Republic of China, "Guowuyuan guanyu yinfa xin yidai rengong zhineng fazhan guihua de tongzhi" [State Council issues notice of new generation artificial intelligence development plan] (July 8, 2017), www.gov. cn/zhengce/content/2017-07/20/content_5211996.htm, italics added; "Trump targets China's push to make its economy high-tech," *Bloomberg,* March 28, 2018, www.bloomberg.com/news/articles/2018-03-28/u-s-targets-made-in-china-2025-in-fight-for-high-tech-economy.

20. Fallows, *China Airborne,* 99. See also Luo Wangshu, "China's high-speed railway changes civil aviation," *People's Daily,* September 12, 2017, http://en.people.cn/ n3/2017/0910/c90000-9266982.html.

21. Chris Buckley, "China's new bridges: Rising high, but buried in debt," *New York Times,* June 10, 2017.

22. Philip Stephens, "A train that proclaims China's global ambitions," *Financial Times*, July 20, 2017, www.ft.com/content/edo33dae-6c69-11e7-b9c7-15af748b 60do; Paul Schemm, "Ethiopia has a lot riding on its new Chinese-built railroad to the sea," *Washington Post*, October 3, 2016, www.washingtonpost.com/world/ africa/ethiopia-has-a-lot-riding-on-its-new-chinese-built-railroad-to-the-sea/2016/10/03/c069d4da-84be-11e6-b57d-dd49277afo2f_story.html; "China transforms smaller Southeast Asian neighbors with railway, power plant and property investment," *South China Morning Post*, December 6, 2016, www.scmp. com/news/china/diplomacy-defence/article/2052126/china-transforms-smaller-southeast-asian-neighbours.

23. Buckley, "China's new bridges."

24. Mark DeWeaver, *Animal Spirits with Chinese Characteristics: Investment Booms and Busts in the World's Emerging Economic Giant* (London: Palgrave, 2012), 77–78. I am much obliged to Mark for his insightful analysis of the local drivers of overinvestment and corruption in China.

25. See for example Jinglian Wu, *Understanding and Interpreting Chinese Economic Reform* (Mason, Ohio: Thompson Educational, 2005).

26. Richard Smith, "Class structure and economic development: The contradictions of market socialism in China" (PhD diss., UCLA, 1989); Smith, "The Chinese road to capitalism." Both are available at www.richardanthonysmith.org.

27. Minxin Pei, *China's Trapped Transition: The Limits of Developmental Autocracy* (Cambridge Mass.: Harvard University Press, 2006).

28. Smith, "Class structure," Chapters 3–5; Smith, "The Chinese road to capitalism"; Bruce L. Reynolds, *Reform in China* (Armonk: M.E. Sharpe, 1987); Wu, *Understanding and Interpreting*, Chapter 4; Pei, *Trapped Transition*; Alexandra Stevenson and Cao Li, "How bad is China's debt? A city hospital is asking nurses for loans," *New York Times*, November 10, 2019.

29. Quoted in Michael Schuman, "The zombie factories that stalk China's economy," *New York Times*, August 30, 2015.

30. Quoted in Smith, "The Chinese road to capitalism," 67.

31. Scott Cendrowski, "Chinese aluminum giant is tied to a $2 billion mystery Mexican stockpile," *Fortune*, September 9, 2016.

32. Frank Langfitt, "China's white elephants: Ghost cities, lonely airports, desolate factories," *NPR*, October 15, 2015, www.npr.org/sections/parallels/2015/10/15/ 446297838/chinas-white-elephants-ghost-cities-lonely-airports-desolate-factories; Alexandra Stevenson and Cao Li, "Chasing white elephants," *New York Times*, November 11, 2019.

33. DeWeaver, *Animal Spirits*, 144–145; Liu Zhihua and Zou Shuo, "Overcapacity campaign faces its toughest challenge this year," *China Daily*, March 9–11, 2018; "China bans capacity expansion in cement, glass sectors," *People's Daily*, August 14, 2018, http://en.people.cn/n3/2018/0814/c90000-9490709.html.

34. Schuman, "Zombie factories."

35. Sun Lizhao et al., "China Railway Corp. struggles to adapt in era of air travel," *Caixin*, February 24, 2017, www.caixinglobal.com/2017-02-24/101058912.html, italics added.

36. China accounts for 80 percent of the world's $461 billion market in counterfeit goods. This industry could not thrive and grow decade after decade without explicit or tacit protection from China's communist-gangster-capitalist state which profits directly and indirectly from this "industry." See Daxue Consulting,

"The counterfeit good industry in modern China" (April 2019), https://daxueconsulting.com/counterfeit-products-in-china.

37. Benedict Rogers, "The nightmare of human organ harvesting in China," *Wall Street Journal*, February 5, 2019.

38. Bryce Pardo, "Evolution of the U.S. overdose crisis: Understanding China's role in the production and supply of synthetic opioids" (Rand Corporation, September 2018), www.rand.org/pubs/testimonies/CT497.html.

39. Official quoted in DeWeaver, *Animal Spirits*, 88. The locus classicus on this tendency is Audry Donnithorne, "China's cellular economy: Some economic trends since the Cultural Revolution," *China Quarterly*, no. 52 (October–December 1972): 605–619.

40. Smith, "Class structure," Chapters 3–5; DeWeaver, *Animal Spirits*, Chapters 5–8. Minxin Pei, *Trapped*, 127–130.

41. Lu Zhang, Inside China's Automobile Factories (Cambridge: Cambridge University Press, 2015), 26, 28; Smith, "Class structure," 208–214, 259–266; Alwyn Young, "The razor's edge: Distortions and incremental reform in the Peoples Republic of China," *National Bureau of Economic Research*, working paper no. 7828 (August 2000), www.nber.org/papers/w7828; Pei, *Trapped Transition*, 127.

42. Pei, *Trapped Transition*, 126.

43. Alexandra Ho, "Too many car factories in China?" *Bloomberg*, February 12, 2015, www.bloomberg.com/news/articles/2015-02-12/china-s-car-factory-binge-risks-hurting-automakers-margins; Michael Schuman, "China's car sector needs a shakeup," *Bloomberg*, August 27, 2017, www.bloomberg.com/view/articles/2017-08-29/china-s-car-sector-needs-a-shakeup-not-buyouts; "China to clamp down on new car plants in fight against capacity glut, pollution," *Reuters*, June 12, 2017; Pei, *Trapped Transition*, 129–130.

44. Trefor Moss, "China bets big on electric cars," *Wall Street Journal*, July 20, 2018.

45. Joe McDonald, "China car dilemma: Beijing wants electric, buyers want SUVs," *Boston Globe*, April 18, 2017; Trevor Moss and Brian Spegele, "Gas guzzlers rule in China," *Wall Street Journal*, May 21, 2017; Adam Mintner, "China's electric cars hit some potholes," *Bloomberg*, March 19, 2019, www.bloomberg.com/opinion/articles/2019-03-20/quality-issues-plague-china-s-electric-car-industry.

46. An Limin and Coco Feng, "China pulls plug on electric vehicle fraud," *Caixin*, February 6, 2016, www.caixinglobal.com/2017-02-06/101050629.html; "China to clamp down on new car plants in fight against capacity glut, pollution," *Reuters*, June 12, 2017, www.reuters.com/article/us-china-autos-overcapacity/china-to-clamp-down-on-new-car-plants-in-fight-against-capacity-glut-pollution-idUSKBN19314U; Trefor Moss, "China cuts electric-car aid," *Wall Street Journal*, March 28, 2019.

47. DeWeaver, *Animal Spirits*, 82.

48. Mo Yelin, "China seeks to rein in ambitious high-speed rail projects," *Caixin*, May 9, 2018, www.caixinglobal.com/2018-05-09/china-seeks-to-rein-in-ambitious-high-speed-rail-projects-101246540.html.

49. Elizabeth C. Economy, *The River Runs Black: The Environmental Challenge to China's Future* (Ithaca, NY: Cornell University Press, 2004), 70–71.

50. Ibid., 73.

51. DeWeaver, *Animal Spirits*, 84–85.

52. Ibid., 84; and sources cited therein.

53. Ibid., 83, 147.
54. Ibid., 85.
55. Buckley, "China's new bridges."
56. "Top 10 Chinese tech and engineering marvels that amaze the world," *People's Daily*, October 16, 2016, http://en.people.cn/n3/2016/1013/c90000-9126730. html; Chris Buckley and Adam Wu, "China hunts for scientific glory, and aliens, with new giant telescope," *New York Times*, September 26, 2016; Du Xiaofe, "Massive Chinese container ship sets new record on east coast of U.S." *People's Daily*, May 17, 2017, http://en.people.cn/n3/2017/0517/c90000-9216987.html; Edward Wong, "China launches satellite in bid to lead quantum research," *New York Times*, August 17, 2016; "Super yachts for China's super rich" *Caixin*, July 22, 2016, www.caixinglobal.com/2016-07-22/101011500.html; Mark McDonald, "'Ruin porn'—the aftermath of the Beijing Olympics," *New York Times*, July 15, 2012; "First home grown cruise ship takes shape," *People's Daily*, June 10, 2017, http://en.people.cn/n3/2017/0610/c90000-9226859.html.
57. DeWeaver, *Animal Spirits*, 82–83.
58. Ibid., 93.
59. Ibid., 95–96.
60. He Qinglian, "The land-enclosure movement of the 1990s," *The Chinese Economy*, vol. 33, no. 3 (May–June 2000): 57–88. In truth, China's peasants have been legally defenseless against state dispossession because they had already been dispossessed in the 1950s as Mao's nationalization and collectivization abolished private property in China.
61. DeWeaver, *Animal Spirits*, 19–20. See also Nancy Holmstrom and Richard Smith, "The necessity of gangster capitalism: Primitive accumulation in Russia and China," *Monthly Review*, vol. 51, no. 9 (February 2000): 1–15.
62. He Qinglian, "The land-enclosure movement," 58–59.
63. Robin Visser, *Cities Surround the Countryside: Urban Aesthetics in Postsocialist China* (Durham: Duke University Press, 2010), Chapter 1.
64. These decrees are listed and described in Xiao-xi Hui, "The Chinese housing reform and the following new urban question," paper presented at the Fourth International Conference of the International Forum on Urbanism, Amsterdam, 2009, http://newurbanquestion.ifou.org/proceedings. Hui writes that after the Asian financial crisis of 1997, the government determined that it would

> Completely marketise urban housing stock and to promote real estate development . . . in order to sustain economic growth . . . The *danwei* welfare housing distribution was totally abolished [and], the socialistic public housing system thereby finally ended, so that the urban housing policy changed from the state guaranteed public rental system toward owner-occupation dependent upon the housing market. As a direct consequence of the radical housing reform in 1998, most public housing was privatised within a few years. The government almost completely withdrew from direct intervention in the housing stock [and] private housing ownership was legally recognised and protected according to the Constitutional amendment (2004) and the promulgation of Property Law (2007).

See also Hui, "The Chinese housing reform," 384.
65. Hui, "The Chinese housing reform," 384.
66. Ibid., 387.

67. Ibid.

68. Henry Sanderson and Michael Forsythe, *China's Superbank: Debt, Oil and Influence—How China Development Bank is Rewriting the Rules of Finance* (Singapore: John Wiley/Bloomberg Press, 2013), 7, 76.

69. National Bureau of Statistics of the People's Republic of China, *China Statistical Yearbook 2016* (Beijing: Zhongguo tongji chubanshe, 2016).

70. Ian Johnson, "Pitfalls abound in China's push from farm to city," *New York Times*, July 23, 2013; Ian Johnson, "China's great uprooting: moving 250 million into cities," *New York Times*, June 15, 2013.

71. Sanderson and Forsythe, *China's Superbank*, 7.

72. Ian Johnson, "New China cities: Shoddy homes, broken hope," *New York Times*, November 9, 2013.

73. Zhao Shuting, "Hubei family reflects on generations of relocation," *Sixth Tone*, March 30, 2018, www.sixthtone.com/news/1002010/Hubei%20Family%20 Reflects%20on%20Generations%20of%20Relocation.

74. See for example Ian Johnson, "Picking death over eviction," *New York Times*, September 8, 2013.

75. Barbara Demick, "Protests in China over local grievances surge, and get a hearing," *Los Angeles Times*, October 10, 2011.

76. Miller, *China's Urban Billion*, 27. David Bandurski tells the harrowing stories of dispossessed Guangdong villagers and their courageous resistance in his superb *Dragons in Diamond Village and Other Tales from the Back Alleys of Urbanising China* (New York: Melville House, 2016).

77. Jeremy Page and Brian Spegele, "Beijing set to 'strike hard' at revolt," *Wall Street Journal*, December 16, 2011; Cai Wong, "Wukan stirs again," *The Diplomat*, June 30, 2016, http://thediplomat.com/2016/07/wukan-stirs-again. The Wukan uprising also went on to inspire others, see Scott Greene, "Wukan 2.0? Zhejiang villagers protest land grabs," *China Digital Times*, February 8, 2012, http:// chinadigitaltimes.net/2012/02/wukan-2-0-zhejiang-villagers-protest-land-grabs.

78. Johnson, "New China cities."

79. Johnson, "New China cities," and "Pitfalls abound."

80. Ian Johnson, "In China, once the villages are gone, the culture is gone," *New York Times*, February 1, 2014.

81. Shepard, *Ghost Cities*, 17.

82. On the whole process, from dispossession to development, see Sanderson and Forsythe, *China's Superbank*, Chapter 1.

83. Qin Shao, *Shanghai Gone*; He Qinglian, "The land-enclosure movement"; Stuart Levenworth and Kiki Zhao, "In China, homeowners find themselves in a land of doubt," *New York Times*, May 31, 2016.

84. Shepard, *Ghost Cities*, 16. For photos see Shepard, "Half the houses will be demolished in 20 years."

85. For one take on the alienated life of Beijingers today see Zhang Wumao, "Beijing has 20 million people pretending to live here," *What's on Weibo*, July 26, 2017, www.whatsonweibo.com/beijing-20-million-people-pret-live-full-translation.

86. Tom Phillips, "China plans to build new city nearly three times the size of New York," *Guardian*, April 4, 2017, www.theguardian.com/world/2017/apr/04/china-plans-build-new-city-nearly-three-times-the-size-of-new-york; Shepard, *Ghost Cities*, Chapter 3; Krutika Pathi, "Is China's latest major construction project

destined to be a ghost town?" *Citilab*, May 1, 2017, www.citylab.com/equity/2017/05/xiongan-new-area-construction-plan/524766.

87. Tan Damin, "Climate change may temper grand plans for Xiong'an," *Chinadialogue*, April 7, 2017, www.chinadialogue.net/blog/9727-Climate-change-may-temper-grand-plans-for-Xiong-an/en; Liu Qin, "Water scarcity might be Xiong'an's undoing," *Chinadialogue*, April 2017, www.chinadialogue.net/article/show/single/en/9756-Water-scarcity-might-be-Xiong-an-s-undoing-; An Shuwei and An Ran, "Xiongan must test, and save, the waters," *China Daily*, May 12, 2017.

88. Chris Weller, "China is building a megacity that will be larger than all of Japan," *Business Insider*, July 22, 2015, www.businessinsider.com/china-megacity-in-beijing-will-be-larger-than-japan-2015-7.

89. Sarosh Kuruvilla et al., *From Iron Rice Bowl to Informalization: Markets, Workers, and the State in a Changing China* (Ithaca: Cornell, 2011), 4–6.

90. Ching Kwan Lee, *Against the Law: Labor Protests in China's Rustbelt and Sunbelt* (Berkeley: UC Press, 2007); China Labour Bulletin, "Standing up: The workers movement in China, 2000–2004" (July 2007), www.clb.org.hk/en/content/standing-workers-movement-china-2000-2004.

91. Max Fisher, "How China stays stable despite 500 protests every day," *The Atlantic*, January 5, 2012, www.theatlantic.com/international/archive/2012/01/how-china-stays-stable-despite-500-protests-every-day/250940; Hou Liqiang, "Report identifies sources of mass protests," *China Daily*, April 9, 2014, www.chinadaily.com.cn/china/2014-04/09/content_17415767.htm.

92. Quoted in Keith Bradsher, "China's leaders confront economic fissures," *New York Times*, November 5, 2013.

93. Shi Futian, "Video gaming hitting new highs," *China Daily*, November 8, 2017; Andrew Polk, "Chinese taking on too much consumer debt," *Bloomberg*, February 14, 2018, www.bloomberg.com/opinion/articles/2018-02-15/chinese-consumers-are-building-up-too-much-household-debt.

94. Daniel Johnson, "Declining audiences and a complete lack of interest—how much longer can the Chinese Grand Prix go on?" *Telegraph*, April 16, 2016.

95. William Wan, "China's Xi Jinping loves football so much he's put it on the national curriculum—but can he secure the World Cup?" *Independent*, February 25, 2015; Chen Jingnan, "Parents plead with government to give their kids more homework," *Sixth Tone*, April 12, 2018, www.sixthtone.com/news/1002084/Parents%20Plead%20With%20Government%20to%20Give%20Kids%20More%20Homework.

96. Cindy Sui, "What the world's largest shopping day says about China," *BBC News*, November 11, 2011, www.bbc.com/news/world-asia-china-41954591.

97. Liu Jianqiang, "China's environment ministry an 'utter disappointment,'" *Chinadialogue*, March 7, 2013, www.chinadialogue.net/article/show/single/en/5788-China-s-environment-ministry-an- utter-disappointment-; Tang Hao, "China's food scares show the system is bust," *Chinadialogue*, August 31, 2012, www.chinadialogue.net/article/show/single/en/5142-China-s-food-scares-show-the-system-is-bust.

98. Deng Yaqing, "Making too much," *Beijing Review*, October 31, 2013, www.bjreview.com.cn/business/txt/2013-10/28/content_574390.htm.

99. Chuin-Wei Yap, "China can't curb steel mills," *Wall Street Journal*, March 13, 2013, italics added.

100. See the following articles by Chuin-Wei Yap: "China's steel industry still overproducing," *Wall Street Journal*, July 16, 2014, https://blogs.wsj.com/economics/2014/07/16/chinas-steel-industry-still-overproducing/8; "China's steelmakers adding, not cutting, capacity," *Wall Street Journal*, February 27, 2014; "China's steel cutbacks look deeper than they are," *Wall Street Journal*, March 6, 2017. See also "China's slow steel industry cuts unlikely to satisfy Trump," *South China Morning Post*, March 12, 2018, www.scmp.com/news/china/economy/article/2136807/chinas-slow-reforms-steel-industry-unlikely-satisfy-trumps.

101. Zhou Xin, "The zombies return: Why are steel firms in China coming back from the dead?" *South China Morning Post*, May 14, 2016, www.scmp.com/news/china/economy/article/1944568/zombies-return-why-are-steel-firms-china-coming-back-dead; Michael Schuman, "Zombie factories stalk the sputtering Chinese economy," *New York Times*, August 28, 2015.

102. Zhou Chen and Li Rongde, "Cities' pollution violations have inspectors fuming," *Caixin*, April 13, 2017, www.caixinglobal.com/2017-04-13/101078097.html.

103. Alice Yan, "Thousands of polluters in northern China fake emissions data, resist checks," *South China Morning Post*, March 31, 2017, www.scmp.com/news/china/policies-politics/article/2083780/thousands-polluters-northern-china-fake-emissions-data; Yan Xiaowei, "The waste-to-power reality: Faked emissions data and huge profits," *Chinadialogue*, July 24, 2014, www.chinadialogue.net/article/show/single/en/8971-The-waste-to-power-reality-faked-emissions-data-and-huge-profits; Huang Shumao, "Chinese companies caught falsifying environmental data," *Chinadialogue*, January 6, 2016, www.chinadialogue.net/blog/7161-Chinese-companies-caught-falsifying-environmental-data-/en.

104. Chuin-Wei Yap, "China's zombie companies stay alive despite defaults," *Wall Street Journal*, July 12, 2016; Chuin-Wei Yap, "China state steel merger taps old theme: Bigger is better," *Wall Street Journal*, September 20, 2016; DeWeaver, *Animal Spirits*, 148.

105. Yan, "Polluters fake emissions"; Nectar Gan, "12,000 officials disciplined and 18,000 companies punished in China's sweeping crackdown against pollution," *South China Morning Post*, September 2, 2017, www.scmp.com/news/china/policies-politics/article/2109342/top-level-china-pollution-inspections-wrapping.

106. Yuan Suwen et al., "Northern China fakes emissions data," *Caixin*, April 6, 2017, www.caixinglobal.com/2017-04-06/101075101.html; Edward Wong and Vanessa Piao, "When China wants better air readings, cotton does the trick," *New York Times*, October 28, 2016; Zhao Xuan and Li Rongde, "What bad air? Hunan officials use mist cannons to fool pollution meters," *Caixin*, February 2, 2018, www.caixinglobal.com/2018-02-02/what-bad-air-hunan-officials-use-mist-cannons-to-fool-pollution-meters-101206784.html.

107. Zhou Chen and Li Rongde, "Beijing fails to implement anti-pollution measures, MEP Says," *Caixin*, October 17, 2016, www.caixinglobal.com/2016-10-17/101053025.html.

108. Zhou Tailai and Li Rongde, "Five local environment officials investigated on allegations of tampering with air-quality readings," *Caixin*, October 26, 2016, www.caixinglobal.com/2016-10-26/five-local-environment-officials-investigated-on-allegations-of-tampering-with-air-quality-readings-101000848.html; Liu Qin, "China's environment ministry launches anti-graft reforms,"

Chinadialogue, March 11, 2015, www.chinadialogue.net/article/show/single/en/7771-China-s-environment-ministry-launches-anti-graft-reforms.

109. John McGarrity, "China promises crackdown on fake air quality data," *Chinadialogue*, February 4, 2015, www.chinadialogue.net/blog/7828-China-promises-crackdown-on-fake-air-quality-data/en; Zhou Chen and Li Rongde, "Tianjin authorities lambasted for letting air, water quality worsen," *Caixin*, July 31, 2017, ww.caixinglobal.com/2017-07-31/tianjin-authorities-lambasted-for-letting-air-water-quality-worsen-101124445.html; "Watchdog raps Shanghai for 'slacking' on environment," *Caixin*, April 12, 2017, https://k.caixinglobal.com//web/detail_17657.

110. Many of these are discussed in Zhang Linshan and Sun Fenyi, *Gaige gengzu xianxiang: Biaoxian, genyuan yu zhili* [Phenomenon of Reform Obstruction: Symptoms, Origin and Control] (Beijing: Shehui kexue wenxian chubanshe, 2017), 5–7. See also *China Quarterly*, vol. 231 (September 2017), special section "Central–local relations and environmental governance in China," which explores systematic resistance up and down the bureaucratic hierarchy to Beijing's environmental initiatives. In particular see Sarah Eaton and Genia Kosta, "Central protectionism in China: The 'central SOE problem' in environmental governance" (685–704); Benjamin van Rooij et al., "Centralizing trends and pollution law enforcement in China" (583–606); Christine Wong and Valerie J. Karplus, "China's war on air pollution: Can existing governance structures support new ambitions?" (662–684); Xuehua Zhang, "Implementation of pollution control targets in China: Has a centralized enforcement approach worked?" (749–774). The authors generally conclude that, as Xuehua Zhang says, "centralized enforcement . . . is arguably ineffective in addressing China's long-standing problem of weak environmental policy implementation"; Zhang, "Implementation of pollution control," 749.

111. *Qiongding zhi xia* [Under the Dome] (2015), directed by Chai Jing; censored in China but available at http://sensesofcinema.com/2015/documentary-in-asia/under-the-dome-chinese-documentary.

112. Gan, "12,000 officials disciplined."

113. "Environmental inspectors locked in by factory boss," *Sixth Tone*, April 18, 2017, www.sixthtone.com/news/1000076/environment-inspectors-locked-in-by-factory-boss; "MEP Inspectors 'abducted' by factory bosses," *South China Morning Post*, April 17, 2017, www.scmp.com/news/china/policies-politics/article/2088149/chinas-smog-police-held-captive-during-checks-polluting.

114. Xuehua Zhang, "Implementation of pollution control," 750–751.

115. Ibid., 756; Kosta, "Command without control."

116. Chuin-Wei Yap, "China defends its steel exports," *Wall Street Journal*, May 15, 2015.

117. Eaton and Kostka, "Central protectionism," 694.

118. Ibid.

119. Min Zhang and Tom Daly, "China crude steel output jumps 8.3%, sets second straight annual record," *Reuters*, January 16, 2020, www.reuters.com/article/us-china-economy-output-steel/china-2019-crude-steel-output-jumps-8-3-sets-second-straight-annual-record-idUSKBN1ZG08E.

120. Emily Feng, "Surging China steel output defies Trump pressure," *Financial Times*, April 16, 2018, www.ft.com/content/1dc206ac-4160-11e8-803a-295c97e6fdob; Liu and Zou, "Overcapacity campaign faces its toughest year." Rob Davies, "What

went wrong with British steel," *Guardian*, May 22, 2019, www.theguardian.com/business/2019/may/22/what-went-wrong-at-british-steel.

121. Eaton and Kostka, "Central protectionism," 690–91.

CHAPTER 6

1. Kerry Brown says that the "high-level cadres" who run the ministries, the state conglomerates, and the administration, all of whom are concentrated in Beijing, total no more than 2,562. This means that China is effectively "run by a group of people that is smaller than most villages in Europe"; *The New Emperors: Power and the Princelings in China* (New York: I.B. Tauris, 2014), 20–21.

2. See the map of Zhongnanhai and environs, with official residences noted (as of 1989), in Andrew J. Nathan and Perry Link (eds.), *The Tiananmen Papers* (London: Little Brown & Co., 2001).

3. Richard McGregor, *The Party: The Secret World of China's Communist Rulers* (New York: Harper, 2010); Carl E. Walter and Fraser J.T. Howie, *Red Capitalism: The Fragile Financial Foundation of China's Extraordinary Rise* (Singapore: John Wiley & Sons, 2012), 22–25.

4. Brown, *New Emperors*, 4. By common agreement, each of the elders was permitted to have one son replace him in the leadership.

5. While China's gangs were suppressed under Mao, the "black societies" enjoyed a revival with Deng's market reforms. Marketization opened up vast new opportunities for officials to get rich colluding with organized gangs to set up illegal businesses and engage in smuggling, extortion, drug trafficking, prostitution, kidnapping, human trafficking, counterfeiting, and murder—the usual fare of mobsters. See He Qinglian, "Chapter 10. The Resurgence of Secret Societies and an Underground Economy," *The Chinese Economy*, vol. 35, no. 1 (January–February 2002): 51–63. Some gangs are even run by the police. These days, China's gangs have gone global, smuggling China's illegal drugs including fentanyl and opiates to the US and world markets. See Peter Holey and William Wan, "Deadly Chinese drugs are flooding the U.S. and the police can't stop them," *Washington Post*, June 22, 2015. With the Hong Kong handover, the Beijing government partnered with Triad mobsters to police Hong Kong and Xi Jinping is said to have employed them to kidnap his own targets including bookstore owners, tycoons, and corrupt officials on the lam.

6. See Louisa Lim, *The People's Republic of Amnesia: Tiananmen Revisited* (Oxford: Oxford University Press, 2014), Chapter 7.

7. See for example Shi Jiangtao, "Struggle for supremacy by party factions now on display," *South China Morning Post*, October 13, 2012. On the rumored threat to Xi Jinping's life by the Bo Xilai faction see Matthew Robertson, "China's 'hatchet man' set to be purged in party struggle," *Epoch Times*, May 30–June 3, 2014; Teddy Ng, "Rising star Li Yuanchao forges ties with all political factions in China," *South China Morning Post*, October 2012.

8. Brown, *New Emperors*, 36–37.

9. Michel Oksenberg, "Economic policymaking in China: Summer 1991," *China Quarterly*, no. 90 (June 1982): 184.

10. Minxin Pei was quoted in David Barboza, "The corruptibles," *New York Times*, September 3, 2009. See also Robertson, "China's 'Hatchet Man.'"

11. Austin Ramzy, "Ousted Chinese official is accused of plotting against Communist Party," *New York Times*, October 20, 2017; V. Mahalingam, "Xi Jinping's fight against coups and assassination bids," *Indian Defense Review*, August 19, 2017, www.indiandefencereview.com/spotlights/xi-jinpings-fight-against-coups-and-assassination-bids; Katsuji Nakazawa, "Power struggle has Xi leery of coup, assassination attempts," *Nikkei Asian Review*, May 23, 2015, https://asia.nikkei.com/Features/China-up-close/Power-struggle-has-Xi-leery-of-coup-assassination-attempts.

12. "Xi Jinping millionaire relations reveal fortunes of elite," *Bloomberg*, June 29, 2012,www.bloomberg.com/news/articles/2012-06-29/xi-jinping-millionaire-relations-reveal-fortunes-of-elite.

13. Chris Buckley, "A chilling phone call adds to hurdles of publishing Xi Jinping book," *Sinophere*, February 19, 2014, http://sinosphere.blogs.nytimes.com/2014/02/19/a-chilling-phone-call-adds-to-hurdles-of-publishing-xi-jinping-book/#more-6510.

14. Kris Cheng, "Publisher suspends launch of dissident's new book on Xi Jinping due to 'fear and pressure,'" *Hong Kong Free Press*, January 12, 2016, www.hongkongfp.com/2016/01/12/publisher-suspends-launch-of-dissidents-new-book-on-xi-jinping-due-to-fear-and-pressure.

15. On the many and growing sources of state income see Joe Zhang, *Party Man, Company Man* (Honolulu: Enrich Professional Publishing, 2014), Chapter 11.

16. McGregor, *The Party*, 78, 81. John P. Burns, *The Chinese Communist Party's Nomenklatura System* (London: M.E. Sharpe, 1989).

17. "Chinese President Xi Jinping given 62% pay rise," *BBC News*, January 20, 2015, www.bbc.com/news/business-30896205; Russell Leigh Moses, "When it comes to corrupt Chinese officials, you get what you pay for," *Wall Street Journal*, March 10, 2014,https://blogs.wsj.com/chinarealtime/2014/03/10/when-it-comes-to-corrupt-chinese-officials-you-get-what-you-pay-for.

18. Feifei Wang, "What is the pay scale for China's top leadership? What does the secretary general, premier, paramount leader, etc. make?" *Quora*, November 14, 2012,www.quora.com/What-is-the-pay-scale-for-Chinas-leadership-What-does-the-Secretary-General-Premier-Paramount-Leader-etc-make.

19. Wen Jiabao, Xi Jinping, and other wealthy princelings were profiled in *Bloomberg* and the *New York Times* in 2012 and 2013 which got both papers shut down in China and their reporters denied visa renewals in 2013. See "Heirs of Mao's comrades rise as new capitalist nobility," *Bloomberg*, December 26, 2012, www.bloomberg.com/news/2012-12-26/immortals-beget-china-capitalism-from-citic-to-godfather-of-golf.html. Further citations below are from the articles in this collection. See also McGregor, *The Party*; Brown, *The New Emperors*.

20. David Barboza, "Billions in hidden riches for family of Chinese leader," *New York Times*, October 25, 2012.

21. Ibid.

22. Ibid. See also "The Wen family empire" graphic, *New York Times*, October 25, 2012, www.nytimes.com/interactive/2012/10/25/business/the-wen-family-empire.html.

23. He Qingliang, "China's listing social structure," *New Left Review*, September 5, 2000, 73. For detailed analysis of the brilliantly devious methods of asset stripping and privatization to cadres see X. L. Ding, "The illegal asset stripping of Chinese state firms," *China Journal*, no. 43 (January 2000): 1–28.

24. "Xi Jinping millionaire relations reveal fortunes of elite."

25. Michael Forsythe, "As China's leader fights graft"; Cary Huang, "Xi Jinping tightens reins on business ties of Chinese officials' families in wake of Panama Papers," *South China Morning Post*, April 19, 2016, www.scmp.com/news/china/policies-politics/article/1936992/xi-jinping-tightens-reins-business-ties-chinese; Zheping Huang, "China's elite—including Xi Jinping—are linked to offshore deals that hid millions of dollars," *Quartz*, April 4, 2016, https://qz.com/653836/chinas-elite-including-xi-jinping-are-linked-to-offshore-deals-that-hid-millions-of-dollars.

26. John Lee, "China's rich lists riddled with Communist Party members," *Forbes*, September 14, 2011, www.forbes.com/2011/09/14/china-rich-lists-opinions-contributors-john-lee.html#3ec28c2d210b.

27. It has never been firmly established that Deng actually said this, his most famous quotation, but neither did he deny it, and the aphorism certainly expressed the essence of his program in the 1980s and 1990s. See Evelyn Iritani, "Great idea but don't quote him," *Los Angeles Times*, September 9, 2004.

28. He Qinglian, *Zhongguo de xianjing* [China's Pitfalls] (Hong Kong: Mingjing chubanshe, 1997). He Qinglian's book was translated and serialized in *The Chinese Economy*, vols. 33–35 (2000–2002), some of which I cite here and elsewhere. On the long history of CCP corruption from Mao to now see Xiaobo Lü, *Cadres and Corruption: The Organizational Involution of the Chinese Communist Party* (Stanford: Stanford University Press, 2000); Yan Sun, *Corruption and Market in Contemporary China* (Ithaca: Cornell University Press, 2004); Melanie Manion, *Corruption by Design: Building Clean Government in Mainland China and Hong Kong* (Cambridge Mass.: Harvard University Press, 2004).

29. "Heirs of Mao's comrades rise as new capitalist nobility," 11; Zheping Huang, "China's elite."

30. Yan Sun, *Corruption and Market*, Chapter 1, and 101–102.

31. In one case, executives of one SOE reportedly spent $193,000 on a single meal. See "Unseemly purchases: Chair of Chinese state behemoth brought down in scandal," *Epoch Times*, April 22, 2014, www.theepochtimes.com/chair-of-chinese-state-behemoth-felled-in-scandal_634208.html.

32. Perry Link, *Evening Chats in Beijing: Probing China's Predicament* (New York: Norton, 1992), 55–56.

33. Minxin Pei, *China's Crony Capitalism: The Dynamics of Regime Decay* (Cambridge, Mass.: Harvard University Press, 2016).

34. "My daddy's rich and my Lamborghini's good-looking" is cited in Dan Levin, "Chinese scions' song: My daddy's rich and my Lamborghini's good-looking," *New York Times*, April 12, 2016.

35. On these institutional changes see State Council of the People's Republic of China, "Zhonghua renmin gongheguo chengzhen guoyou tudi shiyong quan churang he zhuanrang zhanxing tiaoli" [Interim regulations of the People's Republic of China concerning the assignment and transfer of the right to the use of the state-owned land in urban areas] (May 9, 1990), www.law-lib.com/law/law_view.asp?id=6611.

36. Pei, *Crony Capitalism*, Chapters 1–2.

37. Tyler Stiem, "Race and real estate: How hot Chinese money is making Vancouver unlivable," *Guardian*, July 16, 2016, www.theguardian.com/cities/2016/jul/07/vancouver-chinese-city-racism-meets-real-estate-british-columbia; Lu Chen, "Your rich neighbor might be a corrupt Chinese official," *Epoch Times*, February

25, 2015, www.theepochtimes.com/your-rich-neighbor-might-be-a-corrupt-chinese-official_1263621.html.

38. Pei, *Crony Capitalism,* 151–152, 154.

39. Premier Zhu Rongji, quoted in McGregor, *The Party,* 45.

40. Quoted in Walter and Howie, *Red Capitalism,* 23.

41. Quoted in McGregor, *The Party,* 140–41.

42. Henry Sender, "Chinese princelings profit from corruption," *Financial Times,* November 27, 2012.

43. Edward Wong, "An online scandal underscores Chinese distrust of state charities," *New York Times,* August 4, 2011.

44. Sharon LaFraniere, "Officials in China seized infants for black market," *New York Times,* August 5, 2011; "Heirs of Mao's comrades rise as new capitalist nobility," 11.

45. Keith Bradsher, "Antigraft inquiry targets senior Chinese official," *New York Times,* December 6, 2012. One lowly county secretary sold more than 200 posts during his tenure; He Qingliang, "China's Listing social structure," 95.

46. James Ball et al., "China's princelings storing riches in Caribbean offshore haven," *Guardian,* January 21, 2014, www.theguardian.com/world/ng-interactive/2014/jan/21/china-british-virgin-islands-wealth-offshore-havens.

47. Lu, *Cadres and Corruption,* Chapter 6; McGregor, *The Party,* Chapter 5; Holmstrom and Smith, "The necessity of gangster capitalism."

48. David Barboza, "Chinese regulator's relatives profited from stake in insurer," *New York Times,* December 31, 2012.

49. CITIC was founded in 1979 by Rong Yiren, one of China's richest businessmen, and one of the few capitalists who stayed on in China after the revolution. Wang Jun, son of revolutionary general Wang Zhen, was appointed head of operations. CITIC was set up to attract overseas investment and modern technology at a time when China had only $840 million in foreign exchange reserves. Rong and Wang turned CITIC into a sprawling empire with investments in securities, real estate and other assets. By 2012 China's foreign exchange reserves stood at $3.3 trillion (see Table 6.1 in the Appendix). See also "Heirs of Mao's comrades rise as new capitalist nobility."

50. "Families benefited from their control of state companies, amassing private wealth as they embraced the market economy. Forty-three of the 103 ran their own business or became executives in private firms . . . The third generation—grandchildren of the Eight Immortals and their spouses, many of whom are in their 30s and 40s—have parlayed family connections and overseas education into jobs in the private sector. At least 11 of the 31 members of that generation tracked by *Bloomberg News* ran their own businesses or held executive post, most commonly in finance and technology"; "Heirs of Mao's comrades rise as new capitalist nobility," 3.

51. Ibid., 9, 13, 14.

52. Ibid.

53. Former railway minister Liu Zhijun had eighteen (he received a suspended death sentence in July 2013 for corruption). The mayor of Hangzhou, Xu Maiyong ("Triple Plenty Xu") reportedly had dozens (he was executed for bribery and embezzlement of more than $30 million in 2011). Dan Levin, "For China's newly rich, status is a woman on the side," *New York Times,* August 16, 2011. In 2007 China's top prosecutor's office said that 90 percent of senior officials felled by

corruption scandals kept mistresses. Whole industries, like the "college concubine agencies," have sprung up to set up poor but aspiring (and attractive) young girls with wealthy cadres and capitalists; Choi Chi-yuk, "'Triple Plenty' crooked vice-mayor sentenced to death," *South China Morning Post*, May 13, 2011.

54. Pei, *Crony Capitalism*, 134–135.

55. Andrea Chen, "Corrupt coal official had 200 million yuan in cash stashed at home, prosecutors say," *South China Morning Post*, November 1, 2014.

56. "Senior general tangled in corruption, magazine says," *China Daily*, January 17–19, 2014.

57. Zhao Fuduo and Cui Xiankang, "The low official found with towering pile of cash, gold, and properties," *Caixin*, November 20, 2014, www.caixinglobal. com/2014-11-20/101012900.html.

58. X. L. Ding, "Illegal asset stripping," 1–28.

59. X. L. Ding, "Who gets what, how?" *Problems of Post-Communism*, vol. 46, no. 3 (May–June 1999): 32–41. See also Barboza, "Chinese regulator's relatives."

60. X. L. Ding, "Illegal asset stripping," 19.

61. "The army that makes money," *The Economist*, October 5, 1991, 38. "Heirs of Mao's comrades rise as new capitalist nobility," 13.

62. Tai Ming Cheung, *China's Entrepreneurial Army* (Oxford: Oxford University Press).

63. Pei, *Crony Capitalism*, 262. Bruce J. Dickson, *The Dictator's Dilemma* (Oxford: Oxford University Press, 2016), 86–87.

64. Minnie Chan and Choi Chi-yuk, "Top Chinese general linked to disgraced security tzar Zhou Yongkang arrested for corruption," *South China Morning Post*, August 26, 2016, www.scmp.com/news/china/policies-politics/article/2009370/ top-chinese-general-linked-disgraced-security-tsar-zhou.

65. Chris Buckley, "Chinese general under investigation, joining a long line of fallen commanders," *New York Times*, January 9, 2018.

66. David Barboza and Jessica Silver-Greenberg, "JP Morgan's fruitful ties to a member of China's elite," *New York Times*, November 13, 2013.

67. "US probe highlights hiring of Chinese 'princelings,'" *Straits Times*, August 23, 2013, www.straitstimes.com/asia/us-probe-highlights-hiring-of-chinese-princelings.

68. David Barboza, "Billions massed in the shadows by the family of China's premier," *New York Times*, October 26, 2012.

69. Jessica Silver-Greenberg and Ben Protess, "Chinese official made job plea to Chase chief," *New York Times*, October 26, 2012.

70. Nectar Gan, "First he swept up corrupt officials, now he is tightening party control," *South China Morning Post*, January 12, 2018, www.scmp.com/news/ china/policies-politics/article/2127871/xi-demands-pragmatism-and-absolute-loyalty-communist.

71. Pei, *Crony Capitalism*, 184–185.

72. Ibid., 184, 187.

73. Ibid., 243.

74. Ibid., 97.

75. Dev Kar and Sarah Freitas, "Illicit financial flows from China and the role of trade misinvoicing," *Global Financial Integrity*, October 25, 2012, www.gfintegrity.org/ report/illicit-financial-flows-from-china-and-the-role-of-trade-misinvoicing.

76. Jane Cai, "Revealed: The sneaky ways Chinese are moving money across the border," *South China Morning Post*, May 29, 2017, www.scmp.com/news/china/economy/article/2096032/chinas-watchdog-tracks-underground-cash-trail.

77. "Chinese fly cash to North America, by the suitcase," *Wall Street Journal*, January 2, 2013; Shen Ming, "Chinese military officers secretly moving money offshore," *Epoch Times*, June 28, 2012; Benjamin Robertson, "US1.25 Trillion moved out of mainland China illegally in 10 years, says report," *South China Morning Post*, December 16, 2014.

78. Natalie Ornell, "1,000 'naked officials' found in Guangdong," *China Digital Times*, June 8, 2014: https://chinadigitaltimes.net/2014/06/1000-naked-officials-found-guangdong.

79. Ball et al., "China's princelings"; "Heirs of Mao's comrades rise as new capitalist nobility," 6.

80. "China murder suspect's sisters ran $126 million empire," *Bloomberg*, April 13, 2012.

81. Patrick Boehler, "China's elite hiding billions overseas, US report says," *Guardian*, April 5, 2016, www.scmp.com/news/china/article/1411335/chinas-elite-hiding-billions-overseas-us-report-says.

82. "Heirs of Mao's comrades rise as new capitalist nobility," 1, 5.

83. Ibid.

84. Ibid.

85. Ibid.

86. Quoted in He Qingliang, "On contemporary primitive capital accumulation," *The Chinese Economy*, vol. 34, no. 2 (March–April 2001): 80–81.

87. Xinyuan Wang, "Hundreds of Chinese citizens feel just fine about the controversial social credit system," *The Conversation*, December 19, 2019, www.pri.org/stories/2019-12-19/hundreds-chinese-citizens-feel-just-fine-about-controversial-social-credit-system.

88. On the student activists who led the Tiananmen protests in 1989 and later sold out to get rich see Lim, *Amnesia*, Chapters 2–3. See also Javier C. Hernandez, "In 1989, a Tiananmen marcher: Now, a megaphone for the party," *New York Times*, August 1, 2019.

89. Quoted in "Heirs of Mao's comrades rise as new capitalist nobility."

90. Quoted in Margaret Wente, "The real cost of China rising," *Globe and Mail*, November 26, 2010, https://journal.probeinternational.org/2010/11/02/the-real-cost-of-china-rising. See also Mark Kitto, "A Briton's bitter farewell to China echoes loudly," *New York Times*, June 15, 2013.

91. Link, *Evening Chats*, 112–118. Han Dongfang, "China's uncivil society," *Wall Street Journal*, May 3, 2005; Robert Foyle Hunwick, "Desperate Chinese are turning to mass suicide to get their government's attention," *PRI.org*, May 19, 2015, www.pri.org/stories/2015-05-19/desperate-chinese-are-turning-mass-suicide-get-their-governments-attention; Philip Jacobson, "These desperate girls were abducted and sold in China. One daring group of do-gooders kidnapped them back," *Narratively*, September 3, 2017, https://narratively.com/these-vietnamese-girls-were-abducted-and-sold-in-china-one-daring-group-of-do-gooders-kidnapped-them-back; Charles Custer, "Missing, kidnapped, trafficked: China has a problem with its children," *Guardian*, March 12, 2015, www.theguardian.com/commentisfree/2015/mar/12/missing-kidnapped-trafficked-china-children; Alice Yan, "Chinese kindergarten head sacked for watering down

children's milk in latest food scandal to hit China," *South China Morning Post*, November 6, 2018, www.scmp.com/news/china/society/article/2171993/chinese-kindergarten-head-sacked-watering-down-childrens-milk; "Chinese man attacks 22 children 1 adult with knife outside primary school," *Daily News*, December 14, 2012; Ni Dandan, "Beijing doctor brutally killed by patient's son," *Sixth Tone*, December 28, 2019, www.sixthtone.com/news/1005020/Beijing%20Doctor%20 Brutally%20Killed%20by%20Patient's%20Son; Borge Bakken, *Crime and the Chinese Dream* (Hong Kong: Hong Kong University Press, 2018).

92. Min Jiang and Ashley Esarey, "Uncivil society in digital China: Incivility, fragmentation, and political stability," *International Journal of Communication*, no. 12 (2018): 1928–1944; C. M. Clark, "Faculty and student perception of academic incivility in the People's Republic of China, *Journal of Cultural Diversity*, no. 19, vol. 3 (Fall 2012): 85–93; Gabriele de Seta, "Wenming bu wenming: The socialization of incivility in postdigital China," *International Journal of Communication*, no. 12 (2018): 2010–2030.

93. Link, *Evening Chats*, 58, 61.

94. Ibid., 64.

95. Ibid., 67.

96. Echo Huang, "China publishes more science research with fabricated peer-review than everyone else put together," *Quartz*, May 8, 2017, https://qz.com/978037/ china-publishes-more-science-research-with-fabricated-peer-review-than-everyone-else-put-together.

97. Andrew Jacobs, "Rampant fraud threat to China's brisk ascent," *New York Times*, October 6, 2010; Amy Qin, "Fraud scandals sap China's dream of becoming a science superpower," *New York Times*, October 13, 2017.

98. Stephen Chen, "China is offering more than a million dollars for a foreigner to run the world's largest telescope, so why is nobody applying?" *South China Morning Post*, August 3, 2017; Stephen Chen, "How noisy Chinese tourists may be drowning out aliens at the world's biggest telescope," *South China Morning Post*, August 24, 2017, www.scmp.com/news/china/society/article/2107893/how-noisy-chinese-tourists-may-be-drowning-out-alien-signals. Four million tourists visited this remote rural site in the first half of 2017.

99. Link, *Evening Chats*, 76.

100. See Pei, *Crony Capitalism*, 216–242.

101. Qin Shao, *Shanghai Gone*, 17–18.

102. He Qingliang, "China's listing social structure," 92.

103. Pei, *Crony Capitalism*, Chapter 7, 262.

104. Ibid., 218–219

105. Didi Kirsten Tatlow, "In China: A climate of mistrust in medicine," *New York Times*, April 8, 2015, https://sinosphere.blogs.nytimes.com/2015/04/08/in-china-a-climate-of-mistrust-in-medicine.

106. Sui-Lee Wee, "China's healthcare crisis: Lines before dawn, violence and 'no trust,'" *New York Times*, September 30, 2018.

107. Juliet Song, "Fake Chinese medical facility lures in patients by stealing the identity of a well-respected hospital," *Epoch Times*, May 8, 2016, www.theepochtimes. com/fake-chinese-medical-facility-lures-in-patients-by-stealing-the-identity-of-a-well-respected-hospital_2059802.html.

108. Manya Koetse, "Another hospital scandal: Nanchang doctor asks for more money during abortion," *What's on Weibo*, April 11, 2017, www.whatsonweibo.com/

doctor-asks-female-student-money-abortion. Koetse has written extensively on China's medical system since privatization: "Shanghai plastic surgery nightmare: Doctor's sexual abuse scandal exposed on Chinese social media," *What's On Weibo*, December 11, 2016, www.whatsonweibo.com/shanghai-plastic-surgery-nightmare-goes-viral; "Updated: National outrage after woman is made to pay $700 for hospital appointment," *What's On Weibo*, February 2, 2016, www.whatsonweibo.com/700-for-hospital-appointment; "Nanchang doctor stirs controversy after bragging about bribes on Weibo," *What's On Weibo*, December 27, 2017, www.whatsonweibo.com/nanchang-doctor-stirs-controversy-bragging-bribes-weibo. See also "Woman decries hospital scalpers, reigniting debate," *Global Times*, January 26, 2016, www.globaltimes.cn/content/965806.shtml.

109. Didi Kirsten Tatlow, "Chinese doctors becoming the targets of patient anger," *New York Times,* November 1, 2013, https://sinosphere.blogs.nytimes.com/2013/11/01/doctors-the-targets-of-patients-anger.

110. Tatlow, "Climate of distrust."

111. Xinyuan Wang, "Chinese feel just fine about the social credit system."

112. "Rights lawyer says license revoked over open letter," *China Digital Times*, January 14, 2018. The translated text of his letter is available at https://chinadigitaltimes.net/2018/01/rights-lawyer-says-license-revoked-retaliation-open-letter.

113. Including 6 members of the Politburo; 2 members of the Central Military Commission; 2 vice chairs of the Chinese People's Political Consultative Congress; 36 PLA generals; 31 current and former members of the Central Committee; dozens of heads of ministries; chairmen and senior executives of state-owned companies including Sinopec, Sinochem, China Telecom, China Unicom, Wuhan Steel, Dongfang Motors, China Resources, and China Southern Airlines; provincial governors and vice governors; the mayors of Beijing, Shanghai, and other cities; and the prosecutor general of Shanghai, chief economist of the State Administration of Taxation, the director of the National Energy Administration, the director of the China Banking Regulatory Commission, several directors of China Development Bank and Agricultural Bank of China, the government's chief internet regulator, and several Party secretaries; Wikipedia, "Officials implicated by the anti-corruption campaign in China (2012–2017)," https://en.wikipedia.org/wiki/Officials_implicated_by_the_anti-corruption_campaign_in_China_(2012–2017). "China's pride," Meng Hongwei, the first Chinese to head Interpol, was taken down in October 2018; Steven Lee Myers and Chris Buckley, "Interpol chief was China's pride. His fall exposes the country's dark side," *New York Times*, October 8, 2018.

114. Huang Kaiqian, "Interpol issues red alert notices for 3 Sinopec executives, Reuters says," *Caixin*, March 22, 2017, www.caixinglobal.com/2017-03-22/interpol-issues-red-notices-for-3-sinopec-executives-reuters-says-101068675.html.

115. Murong Xuecun, "Xi's selective punishment," *New York Times*, January 16, 2015.

116. Pei, *Crony Capitalism*, 121.

117. "Disciplinary watchdogs seek to fight factionalism within the Party," *People's Daily*, January 12, 2015, http://en.people.cn/n/2015/0112/c90785-8834538.html.

118. Kinling Lo, "Vow to 'dig deep' to find corrupt police amid Xi Jinping's anti-mafia sweep," *South China Morning Post*, February 2, 2018, www.scmp.com/news/china/policies-politics/article/2131626/vow-dig-deep-find-corrupt-police-amid-xi-jinpings-anti; Guo Boxiong, "Man who ran world's largest army charged with taking US$12.3 million worth of bribes," *South China Morning Post*, April 4,

2016; www.scmp.com/news/china/policies-politics/article/1933524/man-who-ran-worlds-largest-army-charged-taking-us123; "China's Communist Youth League pledges to stamp out corruption among officials," *South China Morning Post*, April 26, 2016, www.scmp.com/news/china/policies-politics/article/1938 512/chinas-communist-youth-league-pledges-stamp-out.

119. Dickson, *Dictator's Dilemma,* 91–93, Tables 2.5 and 2.6.

120. Pei, *Crony Capitalism,* Appendix, Tables A.1.–A.6. Amnesty International, "Death sentences and executions, 2017" (2018), 20–21, https://amnesty.org.pl/wp-content/uploads/2018/04/Death-Penalty-REPORT-web-FINAL.pdf.

121. Samuel Wade, "Punished officials bounce back," *China Digital Times,* August 14, 2013.

122. Alice Yan, "Don't go back on your old ways when our backs are turned, CCDI warns cadres," *South China Morning Post,* November 5, 2014. See also Angela Meng, "'Don't lie about your assets' China's anti-corruption agency warns officials," *South China Morning Post,* February 10, 2015, www.scmp.com/news/china/article/1709166/chinese-anti-corruption-agency-warns-government-officials-dont-lie-about.

123. Andrea Chen, "Some cadres shrugging off anti-corruption campaign, graft-buster warns," *South China Morning Post,* October 25, 2014. Stamping out corruption may be impossible but there is at least this to be said for it, see Nectar Gan, "Communist Party's crackdown on corruption is great . . . it keeps my husband home," *South China Morning Post,* June 1, 2016.

124. Drew Hinshaw and Bradley Hope, "China's top cop led Interpol. Then he disappeared," *Wall Street Journal,* April 26, 2019.

125. Sophie Beach, "Amid debt crisis, HNA faces questions about ownership, *China Digital Times,* February 2, 2018, https://chinadigitaltimes.net/2018/02/amid-debt-crisis-hna-faces-continued-questions-ownership; Chris Buckley, "Xi starts new term in China, with trusted deputy to deal with Trump," *New York Times,* March 16, 2018.

126. Barmé is quoted in Andrew Jacobs, "In China's antigraft campaign, small victories and bigger doubts," *New York Times,* January 16, 2015.

127. "Hotel-style prison awaits Bo Xilai," *South China Morning Post,* September 22, 2013, www.scmp.com/news/china/article/1315259/hotel-style-prison-awaits-chinas-bo-xilai. Bo remains in Qincheng, but Zhang Xiaojun, the family aide who helped Bo's wife murder Neil Heywood has been released. See Choi Chi-yuk, "Former Bo Xilai family aide jailed over murder of UK businessman Neil Heywood 'released early,'" *South China Morning Post,* January 20, 2018, www.scmp.com/news/china/policies-politics/article/2129724/former-bo-xilai-family-aide-jailed-over-murder-uk.

128. "Hotel-style prison."

129. Mandy Zuo, "Revealed: Photos claim to show life inside China's 'luxury prison' holding jailed wife of disgraced leader Bo Xilai," *South China Morning Post,* April 29, 2016, www.scmp.com/news/china/society/article/1939947/revealed-photos-claim-show-life-inside-chinas-luxury-prison.

130. Dai Qing, *Tiananmen Follies: Prison Memoirs and Other Writings* (Taipei: Eastbridge, 2004). See also Jonathan Mirsky's critical review "China: The uses of fear," *New York Review of Books,* October 6, 2005.

131. Jane Perlez, "Corruption in military poses a test for China," *New York Times,* November 14, 2012.

132. "Anti-graft fight never ending," *China Daily,* November 23, 2017.

CHAPTER 7

1. Jason Samenow, "Red-hot planet: All-time heat records have been set all over the world during the past week," *Washington Post*, July 5, 2018.

2. Nathaniel Rich, "Losing Earth: The decade we almost stopped climate change," *New York Times Magazine*, August 1, 2018, www.nytimes.com/interactive/2018/08/01/magazine/climate-change-losing-earth.html.

3. Mark Kinver, "Shanghai 'most vulnerable to flood risk,'" *BBC News*, August 21, 2012, www.bbc.com/news/science-environment-19318973.

4. Johnathan Watts, "From Miami to Shanghai: 3°C of warming will leave world cities below sea level," *Guardian*, November 3, 2017, www.theguardian.com/cities/2017/nov/03/miami-shanghai-3c-warming-cities-underwater. For a graphic view of what China's coastal cities would look like if the ice caps melt see the interactive maps in Jeffrey Linn, "Submerged," *China File*, May 18, 2015, www.chinafile.com/infographics/submerged.

5. Matthew Walsh, "China's scorching heat wave brings a glimpse of the future," *Sixth Tone*, August 10, 2018, www.sixthtone.com/news/1002747/China's%20Scorching%20Heat%20Wave%20Brings%20a%20Glimpse%20of%20the%20Future.

6. David L. Chandler, "China could face deadly heat waves due to climate change," *MIT News*, July 31, 2018, http://news.mit.edu/2018/china-could-face-deadly-heat-waves-due-climate-change-0731.

7. Ibid. In April 2019, the China Meteorological Administration reported "alarming" temperature changes and accelerating glacial melting and sea level rise; Liang Chenyu, "Govt report details alarming effects of climate change in China," *Sixth Tone*, April 4, 2019, www.sixthtone.com/news/1003802/Govt%20Report%20Details%20Alarming%20Effects%20of%20Climate%20Change%20in%20China.

8. Somini Sengupta et al., "How record heat wreaked havoc on four continents," *New York Times*, July 30, 2018; Christina Anderson and Alan Cowell, "Heat wave scorches Sweden as wildfires rage in the Arctic Circle," *New York Times*, July 19, 2018; Somini Sengupta, "In India, summer heat may soon be literally unbearable," *New York Times*, July 17, 2018.

9. For a readable summary of the scientific literature on what the world will look like if global temperatures rise beyond 2°C see Mark Lynas, *Six Degrees: Our Future on a Hotter Planet* (New York: HarperCollins, 2007).

10. Somini Sengupta and Nadja Popovich, "Global warming in South Asia: 800 million at risk," *New York Times*, June 28, 2018, www.nytimes.com/interactive/2018/06/28/climate/india-pakistan-warming-hotspots.html.

11. Stockholm Resilience Centre, "Earth at risk of heading towards 'hothouse Earth' state," *EurekAlert.org*, August 6, 2018, www.eurekalert.org/pub_releases/2018-08/src-ear080118.php.

12. Lauri Myllyvirta, "China's smokestack economy makes a roaring comeback in 2017," *Greenpeace*, July 17, 2017, https://unearthed.greenpeace.org/2017/07/17/china-economic-growth-industry-2017; "Air pollution in Jing-Jin-Ji worsened in first half of 2017," *Caixin*, July 20, 2008, http://k.caixinglobal.com//web/detail_19528; Le Rongde, "Beijing area sees fewer 'blue-sky days' this year," *Caixin*, November 17, 2017, www.caixinglobal.com/2017-11-17/beijing-area-sees-fewer-blue-sky-days-this-year-101172743.html.

13. Barbara Finamore, "China pledges to tackle air pollution with new plan," *NRDC*, September 13, 2013, www.nrdc.org/experts/barbara-finamore/china-pledges-tackle-air-pollution-new-plan.

14. Jane Cai, "It's war on smog! China pledges pollution battle 'for the nation's future,'" *South China Morning Post*, March 5, 2014, www.scmp.com/news/china/article/1440784/its-war-smog-china-pledges-pollution-battle-nations-future.

15. Li Jing, "Pollution-free days of Beijing Olympics now just a happy memory," *South China Morning Post*, August 10, 2013, www.scmp.com/news/china/article/1295644/pollution-free-days-beijing-olympics-now-just-happy-memory; Jonathan Kaiman, "After 'military parade blue' skies, pollution returns to Beijing," *Los Angeles Times*, September 7, 2015, www.latimes.com/world/asia/la-fg-china-air-quality-parade-20150907-story.html; Li Jing, "How China's quick blue-sky fixes make pollution worse," *South China Morning Post*, December 9, 2016, www.scmp.com/news/china/policies-politics/article/2053023/how-chinas-quick-blue-sky-fixes-make-pollution-worse.

16. John McGarrity, "One year on after 'war' declared on pollution, Beijing air scarcely improves," *Chinadialogue*, February 2, 2015, www.chinadialogue.net/blog/7695-one-year-on-after-war-declared-on-pollution-Beijing-air-scarcely-improves/en; Xu Nan, "China's noxious air 'as deadly as smoking': Study," *Chinadialogue*, February 4, 2015, www.chinadialogue.net/blog/7697-China-s-noxious- air-as-deadly-as-smoking-study/en.

17. Tom Philips, "Beijing smog: Pollution red alert declared in China capital and 21 other cities," *Guardian*, December 16, 2016, www.theguardian.com/world/2016/dec/17/beijing-smog-pollution-red-alert-declared-in-china-capital-and-21-other-cities; Erin McCann, "Life in China, smothered by smog," *New York Times*, December 16, 2016. See also Tan Yinghong, "The age of smog," *China Digital Times*, January 3, 2017, https://chinadigitaltimes.net/2017/01/tang-yinghong-age-smog.

18. "Beijing fails to implement anti-pollution measures, MEP says," *Clean Air Alliance of China*, October 17, 2017, http://en.cleanairchina.org/product/8234.html.

19. Zheng Jinran, "Lax anti-pollution efforts highlighted," *China Daily*, August 2, 2017, www.chinadaily.com.cn/cndy/2017-08/02/content_30325231.htm; Gan, "12,000 officials disciplined."

20. Nectar Gan, "China firing blanks in 'war on pollution' as smog worsens," *South China Morning Post*, February 2, 2017, www.scmp.com/news/china/policies-politics/article/2066503/china-firing-blanks-war-pollution-smog-worsens.

21. David Stanway et al., "A pollution crackdown compounds slowdown woes in China's heartlands," *Reuters*, May 23, 2019, www.reuters.com/article/us-china-economy-henan-pollution-insight/a-pollution-crackdown-compounds-slowdown-woes-in-chinas-heartland-idUSKCN1SU025.

22. David Blair, "Change in the air," *China Daily*, April 6–8, 2018.

23. Te-Ping Chen, "Air quality improves in Beijing," *Wall Street Journal*, January 1, 2018.

24. Mimi Lau, "Smog returns across north days after China claims progress in winter pollution campaign," *South China Morning Post*," January 15, 2018, www.scmp.com/news/china/policies-politics/article/2128311/smog-returns-across-north-days-after-china-claims; Charmy Zhang, "Beijing to halt construction as smog closes in just weeks after clearest skies in five years," *South China Morning Post*,

January 12, 2018, www.scmp.com/news/china/society/article/2127950/beijing-halt-construction-smog-closes-just-weeks-after-clearest.

25. "Beijing fears relapse in anti-smog battle," *Caixin*, April 20, 2018, www.caixinglobal.com/2018-04-20/beijing-fears-relapse-in-anti-smog-battle-101237230.html.

26. Greenpeace, "Analysis of air quality trends in 2017" (January 2018), www.greenpeace.org/eastasia/Global/eastasia/publications/campaigns/Climate%20and%20Energy/Analysis%20of%20air%20quality%20trends%20in%202017.pdf.

27. Ibid.

28. Li Rongde, "Beijing breathes easy while neighbors suffocate," *Caixin*, December 22, 2017, www.caixinglobal.com/2017-12-22/beijing-breathes-easy-while-neighbors-suffocate-101188579.html; David Stanway, "Major China regions see smog worsen, adding to fears polluters are moving south," *Reuters*, February 12, 2018, www.reuters.com/article/us-china-pollution/major-china-regions-see-smog-worsen-adding-to-fears-polluters-are-moving-south-idUSKBN1FW0H3; "PM2.5 in Beijing down 54%, but nationwide air quality improvements slow as coal use Increases," *Greenpeace*, www.greenpeace.org/eastasia/press/releases/climate-energy/2018/PM25-in-Beijing-down-54-nationwide-air-quality-improvements-slow-as-coal-use-increases; Greenpeace, "Analysis of air quality trends in 2017."

29. Liu Zhen, "Beijing meets national air pollutant standard for first time," *South China Morning Post*, February 7, 2018, www.scmp.com/news/china/society/article/2132406/beijing-meets-national-air-pollutant-standard-first-time; "Smog levels rise 20pc in China's Yangtze Delta in January, raising fears pollution is moving south," *South China Morning Post*, February 13, 2018, www.scmp.com/news/china/policies-politics/article/2133164/smog-levels-rise-20pc-chinas-yangtze-river-delta; Catherine Lai, "'Moderate to very high' health risk warning, as Hongkongers awake to choking air pollution," *Hong Kong Free Press*, January 17,2018,www.hongkongfp.com/2018/01/17/moderate-high-health-risk-warning-hongkongers-awake-choking-air-pollution.

30. Echo Xie, "Small factories in northern China count the cost of Beijing's war on pollution," *South China Morning Post*, April 7, 2019, www.scmp.com/news/china/politics/article/3004981/small-factories-northern-china-count-cost-beijings-war.

31. Huang Kaixi et al., "Farmers freeze as coal cleanup campaign backfires," *Caixin*, December 6, 2017, www.caixinglobal.com/2017-12-07/rural-farmers-freeze-as-coal-cleanup-campaign-backfires-101182005.html; Zhou Chen et al., "Thousands in rural China secretly burn coal as gas prices soar," *Caixin*, December 8, 2017, www.caixinglobal.com/2017-12-08/thousands-in-rural-china-secretly-burn-coal-as-gas-prices-soar-101182697.html.

32. Viola Zhou, "China's polluting factories run around the clock while villagers are told to cut household emissions," *South China Morning Post*, September 21, 2018, www.scmp.com/news/china/society/article/2112011/chinas-polluting-factories-run-around-clock-while-villagers-are. See also Huang Kaixi et al., "Drive for clean air creates 'chaos,' leaves thousands shivering," *Caixin*, December 11, 2017, www.caixinglobal.com/2017-12-11/drive-for-clean-air-creates-chaos-leaves-thousands-shivering-101183499.html.

33. Li Rongde, "Smog smothers north China," *Caixin*, March 26, 2018, www.caixinglobal.com/2018-03-26/quick-take-smog-smothers-north-

china-101226722.html; Li Rongde, "Sandstorm, smog strangle Beijing," *Caixin,* March 28, 2018, www.caixinglobal.com/2018-03-28/sandstorm-smog-strangle-beijing-101227782.html.

34. Finbarr Bermingham, "China 'yet to hit bottom' as economic downturn plumbed new depths in October," *South China Morning Post,* November 14, 2019.

35. "China's air quality worsens as national PM2.5 level rises 5.2 percent in January and February," *South China Morning Post,* March 21, 2019, www.scmp.com/news/china/politics/article/3002655/chinas-air-quality-worsens-national-pm25-level-rises-52pc; "Northern Chinese cities fail to meet winter smog targets," *South China Morning Post,* April 1, 2019, www.scmp.com/news/china/society/article/3004147/northern-chinese-cities-fail-meet-winter-smog-targets; Hou Liqiang, "Why is air pollution worse in places? Inspectors in new round will find out," *China Daily,* April 30, 2019.

36. Lauri Myllyvirta, "China ozone pollution levels hit record high amid industrial output surge," *Ecologist,* July 19, 2018, https://theecologist.org/2018/jul/19/china-ozone-pollution-levels-hit-record-high-amid-industrial-output-surge.

37. Greenpeace, "Analysis of air quality trends in 2017"; "Harmful ozone pollution worsening in northern China," *South China Morning Post,* April 11, 2018, www.scmp.com/news/china/policies-politics/article/2141259/harmful-ozone-pollution-worsening-northern-china-says; Guo Rui, "China's fight for clean air gets more complicated after scientists link fall in PM2.5 pollutants to rise in crop-damaging ground-level ozone," *South China Morning Post,* January 7, 2019, www.scmp.com/news/china/article/2181071/chinas-fight-clean-air-just-got-more-complicated-after-scientists-link.

38. Zhang Chun, "Hebei's lung cancer spike raises questions about role of pollution," *Chinadialogue,* February 15, 2016, www.chinadialogue.net/article/show/single/en/8620-Hebei-s-lung-cancer-spike-raises-questions-about-role-of-pollution-.

39. David Stanway, "China cuts smog but health damage already done: Study," *Reuters,* April 17, 2018, www.reuters.com/article/us-china-pollution-health/china-cuts-smog-but-health-damage-already-done-study-idUSKBN1HO0C4.

40. Myllyvirta, "China's CO2 emissions surged in 2018."

41. Guo Rui, "China still facing an uphill struggle in fight against pollution, warns environment minister," *South China Morning Post,* March 11, 2019, www.scmp.com/news/china/politics/article/2189598/china-still-facing-uphill-struggle-fight-against-pollution-warns. "China launches environmental investigation in pollution-prone Hebei," *South China Morning Post,* October 11, 2019, www.scmp.com/news/china/politics/article/3032506/china-launches-environmental-investigation-pollution-prone.

42. "China's smog-prone regions see clearer skies but pollution worse elsewhere," *South China Morning Post,* January 16, 2020, www.scmp.com/news/china/society/article/3046345/chinas-smog-prone-regions-see-clearer-skies-pollution-worse.

43. "China's environmental ministry finds patchy progress on water and soil pollution," *Reuters,* April 24, 2017, www.reuters.com/article/us-china-pollution/chinas-environment-ministry-finds-patchy-progress-on-water-and-soil-pollution-idUSKBN17R02V; Deng Tingting, "In China, the water you drink is as dangerous as the air you breathe," *Guardian,* June 2, 2017, www.theguardian.com/global-development-professionals-network/2017/jun/02/china-water-dangerous-pollution-greenpeace.

44. Gao Baiyu, "Half of Yangtze provinces are water stressed," *Chinadialogue,* October 3, 2019, www.chinadialogue.net/article/show/single/en/11554-Half-of-Yangtze-provinces-are-water-stressed.

45. "China plans crackdown on illegal dumping," *South China Morning Post*, October 21, 2019, www.scmp.com/news/china/society/article/3033859/china-plans-crackdown-illegal-chemical-dumping; Zou Shuo, "Cities fail to improve water quality," *China Daily*, March 1, 2018; Echo Xie, "What China must do to clean up its act on waste water," *South China Morning Post*, May 26, 2019, www.scmp.com/news/china/politics/article/3011820/why-chinas-waste-water-plants-are-some-its-biggest-polluters.

46. "New 'Water ten plan' to safeguard China's waters," *China Water Risk*, April 16, 2015, http://chinawaterrisk.org/notices/new-water-ten-plan-to-safeguard-chinas-waters; Li Ruohan, "Govt boosts measures to tackle country's polluted water system," *Global Times*, May 11, 2015, www.globaltimes.cn/content/1073632.shtml.

47. Congbin Xu et al., "Remediation of polluted soil in China: Policy and technology bottlenecks," *Environmental Science & Technology*, vol. 51, no. 24 (2017): 14027–14029, https://pubs.acs.org/doi/pdfplus/10.1021/acs.est.7b05471.

48. Zhou Chen et al., "China's tainted soil initiative lacks pay plan," *Caixin*, June 8, 2016, www.caixinglobal.com/2016-06-08/101011627.html.

49. Ibid.

50. Ariel Wittenberg, "EPA cleans up superfund sites but leaves toxins behind," *The Norwich Bulletin,* August 9, 2014, www.norwichbulletin.com/article/20140809/News/140809577. US EPA, "Superfund: National Priorities List," www.epa.gov/superfund/superfund-national-priorities-list-npl.

51. David Stanway, "After China's multibillion-dollar cleanup, water still unfit to drink," *Reuters*, February 20, 2013, www.reuters.com/article/us-china-pollution-water/after-chinas-multibillion-dollar-cleanup-water-still-unfit-to-drink-idUSBRE91J19N20130220.

52. Eugene Simonov, "Lake Baikal pipeline threatens critical ecosystem," *Chinadialogue*, April 7, 2017, www.chinadialogue.net/article/show/single/en/9723-Lake-Baikal-pipeline-threatens-critical-ecosystem; "World's largest water diversion plan won't quench China's thirst," *Bloomberg*, December 10, 2017, www.bloomberg.com/news/articles/2017-12-10/world-s-largest-water-diversion-plan-won-t-slake-china-s-thirst; Tom Philips, "'Parched' Chinese city plans to pump water from Russian lake via 1,000km pipeline," *Guardian*, March 7, 2017, www.theguardian.com/world/2017/mar/07/parched-chinese-city-plans-to-pump-water-from-russian-lake-via-1000km-pipeline; "All Dried Up," *The Economist*, October 10, 2013, www.economist.com/news/china/21587813-northern-china-running-out-water-governments-remedies-are-potentially-disastrous-all; "China has built the world's largest water-diversion project," *The Economist,* April 5, 2018, www.economist.com/news/china/21740011-channelling-water-south-north-does-more-harm-good-china-has-built-worlds-largest.

53. Li Jing, "China's 'iron fist' against pollution is softening," *Chinadialogue,* March 14, 2019, www.chinadialogue.net/article/show/single/en/11139-China-s-iron-fist-against-pollution-is-softening.

54. Justin Gillis, "A prophet of doom was right about the climate," *New York Times*, June 23, 2018; Nathaniel Rich, "Losing the Earth: The decade we almost stopped climate change, a tragedy in two acts," *New York Times Magazine*, August 1, 2018,

www.nytimes.com/interactive/2018/08/01/magazine/climate-change-losing-earth.html.

55. Kevin Anderson, "The emission case for a radical plan," presentation at the Radical Emissions Reduction Conference, Tyndall Centre for Climate Research, Norwich, UK, December 10–11, 2013, www.tyndall.ac.uk/sites/default/files/anderson_-_radical_plan_conf.pdf. The IEA quotation is from the same source.

56. Ibid., 5, italics added.

57. James Hansen et al., "Assessing 'dangerous climate change': Required reduction of carbon emissions to protect young people, future generations and nature," *Plos One*, vol. 8, no. 12 (December 2013): no pagination, http://journals.plos.org/plosone/article?id=10.1371/journal.pone.0081648.

58. Naomi Klein, *This Changes Everything: Capitalism vs. The Climate* (New York: Simon & Schuster, 2014), 87.

59. David Wells-Wallace, *Uninhabitable Earth: A Story of the Future* (New York: Penguin, 2019).

60. Kevin Anderson, "Avoiding dangerous climate change demands de-growth strategies form wealthier nations," *Kevinanderson.info*, November 25, 2013, http://kevinanderson.info/blog/avoiding-dangerous-climate-change-demands-de-growth-strategies-from-wealthier-nations.

61. "China's Xi says GDP growth no less than 6.5% until 2020: Reports," *CNBC News*, November 3, 2015, www.cnbc.com/2015/11/03/chinas-xi-says-gdp-growth-no-less-than-65-until-2020-reports.html.

62. Calculating Chinese emissions is fraught with difficulty and estimates vary widely because they are poorly documented and because the government does not publish regular annual emissions reports. Here I follow the accounts presented by Yuli Shan et al., "China CO_2 emission accounts 1997–2015," *Scientific Data*, vol. 5, article no. 170201 (2018), www.nature.com/articles/sdata2017201#t1.

63. Shan et al., "China CO_2 emission accounts." See also Table 5.3 in the Appendix of the same.

64. Some Western economists think China's GDP hardly grew at all in 2018 or may even have been negative. Sidney Leng, "China's GDP growth could be half of reported number, says US economist at prominent Chinese university," *South China Morning Post*, March 10, 2019, www.scmp.com/economy/china-economy/article/2189245/chinas-gdp-growth-could-be-half-reported-number-says-us.

65. Richard Smith, "Essay 3 (2011): Green capitalism: the god that failed" in *Green Capitalism*; Smith, "An ecosocialist path."

66. Lauri Myllyvirta and Fergus Green, "China's carbon trading scheme: Smoke and mirrors," *Lowy Interpreter*, October 17, 2019, www.lowyinstitute.org/the-interpreter/china-s-carbon-emissions-trading-scheme-not-where-action.

67. Somini Sengupta, "Why build Kenya's first coal plant? Hint: Think China," *New York Times*, March 1, 2018; "Arctic gas terminal begins ice silk road," *China Daily*, December 11, 2017; Eva Dou, "Beijing stakes an arctic claim," *Wall Street Journal*, January 27–28, 2018.

68. Leslie Hook and Lucy Hornby, "China's solar desire dims," *Financial Times*, June 8, 2018, www.ft.com/content/985341f4-6a57-11e8-8cf3-0c230fa67aec; Ke Dawei, "China becomes largest natural gas importer," *Caixin*, June 26, 2018, www.caixinglobal.com/2018-06-26/china-becomes-largest-natural-gas-importer-101284633.html.

69. Fang Hao, "Efforts to cut steel capacity not working," *Chinadialogue*, February 3, 2017, www.chinadialogue.net/article/show/single/en/9642-efforts-to-cut-steel-capacity-not-working; Bethany Allen-Ebrahimian, "Chinese steel output hits all-time high," *Foreign Policy*, July 19, 2017, http://foreignpolicy.com/2017/07/19/chinese-steel-output-hits-all-time-high; Muyu Xu and Melanie Burton, "Chinese steel, aluminum output at record as US mulls penalties," *Reuters*, February 23, 2017, www.reuters.com/article/us-china-economy-output-steel/chinas-steel-aluminum-output-at-record-as-u-s-mulls-penalties-idUSKBN1A2096.

70. Zheping Huang, "China's economic growth is driven by all the things it says it wants to get rid of," *Quartz*, July 17, 2017, https://qz.com/1030268/chinas-gdp-growth-is-driven-by-all-the-things-it-says-it-wants-to-get-rid-of.

71. Zheng Bo, "Cars a threat to China's 2030 CO2 peak," *Chinadialogue*, August 14, 2015, www.chinadialogue.net/article/show/single/en/8115-Cars-a-threat-to-China-s-2-3-CO2-peak; George Monbiot, "Cars are killing us. Within 10 years, we must phase them out," *Guardian*, March 7, 2019, www.theguardian.com/commentisfree/2019/mar/07/cars-killing-us-driving-environment-phase-out.

72. "China to ban production of petrol and diesel cars 'in the near future,'" *Guardian*, September 11, 2017, www.theguardian.com/world/2017/sep/11/china-to-ban-production-of-petrol-and-diesel-cars-in-the-near-future.

73. Ji-Feng Li et al., "Analysis on energy demand and CO2 emissions in China following the Energy Production and Consumption Revolution Strategy and China Dream target," *Advances in Climate Change Research*, vol. 9, no. 1 (March 2018): 16–26. In its 2017 annual energy outlook, China National Petroleum Corporation (CNPC) projected that "by 2050, coal, non-fossil energy, and oil and gas will each take up one-third of China's energy mix." Counting methane as "clean" energy, the CNPC can thus say that by 2050 "new energy will account for more than half of China's energy mix," when in fact fossil fuels will still provide two-thirds of China's energy; Zheng Xin, "New energy to play a dominant role by 2030," *China Daily*, August 17, 2017. See also "Electric vehicles' dirty secret: China's huge coal production powers the world's largest but not the cleanest EV fleet," *Wall Street Journal*, October 12–13, 2019.

74. Ji Shuguang et al., "Electric vehicles in China: Emissions and health impacts," *Environmental Science & Technology*, vol. 46, no. 4 (2012): 2018–2024, https://pubs.acs.org/doi/abs/10.1021/es202347q.

75. Emma Foehringer Merchant, "Lithium-ion battery production is surging, but at what cost?" *Green Tech Media*, September 20, 2017, www.greentechmedia.com/articles/read/lithium-ion-battery-production-is-surging-but-at-what-cost; Niclas Rolander et al., "The dirt on clean electric cars," *Bloomberg*, October 15, 2018, www.bloomberg.com/news/articles/2018-10-16/the-dirt-on-clean-electric-cars; Max Opray, "Nickel mining: The hidden environmental cost of electric cars," *Guardian*, August 24, 2017, www.theguardian.com/sustainable-business/2017/aug/24/nickel-mining-hidden-environmental-cost-electric-cars-batteries.

76. Miles Berners-Lee and Duncan Clark, "What's the carbon footprint of . . . a new car?" *Guardian*, September 23, 2010, www.theguardian.com/environment/green-living-blog/2010/sep/23/carbon-footprint-new-car.

77. Union of Concerned Scientists, "Cleaner cars from cradle to grave" (November 2015), 3, 5, www.ucsusa.org/sites/default/files/attach/2015/11/Cleaner-Cars-from-Cradle-to-Grave-full-report.pdf

78. For more on this see Smith, "An ecosocialist path," 159–160.

79. Christopher Ross, "The vintage Volkswagen beetle goes electric," *Wall Street Journal*, April 23, 2015.

80. Walter Benjamin, *The Arcades Project* (Cambridge, UK: Belknap Press, 2002).

81. Zhang Chun, "Downsizing China's consumer dream could bring huge carbon cuts, report says," *Chinadialogue*, July 6, 2016, www.chinadialogue.net/article/show/single/en/9073-Downsizing-China-s-consumer-dream-could-bring-huge-carbon-cuts-report-says.

82. Sui-Lee Wee, "Inside China's predatory health care system," *New York Times*, September 30, 2018.

83. Brad Plumer, "Wildlife facing extinction risk all over the globe," *New York Times*, May 7, 2019. See also the "Share the World's Resources" campaign, at www.sharing.org.

84. IPCC, "Global Warming of 1.5°C."

85. See Smith, *Green Capitalism*; Smith, "An ecosocialist path."

86. "Chinese flight to Antarctica a success, signal of new era in tapping polar travel," *People's Daily*, December 18, 2018, http://en.people.cn/n3/2017/1218/c90000-9305376.html.

87. Du Xiaofei, "Massive Chinese container ship sets new record on east coast of US," *People's Daily*, May 17, 2017, http://en.people.cn/n3/2017/0517/c90000-9216987.html.

88. John Vidal, "The world's largest cruise ship and its supersized pollution problem," *Guardian*, May 21, 2016, www.theguardian.com/environment/2016/may/21/the-worlds-largest-cruise-ship-and-its- supersized-pollution-problem.

89. Zhong and Zhang, "China chokes on takeout plastic"; Matt Prichard, "Throwaway world chokes on convenience," *China Daily*, April 13–15, 2018; David Stanway, "On Singles Day, green groups warn of China's surge in packaging waste," *Reuters*, November 10, 2019, www.reuters.com/article/us-singles-day-pollution-idUS KBN1XL0A4; Izabella Shealy, "The abundance of less," *Chinadialogue*, July 19, 2018, https://chinadialogue.net/culture/10738-Book-review-The-Abundance-of-Less/en; Vanessa Friedman, "Who needs so many clothes?" *New York Times*, May 3, 2018.

90. Charlie Parton, "China's looming water crisis" (Chinadialogue, April 2018), https://chinadialogue-production.s3.amazonaws.com/uploads/content/file_en/10608/China_s_looming_water_crisis_v.2__1_.pdf; Hou Liqiang, "Local authorities told to list illegal dumping sites," *China Daily*, June 8–10, 2018.

91. Tom Levitt, "Chinese cities feel loss of street life and community," *Chinadialogue*, November 5, 2012, www.chinadialogue.net/article/show/single/en/5291-Chinese-cities-feel-the-loss-of-streetlife-and-community-.

92. See for example Chrystia Freeland, "The triumph of the family farm," *The Atlantic*, June 13, 2012. See also Farm Aid, "Rebuilding America's economy with family farm-centered food systems" (2013), www.farmaid.org/makethecase; Alan Bjerga, "Organic lets family farms prosper in industrial-agriculture era," *Bloomberg*, June 28, 2012, www.bloomberg.com/news/2012-06-28/organic-lets-family-farms-prosper-in-industrial-agriculture-era.html.

93. Zhang Wei, "Swapping pesticides for beetles could put money in farmers' pockets," *Chinadialogue*, September 6, 2018, https://chinadialogue.net/article/show/single/en/10805-Swapping-pesticides-for-beetles-could-put-money-in-farmers-pockets.

CHAPTER 8

1. Andrew Jacobs, "Pageant silences beauty queen, a critic of China, at U.S. event," *New York Times,* December 13, 2016, www.nytimes.com/2016/12/13/world/asia/anastasia-lin-miss-world-china-censorship.html. See also Anastasia Lin, "The Cultural Revolution comes to North America," *New York Times,* April 8, 2019.
2. "The Long March abroad," *The Economist,* July 7, 2016.
3. Zheping Huang, "Xi Jinping says China's authoritarian system can be model for the world," *Quartz,* March 9, 2018, https://qz.com/1225347/xi-jinping-says-chinas-one-party-authoritarian-system-can-be-a-model-for-the-world. Some Chinese have doubts. See David Bandurski, "In translation: China needs to check its inflated national ego," *Hong Kong Free Press,* August 1, 2018, www.hongkongfp.com/2018/08/01/translation-china-needs-check-inflated-national-ego.
4. "China holds ethnic Mongolian historian who wrote 'genocide' book," *Radio Free Asia,* July 23, 2018, www.rfa.org/english/news/china/mongolian-historian-0723 2018123931.html; Liu Xuanzun, "Tibet underage students banned from religious activities in accordance with law," *Global Times,* July 23, 2018, www.globaltimes.cn/content/1112052.shtml; Chris Buckley, "Tibetan man pushing to save his native language gets five years in prison," *New York Times,* May 23, 2018; Javier C. Hernandez, "Bold displays of art in support for migrants in Beijing," *New York Times,* March 11, 2018; Amy Qin, "Liu Xiaobo's death pushes China's censors into overdrive," *New York Times,* July 17, 2018.
5. Karen Lim, "The epic eye roll from a Chinese reporter is breaking the internet," *Asiaone,* March 13, 2018, www.asiaone.com/china/epic-eye-roll-chinese-reporter-breaking-internet; Paul Mozur, "Reporter rolls eyes and becomes a sensation," *New York Times,* March 14, 2018.
6. Xi is often likened to the cartoon bear, which he evidently hates. Censors apparently banned the letter "N" to pre-empt scientists from expressing dissent mathematically: N<2, with "N" being the number of Xi's terms in office. See Tom Phillips, "Ce*nsored! China bans letter N (briefly) from internet as Xi Jinping extends grip on power," *Guardian,* February 27, 2018, www.theguardian.com/world/2018/feb/28/china-bans-the-letter-n-internet-xi-jinping-extends-power; Amy Qin, "Harmless pig? 'Gangster'? China is taking no chances," *New York Times,* May 11, 2018.
7. Edward Wong, "China frees 5 women's rights activists on bail after holding them for weeks," *New York Times,* April 14, 2015.
8. Yuan Yang, "China's 'MeToo' movement evades censors with #RiceBunny [mi tu]," *Financial Times,* August 8, 2018, www.ft.com/content/61903744-9540-11e8-b67b-b8205561c3fe; Zheng Caixiong, "#MeToo in China: Movement gathers pace amid wave of accusations," *Guardian,* July 30, 2018, www.theguardian.com/world/2018/jul/31/metoo-in-china-movement-gathers-pace-amid-wave-of-accusations.
9. Vincenso La Torre and Elaine Yau, "China bans exports of black clothing to Hong Kong amid protests: All mailings to city to be 'severely investigated,' courier firm worker says," *South China Morning Post,* October 17, 2019, www.scmp.com/lifestyle/fashion-beauty/article/3033312/china-bans-exports-black-clothing-hong-kong-amid-protests.

10. "Charts of the day: China's pension system is out of pocket," *Caixin*, April 19, 2019, www.caixinglobal.com/2019-04-19/charts-of-the-day-chinas-pension-system-is-out-of-pocket-101406390.html; "Old, not yet rich: China's median age will soon overtake America's," *The Economist*, November 2, 2019.

11. Jane Cai, "Minimum wages on the march as labor pool shrinks," *South China Morning Post*, October 13, 2017, www.scmp.com/news/china/economy/article/2115121/minimum-wages-march-china-labour-pool-shrinks.

12. Alexandra Stevenson and Cao Li, "China's slowdown already hit its factories. Now its offices are hurting too," *New York Times*, March 14, 2019.

13. Keith Bradsher, "China's economy, by the numbers, is worse than it looks," *New York Times*, January 20, 2019; "China defaults hit record in 2018. 2019 pace is triple that," *Bloomberg*, May 7, 2019; Alexandra Stevenson and Cao Li, "Chinese firms using I.O.U.s to stay afloat," *New York Times*, August 7, 2019; Mike Bird and Lucy Craymer, "Private data show sharper China slowdown," *Wall Street Journal*, September 8, 2019.

14. He Huifeng, "'We're in trouble': China's middle class frets that the good times are over," *Inkstone*, September 10, 2019, www.inkstonenews.com/business/chinas-rich-are-trying-move-their-wealth-abroad-yuan-weaks-and-price-rises/article/3026498.

15. "Chinese trade surplus hits five-year low as imports rise to record high," *China Banking News*, January 15, 2109, www.chinabankingnews.com/2019/01/15/chinese-trade-surplus-hits-five-year-low-imports-rise-record-high; Frank Tang, "China's first account deficit for 17 years 'could signal fundamental shift,'" *South China Morning Post*, May 4, 2019, www.scmp.com/news/china/economy/article/2144761/chinas-first-current-account-deficit-17-years-could-signal. Moody's Analytics, "China: Current account balance," www.economy.com/china/current-account-balance.

16. Michael Baltensperger, "Why China's current account balance approaches zero," *Breugel*, April 15, 2019, https://bruegel.org/2019/04/why-chinas-current-account-balance-approaches-zero. Morgan Stanley Research, "Facing current-account deficit, China looks abroad for capital" (March 2019), www.morganstanley.com/ideas/china-foreign-capital.

17. Peking University professor Zhang Jian told *Bloomberg*: "I can't find a single example of a superpower growing when its population was falling. . . . [Xi] needs to take care about the domestic situation and worry less about being a great power"; Mark Champion, "What does a Chinese superpower look like? Nothing like the U.S." *Bloomberg*, August 27, 2018, www.bloomberg.com/news/features/2018-08-27/what-does-a-chinese-superpower-look-like-nothing-like-the-u-s.

18. Christopher Balding, "China can't count on consumers to get through the trade war," *Nikkei Asian Review*, July 24, 2018, https://asia.nikkei.com/Opinion/China-can-t-count-on-consumers-to-get-through-trade-war.

19. Li Yuan, "China's consumption downgrade: Skip avocados, cocktails and kids," *New York Times*, August 22, 2018; James T. Areddy, "Consumers pull back, in blow to Xi," *Wall Street Journal*, June 26, 2019.

20. Neil Gough and Owen Guo, "As China's economy slows, Beijing's growth loses punch," *New York Times*, July 15, 2016.

21. See Keith Bradsher, "Street protests in Wuhan, a Chinese city of 10 million, stall an incinerator plant," *New York Times*, July 6, 2019.

22. China Labour Bulletin, "Strike Map" (2018), http://maps.clb.org.hk/strikes/en; Paul Mason, "China's workers are turning from analogue slaves into digital rebels," *Guardian*, September 14, 2014, www.theguardian.com/commentisfree/2014/sep/14/china-analogue-slaves-digital-rebellion; "Crane operators organize momentous nationwide strike," *China Digital Times*, May 9, 2018, https://chinadigitaltimes.net/2018/05/crane-workers-organize-momentous-nationwide-strike; Wang Jiangsong, "The significance of crane operators across China going on strike," *China Change*, May 7, 2018, https://chinachange.org/2018/05/07/the-significance-of-crane-operators-across-china-going-on-strike; "China must release detained crane workers on strike & would-be May 1st protesters," *China Human Rights Defenders*, May 3, 2018, www.nchrd.org/2018/05/china-must-release-detained-crane-workers-on-strike-would-be-may-1st-protesters.

23. Scott Morgan, "Truck drivers strike across China, shout 'overthrow the CPC,'" *Taiwan News*, June 11, 2018, www.taiwannews.com.tw/en/news/3454011; "China's truck drivers strike over stagnant pay, high fuel costs, and arbitrary fines," *China Labour Bulletin*, June 11, 2018, www.clb.org.hk/content/china's-truck-drivers-strike-over-stagnant-pay-high-fuel-costs-and-arbitrary-fines; Chris Buckley, "Marching in pockets across China, army veterans join ranks of protesters," *New York Times*, June 26, 2018.

24. See *Made in China*, vol. 3, no. 2 (April–June 2018). See also Mingqi Li, "Class conflict intensifies as China heads into uncertain times," *Real News Network*, August 21, 2018, https://therealnews.com/stories/class-conflict-intensifies-in-china-as-it-heads-into-uncertain-times; Stella Qiu and Anne Marie Roantree, "Job jitters mount as China's factories sputter ahead of Lunar New Year," *Reuters*, January 17, 2019, www.reuters.com/article/us-china-trade-labour-insight/job-jitters-mount-as-chinas-factories-sputter-ahead-of-lunar-new-year-idUSK CN1PB2WO.

25. Jin Xiaochang, personal communication from Shanghai, October 23 and December 16, 2019.

26. Jenny Chan, "Shenzhen Jasic Technology: Towards a worker-student coalition in China," *New Politics*, September 3, 2018, http://newpol.org/content/shenzhen-jasic-technology-towards-workerstudent-coalition-china; Josh Rudolf, "No one can resist the tides of history: Detained activist Yue Xin on the Jasic workers," *China Digital Times*, August 18, 2018, https://chinadigitaltimes.net/2018/08/no-one-can-resist-the-tides-of-history-detained-activist-yue-xin-on-the-jasic-workers; Michelle Chen, "China's workers aren't fighting a trade war—they're fighting a labor war," *Nation*, September 4, 2018, www.thenation.com/article/chinas-workers-arent-fighting-a-trade-war-theyre-fighting-a-labor-war.

27. Sophie Beach, "Young #MeToo activists broaden calls for equality," *China Digital Times*, September 6, 2018, https://chinadigitaltimes.net/2018/09/young-metoo-activists-broaden-calls-for-equality.

28. Yuan Yang, "Inside China's crackdown on young Marxists," *Financial Times*, February 19, 2019, www.ft.com/content/fd087484-2f23-11e9-8744-e7016697 f225.

29. Edwardo Baptista, "Six Marxist students vanish in the lead up to Labor Day," *CNN*, May 1, 2019, www.cnn.com/2019/05/01/asia/china-students-peking-university-intl/index.html.

30. Gerry Shih, "Everyone is getting locked up: As workers grow disgruntled, China strikes at labor activists," *Washington Post*, December 24, 2019, www. washingtonpost.com/world/asia_pacific/as-workers-grow-disgruntled-in-a-slowing-economy-china-targets-labor-activists/2019/12/24/28a92654-2534-11ea-9cc9-e19cfbc87e51_story.html.

31. "Xi Jinping wanted global dominance. He overshot," *New York Times*, May 7, 2019.

32. Ibid.

33. Chuin-Wei Yap et al., "Huawei's years long rise is littered with accusations of theft and dubious ethics," *Wall Street Journal*, May 25, 2019; "Huawei accused of scheme to steal semiconductor technology from US start-up to help China achieve total dominance," *South China Morning Post*, October 18, 2018, www. scmp.com/business/article/2169224/us-start-accuses-chinas-huawei-trying-steal-semiconductor-technology; Michael Schuman, "Why Alibaba's massive counterfeit problem will never be solved," *Forbes*, November 4, 2015; Kate O'Keefe, "Huawei boss accused of tech theft," *Wall Street Journal*, May 23, 2019; Chuin-Wei Yap, "Huawei propelled by Beijing's billions," *Wall Street Journal*, December 26, 2019.

34. Lulu Yilun Chen, "China claims more patents than any country—most are worthless," *Bloomberg*, September 26, 2018, www.bloomberg.com/news/articles/2018-09-26/china-claims-more-patents-than-any-country-most-are-worthless.

35. Fran Wang, "China's 'weak' research can't break foreign technology 'stranglehold,' legislators warn," *Caixin*, December 25, 2018, www.caixinglobal.com/2018-12-25/chinas-weak-research-cant-break-foreign-technology-stranglehold-legislators-warn-101363320.html; James McGregor, "China's drive for 'indigenous innovation'—a web of industrial policies" (US Chamber of Commerce et al., July 2010), www.uschamber.com/sites/default/files/documents/files/100728china report_0_0.pdf; Lingling Wei and Bob Davis, "How China systematically pries technology from U.S. companies," *Wall Street Journal*, September 26, 2018.

36. Steve Dickinson, "Does China WANT a second decoupling? The Chinese texts say that it does," *China Law Blog*, June 21, 2019, www.chinalawblog.com/2019/06/does-china-want-a-second-decoupling-the-chinese-texts-say-it-does.html.

37. Though there are still gaps. See Heather Somerville, "China presses ahead on Silicon Valley deals," *Wall Street Journal*, October 29, 2019.

38. US Trade Representative (USTR), "Update concerning China's acts, policies and practices related to technology transfer, intellectual property, and innovation" (November 2018), https://ustr.gov/sites/default/files/enforcement/301Investi gations/301%20Report%20Update.pdf; Rob Barry and Dustin Voltz, "Inside China's major corporate hack," *Wall Street Journal*, December 31, 2019; David E. Sanger, "Chinese cyberthieves step up efforts to snag U.S. technology," *New York Times*, November 30, 2018; Brian Spegele and Kate O'Keefe, "China maneuvers to snag American space technology," *Wall Street Journal*, December 5, 2018; Ellen Nakashima and Paul Sonne, "China hacked a Navy contractor and secured a trove of highly sensitive data on submarine warfare," *Washington Post*, June 8, 2018; "China's military built with cloned weapons," *USNI News*, October 27, 2015, https://news.usni.org/2015/10/27/chinas-military-built-with-cloned-weapons. Crowdstrike, "'Huge fan of your work': How Turbine Panda and China's top spies enabled Beijing to cut corners on the C919 passenger jet" (October 2019), www.

crowdstrike.com/resources/wp-content/brochures/reports/huge-fan-of-your-work-intelligence-report.pdf.

39. Hal Brands, "How China went from a business opportunity to enemy no. 1," *Financial Times*, September 6, 2018, www.bloomberg.com/view/articles/2018-09-06/how-china-went-from-a-business-opportunity-to-enemy-no-1.

40. David Lawder et al., "Exclusive: China backtracked on almost all aspects of U.S. trade deal—sources," *Reuters*, May 8, 2019, www.reuters.com/article/us-usa-trade-china-backtracking-exclusiv/exclusive-china-backtracked-on-almost-all-aspects-of-us-trade-deal-sources-idUSKCN1SE0WJ; Michael Nienaber, "Germany to create fund to foil foreign takeovers after China moves," *Reuters*, March 20, 2019, www.reuters.com/article/us-germany-industry-exclusive/exclusive-germany-to-create-fund-to-foil-foreign-takeovers-after-china-moves-idUSKCN1R10IR; Arne Delfs, "Germany toughens stance and blocks China deal," *Bloomberg*, August 1, 2018, www.bloomberg.com/news/articles/2018-08-01/germany-said-to-block-company-purchase-by-chinese-for-first-time.

41. "U.S. businesses no longer 'positive anchor' for U.S.-China relations: Chamber," *Reuters*, April 17, 2019, https://in.reuters.com/article/usa-trade-china/us-businesses-no-longer-positive-anchor-for-us-china-relations-chamber-idINKCN1RT0D3.

42. Dimitri Simes, "Russia up in arms over Chinese theft of military technology," *Nikkei Asian Review*, December 20, 2019, https://asia.nikkei.com/Politics/International-relations/Russia-up-in-arms-over-Chinese-theft-of-military-technology.

43. Austin Ramzy and Chris Buckley, "'Show absolutely no mercy': Inside China's mass detentions," *New York Times*, November 17, 2019; David Stavrou, "A million people are jailed in China's gulags. I managed to escape. Here's what really goes on inside," *Haaretz*, October 17, 2019, www.haaretz.com/world-news/.premium. MAGAZINE-a-million-people-are-jailed-at-china-s-gulags-i-escaped-here-s-what-goes-on-inside-1.7994216.

44. China's ambassador to Denmark reportedly threatened to drop a trade agreement if the Faroe Islands did not sign a 5G contract with Huawei. Simon Kruse and Lene Winther, "Banned recording reveals China ambassador threatened Faroese leader at secret meeting," *Berlingske*, December 29, 2019, www.berlingske.dk/internationalt/banned-recording-reveals-china-ambassador-threatened-faroese-leader. Also in December 2019, the Chinese ambassador to Sweden threatened "bad consequences" for Sweden after its cultural minister presented a free speech prize to Gui Minhai, one of the Hong Kong booksellers that was kidnapped by China. Gui was represented by an empty chair. See Keegan Elmer and Wendy Wu, "China cancels trade visit to Sweden over detained bookseller Gui Minhai's free speech award," *South China Morning Post*, December 10, 2019, www.scmp.com/news/china/diplomacy/article/3041486/china-cancels-trade-visit-sweden-over-detained-bookseller-gui. In the same month, the Chinese ambassador to Germany threatened Berlin, again over 5G. See Tony Czuczka and Steven Arons, "China threatens retaliation should Germany ban Huawei 5G," *Bloomberg*, December 16, 2019, www.bloomberg.com/news/articles/2019-12-14/china-threatens-germany-with-retaliation-if-huawei-5g-is-banned.

45. "Efforts to split China will end in 'bodies smashed and bones ground to powder,' says Chinese president Xi Jinping," *Hong Kong Free Press*, October 14, 2019, www.

hongkongfp.com/2019/10/14/efforts-split-china-will-end-bodies-smashed-bones-ground-powder-says-chinese-president-xi-jinping.

46. Raymond Zhong and Li Yuan, "Wary of trade fight, China mutes its aims of tech glory," *New York Times*, June 27, 2018; Tianyu Fang, "China should stop exaggerating its technological advancements, says state-owned newspaper editor," *SupChina*, June 28, 2018, https://supchina.com/2018/06/28/china-should-stop-exaggerating-its-technological-advancements; Bandurski, "In translation."

47. Willy Wo-Lap Lam, "Xi's grip loosens amid trade war policy paralysis," *Jamestown Foundation*, August 1, 2018, https://jamestown.org/program/xis-grip-on-authority-loosens-amid-trade-war-policy-paralysis.

48. Deng Yuwen, "Trade war raises the spectre of a 'China collapse,' and Beijing should worry," *South China Morning Post*, August 15, 2018, www.scmp.com/comment/insight-opinion/united-states/article/2159628/trade-war-raises-spectre-china-collapse-and.

49. Li Yuan, "Cheering on Trump in China," *New York Times,* April 17, 2019.

50. "Basic Law of the Hong Kong Special Administrative Region of the People's Republic of China," www.basiclaw.gov.hk/en/basiclawtext/images/basiclaw_full_text_en.pdf. The law was adopted on April 4, 1990.

51. The Legislative Council of Hong Kong, which elects the chief executive, apportions half of its 1,200 seats to "functional constituencies" comprised of China-friendly businessmen and other pro-China groups, ensuring that pro-Beijing forces are in the majority regardless of the results of legislative elections.

52. Zheping Huang and Echo Huang, "A brief history: Beijing's interpretations of Hong Kong's Basic Law, from 1999 to the present day," *Quartz*, November 7, 2016, https://qz.com/828713/a-brief-history-beijings-interpretations-of-hong-kongs-basic-law-from-1999-to-the-present-day.

53. Cui Tiankai, "One country, two systems is the best system for Hong Kong, China and the world—including America," *Newsweek*, August 2, 2019, www.newsweek.com/one-country-two-systems-hong-kong-china-1452317.

54. For example, in a brilliantly inventive coup—a sort of "popup democracy" with lessons for democracy activists worldwide—Occupy Central held an online plebiscite at www.popvote.hk in June 2014 to give the general public a say in who should have the right to nominate candidates for the office of chief executive in the 2017 election. Beijing had pledged that the Hong Kong public would directly choose its chief executive, but only from a list of candidates selected by a CCP-controlled nominating committee. Over a ten-day period, and despite fierce CCP cyberattacks that tried to shut the site down, 792,808 voters (28 percent of the registered electorate) voted on three proposals, all of which would have allowed citizens to directly nominate candidates. The winning proposal, put forth by the Alliance for True Democracy, would have allowed candidates to be nominated by 35,000 registered voters, or by any political party which secured at least 5 percent of the vote in the last election for Hong Kong's legislative committee. The proposal was put forward to the government and, unsurprisingly, rejected. Tony Cheung et al., "Alliance for True Democracy proposal wins Occupy Central poll as nearly 800,000 Hongkongers vote," *South China Morning Post*, June 29, 2014, www.scmp.com/news/hong-kong/article/1543231/alliance-true-democracy-proposal-wins-occupy-central-poll-nearly. See also Alice Woodhouse and Nicolle Liu, "Hong Kong protesters go into creative overdrive," *Financial Times*, October 16, 2019, www.ft.com/content/526e2d46-ee97-11e9-bfa4-b25f11f42901.

55. Kinling Lo and Jun Mai, "Beijing to prioritize turning Hong Kongers into patriots," *Inkstone,* November 1, 2019, www.inkstonenews.com/politics/beijing-prioritize-turning-hongkongers-patriots/article/3035920.

56. Alex Palmer, "The case of Hong Kong's missing booksellers," *New York Times,* April 3, 2018, www.nytimes.com/2018/04/03/magazine/the-case-of-hong-kongs-missing-booksellers.html; Tony Cheung and Christy Leung, "Hong Kong police investigate democracy activist's claim he was kidnapped and tortured by mainland China agents," *South China Morning Post,* August 11, 2017, www.scmp.com/news/hong-kong/politics/article/2106391/hong-kong-pro-democracy-activist-claims-he-was-abducted.

57. "Hong Kong's future leader must 'love China,'" *Wall Street Journal,* March 26, 2013.

58. Kevin Lui, "Four more Hong Kong lawmakers ousted in blow to democratic hopes," *Time,* July 14, 2017, https://time.com/4856181/hong-kong-lawmakers-oath-china-disqualified; Austin Ramzy, "Hong Kong bars another democracy supporter from running for office," *New York Times,* October 12, 2018; Alvin Lum et al., "Democracy activist Joshua Wong slams 'politically driven decision' to bar him from running in Hong Kong district council election," *South China Morning Post,* October 19, 2019, www.scmp.com/news/hong-kong/politics/article/3035285/democracy-activist-joshua-wong-banned-running-hong-kong.

59. Joshua Wong and Alex Crow, "Hong Kongers will not be cowed by China," *New York Times,* September 4, 2019.

60. On collusion between the CCP and organized crime see Yi-Zheng Lian, "Gangs of Hong Kong," *New York Times,* August 2, 2019.

61. Anna Fifield, "China's army just released a video showing soldiers practicing shooting protesters," *Washington Post,* August 1, 2019, www.washingtonpost.com/world/asia_pacific/chinas-army-just-released-a-video-showing-soldiers-practicing-shooting-protesters/2019/08/01/f884b9a6-b41e-11e9-acc8-1d847bacca73_story.html.

62. Edwardo Baptista, "Writing on the wall: A tour of Hong Kong's protest graffiti," *The Economist 1843 Magazine,* December 6, 2019, www.1843magazine.com/dispatches/writing-on-the-wall-a-tour-of-hong-kongs-protest-graffiti.

63. Anna Fifield, "Taiwan's 'born independent' millennials are becoming Xi Jinping's lost generation," *Washington Post,* December 26, 2019, www.washingtonpost.com/world/asia_pacific/taiwans-born-independent-millennials-are-becoming-xi-jinpings-lost-generation/2019/12/24/ce1da5c8-20d5-11ea-9c2b-060477c13959_story.html.

64. Michele Chen, "Hong Kong protesters and militant Chinese workers point the way to a new kind of internationalism," *Common Dreams,* July 30, 2019, www.commondreams.org/views/2019/07/30/hong-kong-protesters-and-militant-chinese-workers-point-way-new-kind.

65. Keith Bradsher et al., "In Hong Kong, a banner day for democracy," *New York Times,* November 25, 2019.

66. "Instigating violence is doomed to fail," *People's Daily,* December 2, 2019, http://en.people.cn/n3/2019/1202/c90000-9637349.html; "Chinese people will not be intimidated by any threats," *People's Daily,* December 2, 2019, http://en.people.cn/n3/2019/1202/c90000-9636970.html.

67. "Hong Kong takes to the streets in massive show of support for pro-democracy movement," *Market Watch,* December 8, 2019, www.marketwatch.com/story/

hong-kong-takes-to-the-streets-in-massive-show-of-support-for-pro-democracy-protest-movement-2019-12-08; Sum Lok-kei, "Nearly a fifth of Hong Kong voters say they support violent actions by protesters, such as attacking opponents or hurling petrol bombs and bricks," *South China Morning Post*, December 21, 2109, www.scmp.com/news/hong-kong/politics/article/3043073/nearly-fifth-voters-say-they-support-violent-actions.

68. Zoe Low, "Hong Kong's uncles and aunties take on role of guardian angels, watching over the young protesters amid violence," *South China Morning Post*, October 5, 2019, www.scmp.com/news/hong-kong/politics/article/3031671/hong-kongs-uncles-and-aunties-take-role-guardian-angels; Tiffany May and Paul Mozur, "Parents of besieged Hong Kong protesters come to the front lines," *New York Times*, November 19, 2019; John Lyons, "'You don't have to face it alone.' Hong Kong protests propelled by hidden support network," *Wall Street Journal*, September 20, 2019.

69. Kris Cheng and Holmes Chan, "Arrest at Uighur solidarity demo in Hong Kong, as riot police point pistol at protesters," *Hong Kong Free Press*, December 22, 2019, www.hongkongfp.com/2019/12/22/arrest-uighur-solidarity-demo-hong-kong-riot-police-point-pistol-protesters.

70. Sue-Lin Wong and Qianer Liu, "Huawei critics inspired by Hong Kong protests," *Financial Times*, December 13, 2019, www.ft.com/content/477ee462-1a3d-11ea-97df-cc63de1d73f4.

71. "Even Taiwan's China-friendly opposition cool to reunification plan," *Straits Times*, January 4, 2019, www.straitstimes.com/asia/east-asia/even-taiwans-china-friendly-opposition-cool-to-beijings-reunification-plan.

72. Fifield, "Taiwan's 'born independent' millennials"; Eva Dou, "Taiwan's president criticizes Beijing, courts support," *Wall Street Journal*, November 11, 2019; K. Thor Jensen, "Taiwan's offer of amnesty for Hong Kong protesters draws fire from mainland China," *Newsweek*, August 19, 2019, www.newsweek.com/taiwan-china-hong-kong-amnesty-1455077.

73. David Bandurski, "'Project Dazzling Snow': How China's total surveillance experiment will cover the country," *Hong Kong Free Press*, August 12, 2018, www.hongkongfp.com/2018/08/12/project-dazzling-snow-chinas-total-surveillance-experiment-set-expand-across-country. Paul Mozur and Aaron Kruolik, "China's blueprint for a digital totalitarian state," *New York Times*, December 18, 2019.

74. Folk singer Li Zhi, whose songs "Goddess" and "Square" allude to the 1989 Tiananmen democracy protests, has been silenced and his performances banned. On April 3, 2019 the popular singer's entire musical catalogue was scrubbed from the internet and his Sina Weibo account, with more than a million followers, was deleted. See Geremie Barmé, "They're afraid," *China Heritage*, April 29, 2019, http://chinaheritage.net/journal/theyre-afraid. See "An introduction to Li Zhi and his music," *China Digital Space*, https://chinadigitaltimes.net/space/Li_Zhi.

75. Javier C. Hernandez, "In China, spies in classrooms inhibit speech," *New York Times*, November 1, 2019.

76. Anna Fifield, "In Xi Jinping's China, a top university can no longer promise freedom of thought," *Washington Post*, December 18, 2019, www.washingtonpost.com/world/asia_pacific/in-xi-jinpings-china-a-top-university-can-no-longer-promise-freedom-of-thought/2019/12/18/59f4d21a-215d-11ea-b034-de7dc2b5199b_story.html.

77. In mid-April 2018 the US government banned American firms from selling parts and software to China's ZTE, a maker of smartphones and telecoms gear, for seven years. The US Department of Commerce imposed the ban following ZTE's violation of an agreement on punishing employees that was reached after it was caught illegally shipping US goods to Iran. ZTE had previously been fined for violating sanctions but it had persisted. The ban was a virtual death sentence for the company, which immediately shut down its production lines because it depended on US chips from Qualcomm, and Android software from Google. President Trump lifted the ban in May after levying a $1.3 billion fine and forcing ZTE to provide "high-level security guarantees" against further violations. See Steve Stecklow et al., "U.S. ban on sales to China's ZTE opens fresh front as tensions escalate," *Reuters*, April 16, 2018, www.reuters.com/article/us-china-zte/u-s-ban-on-sales-to-chinas-zte-opens-fresh-front-as-tensions-escalate-idUSKBN1HN1P1. The political upshot of this affair was that the company's critical dependence on US tech humiliated Xi and Communist Party nationalists who, up until April, had been bragging about how China was a rising tech superpower that would soon overtake the US; see for example Wang Yanfei, "China leads in industrial revolution," *China Daily*, December 6, 2017; Ma Si et al., "Breakthroughs confirm China's rise as a global high-tech player," *China Daily*, October 20, 2017; Ma Si, "China a pioneer in AI innovation," *China Daily*, March 27, 2018.

78. Li Yang, "Vaccine scandal has shattered public trust in supervision," *China Daily*, July 25, 2018; Javier C. Hernandez, "In China, vaccine scandal infuriates parents and tests government," *New York Times*, July 23, 2018; Laurie Chen and Kristen Huang, "Chinese president Xi Jinping orders crackdown on 'appalling' vaccine scandal," *South China Morning Post*, July 23, 2018, www.scmp.com/news/china/policies-politics/article/2156431/chinese-premier-li-keqiang-promises-clean-vaccine; Echo Huang, "The world is getting a harsh taste of China's unsafe medicine supply chain," *Quartz*, August 9, 2018, https://qz.com/1352071/the-world-is-getting-a-harsh-taste-of-chinas-unsafe-medicine-supply-chain. In 2019 parents were outraged once again, this time at rotting, "disgusting" food served to their children in public schools; see "Anger over 'disgusting' food found in Chinese school kitchen," *BBC News*, March 14, 2019, www.bbc.com/news/world-asia-china-47565092.

79. "Woman who splashed Xi Jinping poster sent to psychiatric hospital," *Radio Free Asia*, July 23, 2018, www.rfa.org/english/news/china/hospitalized-07232018105734.html.

80. "Chinese commentators take aim at Xi Jinping's unlimited presidency, lack of reform," *Radio Free Asia*, August 1, 2018, www.rfa.org/english/news/china/commentators-08012018114312.html.

81. Translation by Geremie Barmé published as "Imminent fears, immediate hopes—a Beijing jeremiad," *China Heritage*, August 1, 2018, http://chinaheritage.net/journal/imminent-fears-immediate-hopes-a-beijing-jeremiad. See also "Xu Zhangrun's China: 'Licking carbuncles and sucking abscesses,'" *China Change*, August 1, 2018, https://chinachange.org/2018/08/01/xu-zhangruns-china-licking-carbuncles-and-sucking-abscesses.

82. Jerome A. Cohen, "Xi Jinping sees some pushback against iron-fisted rule," *Washington Post*, August 2, 2018.

83. Qiao Long, "China launches 'patriotic struggle' campaign targeting intellectuals," *Radio Free Asia*, August 3, 2018, www.rfa.org/english/news/china/campaign-08032018104859.html; "Amid economic uncertainty, Beijing silences critics," *China Digital Times*, July 18, 2018, https://chinadigitaltimes.net/2018/07/as-economic-uncertainty-looms-beijing-silences-critics.

84. Translation published as "I will not submit, I will not be cowed," *China Heritage*, October 10, 2019, https://chinaheritage.net/journal/i-will-not-submit-i-will-not-be-cowed.

85. Ministry of Education of the People's Republic of China, "Fudan daxue zhangcheng xiuzheng an" [Amendments to Fudan University articles of association] (December 5, 2019), www.moe.gov.cn/srcsite/A02/zfs_gdxxzc/201912/t20191216_412276.html. For background and detail on the Communist Party's shackling of academia see Carl Minzner, "Intelligentsia in the crosshairs: Xi Jinping's ideological rectification of higher education," *China Leadership Monitor*, December 1, 2019, www.prcleader.org/carl-minzner.

86. Javier C. Hernandez, "Taking risk, Chinese students protest limits on free speech," *New York Times*, December 19, 2019.

87. Philip Wen, "Demand for absolute loyalty to Beijing at Chinese universities triggers dissent," *Washington Post*, December 18, 2018, www.wsj.com/articles/demand-for-absolute-loyalty-to-beijing-at-chinese-universities-triggers-dissent-11576674047.

88. Ministry of Education, "Guanyu kaizhan quanguo zhong xiaoxue tushuguan tushu shencha qingli zhuanxiang xingdong de tongzhi" [Notice on carrying out the special review and cleanup of library books in primary and middle schools nationwide] (October 15, 2019), www.moe.gov.cn/s78/A06/A06_gggs/A06_sjhj/201910/t20191021_404580.html; Phoebe Zhang, "Chinese library sparks outrage over report staff burned 'banned books,'" *South China Morning Post*, December 9, 2019; Gerry Shih, "China's library officials are burning books that diverge from Communist Party ideology," *Washington Post*, December 9, 2019, www.washingtonpost.com/world/asia_pacific/in-china-library-officials-burn-books-that-diverge-from-communist-party-ideology/2019/12/09/5563ee46-1a43-11ea-977a-15a6710ed6da_story.html.

89. Elaine Yau, "The Bookworm, a centre of literary life in Beijing, to close, unable to renew its lease amid crackdown on 'illegal structures,'" *South China Morning Post*, November 5, 2019, www.scmp.com/lifestyle/arts-culture/article/3036439/bookworm-centre-literary-life-beijing-close-unable-renew-its; Eva Li, "Why Shanghai's best-known liberal bookshop is closing down," *South China Morning Post*, July 16, 2017, www.scmp.com/news/china/policies-politics/article/2100533/why-shanghais-best-known-liberal-bookshop-closing-down.

90. Brian Wang, "China defense budget increases by 8.1% but police state budget is still 20% more," *Next Big Future*, March 7, 2008, www.nextbigfuture.com/2018/03/china-defense-budget-increases-by-8-1-but-police-state-budget-is-still-20-more.html.

91. As Xi was intensifying repression of free thinkers, activists, human rights lawyers and others in 2015, Li Keqiang complained that "some officials would rather stand idle than do work to prevent making mistakes. They hold onto their posts but make only perfunctory efforts. Aren't they like dead wood?" Better safe than sorry. As one study showed, when cadres "can't be certain about what actions would be deemed disloyal from one month to the next," they "don't' dare to do

things, as they worry about making mistakes." See Zhao Yinan, "Li calls for a 'new attitude' by officials," *China Daily,* March 6–8, 2015; "China's bummed out bureaucrats," *Blooomberg Businessweek,* March 2019, 44–45.

92. Yi-Zheng Lian, "Could there be another Chinese revolution?" *New York Times,* September 7, 2018, www.nytimes.com/2018/09/07/opinion/china-xi-revolution-red-aristocrats.html.

93. Ramzy and Buckley, "'Show absolutely no mercy'"; International Consortium of Investigative Journalists (ICIJ), "Exposed: China's operating manuals for internment and arrest by algorithm" (November 2019), www.icij.org/investigations/china-cables/exposed-chinas-operating-manuals-for-mass-internment-and-arrest-by-algorithm.

94. David Connett et al., "Pinochet arrested in London," *Guardian,* October 17, 1998, www.theguardian.com/world/1998/oct/18/pinochet.chile. Azeem Ibrahim, "China must answer for cultural genocide in court," *Foreign Policy,* December 3, 2109,https://foreignpolicy.com/2019/12/03/uighurs-xinjiang-china-cultural-genocide-international-criminal-court.

95. Javier C. Hernandez, "Wealthy Chinese scramble for imperiled commodity: American 'golden visa,'" *New York Times,* April 28, 2017; Robert Frank, "More than a third of Chinese millionaires want to leave China: Here's where they want to go," *CNBC,* July 5, 2018, www.cnbc.com/2018/07/05/more-than-a-third-of-chinese-millionaires-want-to-leave-china.html; Rachel Wang, "Why China's rich want to leave," *The Atlantic,* April 11, 2013, www.theatlantic.com/china/archive/2013/04/why-chinas-rich-want-to-leave/274920; Wang Zhuoqiong, "Chinese students head overseas at younger ages," *China Daily,* August 2, 2013; Hurun Research Institute and Visas Consulting Group, "Immigration and the Chinese HNWIs 2018" (June 2018), www.hurun.net/EN/Article/Details?num=670D27DA6723.

96. Michael Cole, "Canada slams door on 45K Chinese millionaires with end of visa program," *Forbes,* February 13, 2014.

97. Paul Viera et al., "Western cities want to slow flood of Chinese home buying. Nothing works," *Wall Street Journal,* June 6, 2018, www.wsj.com/articles/western-cities-want-to-slow-flood-of-chinese-home-buying-nothing-works-1528294587; Yuan Yang and Emily Feng, "China's buyers defy law to satisfy thirst for foreign homes," *Financial Times,* March 13, 2018.

98. Laura He, "Money has been leaving China at a record rate. Bejing is battling to stem the tide," *CNN,* December 19, 2019, www.cnn.com/2019/12/19/business/china-capital-flight-trade-war-us/index.html.

99. Birtles, "If China's on the rise, why do many want out?"

100. "Hundreds ill at 'toxic school' near chemical plants," *China Digital Times,* April 18, 2016, https://chinadigitaltimes.net/2016/04/hundreds-fall-ill-toxic-school-near-chemical-plants; "Anger over 'disgusting' food found in Chinese school kitchen," *BBC News,* March 14, 2019, www.bbc.com/news/world-asia-china-47565092; Wang Yiwei, "Parents fuming over investigation into school's toxic track," *Sixth Tone,* January 23, 2019, www.sixthtone.com/news/1003487/parents-fuming-over-investigation-into-schools-toxic-track.

101. He Huifeng, "Desperate Chinese middle class take big risks to move money, themselves, overseas," *South China Morning Post,* October 14, 2018, www.scmp.com/economy/china-economy/article/2167731/desperate-chinese-middle-class-take-big-risks-move-money-and-themselves; Phoebe Zhang, "Why West means

best for middle-class parents fleeing the Chinese educational system," *South China Morning Post*, June 29, 2019, www.scmp.com/news/china/society/article/3016600/why-west-means-best-middle-class-parents-fleeing-chinese.

102. Liu Xiaobo, "Charter 08," Perry Link trans. and commentary, *New York Review of Books*, January 15, 2009, www.nybooks.com/articles/2009/01/15/chinas-charter-08.

103. Smith, "Green capitalism," 49; Smith, "Six theses"; Smith, "An ecosocialist path." See also Olivia Boyd, "Civil society needed to enforce environmental law," *Chinadialogue*, October 20, 2016, www.chinadialogue.net/article/show/single/en/9324-Civil-society-needed-to-enforce-environmental-law.

104. Kim Stanley Robinson, *Red Moon* (New York: Orbit, 2019).

105. Bruce Gilley, *China's Democratic Future* (New York: Columbia University, 2004).

106. "Can Hong Kong's resistance win?" *New York Times*, July 12, 2019.

107. See for example Eric Fish, "1919–2019: A century of youth protest and ideological conflict around May 4," *SupChina*, May 1, 2019, https://supchina.com/2019/05/01/a-century-of-youth-protest-and-ideological-conflict-around-may-4; David Bandurski, "Burying Mr. Democracy," *China Media Project*, May 3, 2019, http://chinamediaproject.org/2019/05/03/burying-mr-democracy; Ian Johnson, "A spectre is haunting Xi's China: 'Mr. Democracy,'" *New York Review of Books*, April 19, 2019, www.nybooks.com/daily/2019/04/19/a-specter-is-haunting-xis-china-mr-democracy.

108. Denise Lu and Christopher Flavelle, "Erased by rising seas by 2050," *New York Times*, October 30, 2019; Damian Carrington, "Climate crisis: 11,000 scientists warn of 'untold suffering,'" *Guardian*, November 5, 2019, www.theguardian.com/environment/2019/nov/05/climate-crisis-11000-scientists-warn-of-untold-suffering.

109. Steven Mufson, "This documentary went viral in China. Then it was censored. It won't be forgotten," *Washington Post*, March 16, 2015, www.washingtonpost.com/news/energy-environment/wp/2015/03/16/this-documentary-went-viral-in-china-then-it-was-censored-it-wont-be-forgotten.

Index

Thanks to our Patreon Subscribers:

Abdul Alkalimat
Andrew Perry

Who have shown their generosity and comradeship in difficult times.

Check out the other perks you get by subscribing to our Patreon – visit patreon.com/plutopress.

Subscriptions start from £3 a month.

CPSIA information can be obtained
at www.ICGtesting.com
Printed in the USA
BVHW072036210720
584158BV00010B/59